MATTERS OF INTERPRETATION

MATTERS OF INTERPRETATION

Reciprocal Transformation in Therapeutic and Developmental Relationships with Youth

Michael J. Nakkula

Sharon M. Ravitch

•

[handwritten inscription]
Thanks for all your commitment, Sahar!
with affection,
Mike

Jossey-Bass Publishers
San Francisco

Substantial discounts on bulk quantities of Jossey-Bass books are available to corporations, professional associations, and other organizations. For details and discount information, contact the special sales department at (415) 433-1740; Fax (800) 605-2665.

For sales outside the United States, please contact your local Simon & Schuster International Office.

Jossey-Bass Web address: http://www.josseybass.com

Manufactured in the United States of America on Lyons Falls D'Anthology paper, which is a special blend of nontree fibers and totally chlorine-free wood pulp.

Library of Congress Cataloging-in-Publication Data

Nakkula, Michael J.
    Matters of interpretation : reciprocal transformation in
  therapeutic and developmental relationships with youth /
  Michael J. Nakkula, Sharon M. Ravitch.
      p. cm.
    Includes bibliographical references and index.
    ISBN 0-7879-0957-2 (hardcover : alk. paper)
    1. Youth—Counseling of. 2. Social work with youth.
  3. Counselor and client. 4. Hermeneutics. I. Ravitch, Sharon
  M. II. Title.
  HV 1421.N35 1997
  362.7—dc21
                                           97-29503
                                            CIP

FIRST EDITION

HB Printing 10 9 8 7 6 5 4 3 2 1

The Jossey-Bass
Psychology Series

To our parents
Arvid and Joyce Nakkula
and
Carl and Arline Ravitch

CONTENTS

PART THREE
Interpretations of the Missing

PART FOUR
The Socializing Influence of Language

ETHICAL PREFACE: THE ETHICS OF INTERPRETATION

EVERY ACT OF APPLIED development work[1] is an act of interpretation. And every interpretation made in such work is an ethical act, because people's lives are the focus of these interpretations and of the intervention strategies that result from them.

Interpretations shape and are shaped by society, culture, race, class, gender, and sexual orientation; by our histories, experiences, sense of self, and relationships; and by power differentials. Who we are and how we understand ourselves, others, and the world around us are implicit yet powerful parts of all interpretive action. Likewise, we understand present and future events on the basis of what we have known and how we have known up to the present, including how we have known ourselves. In turn, our interpretations of present and future events revise, to some extent, the way we see ourselves, others, and the world. In human service practice, in which there are often power differentials between "expert" and "client," this reciprocal influence between ourselves and our interpretations carries an extra layer of responsibility—an ethical layer.

From this perspective, the systematic deconstruction (critical taking apart) of our interpretations is an ethical responsibility because it allows for an increased understanding of the values and biases that underlie and direct our efforts. Thus, we argue, critical self-reflection is essential for an ethical approach to applied developmental practice, theory making, and research. In this book, we approach ethical youth service practice from a perspective informed by hermeneutics. Hermeneutics, broadly defined, is a framework for conceptualizing the circular process of interpretation in a manner that contextualizes ourselves, others, and our interactions more fully.[2]

Contrary to the belief that hermeneutics is an academic discipline that deals only with the interpretation of written texts and is therefore abstract and removed from real-life concerns, the hermeneutic framework presented here is a practical and ethically responsible approach to working with youth, and with human beings in general. Our framework is based on the acknowledgment that interpretations of human action are value- and morality-laden acts (Gadamer, [1960] 1993; Fowers and Richardson, 1996). Because such value-laden interpretations in applied development work include implications for how practitioners see our clients and how clients may come to view themselves, we believe that hermeneutic praxis (reflective practice designed to promote change and human emancipation) is among the *least* abstract activities in which applied developmentalists can engage.

Ethics has long been a central part of theory, research, and practice in such applied developmental fields as psychology, education, and social work, as well as in various forms of qualitative research. Yet discussions of ethics are fairly restricted in this literature, relegated largely to such issues as confidentiality, appropriate relational boundaries for professional practice, and guidelines for reporting abuse or threat of harm. Although these concerns are immensely important for youth development work, one purpose of this book is to expand and reframe the parameters of ethics in applied development work with youth. Ethics are more than bylaws or legal guidelines for professional conduct; they constitute the moral fabric that binds together the philosophy, approach to, and assessment of youth development work. How people conceive of, evaluate, and apply their work is steeped in what they view as their philosophy. Each aspect of youth development work, from its origins in personal and political stances through its development and application, is laden with ethical influences and implications.

This book addresses the ethical implications of a hermeneutic approach to applied development work with youth, and the various considerations that influence professionals' interpretations of children's lives. In our opinion, few human activities come with such a distinct ethical responsibility. We have therefore grounded this book in ethics from the beginning. By placing ethics front and center in our presentation, we attempt to highlight the wide-reaching ethical significance of interpretation. In doing so, we hope to complement existing ethical codes of practice (such as the Ethics Guidelines of the American Psychological Association) with an awareness of the broader ethical foundations that help guide every aspect of applied development work, not simply those areas that require specific rule-based guidance.

THE ETHICS OF PREJUDICE AND MISUNDERSTANDING

As we describe in more detail throughout this book, prejudice and misunderstanding have a specific meaning and place within philosophical hermeneutics (Gadamer, [1960] 1993) and are central to our hermeneutic framework.[3] Within this paradigm, prejudice and misunderstanding are necessarily a part of being human. That is, we all become grounded in certain views and opinions (prejudgments or prejudices) by virtue of our experiences in the world. These perspectives contribute to our understanding and misunderstanding the experiences of others. Accordingly, biases and prejudices, as used within the framework presented in this book, should not be viewed as markers of social ignorance or flawed character. Rather, they are considered to be openings for increased self- and other-understanding and for more honest and aware communication. To be useful in this manner, biases must be continuously revised through an explicit process of *uncovering* and confrontation through dialogue and critical self-reflection. The process of uncovering that we describe in this book comes from a distinctly hermeneutic perspective that is inherently political and sociophilosophical. Human beings—our thoughts, communications, interactions, and interpretations—cannot be abstracted from the constraints and possibilities of the larger societal forces in which we are embedded. In this sense, uncovering is intended to make explicit those societal forces that shape the interpretations that influence social action.

From this perspective, it becomes unethical for us, as applied developmentalists, not to explore our own biases and prejudices and the contexts that shape (and misshape) them. The lack of such exploration impedes serious (and often uncomfortable) consideration of the (mis)understandings that result from our biased interpretations. Without careful consideration of our preconceived notions about others, applied developmentalists work from an overly constricted worldview, and consequently from a limited understanding of the various influences on the work we do and the relationships we form with youth. Given the vicissitudes of experience that influence interpretation, there is infinite room for both misunderstanding others and being misunderstood.

Misunderstanding and miscommunication occur even within the closest relationships and between people from similar ethnic or cultural backgrounds. Given the way our society is structured, these phenomena can become more prevalent and troubling in cross-cultural, cross-generational, cross-racial, and cross-class applied development work. Within these professional contexts, differences in interpretive authority, privilege, and institutional power can exacerbate possibilities for acting from misunderstanding. Because applied developmentalists deal with something as serious as youths' lives, the possibilities for negative influence (even if unconscious) stemming from prejudices and misunderstandings, and from the assumptions these generate, must be rigorously and continuously reexamined.

The hermeneutic framework presented in this book is a conceptual guide for considering how one's social and psychological situatedness affect interpretation, or processes of meaning making, and how they shape what one looks for and finds in applied developmental practice, research, and theory building. We hope that a critical reading of this book, with its focus on processes of interpretation and the ethical implications of making these processes explicit, will provide new ways to improve communication and build possibilities for mutually transformative relationships. Further, the hermeneutic approach can be used as a metaframework for joining as well as critiquing applied developmentalists' existing ethical, theoretical, and methodological approaches to youth development work.

CRITICAL REFLECTION AS A PATHWAY TO MORE ETHICAL PRAXIS

Because there are infinite possibilities for the misunderstanding and misappropriation of others' meanings, even when guided by the best intentions, is there realistic hope in youth development work for mutual transformation through genuine understanding?

Actualizing hope for growth or change within the hermeneutic framework requires committing to a process of critical self-reflection, that is, reflecting on our biases and prejudices, background, worldview, and perspectives on others. It also requires ongoing analysis of how these issues get played out in communication during counseling sessions, supervision, and teaching, as well as within other professional relationships. We can never (and we would argue, should not want to) secure ourselves with the belief that our developmental practice or research is "neutral," "objective," or unencumbered by experiences with and notions about particular individuals or groups. Instead, we must recognize that our work always holds the possibility of being influenced by counterproductive prejudices, some of which lay outside of our awareness.

By increasing self-reflection, however, via a continual effort to contextualize ourselves and others within the multiple and guiding contexts of life—constructions of race, class, ethnicity, gender, politics, and culture, as well as relational and individual particulars—there is an opportunity for our self-awareness and perspective-taking abilities to grow. As a result of such growth, applied development work is more likely to enhance options for human emancipation, and less likely to minimize or pathologize those individuals in our care.

HERMENEUTIC IMPLICATIONS FOR ETHICAL THEORY, RESEARCH, AND PRACTICE

Interpretation crosses over disciplines and over the "boundaries"[4] of research, theory, and practice. It reaches into our psychological worlds and our relationships, and shapes our schools, our politics, our styles of communication, and society at large. Because acts of interpretation are so pervasive and subtle, and because we often take our views for granted as "the way things are" or "the right perspective," the ethical focus of applied developmental theory, research, and practice should be on the uncovering and transformation of underlying assumptions that inform interpretations. Transformation in this sense does not imply trying to "do away" with our biases; rather, it implies actively modifying them in the face of additional or contradictory awareness. Such transformation of our perspectives (even those that are cherished) can lead toward more informed and responsible practice, be it serving children and youth directly, building theory, training practitioners, or conducting research.

The hermeneutic framework presented in this book is an attempt to embody applied development work in theory-practice connections that are ethically driven. We place the onus of responsibility for change within the relationship between the practitioner and client (or student) rather than exclusively within one party or the other. Nonetheless, the adult professional is responsible for leading the process of uncovering and transforming biases that help shape the relationship. From a theoretical perspective, the exchange of interpretations stemming from the attempt to uncover biases would lead to growth and the mutual enhancement of well-being for both the youth and the adult worker. Within the hermeneutic framework, theory is not abstract thinking about detached objects; rather, it focuses on the quality of human relatedness for the enhancement of human well-being. In this sense, hermeneutic theory is theory based in ethics.

We believe, as we discuss in more depth throughout the following chapters, that hermeneutic research has meaningful implications for other forms of qualitative research, including (but not limited to) ethnographic, multicultural/culture-based, feminist, Afrocentric, and action research. Like these more specific approaches, hermeneutics assumes and emphasizes the inextricable ties between researchers' biased views of the world and their interpretations, while simultaneously problematizing (making conscious for critique) and reframing this intersection. The hermeneutic framework, while consistent with these specific approaches, diverges from them by virtue of the distinction that Heidegger ([1927] 1962) called "localized" versus "general" hermeneutics. For training purposes, we have intentionally chosen a more generalized approach to interpretive work. By starting from basic principles, trainees can notice and begin to appreciate how (and why) more specific or localized approaches, particularly those grounded in carefully articulated ideological stances such as feminism and Afrocentrism, work from specific, consciously selected biases. We want to be clear that we are not suggesting that our more general approach is superior to a more localized method; quite to the contrary, we believe a hermeneutic approach interacts with and learns from these more focused approaches, that it both informs and is informed by them.

We conceive of the interaction between hermeneutics and other standpoint epistemologies in this way: our overarching framework contextualizes the need for and implications of specific, ideologically based methods while it provides a critical context for comparing and critiquing them. A hermeneutic framework is a metaframework that aims to support different perspectives by contextualizing them within a broader landscape of approaches and methodologies and within larger societal forces, including politics, economics, race, class, ethnicity, gender, and the power structures that shape them. Our phenomenological methodology, which is the outgrowth of our hermeneutic perspective, is designed to explore systematically the implications of biases for research participants and for clinical or educational interventions derived from research findings.

ETHICS AS THE FOUNDATION FOR ALL APPLIED DEVELOPMENTAL PRACTICE

Although we do not explicitly discuss ethical implications within each chapter of this book, those implications are inherent in the various forms of interpretive work we associate with applied developmental practice. Ethics inform *everything* we describe because, as we have suggested, they cannot be separated from the interpretive acts that construct relationships and drive our work. We are not suggesting that our framework is unique in this regard; what is unique is our recognition of and emphasis on ethical underpinnings. Such underpinnings exist in all approaches. Our approach attempts to make these ethical underpinnings more explicit, because raising one's ethical consciousness enables one to act in a more ethical manner.

This book is structured around what we call *phenomenological case studies* that were written by graduate students training as counselors, educators, and other applied developmentalists. The student contributors have written phenomenological investigations focused on uncovering interpretations of their fieldwork. These case studies are placed within broader thematic contexts or clusters, which are defined in part by particular ethical concepts. The case studies in the first cluster, or Part Two of this book, "The Transformational Role of Interpretation," address the mutual development that occurs in youth work through the simultaneous transformation of the counselor/educator and youth in areas of self-awareness and perspective taking. One aspect of hermeneutic transformation is the growth that occurs through uncovering prejudices and by becoming increasingly aware of how we affect and are affected by those around us. Such transformation is in the service of providing more responsible practice with youth.

The studies in the second cluster, or Part Three of the book, "Interpretations of the Missing," address the ethical importance of looking beyond what can be readily observed in interactions with and observations of youth. Responding only to superficial manifestations of behavior leads to interventions of limited effectiveness at best, and at worst, to acts that are demeaning, hurtful, or oppressive. The studies in the third cluster, or Part Four of the book, "The Socializing Influence of Language," focus on an explication of the rules of the game of life in order to help youth recognize and uncover the more implicit rules of education in a society built in part on the systematic oppression of people of color, immigrants, and low-income populations. This focus has important ethical implications because, we argue, it is the responsibility of educators and counselors to give all youth, and particularly socioeconomically disenfranchised youth, a fair chance to play the game as empowered competitors or to create healthy alternatives. Politics and power, as well as the socializing influence of language, are important ethical issues that should be central considerations in applied development work, because they are larger contexts that can control and debilitate students even as practitioners attempt to help them.

Our assumption is that readers will come to this text having already thought through and dealt with issues of ethics, racism, sexism, and other concerns related to power and authority. Nevertheless, we have written this book from the belief that wherever one is in one's personal and professional development, consideration of these issues can and must always be deepened. Our hope is that reading this book and discussing its guiding themes will contribute to readers' growth toward increasingly aware and informed insight, communication, and praxis.

August 1997   Michael J. Nakkula
Cambridge, Massachusetts   Sharon M. Ravitch

NOTES

1. Throughout the book we use the terms *counseling, applied development work,* and *youth work* somewhat interchangeably. In general, however, the term *applied development work* represents the overall work in the related areas of counseling, clinical practice, social work, education, youth work, and applied research, and the term *applied developmentalist* refers to the practitioner who works in these areas.
2. A more in-depth and operational definition of hermeneutics is provided in the second preface.
3. When we use the term *hermeneutic framework* in this book, we mean the symbiotic integration of hermeneutic theory, research, and practice. We do not view hermeneutical work as theory alone, research alone, or practice alone, but always as the mutually informing integration of all three.
4. The term *boundaries* is placed in quotation marks to highlight our belief that the firm distinctions generally attributed to theory, research, and practice are often false because they treat these entities as discrete when actually they are interconnected.

PREFACE

ALTHOUGH HERMENEUTICS, most commonly defined as the systematic interpretation of written texts, has edged its way into the human sciences, the utility of a hermeneutic framework as a practical tool for the promotion of human well-being has remained largely undeveloped. This is so despite the fact that through its origins as a mechanism for clarifying misunderstanding, hermeneutics has always existed within the realm occupied by counselors and other interpreters of the human condition, particularly as that condition is experienced and expressed through language. Hermeneutics is about clarifying the meaning of messages—hidden messages, messages with multiple meanings, messages that carry essential importance for the ways we live. Counseling and other forms of applied development work are about similar things, and more.

Our primary goal in this book is to bring hermeneutics and various forms of applied development work closer together. From our perspective, this is an important and overdue task, because we believe that hermeneutics, when connected to human interactions, opens up important possibilities for deeper understanding and respect in relationships. The hermeneutic literature is extremely dense, for the most part, which likely contributes to its alienated position among human service practitioners and applied researchers. Therefore, central to our job as authors will be to serve as modern-day counterparts of Hermes, the messenger of the gods in ancient Greece, after whom the long tradition of hermeneutics was named. We will translate what we believe are core components of this literature as they relate to the theory, research, and practice of applied development work.

But serving as translators is only the beginning of our mission. Through translation we hope also to teach and model, thereby suggesting to students, counselors, educators, and other youth development practitioners that the work of interpreting complicated, seemingly impenetrable texts not only parallels the work of youth development but also facilitates it. In a certain sense, making connections is making connections, wherever and however that practice occurs. The more adept one becomes at this art, science, skill, craft, and way of being, the more broadly and flexibly one can make sense of things and, accordingly, the more options one sees for living. In this vein, we see applied development work as metahermeneutical, that is, as interpreting and promoting interpretation across multiple contexts of being, and doing much of it simultaneously and in the moment.

INTERPRETATION IN APPLIED DEVELOPMENT WORK

Interpretation in applied development work is not timed by convenience. Unlike theologians and literary critics, applied developmentalists, such as psychologists and social workers, do not usually have the luxury of deciding when to pick up a text for interpretation, or even which texts to interpret. In the work of applied developmentalists, interpretation happens all at once, in the moment of every interaction. The texts interpreted by applied developmentalists are not static, permanent, already-drafted manuscripts; they are the constantly emerging and evolving composites of human interaction that are presented through various forms of openness and disguise. In addition, applied developmental interpretation is intended to move beyond merely understanding these human texts. Interpretation in this work attempts to move understanding to action by facilitating others' interpretations—the self-interpretations of clients, including interpretations of their location within the social structure and the effects this has on their functioning in the world.

Applied developmental interpretations are intended to promote change and growth—or in the language of our hermeneutic framework, the development of the text of one's self. This self-text—the internalized story of one's life—is in ongoing revision. Applied development work can play a critical role in that developmental process of revision. In an important sense, youth developmentalists become coauthors and editors of their students' or clients' life texts. Generally these roles come by invitation, but at times they are imposed, as in the case of children and youth referred for counseling or therapy by teachers, parents, or other authority figures. In extreme cases, counseling or residential treatment may be mandated by the legal system. Regardless of how it is initiated, counseling and related forms of prevention, intervention, and applied development work are multileveled, multicomplicated, sacredly important, ethically grounded, action-oriented matters of interpretation.

As our language might suggest, we take the unequivocal stance that work of this sort—that is, interpretation toward the development of human growth and well-being—is the preeminent hermeneutical act. Its preeminence stems from the fundamental task of applied development work: interpreting and influencing the human condition. Yet hermeneutics remains estranged from counseling and other forms of applied development work, or is seen as a distant cousin at best. Our task is to change that, to bring these interpretive cousins closer together.

To clarify our previous reference to applied development work as a metahermeneutical process of organizing multiple intersecting interpretive acts, we provide the following example of an everyday counseling scenario. This example foreshadows what the student-authors of Chapters Five through Eight, Ten through Thirteen, and Fifteen through Eighteen experienced through their training, and what all human service trainees and practitioners engage in all the time on multiple levels. The interpretive acts in this scenario are representative of the everydayness of hermeneutics for counseling and youth development work. They are not dramatic acts but, rather, ordinary ones that, when explicitly articulated, depict the immediacy and pervasiveness of interpretation as it exists in the daily work of applied developmentalists.

•

Interpretive Act 1

Tania, a school counselor, comes into work on Monday and finds that one of her students has a slightly bruised face. The student says she got into a fight over the weekend. She says this with a trembling voice that seems inconsistent with her usual "tough" affect around fighting. Tania wonders if the student is being honest, but because their relationship is just forming, and because this student is particularly wary of trusting adults, Tania realizes she must carefully consider just how far to go in overtly questioning the student's story.

Interpretive Act 2

As she leaves the scene of this brief interaction, Tania thinks back to an earlier session in which the student discussed her father's drinking and alluded to him being scary when he drinks too much. The student did not say that her father had ever hit her, but she appeared uncomfortable when the subject was discussed: "He just scares me when he drinks—I don't really like talking about it." Tania wonders if there is a connection between the student's bruised face and her father's drinking.

Interpretive Act 3

As Tania walks back to her office, she remembers a previous case in which she suspected child abuse, questioned the suspected victim, was not comfortable with the answers provided, involved the Department of Child Protective Services, initiated an investigation, enraged the family, alienated the child, and lost the relationship. She suddenly becomes fearful that something similar could happen in the current situation.

Interpretive Act 4

In weighing the development of the relationship against her concern for the student's safety, Tania considers the legal and ethical implications of the situation. She knows she must report the case to the Department of Child Protective Services if she has firm suspicions that the student has been abused or is in danger of being harmed. She wonders how firm her suspicions are, and in what they are rooted. Is this a reportable case? She feels that additional information is necessary for her to make that judgment.

Interpretive Act 5

In planning her next step, Tania flashes back to her own childhood with its history of family violence. She remembers wishing that someone would have intervened on her behalf and helped with the family's pain somehow. This memory is not crystallized (or fully conscious) in the moment of her work, but it is clearly there, having an impact on her decision-making process.

Interpretive Act 6

Tania realizes she needs to talk to the school nurse about the incident. She knows the nurse will ask for background information. She wonders what to tell: Which pieces of the student's divulged history are confidential? Tania knows that the nurse is highly conservative in making reporting decisions and will likely press to file a report with the Department of Child Protective Services, even if that report is based on not-quite-firm suspicions. She tentatively proceeds toward the nurse's office.

Interpretive Act 7

On the way to the nurse's office, Tania begins questioning her competency because of her difficulty making a decision. She feels that with her level of experience this should be an ordinary scenario, one in which she should clearly know what actions would be most ethical and supportive for the student. After all, had she not been through this several times before?

Interpretive Act 8

In the midst of her self-doubting, Tania hears her name over the public address system; she is being summoned to the principal's office. She snaps out of her hazy self-reflection and heads down the hall toward the office. When she arrives, two students are crying, cursing each other out, and being held apart by the principal. The student with the bruised face has just gotten into a fight and is about to be suspended. In a millisecond, Tania questions whether she has created the whole abuse scenario out of her own not-quite-resolved family issues. Still, whatever is going on, she must now speak with the student about the impending suspension and the possibility of being sent home to her father. How will he react to her misbehavior? How should the news be delivered? Even if she did get the bruised face from a classmate, why was she fighting? Is she calling out for attention because there is abuse at home?

———————————————————————— • ————————————————————————

These eight interpretive acts represent middle-of-the-road matters of interpretation that school counselors, therapists, and applied developmentalists in all settings encounter on an everyday basis. They are neither dramatic by comparison to more serious concerns that arise regularly, such as disclosures of suicidal ideation or sexual abuse, nor more intense than the infinite number of smaller matters that occupy interpretive time and space, such as decisions about referral for counseling services, matching time and energy with grant-writing opportunities to fund student support projects, and making choices of word usage in the middle of a therapy session. These acts represent only the tip of a youth developmentalist's interpretive process. We have portrayed a largely conscious construction of and reflection on this process by making explicit connections between fragments of thoughts, memories, feelings, and actions. In actual life, the process generally is less conscious and is reflected on less explicitly. More typically, an educator's interpretive acts are carried out instinctively through the guidance of internalized rules, personal and professional experiences, and repetitiously practiced ways of being. The complexity of the presented scenario is magnified many times over when the thoughts must be made conscious and then organized and presented in spoken language for the purpose of constructively influencing a current situation. And only when the thinking and speaking of others interacts with one's own interpretive process, with infinite varieties of complexity, ambiguity, and confusion, does the scope of an applied developmentalist's interpretive challenge begin to emerge.

Tania's dilemma, although incomplete and somewhat superficial, points to several aspects of the goodness of fit between applied developmental work and the hermeneutic model presented in this book. It points to the interrelationship of the interpretation of self and others;

to the ethics of interpretation, especially where children are involved; to notions of competing interpretations and the validity of interpretation; and to the dialectical relationship between interpretation and action.

So, one might ask, what is new or different about the hermeneutic view of this interpretive process, and how is this perspective uniquely helpful to applied developmentalists? In applied development work, hermeneutics places the focus of interpretation on context—the multiple and interacting contexts of human interactions. Careful consideration of such contexts is necessary for understanding the construction of human thought, feeling, and action in particular situations.

In the realm of applied developmental interpretation, the more clearly a person conceptualizes and comprehends the multiple contexts that influence behavior and interactions, the more likely she or he is to understand the multiple contributions to and meanings of these phenomena. A potentially infinite variety of contexts influence human interaction, including different aspects of individual life histories, places of interaction, times of interaction, and the histories of other people involved. Unquestionably, the contexts of race, class, religion, sexuality, gender, culture, and larger sociopolitical forces are critical to many interpretive scenarios. Where one comes from, in every sense of the phrase, is essential to the unfolding of any human action and to every act of interpretation. We contend that thoroughly contextualizing youths' experiences lessens the likelihood of misappropriating the meanings of their words and actions, and of pathologizing their behavior on the basis of generalized and unchecked prejudices. Our hermeneutic approach to applied development work is centered in the ongoing contextualization of human *being,* with a particular emphasis on emerging contexts—the contexts of one's plans, hopes, and expectations for the future.

It is important to reemphasize the perhaps obvious point that applied developmentalists attempt to develop ever-clearer interpretations of clients' situations, not simply for the purpose of better understanding those clients but also to help foster the clients' self-interpretations and associated thoughts, feelings, and behaviors when they are overly self-critical or damaging. In the language of critical hermeneutics, which focuses on interpretation as a means of fomenting individual and social change, our increased insight into the interpretive processes of our clients allows us to participate more effectively in their emancipation from damaging self-interpretations and from the oppressive conditions in which they often live. But helpful participation in clients' emancipatory processes requires a prior commitment to investing in our own emancipation from conscious and unconscious constraints on self-understanding. These constraints can significantly impair the conduct of our lives, our views of the world, and thus our approaches to applied development work with youth. We recommend a commitment to this ongoing investment—ongoing because human emancipation is never complete but rather is a lifelong developmental process. This process becomes stunted when we mistakenly think of it as completed.

Enhanced self-interpretation and the corresponding capacity to understand others better are parallel and interacting goals for both adult and youth within our hermeneutic framework. As the title of our book suggests, these interacting goals are mutually influenced by the development of youths and applied developmentalists through the reciprocity of working together. Applied developmentalists work to empower others by being earnestly empowered and enlightened ourselves. The emphasis that a hermeneutic approach places on healthy mutual influence is part of what makes this approach to applied development work unique.

THE CONTEXTS OF OUR WORK

Consistent with the hermeneutic approach, we want to say a little about the origins and language of our message and about its intended audiences.

Origins

The material in this book comes out of the Risk and Prevention Program at the Harvard Graduate School of Education (HGSE). The Risk and Prevention Program is an interdisciplinary master's specialization within HGSE's Department of Human Development and Psychology. It draws primarily from the fields of education, applied and developmental psychology, public health, social policy, sociology, and anthropology. The primary goals of the program include exposing students to multiple perspectives on child and adolescent development and providing them with training experiences in the prevention of risky behavior and the promotion of the health and well-being of children and youth.

Since the program's inception in 1992, Michael Nakkula has taught the Risk and Prevention Adolescent Practicum Course. This course places students in a range of school- and community-based training sites, where lessons from the Harvard classroom are applied to real-world problems under the guidance of professional supervision. Because of the Risk and Prevention Program's interdisciplinary design, it is neither a counseling program in the traditional sense nor a traditional education or youth development program. It is none of these things by intent, not by accident. It is explicitly meant to be an integrationist program in which different approaches to prevention and to child and youth development can be constructed, studied, and applied. This integrationist and cross-disciplinary stance is directly connected with the development and application of the hermeneutic approach.

Because the practicum training sites are so varied in focus and design, adoption of a standard counseling or educational approach would not be appropriate. For example, students at the Urban Youth Connection site focus primarily on individual and group counseling within a fairly clinical school-based model; those at the Prevention Center of Boston's Medical Foundation engage primarily in peer-leadership training, in which there is little direct focus on counseling intervention; and students placed with Concilio Hispano's Primavera program provide a combination of services, including teaching, tutoring, and life-skills counseling for young women who have dropped out of high school because of restrictions placed on them as a result of pregnancy and its attendant responsibilities.

The students placed at these sites, and at others with equally diverse agendas, face very different challenges, and they bring with them very different approaches to practice. They are all, however, immersed in explicit processes of interpretation. They each see as a training goal the promotion of growth and the recognition of change—in their students or clients, in their own skill levels, and in themselves as developing professionals committed to their work. The hermeneutic framework is designed to address and clarify these various acts of interpretation at the level of practice (by promoting critical thinking, flexible decision making, healthy self-reflection, and empathy and respect for others), at the level of research (by evaluating the effects of interpretive action on the self and others through systematic, phenomenological investigation), and at the level of theory building (by combining practice, phenomenological note taking, and complex readings on hermeneutics with critical self-reflection and active debate).

A question within the larger field of hermeneutics is whether hermeneutics is practical for everyday and professional action or whether it should retain a more comfortable existence within the narrower confines of philosophical debate and literary criticism. This book is an answer to that question. Sharon Ravitch is a doctoral student in human development and psychology focusing on cultural and psychosocial development at HGSE and has devoted several years of focused study to hermeneutic theory, research, and practice. Her training chapter (Chapter Five, written during her master's year), as well as the chapters by her junior peers in the Risk and Prevention Program, attests to the learnability of the hermeneutic framework over a fairly short period. We find the student papers featured in this volume to be compelling evidence—real-life, hermeneutic data—for the value of this model for practice. But "practice," in the hermeneutic sense, is not a distinct set of skills or techniques separate from the reflective work of theory or the rigorous efforts of research. To separate practice from research and theory is to compartmentalize artificially. As we discuss throughout this volume, strong hermeneutic practice entails systematic evaluation (self-reflection, in part) and an understanding of an interpretation-based theory of human *being*.

The Phenomenological Case Studies

In an effort to communicate the accessibility of the hermeneutic framework for applied development work and for the training of advanced college and graduate-level practitioners, we have structured the book around the research and writing of student trainees. We refer to the student papers as *phenomenological investigations* or *phenomenological case studies*. By phenomenological we mean the uncovering and interpreting of meaning. The meaning uncovered and interpreted is that which is encountered through the trainees' work with youth in their various training contexts. The authors interpret meaning made by themselves, their supervisors, the youth, their teachers, parents, and others who play a role in the work being examined. Observations and interpretations of these meaning-making endeavors are organized through a combination of note taking and ethnographic memo writing, which are explained in detail in Chapter Two.

The students who authored the case studies included here come from a range of academic and personal backgrounds. Some are young students nearly straight out of college. Others are experienced professionals who came to the Risk and Prevention Program for a sabbatical of sorts from their work as counselors, teachers, or youth development workers. All of them, as will become apparent, are highly talented. In fact, the decision to publish this book emerged from our observation of the extraordinary ways in which students had been interpreting and writing about their experiences using the tools and philosophy of the hermeneutic framework. We believe that these chapters are among the most inspiring exemplars available in the overlapping areas of education, counselor training, youth development, qualitative research, and hermeneutics. They have much to teach precisely because they were written by actual trainees doing real-world work. If they had been written by academics or advanced professionals, they would still be important, but the replicability of their lessons would be more questionable.

Audiences

We believe that this book is relevant and accessible to several important audiences. At one end of a continuum are theoreticians, who may be skeptical of a genuine application of hermeneutics to professional practice and who, we believe, will find this an interesting experiment to critique. At the center are academics, who have considered and written about hermeneutic connections to practice but who have not witnessed those connections so thoroughly applied. Also near the center are qualitative researchers doing action research and ethnographic fieldwork. Such researchers, who likely come from social science and humanities backgrounds, can read from and into this work reasons to contextualize communication more thoroughly and to place interviews within their contexts of time, relationship, place, subjectivity, and misunderstanding. At the other end of the continuum, where we hope to have the largest impact, are the professors, supervisors, practitioners, and students committed to human development, who will find here a different approach to thinking about and conducting their work.

We envision master's and doctoral students of psychology, education, counseling, social work, and the related human service professions as primary audiences. We view the book as useful for classes and internship programs in those areas. This text would be best utilized to complement a more traditional skills-oriented training text, because it builds from basic skills and uses case studies to exemplify the challenges and benefits of its application to youth work. We also foresee it being read for the benefit of professional and personal development by those already immersed in their professions. In terms of our own work with student trainees, we view this book in a twofold manner: (1) as providing an overarching interpretive framework in which to integrate and critique other theories of and approaches to counseling and applied human development, and (2) as a theory, practice, and research guide—the only such guide available—for the conduct of hermeneutic counseling and applied human development practice.

To a certain extent, we hope to create—or perhaps more accurately, to name—an audience that generally goes unidentified, that is, the audience of professionals working with children and youth who see themselves fitting somewhere between education, counseling, and social work. Some of these people work in residential treatment centers as "line staff," in recreation and youth centers as "youth workers," in community health centers as "human service providers," and in after-school programs and day-care centers as aides or mentors. We believe that this book may serve as an organizing framework that does not pigeonhole this large and diverse range of people into one particular discipline or set of techniques.

As mentioned earlier, we refer to this audience throughout the preface and the remainder of the book as *applied developmentalists* and to its work as *youth development work* and *applied human development*. We also often use these terms interchangeably with *counselor* and *counseling*. Applied developmentalist, however, is the name that we believe most accurately captures our primary audience. All of the work addressed in this book has the aim of promoting human development, that is, the development of youth and of the adults working with them. Frequently, however, we use the term *counselor* when we select an example from a particular profession, because counseling is a fairly broad and widely recognizable activity, and it is highly relevant to many of the contexts about which we write. Not only do line staff in residential treatment view their work as a variation of counseling, but psychologists, social workers, and psychiatrists also can make connections between counseling and the work of their professions.

Whatever your discipline, a goal of this book is to place you, the reader, at its center. The hermeneutic approach places the interpreter, whether it be a counselor or other human service provider, at the core of the interpretive process. Most professionals enter their training looking outward, toward the problems and situations of others. Our approach begins by looking inward, toward one's own biases and prejudices, and does so from the recognition that everyone sees the world differently, with views colored by one's own history, values, disposition, and professional training. Because everyone sees the world uniquely, it is little wonder that there are so many theoretical lenses through which to understand human behavior and human problems.

The hermeneutic approach acknowledges the validity of differing perspectives but requires that we take responsibility for our own biases

and assumptions by grounding our practice in ongoing and contextualized self-reflection. Critical reflection on where we come from and
what we bring is considered the key to making responsible interpretations in our work and in everyday life. In hermeneutic work there is an
explicit focus on the co-construction of meaning and interpretation in
tandem with an emphasis on how one's background and opinions
affect current situations. A rigorous methodology, presented in
Chapter Two, helps to facilitate the process of uncovering the layers of
bias and preconception that shape our interpretations.

In this book's introductory chapter we thoroughly articulate the theory, research, and practice implications of the overarching model. This
overview, combined with the methodology chapter, the student-written
phenomenological case studies, and our contextualization of the case
studies within broad hermeneutical themes, constitutes an opportunity
for an important advancement in the fields of counseling and applied
human development, and in the general area of hermeneutics. We hope
that in the realms of counseling and applied human development the
book will be used as an organizing framework for building on existing
approaches to theory, research, and practice, and that in the general
study of hermeneutics it will be viewed as a unique contribution to the
application of theory to real-world research and practice. Finally, and
perhaps most importantly, we hope that you, the readers, from all
backgrounds and disciplines, will gain from this book a deeper appreciation of the complicated nature of your work, of the multiple and
guiding contexts that shape communication and understanding, and of
the complexity and depth of your everyday lives.

ACKNOWLEDGMENTS

WE LEARN ABOUT POSSIBILITY through experiencing ourselves in relationships with others. This book has been made possible because of many relationships, personal and professional. We are fortunate to have been taught, mentored, nurtured, and inspired by many people throughout our lives and during the process of writing this book. At this time we want to honor and thank some of these individuals.

Together, we wish to thank the following people:

Robert Selman, for supporting and creating possibilities for us through his presence and guidance as friend, mentor, and director of the Harvard Graduate School of Education's Risk and Prevention Program, through which the work for this book was developed. Bob's relentless perspective taking on all matters of interpretation—personal, professional, and political—combined with his nonjudgmental support, have for many years informed our internal working models for this book, and for life more generally.

Nancy Hoffman, who brought us together as professor and student. In a variety of ways Nancy has been a tremendous supporter of each of our individual life projects, which has been inordinately helpful to the joint project of completing this book.

Meg Turner, for her profound and authentic way of living and teaching. Meg's early lessons helped validate Mike's initial ventures into the relationship between hermeneutics and psychology, and Sharon's views on a critical feminist psychology.

The twelve contributors to this book. Their extraordinary insight, humanity, and creativity, displayed in their writing, kept this book alive when we had doubts regarding the validity of our efforts. We also want to thank the many students who submitted their work for review; because of the constraints of space we were able to include only a small sample of the many stellar works available.

The many people who assisted us by reading drafts of this book and providing invaluable critiques: Peg McAdam, Diamond Cephus, and Donna San Antonio. In addition, we want to thank Frank Richardson,

Lisa Delpit, and Robert Woolfolk for their formal review and critique of the manuscript.

The editorial and publishing team at Jossey-Bass Publishers—Leslie Berriman, Bill Hicks, and Cathy Mallon—who were unfailing in their support and patience throughout this process. We thank each of them, with special gratitude to Leslie Berriman, our editor and coshaper of this book, for her belief in our work, in this project, and in us. It has been a pleasure working with you, getting to know you, and building this book together, piece by piece, one supportive argument at a time.

Our research for this book was funded, in part, by the Harvard Graduate School of Education Faculty Research and Innovation Fund. We are grateful for this support, and for the support of the school administration in general.

Finally, our greatest joint thank you goes to Christina Nikitopoulos for coming through for us again and again, sacrificing her time and energy to help pull this book together, and laughing with us each step of the way.

Mike also wishes to thank:

All of the practicum students who over the past five years have helped shape and revise the approach to interdisciplinary youth development presented in this book. Each of these students has challenged my ideas and assumptions in ways that have kept my work alive. They have also reinvigorated my belief in our work with youth through their passion and commitment.

Of course, the teaching fellows who have worked with me as colleagues, supporters, and critics: Sheila O'Keefe, Dorothy Smith, Michael Karcher, Diamond Cephus, Peg McAdam, and Donna San Antonio. Just listing these names helps me understand why I'm here.

The principals, teachers, and other public school personnel who invited us to work with them on our common purpose of enhancing the education and well-being of children: particular thanks go to Valeria Lowe and Charles McAfee, two Boston Public School principals who have been especially inspirational and welcoming over the many years of this work, and to John Dennehey, who has shown me what is possible in school leadership. Additional thanks to John for the mentoring he has provided to so many of my master's and doctoral students.

Maureen McGoldrick and Emily Carrington, school counselors and social workers who, through their commitment to student support, have taught me how to appreciate and navigate the complex systems of public schools.

My partners in the building of community-school-university collaboratives. Niobe Way and Bobbie Gottlieb for their camaraderie in developing the Urban Youth Connection (UYC), from which much of this work was spawned. Steve Keel and Carmen Torres for their running of the UYC and their caring supervision of my students over the years. Ward Cromer, Scott McCloud and Sheila O'Keefe for their development work on Project IF, which has served to help refine and implement the ideas in this book. Mark Taylor and Francois Guilleux, committed loyalists of Project IF, who have helped to shape its mission and facilitated its growth. The community supervisors and site coordinators who have kept me abreast of what's real.

Ultimate thanks go to my family: My parents, Arvid and Joyce Nakkula, whose contributions to the book are briefly delineated in Chapter Three. My brothers and their families: Tim, Tammy, and Ashley; Greg, Kathy, and Nicole; Shawn and Jenny. Their caring from afar makes the loneliness more tolerable. My extended family, the Nakkulas, the Nuranens, and the endless stories they created, stories that directed me to the work presented here. Along these lines, I want to pay special homage to my uncle David Nuranen, whose desire to get the story straight has finally paid off. And to Bert and Roy, who by teaching me the ABCs and going to college opened the door to my teaching at Harvard.

Sharon also wishes to thank:

My parents, Arline and Carl Ravitch, for cherishing me and, through your example, teaching me how to cherish others. The gifts of your unconditional love, respect, support, and faith in me throughout my life continually inspire and sustain me.

My grandfather, Albert Karp, who died during the writing of this book but breathed his life into it. This man, who graduated only from the eighth grade but spent his life educating himself, took great pride in the fact that his grandchildren sought and received formal education. He was a constant source of strength and a springboard for my ideas, and this book is deeply connected to him and to my grandmother, Edith Karp, who continues to be central to who I am.

My brother Frank and sister Elizabeth, for leaving large and friendly footsteps and extending your hands so I could reach up and follow you; and Jamie and Auren, for loving my siblings so deeply and adding spirit to our family.

My dear uncle, Gary Karp, for your continued nurturing and support; the Schwartz family, Aunt Bobbi Tacknoff, and my extended family—the Blyweiss, Berenbaum, Abrams, and Feder families—for helping to raise me.

I want to acknowledge and thank the mentors from whom I have been so fortunate to learn. At Temple University: Norbert Samuelson (for being the first professor to believe in my intellectual abilities), Timothy Corrigan, Laura Levitt, and Rebecca Alpert—each of you provided guidance and invited me into the passionate world of ideas. At Harvard: Carol Gilligan, for your faith in me and your continued encouragement; Charles Ducey, Peg McAdam, and Vicki Magee—each of you has helped me to think more deeply, critically, and relationally about people and life, and to get to know myself better, thereby enabling me to relate with others more generously.

I am fortunate to be engaged in relationships with people who continually support and energize me through their love, friendship, and wisdom: my oldest and dearest friend, Debbie Melincoff, for helping me to take perspective on myself like no one else can and always making me laugh; my soul sister Laura Hoffman, for your generous spirit, courage, and sagelike advice; my divas—Alyssa Levy, Karin Liiv, and Beth Moughty—for showing me, through your dynamic examples, how strong we all can be; Doug Belkin, for helping me to empower myself by believing in me; Jo-Ann Finkelstein, for helping to remind me about the power of living our truths; Amy and Paul Caplan, for taking me under your wings during my years at Harvard and beyond; Aaron Toffler, for inviting me into the beauty of nature; Jodi Grossblatt Saunders, for introducing me to Women's Studies and keeping the flame ignited; Melissa Bloom and Merle Salkin for sharing your vitality with me; Lois and Steve Hirsh, for staying connected through many years and changes.

I want also to thank several people at the University of Pennsylvania Graduate School of Education's program in Education, Culture, and Society for your encouragement since I began my doctoral studies at Penn: Frederick Erickson and Rona Rosenberg, for your support and your faith in my work; Wendy Hobbins, for your wisdom and for being a true example of mindfulness and strength; Meredith de Chabert and Bryan McKinley Brayboy, for your friendship; and Cindy Sawyer, for helping to break down some of the walls between blacks and Jews by opening our vital dialogue.

Finally, I am grateful to the many students and families who have opened your hearts and homes to me over the years. You are my continued grounding and inspiration.

THE AUTHORS

MICHAEL J. NAKKULA is a psychologist specializing in the study and promotion of developmental opportunities available to low-income and working-class youth. He is assistant professor in the Department of Human Development and Psychology at the Harvard Graduate School of Education, where he has helped to create the Risk and Prevention Program, through which his most recent work has been conducted. Nakkula's work in the area of youth development focuses on the interface of psychology and philosophy—specifically, the naturally developing interpretive philosophies that become internalized and help to shape psychological dispositions and behavioral options. Drawing on the hermeneutic framework that informs *Matters of Interpretation,* he has cofounded and evaluated a number of university-community collaborations that support youth development, including Project IF: Inventing the Future, a school- and community-based counseling and mentoring program developed through collaboration with Massachusetts General Hospital's Bunker Hill Health Center, where Nakkula holds an appointment of Clinical Fellow. Additional research and publications are in the areas of adolescent high-risk behavior, pair therapy (Robert Selman's friendship development intervention), program evaluation, and multicultural counseling.

SHARON M. RAVITCH is currently a doctoral student and Dean's Fellow in the Education, Culture and Society Program at the University of Pennsylvania Graduate School of Education. She earned her Ed.M. degree (1994) in education (risk and prevention) and her Certificate of Advanced Study (1995) in human development and psychology (cultural and psychosocial development) at Harvard University's Graduate School of Education. Ravitch began her doctoral studies in human development and psychology at Harvard in 1996, focusing on child and youth development with an emphasis on school-based therapeutic interventions. While at Harvard, she conducted training and counseling in the Boston and Cambridge Public School Systems and acted as a consultant to the Cambridge Public School System's Office of Research, Development and Assessment. She is currently working toward an interdisciplinary doctorate in anthropology, sociology, and education at the University of Pennsylvania, where she studies with Frederick Erickson and conducts research on issues of multicultural education in the Cantor-Fitzgerald Center for Research on Diversity in Education at the University's Center for Urban Ethnography. Grounded in a perspective informed by hermeneutics and critical social theory, Ravitch focuses on combining innovative models of cross-disciplinary theory and practice with ethnographic and other qualitative methodologies to explore the interrelationship between the psychosocial development and identity formation of economically disenfranchised youth and the social and educational institutions in which they interact. She is a graduate lecturer on education at several Philadelphia area colleges, and works as an educational consultant in Philadelphia, New York, and Boston.

The authors who have contributed their phenomenological case studies to this book are former master's students from the Harvard Graduate School of Education's Risk and Prevention Program. Their contributions reflect the hermeneutic approach to psychosocial inquiry conducted through the Risk and Prevention Program's Adolescent Practicum Course, taught by Michael Nakkula. Each of the case studies was originally a paper written for the practicum course and was subsequently edited for inclusion in this volume.

The authors came to their master's training from a variety of professional backgrounds—including teaching, counseling, youth development work, and the creative arts—and from a number of academic disciplines—including education, psychology, religion, literature, sociology, and history. Currently they hold positions in a range of youth-serving capacities, from school administrators to teachers and counselors to community-based positions such as program developers and fundraisers.

MARCO ANTONIO BRAVO is a lecturer on language and literacy in the Teacher Education Program at Santa Clara University in Santa Clara, California.

KRISTIN M. CARVILL is an elementary school prevention coordinator for the Eckerd Family Youth Alternatives, a nonprofit organization in

Brooksville, Florida, dedicated to improving the lives of children and their families.

DEBORAH H. CHENG is currently working for Here and Now, an Asian American Theater company that performs for high school and college audiences in the Riverside, California, community.

TARA EDELSCHICK teaches and provides student advocacy at West Side High School, an alternative school in New York City that serves students who have been unnsuccessful in larger, more traditional settings.

RANDY B. HAYWARD is director of counseling for the Benjamin Banneker Charter School in Boston, Massachusetts.

SHUNA KEENAN is a community health associate, providing technical consultation for Prevention Support Services of the Boston Medical Foundation in Boston, Massachusetts.

ROBERT W. LEARY is a youth and community coordinator through the Vista Volunteer Program at a mutual housing community in the metro Denver area.

KARIN E. LIIV is founder and executive director of Link Youth Alliance, a community development program for urban youth leadership in San Francisco, California.

ANNA MACKEY conducts evaluation research with Committee for Children, a nonprofit agency in Seattle, Washington, that specializes in the development of a wide range of prevention curricula for children and youth.

HUGH MCDONOUGH is a crisis intervention clinician at the Wreath School, a residential school for emotionally disturbed adolescent boys in Middleton, Massachusetts.

JOHN RAMÍREZ JR. is assistant principal of Martin Luther King Jr. Middle School in Seaside, California.

GREGORY SEATON recently completed a position as director of minority recruitment for teacher education at the University of Central Florida. He is currently a doctoral student at Brown University's Graduate School of Education.

PART ONE

AN INTERPRETIVE FRAMEWORK

I

INTRODUCTION

The Forward Arc of Projection

EACH YEAR, WHEN A NEW GROUP of Harvard master's students enrolls in the Risk and Prevention Adolescent Practicum Course, they are propelled into an experience that is foreign, frustrating, alienating, exhilarating, and immediate. The students experience extreme manifestations of what the philosopher Martin Heidegger referred to as "thrownness" in his seminal work *Being and Time* ([1927] 1962). According to Heidegger, active living, or engaged involvement, in the world necessitates being thrown into new situations that challenge our usual ways of knowing and experiencing. Such challenges contribute to a host of changes, from subtle and dramatic shifts in perspective or worldview to a range of feelings including accomplishment, inadequacy, pride, shame, and hope. Each of these changes, whether substantial or insubstantial, revises (or entrenches) in some way the ever-developing text of human experience that we take into subsequent encounters.

On a variety of levels, this book and the hermeneutic framework it presents are about thrownness, about the ongoing experience of being thrown into new ways of thinking, doing, and being, both as a person and as a youth development professional. But the concept of "new ways," as we present it here, is paradoxical, if not presumptuous. We in academe can delight in proclaiming our most recently advanced breakthroughs in understanding. This work is not intended to be a proclamation of that sort, although our enthusiasm for the subject matter might at times lead to such an impression. For what may seem like excessive enthusiasm, we apologize in advance. We do intend, however, and without apology, to provide and induce ongoing discovery, or "dis-covery," in a hermeneutic and phenomenological sense. That is, we hope to uncover and clarify ways of thinking, doing, and being that already exist in the youth development fields and in each of our individual and collective experiences of life. In that sense, the hermeneutic framework presented here is designed to recognize and better understand the "already there" of everyday and professional experience, just as it is intended to uncover and prepare for those insights that are still on the way.

The concept of being thrown into new ways that already exist is confusing, but the paradox within it highlights the essence of our approach to youth development research and praxis (theory-based practice). At its core, our approach is about making the alien familiar and the familiar alien. It is about using a consciously expanding base of familiarity to step into foreign situations with a belief that these contexts and interactions are ultimately understandable, at least in an approximate and subjective way that allows one not to feel too alienated, distanced, and disempowered.

Several of the chapters in this book provide examples of the de-alienating process. They depict the experiences of student trainees thrown into the lives of youth and into the hermeneutic framework, from the students' own points of entry. These entry points are as varied as the new experiences the students encounter. It is this intersection of differences (in background and new experiences) and the interpretations it generates that constitute the "new" here, the *never-before-experienced-in-quite-this-way*, which we think has so much to teach about living, learning, and doing our work.

We believe that the hermeneutic framework introduced in this chapter is uniquely designed to capture the fundamental interrelatedness of living, learning, and doing our work that closely parallels the interaction among theory, research, and practice. In fact, since Heidegger, hermeneutics has been used as a theory for understanding life or human *being*, not just the written word of humans. Hermeneutics as a theory of living, as a means of understanding the essence of human being, might be considered a natural theory of life, one grounded in and derived from two of the most central functions of human development: the ongoing *interpretation* and *articulation* of everyday experience. Interpreting and articulating experience is what we do in all aspects of our existence: from formal learning or the conducting of research to the specialized practice of professional work such as counseling, education, and youth development.

The breadth of the hermeneutic framework allows one to focus on the interrelation of parts in one's work—the theory, research, and practice parts of the experiential gestalt—or if you will, the trees, plants, and underbrush that make up the forest. The challenge for the authors of the following chapters, and for others using this approach, is to keep the parts and whole in focus simultaneously—or more accurately, to move them in and out of focus interchangeably in a manner that allows the parts and whole to interactively shape each other. From this view of the forest, not only every tree but also every shrub, weed, and blade of grass is critical to the overall ecology of human experience.

Most people in human service fields have clearly learned that they must not lose the forest for the trees; they see how the oaks and the redwoods—the major events of a life—fit into the forest or overall history and pattern of functioning. But in many cases, the shrubs, weeds, and blades of grass are not simply neglected; they are thoroughly unrecognized. The ordinariness of life—the little things, which far outnumber the bigger, more obvious events and characteristics—are unseen and unattended as they provide a foothold for viewing the landscape. With their focus on "everydayness," the hermeneutic accounts in this book zoom in below the forest vista and its trees in an effort to capture from a variety of vantage points the texture, shapes, and sounds of ordinary living that hold and give meaning to the extraordinary experiences of youth and the people working to serve them.

Before outlining the specifics of the hermeneutic framework, there are some other aspects of thrownness that we ask the reader to consider. First, we are not thrown into new experiences from nowhere. We are thrown into the new from our histories of experiencing and making sense of everyday life. This point seems obvious, yet it is often forgotten when learners confront new material. Drawing from Heidegger ([1927] 1962) and from his successor Hans-Georg Gadamer (1976, [1960] 1993), we emphasize the notion of a "forestructure" of understanding any seemingly foreign phenomena. This forestructure is what one has already learned and internalized in life, and the manner in which the learning has been organized or contextualized in preparation for the future assimilation of anything new.

This concept is the source of the subtitle of this introductory chapter: "The Forward Arc of Projection." Just as the contributors to the following chapters were not thrown into their training experiences from nowhere—they were projected into them from rich life histories, including previous work with youth—the readers of this book come to the material from particular places. Our writing is intentionally prepared to address, both implicitly and explicitly, assumed aspects of this forestructure, such as traditional models of counseling and youth development work. We expect that our audience will take in and critique the material on the basis of the language, biases, and values of their professions. In that sense, although much of the theory presented here may be new to many readers, it will be read from the angle of a preprepared context, and it will be seen, we hope, as different from but related to that which is already familiar. With that in mind, the following section provides a brief overview of the language of hermeneutics.

THE SUBSTANTIVE AND LINGUISTIC DEVELOPMENT OF HERMENEUTICS

Because it has a long developmental history stemming from and winding through a diverse range of disciplines, hermeneutics has taken on a good deal of jargon over the years. This heavy linguistic baggage has turned many practically oriented students and scholars away from the study, and certainly the practice, of hermeneutics, which they view as an overly abstract and esoteric exercise in relativity play or language games. We believe that this perspective is largely based on an unfortunate and poignantly ironic misunderstanding—unfortunate in that hermeneutics can provide a practical framework for making sense of the ambiguity inherent in everyday life and work activities, and ironic in that hermeneutics has fallen prey to the very problem it has been called upon to rectify: the loss and distortion of meaning that occurs through language.

Originating in Greek mythology, in the story of Hermes, messenger and translator of the gods, hermeneutics has steadily developed as a process of communication and translation of complex and important messages. Continuing within the domain of divine translation, hermeneutics grew into a method of biblical interpretation, a means of placing holy scripture within the historical context in which it was believed to have been written and from which its meaning was believed to have been derived. Hermeneutical exegesis, the analytical process of extracting complex and ambiguous passages from the Bible—and later, other sacred texts—and interpreting their meaning by contextualizing them according to location, time, overall story, and author, became a staple of theological study and practice. The very notion and practice of hermeneutical exegesis contain within them the debates that characterize later conflicts of meaning within religion, philosophy, psychology, literature, and the sciences—debates over the absolute versus the relative nature of truth.

The hermeneutic role in the debates over truth was revolutionized by Heidegger through the publication of *Being and Time* in 1927. Heidegger articulated a number of topics in his philosophical argument that have implications for practitioners of all sorts, including counselors and youth development workers. Three of these topics, which are of central importance for this book, are

1. His shift in attention from the known or potentially knowable to the knower, or from an emphasis on studying what one understands (God's word, or the nature of stars, for example) to emphasizing the study of understanding itself

2. His use of a hermeneutic method to interpret and contextualize the meaning of human experience

3. His view of human being as a fundamentally hermeneutic process, one of ceaselessly contextualizing lived experiences within larger, meaningful stories

Heidegger's development of these three topical areas moved hermeneutics out of the exclusive domain of written texts and into the living story of human being. Still, there was an important step between the use of hermeneutics to study sacred texts and Heidegger's use of it to study—or more precisely, to explain—the nature of human being. That step was Edmund Husserl's ([1900, 1901] 1976) development of phenomenology as both a form of philosophy and a method of studying human experience. Husserl was Heidegger's teacher and mentor, and indeed, *Being and Time* was framed as a phenomenological investigation stemming from the Husserlian tradition. But although Heidegger's thesis in many respects amplifies the themes set out in his mentor's work, in other ways it turns the essence of phenomenology upside down.

"To the things themselves" was the rallying cry of Husserl's phenomenology. This credo was a response to the abstract nature of Western philosophy. It expressed Husserl's belief that the truth of any phenomenon could not be ascertained through removed speculation. The aim of philosophy, he argued, should be to examine those phenomena that can be observed or experienced through various acts and signs that indicate meaning. Phenomenology became a philosophy of the human experience, and the method of phenomenology became one of careful observation rather than metaphysical speculation or the construction of purely logical arguments. In much the same way as it is used in forms of psychological and social inquiry today, the method consisted of gathering information about specific human experiences through direct observation of acts and signs, and reducing that information to its meaningful essence. Complex emotions such as grief and joy, or cultural rituals such as religious ceremonies, were examined carefully with the goal of reducing them to what was believed to be their common, essential meaning.

Although Husserl's phenomenology moved philosophy and eventually the social sciences closer to a careful and less presumptuous study of human experience, it posed important problems for Heidegger. First, it remained focused on the meaning of things "out there" rather than focusing on the meaning-making individual. Husserl took a giant step in moving toward a focus on the individual meaning of real-world, human phenomena, and he helped to show how the meaning of those phenomena are constructed by human sense-making capacities. Nonetheless, his focus remained on understanding the truth of what is understood, not on the understanding process itself. Second, the reduction of phenomena to a core essence was, and is, problematic because of its suggestion of a "universal truth" that potentially blinds the observer to alternative truths. A basic tenet of Heidegger's work became the claim that anything uncovered covers something else. Therefore, any "essence" reached is merely one of many, and is the result of who, how, and when one observes, rather than being an absolute or generalizable truth that holds firm across time and contexts.

Whereas Heidegger followed his mentor to the things themselves, and remained radically focused on real-world signs, symbols, and activities rather than on metaphysical speculation, he dramatically reversed Husserl's notion of the reduction of phenomena to essential meaning. Heidegger instead proposed a metaphor of expansion: *the expansion of horizons*. According to this concept, we see the world only within the horizons in which we exist. By integrating into the familiar that which is alien or unfamiliar in life, or in study, these horizons can be expanded, allowing us to see more and to see differently. Any phenomenological study is limited by the horizons of the researcher, just as any approach to life is restricted by the horizons of the individual. Therefore, central to these arguments, and to the whole of Heidegger's work, are the concepts of time and history: any perspective, however well supported, is only valid for the moment. As horizons shift, so does meaning, and accordingly, so do the perspectives drawn from any process of knowing.

Gadamer (1976, [1960] 1993) has expanded on many of the Heideggerian concepts in a manner that has become central to the application of hermeneutics to a variety of topics and disciplines. In particular, Gadamer has developed Heidegger's emphasis on language not only for the *articulation* of meaning but also for the *construction* of meaning. According to Gadamer, we are socialized into languages that guide our navigation through every aspect of living. This socialization process leads to the formation and perpetuation of biases and prejudices that simultaneously open up and limit our understanding of the world and ourselves.

According to Gadamer's schema, in which notions of prejudice and bias are reframed, we are always projected into new situations with prejudgments—biases and prejudices built from prior experiences and the names we have attached to those experiences. The development of prejudice is a natural and unavoidable process, Gadamer argues, and one that needs to be embraced and reflected on rather than denied and avoided. He refers to this stance as the *rehabilitation of prejudice* ([1960] 1993). This rehabilitation reverses the traditional view of prejudice as unnatural and distorted by presenting it as natural, necessary, and if used properly, capable of opening one up to genuine transformation. In this regard, reflecting on prejudice might be viewed in Gadamer's framework as his road to the unconscious, with "the unconscious" defined as those aspects of self-understanding that have been thoroughly internalized and long forgotten. Gadamer (1976) describes these forgotten aspects of the self as the *forgetfulness of being,* which, he suggests, serves as the primary guide for our everyday activities.

Gadamer places our socialization into language within his larger framework of play and "the game." From this perspective, language functions like forms of play. It is organized according to rules that are learned gradually through immersion into the language game. At first, rules are used rigidly to guide the awkward player, who must think consciously about each step. As the player, or speaker, gains in proficiency, the rules slip into the background, becoming internalized and therefore less conscious. As this process develops further and the player becomes increasingly adept, she loses awareness of the game; rather than playing it, she becomes played by the game. She becomes lost in language, using it effortlessly to gain access to progressively more complex means of linguistically guided functioning.

Gadamer's conceptions of prejudice, bias, the game, and the socializing influence of language are arguably the cornerstones of this book.

Our prominent use of his language is tied to a number of factors. First, he developed important concepts from Husserl and Heidegger's work, such as the intent and historical predisposition of the interpreting being. By framing such concepts within the language of prejudice, bias, and misunderstanding, Gadamer clarified our access to these issues; he made it easier to see how understanding the concepts of *subjectivity* and *postmodernism* have liberating implications for everyday functioning.

A second reason for our steady use of Gadamerian language is that his core concepts closely match the issues of central importance to applied developmentalists. Prejudice, for example, is critical to the promotion of social development. Gadamer's broadening of our view of prejudice makes it easier to address prejudgments of all sorts, including those rooted in class, race, gender, sexual identity, and other cultural experiences. His notion of the game serves as a useful metaphor for understanding child and youth development: children are constantly socialized into new "games," such as school and social groups, that require the ongoing internalization of new rules. These are just two examples of the consistency between Gadamer's language and the language of applied developmentalists. But as important as the match between languages is the unique twist Gadamer applies to his concepts. One is drawn to these concepts through basic recognition, and changed by them through the alternative points of view his language provides.

Finally, Gadamer's work serves as a bridge of sorts between the earlier contributions of Husserl, Heidegger, and others (see Chapter Two) and the more contemporary work of Paul Ricoeur (1981) and Jurgen Habermas ([1983] 1990). Ricoeur's work provides the metaphor of the text as a model for understanding human action. Consistent with Gadamer's views on the socializing influence of language, Ricoeur depicts the texts of human lives as linguistic constructions that encapsulate the traditions people build through the range of their experiences. Rather than seeing the internalization of early relationships with parents, for example, as the primary working model from which people draw conscious and unconscious directions for living, Ricoeur sees people as drawing from the entire text of their evolving life experiences. As Gadamer suggests, these texts are organized around rules, themes, and prominent symbols, each of which are made possible, and likewise limited, by language. The subsequent chapters of this book include various connections between Ricoeur's model of the text and Gadamer's conceptions of building life texts through the interpretive power and limitations of language.

The connection between Gadamer and Habermas also revolves around language. Habermas's writings on communicative competence and communicative action set him apart from others working within the hermeneutic arena. Whereas Gadamer is centered in the postmodern view of the relativity of truth, and the literal impossibility of fully understanding another's truth because of idiosyncratic differences in life history and personal experience, Habermas emphasizes working toward common truths and mutual understanding through consensus building. He argues that communication holds the power to bring people together, just as it is capable of driving them apart. We have an ethical responsibility, from his perspective, to create communicative contexts that allow us to explore personal and political differences through dialogue. By not carrying out this responsibility, we remain snared in misunderstanding, thereby perpetuating power struggles and disparities in power. Such struggles and disparities are the sources of economic, political, and larger societal oppressions, according to Habermas. From his perspective, and ours, it is only through utilizing the power of language that emancipation from oppression can be realized.

There are obvious connections between Habermas's emphasis on communication and power and Gadamer's views on language and prejudice. Those connections might be termed the "politics of prejudice." Societal power and the manner in which it is communicated (or denied) certainly shapes the prejudices into which people are socialized and by which certain members of our society are routinely victimized. A number of the student-written case studies included in this book capture the intersection of power and prejudice, and the role of communication in uncovering and addressing these crucial life concerns.

A HERMENEUTIC FRAMEWORK FOR APPLIED DEVELOPMENT

As outlined in Chapter Two, the framework used in the Risk and Prevention Adolescent Practicum Course and in the phenomenological case studies in this book draws extensively from the substantive and linguistic history of hermeneutics, and it shapes that history into a theory, method, and approach to practice that is applicable to applied development.

The development of the framework begins with the German social scientist Fredreich Schleiermacher's ([1819] 1977) brief and commonly referenced definition of hermeneutics: *the art of understanding*. Although this definition is simultaneously too limited and too broad for applied development work, the art of understanding is at the heart of more comprehensive and specific definitions of hermeneutics. Youth development work has the art of understanding at the core of its fundamental mission: the enhancement of human functioning and well-being. In this book we attempt to link the understanding processes of hermeneutics with the understanding processes of education, counseling, and related human development efforts. This attempt is motivated by our conviction that hermeneutics—although a complicated and abstract theory generally associated with and applied to phenomenological and existential philosophy, linguistics, literary criticism, and to a lesser extent, the social sciences—has tremendous implications for the theory, research, and practice of applied youth development.

As stated earlier, the approach to hermeneutics presented in this book need not serve as a new theory of prevention or intervention, although one might view it as such. Rather, it is intended to be understood as a metatheory—a means by which existing theories can be critiqued, further understood, integrated, revised, or in some cases discarded. The theory presented here is not, from our perspective, mutually exclusive of existing theories of counseling or research. To the contrary, hermeneutics, when utilized effectively, should uncover connections among already existing phenomena and perspectives, including theory. Such uncovering typically leads to revision, but not necessarily to destruction or replacement.

Common contemporary definitions of hermeneutics might be summarized as "the theory of interpretation." Like the definition of the art of understanding, this definition is vague and oversimplified. Through the vagueness, however, one begins to see connections to youth development work. Understanding and interpretation are clearly central to the agendas of the fields of education and psychology in most, if not all, of their various applications. In a previous work, Nakkula and Selman (1991) presented a synthesized definition of hermeneutics derived from Heidegger's *Being and Time* that focuses on the interpretation of human being, or what it means to be human. According to that definition, hermeneutics is the understanding of human being through "one's interpretation of one's connectedness to the world over time" (Nakkula and Selman, 1991, p. 186). But for Heidegger, hermeneutics is more than an understanding of being: *it is being itself.* Most fundamentally, from Heidegger's perspective one *is* one's interpretations of one's connections to the world over time.

A FOUR-PRONGED DEFINITION OF HERMENEUTICS

The four concepts introduced earlier—interpretation, connectedness, world, and time—are interrelated in the working definition of hermeneutics used throughout this book. The absence of any one of these concepts renders all attempts to utilize hermeneutics incomplete, according to our framework. In addition, we would argue, the absence of any of these concepts from an applied developmentalist's efforts to understand human being and facilitate human growth will almost certainly lead to inadequate understanding and misdirected research or preventive or therapeutic action. Having stated our working definition of hermeneutics and some of the biases behind it, in the following sections we will more thoroughly describe the contribution of each part to the definitional whole.

Interpretation

Functioning as a hermeneutically informed youth service provider is anxiety provoking in a peculiarly postmodern way. That is, the hermeneutic counselor must establish and hold onto a staunch and active willingness to view reality as "a matter of interpretation." More precisely, reality must be viewed as a process of interpretation that is continuously and necessarily revised: there is no learnable truth to uncover that will bring final solutions and clarifying solace, except the truth of infinite change. Clients seeking advice or answers can find them only through the intersection of their interpretations, present and emerging, with those of the interventionist and other important people in their lives.

Hermeneutic counseling does not necessarily provide interpretations in the manner of psychodynamic counseling, in which symptoms are connected with intrapsychic relations among the id, ego, and superego. Nor does it necessarily interpret a client's behavior as a consequence of specific stimuli and ongoing reinforcements, or as a matter of cognitive mediation between stimuli and reinforcements, as is the case in many cognitive-behavioral approaches. And unlike client-centered counseling, hermeneutics does not necessarily place the interpretive onus exclusively or even primarily within the purview of the client, because counseling interpretations are generally viewed as mutual constructions between counselor and client.

But while hermeneutic counselors do not necessarily make interpretations similar to those provided by psychodynamic, cognitive-behavioral, or client-centered counselors, they could share interpretive approaches with all of them, as long as the interpretations are not viewed as "true" or "correct" in an objective sense. Consistent with Spence's (1982) notion of "historical truth" and "narrative truth," hermeneutic interpretations can be true to a client's experience without being historically or objectively verifiable or accurate. The critical component of hermeneutic truth is the person's interpretation of it, the meaning it holds for that person within his or her history and current experience.

Interpretation as meaning is the core of everything in hermeneutics, and the hermeneutic youth development process is one of creating, uncovering, revising, and critiquing our interpretations, and even grieving as we let them go. A client begins counseling with a global interpretation of who he is, who the important people in his life are, how the world works, what counseling is, and what it should do for him. His self and everything else in the world are interpreted. These intersecting interpretations constitute what he experiences as reality. While most forms of applied development work begin with the taking of the client's personal history, which creates the foundation of the therapeutic process, hermeneutic counseling begins with a historical interpretation: personal history is reviewed as the client remembers his experience of events, not as a review of events uninterpreted. In addi- tion, historical material is discussed as it was interpreted when it happened, as well as how it is interpreted in the present. This method of grounding personal history in past and present interpretive experience rather than viewing it as objective reality serves as the starting point for the mutual and integrating interpretations that the counseling relationship becomes.

As discussed earlier, one of Heidegger's guiding intentions was to redefine reality itself by moving it from "out there" in the world to "in here," within each person. The core of being human and the key to Heidegger's notion of reality is interpretation. Everything in the world, according to Heidegger, is *as one knows it to be*. Not only are personal or subjective abstractions like love, hate, kindness, and spirituality individually created, but so are the essences of events, and even material objects. The reality of any thing *is* one's understanding or interpretation of that thing. A car, for example, does not just exist out there in the world objectively; it does not have a universally objective quality of "carhood." It is somebody's car, or one that somebody else would like to own, and in that sense the car is defined by what it means to the person who owns it or wants to own it; it might be defined in part by the inconvenience of having to pay insurance and repairs, or by the fantasy of wishing one could afford to purchase it. However defined, the essence or most important quality of the car is what it means to those to whom it is important. Nonmaterial realities, like the phenomenon of "going to school" or "being depressed," are similarly defined; they *are* as they *are interpreted* by those experiencing them.

From this hermeneutic perspective, then, reality is the constitution of the world through one's interpretations. By shifting the essence of reality from the world as an external object to people's internal experiences of the world, Heidegger placed primary emphasis on the interpreter herself. The existence or being of reality can be found only in and through each individual human being. As such, any understanding of reality needs to be human centered: the most fundamental interpretation is the interpreter's understanding of herself. Without knowing how the interpreter understands herself, one cannot genuinely appreciate her understanding of the world. Working from this perspective, hermeneutic applied development work focuses primarily on the client's cumulative interpretations of who and how she is. The uncovering of these interpretations allows for an understanding of how the client perceives her history, her current situation, and her future. In summary, an interpreted self interprets a world that provides experiences of pain, pleasure, nurturance, failure, and success. Each of these experiences is derived from particular connections to the world that shape the interpretations of who one is and what one can do.

Connectedness

How we are connected to the world through relationships and the nature of everyday work, play, and ordinary living is central to our understanding of reality, even those aspects of reality that seem far removed from us. Understanding youth requires an uncovering of the connections they have to particular contexts as well as the disconnections they experience from those contexts. Family, friends, and school are three significant domains in most youths' lives. The manner in which they feel connected and disconnected within these domains is critical to understanding their interpretations of themselves, of others, and of the world in general.

When charting family histories, psychologists and other interventionists often try to elicit a list of experiences, typically those viewed as problematic or difficult in some way. A hermeneutic family history departs from more traditional clinical intakes in that it emphasizes a youth's connections to or disconnections from his family, and looks for episodes or stories of everyday family functioning and the youth's perspective on those stories, particularly his role in them. Where there is a disconnection from one parent or sibling, contributions to that disconnection are explored. When healthy connections to family members or events are not spontaneously named, there is an explicit attempt to find them. In many counseling models, emphasis too frequently remains on problems in families. For many young people, those problems are countered by important connections to relatives, siblings, or family friends. It is critical to uncover these connections and bring them into the counseling text. Without these connections, the reality of the counseling relationship becomes overly influenced by the problems in youths' lives, and underrepresented by their strengths and healthy connections. As this occurs, youth run the risk of taking on a clinically imposed problem-orientation as the predominant story of their family lives.

Interpretations of family connections and disconnections are obviously related to experiences with friends, at school and in other important societal and personal contexts. Alienating family experiences lead many youth to seek primary connections through their peers. What are these connections like? What is the content of their friendship activities, and how are those activities understood? Are the activities responses to life at home—replications of it, escapes from it? Young people's general experiences of connectedness to, and alienation from, the world are often related to the connections they make between family and friends. If they feel adequately accepted and supported in both contexts, they are likely to feel similarly in other relationships and modes of functioning. To understand school performance, for example, it is important to comprehend a student's connections to family and friends. Is school valued by these two groups? Is school performance marked by excessive expectations at home? Does a student's peers look down on studying? Without understanding the complex answers to such questions, it is impossible to appreciate why a student is succeeding or failing in school, and what that means to her.

World

Just as interpretations of self, others, and life in general always occur through interpersonal connections or disconnections of one sort or another, they also occur through connections or disconnections to the world, or more specifically, to particular contexts within the world. In Heidegger's argument that all being is being in the world, he is referring to the everyday reality of being. For some youth, that reality is strongly marked by school achievement or athletic pursuits. For others, it is marked by peer group or gang involvement, street life, family closeness or chaos, and/or religious affiliation. For most youth, it is marked by involvement in many of these contexts, and in all cases it is influenced by larger societal forces. This involvement and the social forces that shape it constitute an individual's world. What Heidegger refers to as the everydayness or ordinariness of involvement in these worlds comes to define the core of self-interpretation: I am as I am connected to my world or worlds; I know myself through my trials and successes as a friend, student, athlete, son, or daughter; I know myself as I am connected to the world of my most meaningful activities.

Hermeneutic applied development work requires both an understanding of the worlds of youth and a construction of the counseling world. Knowing youth should be knowing them in context. In group therapy, for example, six adolescents might come together to discuss concerns with school, family, and friends. The youths and therapist co-construct the world of group therapy—which allows for varying degrees of connectedness and self-exploration—and they do so from the various worlds in which they exist. What and how each participant contributes to the group is related to what and how each experiences in other important contexts. Construction of the group world is facilitated by exploration of the other worlds brought into the group. That exploration can be initiated by sharing stories of other contexts. As each participant shares a little more of the world from which she comes, her status in the group world is altered, and her interpretation of the group as a safe or unsafe environment is affected as well. The relative effectiveness of group therapy is determined by the quality of connectedness that participants feel in the group, and by the interpretations made as a result of those feelings. In short, interpretation is not detached; it occurs through connections to specific contexts. Explicitly contextualizing and discussing these connections creates opportunities for exploration and the development of further connections to a progressively larger world.

Time

The concept of development leads to the final prong of our definition. Not only are all interpretations guided by specific connections to particular worlds, they are also specific to particular points in time. When interpretations occur is as important as where and how they occur. In the group therapy example, interpretations made and shared in the group differ dramatically as group chemistry evolves. It would be inappropriate, for example, to suggest that statements made during the start-up phase of a group necessarily represent feelings and opinions that exist in later phases. For this reason it is crucial that the group facilitator recognize the potential for change and growth and serve as a historian or chronicler of relational and individual changes that occur over time.

 In all human development work, it can be difficult to recognize growth. We often believe that how we feel now is how we have always felt, or how we have felt for an extensive period. Similarly, we can believe that our thoughts and feelings are stable, representing static points of view. It is difficult to remember or track the routes of one's thoughts and feelings accurately as they develop. Yet tracking such change is crucial to believing that there is growth, and believing in growth is at the core of youth development work. Youth (and their counselors) need to feel hope that life can be different, better. But genuine hope requires some degree of evidence that one's efforts will amount to something. As historian, the therapist must capture evidence of change, to show how clients' feelings toward themselves and others and their perceptions of important phenomena have changed over time.

Capturing the evidence of change and the process of facilitating it allows applied developmentalists to articulate models of growth. Articulating growth models, even for fairly young children, is important. Success in virtually all arenas is contingent upon some belief in what one can accomplish over time. Friendship, scholarship, musical accomplishment, and athletic achievement all require development, and the actualization of that development generally requires a belief in the ability to *become* a friend, scholar, musician, or athlete. Hermeneutic providers of youth services attempt to foster interpretations of such beliefs—beliefs in one's ability not simply *to be* what one desires but, more specifically, *to become* what one desires. Interpretations of "who I am" are transformed into interpretations of "who I am becoming" and "who I hope to become." This emphasis on becoming is not meant to nullify an appreciation of one's self-in-the-moment; it is, rather, a recognition that the current self is always a self-in-progress.

As suggested previously, belief and faith in the transformation of self requires reinforcing evidence. Children and youth can feel hopeless, as though the world is poised against them, if there are not ample opportunities to experience and interpret growth. Whether those opportunities are made available through group work, classroom performance, or other contexts, a primary role of hermeneutic youth workers is to seize every moment for interpreting and acknowledging change. Small changes, like report cards that reflect improvement from D's to C's, need to be clearly recognized and celebrated as symbols of the capacity for growth. Seemingly small changes that are built on gradually can be as important to life progress as the dramatic shifts that more easily capture our attention. Unfortunately, in youth development work we too frequently seek out the obvious or dramatic, missing the often slow and steady nature of development.

Time, then, or development, is an important organizer of interpretations of connectedness to the world. For Heidegger, time defines being. He understood how the passage of time makes possible new connections to the world and new interpretations of those connections, which in turn continuously redefine our being-in-the-world. For children and youth, time, when explicated, holds a similar power—the power of possibility. The responsibility of hermeneutic applied developmentalists is to help uncover and develop the power of possibility. This uncovering process is a matter of pointing out and interpreting change where it has already occurred, and using the available samples as evidence to support the belief that an individual can be what she strives to become.

Our four-pronged definition may seem rather straightforward in the abstract. As it is applied to practice, however, each prong becomes shaped, increasingly complicated, and politicized by the life experiences, concerns, and agendas of the interpreters, and each is made even more complex when these elements are brought into relationships. The twelve phenomenological case studies in this book graphically bring to life the complexity and highly individualized interpretive process in action. A number of the studies depict the roles of race and ethnicity as critical to experiences of connectedness and disconnectedness for both counselors and youth. In these studies, one can see the "formula" of hermeneutic interpretation come to life. It becomes apparent how the praxis of hermeneutics helps people to articulate their experiences through a language that explicates modes and functions of power, of communication differences, and of inequality and transformation.

THE EXPANSION AND REVITALIZATION OF HERMENEUTICS FOR PRACTICE

Before we launch more deeply into the development of the hermeneutic framework, we want to locate this book within its historical contexts.

In our efforts to create a bridge between hermeneutic theory and practice, we have learned from the classic hermeneutic theorists—Heidegger, Husserl, Habermas, Ricoeur, Schleiermacher, Dilthey, and Gadamer. In addition to these thinkers, we have learned from current scholars in the field of hermeneutics—Martin Packer and Richard Addison (1989); Stanley Messer, Louis Sass, and Robert Woolfolk (1988); and Shaun Gallagher (1992). Several of these scholars' texts have been extensively used in our practicum course and have shaped our framework in important ways. It is important to acknowledge their contributions to the writing that follows. Packer and Addison's (1989) *Entering the Circle* outlines the benefits of a hermeneutic approach for psychological research; Messer, Sass, and Woolfolk's (1988) *Hermeneutics and Psychological Theory* places hermeneutics within the range of theoretical orientations used by psychotherapists; and Gallagher's (1992) *Hermeneutics and Education* explores connections between educational and hermeneutic theory. The implications of these works for our approach are represented in the phenomenological case studies presented in Parts Two through Four of this book.

There are also many thinkers who are not of the hermeneutic tradition per se whose ideas have helped to shape the intellectual milieu at the Harvard Graduate School of Education. Through their teaching and mentoring and by osmosis, we have been highly influenced by their work. Central among them are Robert Selman (1989), with his work on social perspective taking, and Carol Gilligan (1982), with her ongoing work on girls' and women's development. Their contributions to our framework will be apparent throughout the book. Finally, there are writers on multicultural and culture-based research who have helped to expand our paradigm. Central among these contributors are Charles Taylor (1992), Molefi Kete Asante (1991), Derald Wing Sue (1993), Paulo Freire (1970, 1973), Lisa Delpit (1988, 1995), Farah Ibrahim (1991), Joseph Ponterotto (1991, 1993, 1995), Michelle Fine (1986, 1991, 1992), bell hooks (1994), and Audre Lorde (1984). These scholars and activists, and their groundbreaking ideas, have become part of an internalized ethos that helps to shape the hermeneutic gestalt.

We enter this landscape of hermeneutic inquiry at an important point in the evolution of hermeneutics and the discourse on qualitative research methods. As we reflect on the differences between our perspective and those of many authors who came before us, one important contrast comes to mind: we *assume* rather than argue for a postmodernist perspective, having internalized a bias for postpositivist, interpretive research and practice. Our pioneering predecessors laid the groundwork that makes this possible. We have entered into already-developed, though still-evolving, discussions on the relativity of truth, the subjectivity of research, power differentials, societal inequality, gender differences, the need to attend to what is not said as much as what is, and more.

In part because of the influences of contributors from critical theory and pedagogy, multiculturalism, feminism, Afrocentrism, and post-modern philosophy, hermeneutics continues to be redefined, even reframed. Just as Heidegger used a hermeneutic approach to confront the dogma of Western philosophy, contemporary scholars are challenging the confines of the traditional hermeneutic literature. A hermeneutics for applied developmental practice must address the diversity of human experience. Lisa Delpit (1988, 1995) reveals the necessity of a hermeneutics for practice through her articulation of the errors white teachers often make in their attempts to understand and communicate with black students. Similarly, Michelle Fine's (1986, 1991, 1992) work on the meaning that low-income girls make of school success and failure argues for a hermeneutic approach colored by race, class, and gender.

This book builds on the insights of scholars like Delpit and Fine in its presentation of a hermeneutic framework that begins with the classic contributions from Schleiermacher to Habermas, and continues with more contemporary applications from such ideologies as feminism and Afrocentrism. By integrating this white European male canon with ideas that represent the practical and political challenges of our time, we have developed a hermeneutic framework designed to meet the interpretive demands of everyday life in a diverse and complex society. The outcome of our diversified framework is a gestalt that cuts across time and human contexts.

The theory, research, and practice components of our hermeneutic gestalt are actualized through the methodological approaches discussed in the next chapter. As we enter more deeply into a discussion of the hermeneutic legacy that has informed our methodology, it is important to reinforce the point that our framework is continuously evolving through our interactions with feminist, Afrocentrist, multicultural, and critical qualitative research perspectives. As such, our own perspectives, and each aspect of our hermeneutic framework, have been developed through and challenged by these related disciplines and approaches. With this in mind, we move into the specifics of our methodology.

2

A HERMENEUTIC METHODOLOGY FOR THEORY, RESEARCH, AND PRACTICE

HERMENEUTICS, AS IT IS DESCRIBED HERE, is neither theory alone, research alone, nor practice alone. Nonetheless, we use it for theory building and for uncovering our theoretical stances, as a research methodology or as a guide for methodological application, and as an approach for our counseling work. To disconnect the hermeneutic framework from any part of the theory-research-practice dialogue is to dislodge it from its natural position and dis-locate it exclusively in one domain or another. And to suggest that hermeneutics is an umbrella concept for the integration of theory, research, and practice also misses its essence, at least within our framework. For us, hermeneutics is a particular way of creating theory, or of being a theorist; of conducting research, or of being a researcher; of carrying out various forms of applied developmental practice, or of being a practitioner. In short, within our framework, hermeneutics is both a way of doing and a way of being. It is both a method and a particular way of being a methodologist.

THE DEBATE BETWEEN METHOD AND BEING

The dialectic of doing (that is, applying a method) and being is essential to the work presented throughout this book and is important to highlight for historical as well as descriptive purposes. Mere description of the dialectical interaction of method and being would omit what has been a productive conflict within the broader spectrum of hermeneutic debate, a conflict that has led to the development and utility of the particular hermeneutic framework used in our work. In this chapter we discuss the method/being debate and work from there toward articulating the methodology of our work.

Historically Based Methods: Schleiermacher and Dilthey

As noted in Chapter One, hermeneutics began as a method of deciphering the meaning of sacred texts. An early pioneer who made important contributions to this methodology was Friedrich Schleiermacher ([1819] 1977). His rigorous attempts to place the meaning of sacred texts within its appropriate historical context led to the recognition that interpretation is time bound, or historical, rather than static, or universally valid across time and context (Mueller-Vollmer, 1988). Schleiermacher summarized his approach by coining the term *the hermeneutic circle,* which represents the circular nature of interpretation. He argued that the parts of any text must be interpreted within the whole, and that the whole text, in turn, must be viewed within the larger sociohistorical context.

From this perspective of part/whole interrelationship, just as word choice, sentence structure, and thematic subplots are understood within a larger narrative, the interpretation of an overall story is derived from the intersection of meaning and nuance that is constructed from its individual parts. The whole text, of course, is viewed historically, and the historical tradition is itself influenced by the evolving meaning of its written works. Therefore, as meaning shifts anywhere within the global interactive system of a text and context, parts and whole are mutually influenced, leading to a continuous revision of both textual and historical understanding.

Schleiermacher's approach to historically based textual analysis was further developed for the social sciences by Wilhelm Dilthey ([1900] 1976), who continued to view hermeneutics as a method for deepening understanding. By shifting the locus of interpretation from the written word to the human sciences, Dilthey ushered in the view, developed further by Heidegger ([1927] 1962), Gadamer (1976, [1960] 1993) and Ricoeur (1981), that the meaning of human action could be interpreted, in important respects, similarly to the meaning of a literary text. Referring back to the hermeneutic circle of understanding, Dilthey argued that individual acts or localized social actions are influenced by, and must be interpreted within, larger contexts of behavioral and socialization patterns, which are themselves located within historical epochs or particular periods. As with textual analysis, the larger patterns of behavior and social functioning are reshaped and reunderstood on the basis of the shifting action and meaning of their constituent parts. And just as whole written texts both are understood within history and help to define it, broad interpretations of human action both are understood historically and contribute to the ongoing redefinition of human history.

From Method to Being: Heidegger's Findings

The core of the hermeneutic debate between method and being was introduced by Heidegger in *Being and Time* ([1927] 1962). In an analysis that profoundly influenced the remainder of twentieth-century thought, Heidegger adapted Schleiermacher's and Dilthey's historical methods for his investigation into the very meaning of being human. Heidegger's approach was phenomenological in the sense that it sought an essential meaning: the meaning of being, and in particular, the meaning of human being. But the essential meaning uncovered and interpreted was interpretation itself. The essential meaning of being human, according to Heidegger's phenomenological investigation, is making meaning of the world and of one's being in the world.

Heidegger named his findings "hermeneutical." Humans, he claimed, are hermeneutical beings, that is, beings who constantly interpret what the world means and what it means to be in the world in particular ways. From this perspective, hermeneutics is not a method but a way of being—the fundamental way in which we are human. According to Heidegger, we go about being human and creating human understanding in a manner that approximates the hermeneutic circle described by Schleiermacher and Dilthey. Every insight generated is understood within larger contexts of meaning, and these larger contexts are in turn understood differently as a result of new insights. In this sense, we are always uncovering new ways of being, revised ways of understanding the world and our place within it, which lead to opportunities not only for changing ourselves but also for changing the world. Every revision of self-understanding revises, to some extent, our view of the world, which has implications for our subsequent efforts toward self-development and for our influence on friends, family, and the communities in which we live.

Being-in-Language: Gadamer's Prejudice

Gadamer (1976, [1960] 1993) has been the major proponent of the Heideggerian argument that human being is fundamentally interpretive in nature, and that hermeneutics is this way of being rather than a systematic method for finding truth. Through a further articulation of the hermeneutic circle, Gadamer has presented two arcs, which he uses to describe the manner in which the parts and whole of human experience interact. The first arc is that of *projection*. It represents fairly unreflected-upon movement into and engagement with action. We are projected forward or thrown into new activities with prior expectations based on internalized interpretations of our archive of life experiences. These experiences, the meanings of which have been organized and reorganized over time to such an extent that they are a part of us, part of our interpretive history, are largely taken for granted. This historical backdrop of interpreted experience is our "forestructure of understanding" (Gadamer, 1960, 1976), the meaning base from which we are thrown into all subsequent encounters. Up to the time of the next encounter, this forestructure represents the whole of our experience.

This experiential whole allows us to make sense of the next experience into which we are projected, the next part to be integrated within our larger meaning matrix. In turn, the new experiences, or parts, provide an opportunity to revise the whole to some extent. The extent to which that can happen is dependent on the second arc in Gadamer's model, the return arc of *reflection*. By critically reflecting on the action into which we have recently been projected, we are afforded the opportunity to make more considered interpretations of that action. The more fully or broadly we can interpret the action, the more influence that interpretation can have on revisions of the forestructure that we will use for understanding future actions. According to Gadamer, this process of projection and reflection is ongoing and represents the essential nature of human being. In his framework, hermeneutics is this circular process of everyday interpretation, not a particular methodology for the human or historical sciences.

Two other aspects of Gadamer's work are pivotal to the method/being debate: the linguistic constitution of reality, and Gadamer's notion of prejudice. According to his model, all understanding is made possible by language, which ushers in new information and simultaneously restricts the meaning we can make of it. By virtue of being taught a particular language in which to describe and communicate our experiences, we are limited in our description and communication by the very limits of our linguistic capacities. But this limitation not only influences what we articulate of our experiences; it also limits the experiences themselves. Because of the restrictions of our inner and spoken vocabularies, we have a necessarily reduced awareness of categories for defining reality as we know it. These restricted definitions represent for Gadamer the socializing influence of language—the manner in which language opens us up to, and closes us off from, the vicissitudes of meaning potentially available in the world.

The socialized outcome of our linguistically guided development, according to Gadamer, is our prejudices or biases. Prejudices represent the prejudgments that stem from our forestructures of understanding. In this sense, Gadamer does not view prejudices in the usual fashion, as bigotry or conscious denigration. In his framework they are "biases of our openness to the world" (1976, p. 9), biases that are shaped by the richness and limitations of our experiences, and by the language we have available for describing and understanding those experiences. From this perspective, the hermeneutic work of being human is a matter of engaging with the world from our prejudiced position and reflecting on that engagement for the purpose of revising our prejudices in a manner that makes future engagement healthier and more productive.

Being and Method: Habermas and Ricoeur

Gadamer's reliance on an all-encompassing view of language as the constituting force in human development and human being renders his view of hermeneutics quite understandable: to be human, from his perspective, is to be a linguistic interpreter, an interpreter of one's self and the world within the confines of one's linguistic parameters. Others who followed Gadamer in the method/being debate have taken exception to what they view as an overemphasis on the role of language for structuring reality and understanding the variations in human being. Central among these critics is Jurgen Habermas (1971), who continues to grant language a central role in human functioning but emphasizes the contexts and methods in which language is used to reach mutually agreed-upon ends rather than emphasizing the individual's internal use of language to structure a reality decontextualized from external human conditions.

According to Habermas, a primary role for hermeneutics is as a method for fostering clearer communication among individuals. His method is generally referred to as *consensus building through the development of communicative competence.* But within this model, reaching consensus, or a common understanding, particularly on controversial issues that influence human well-being, requires the development of more ideal speech contexts. Habermas claims that we frequently misunderstand one another because speech is distorted by oppressive societal conditions that restrict open communication. Drawing from Marxist ideology, he argues that such conditions exist to maintain and reinforce current economic power structures. Freeing speaking conditions would result in a shifting of society and a radical change in everyday human being. Gadamer's avoidance of the role of politics in speech, according to Habermas, reduces Gadamer's understanding of the manner in which language is restricted both in its development and in its use as a tool for facilitating human emancipation. Although Habermas agrees that the hermeneutic process represents a way of being human that is grounded in language, he calls for a use of hermeneutic methods to clarify and transform understanding of and access to the speech conditions that influence daily life.

Paul Ricoeur (1989) is the final participant in the method/being debate whose work is central to this book. Drawing from linguistics, psychoanalysis, philosophy, and the human sciences, Ricoeur represents both sides of the debate. He concurs with the view of human development as similar in structure to the development of a written text, and he has contributed extensively to the refinement of the "person as text" metaphor. He is in agreement with Heidegger and Gadamer that language essentially uncovers possibilities for connecting with and interpreting our involvement in the world, and he adds that these interpreted uncoverings are organized into themes and subthemes, which come together to form the coherent structure of our evolving life stories. But just as our lives are constructed hermeneutically, from Ricoeur's perspective, they can also be understood through hermeneutic methods.

In his collection of essays on this topic, *Hermeneutics and the Human Sciences* (1981), Ricoeur articulates the use of hermeneutic methods to organize human action as an evolving text, and for interpreting the meaning of life stories through the decoding of signs and symbols that the text embodies. Consistent with both Heidegger and Freud, Ricoeur argues that the overt meaning of the text shields us from deeper and alternative meanings. As such, hermeneutic methods are required to interpret what the signs point to and what the symbols represent. As with Heidegger, hermeneutics is a process of uncovering; in Ricoeur's work, as with Freud, it is a matter of uncovering not only what is not yet found but also what has been hidden or protected. Although one might argue that the work of Ricoeur and others dehumanizes people by interpreting them as texts, perhaps a more plausible argument is that methods of textual analysis have progressed in a manner that more closely resembles what it means to be human. The metaphor, it might be argued, is reversed: it is not humans who are interpreted as texts; it is texts that are linguistically constructed and interpreted in a manner that approximates the essence of people.

Our use of hermeneutics owes much to the evolution of the method/being debate. We agree with Heidegger and Gadamer that the essence of humanness is very much a matter of interpreting who we are and how the world is, and that these interpretations are ever in flux as we continually revise our fundamental views of reality. Additionally, we see no contradiction between the acceptance of hermeneutics as a way of being and the application of methodological approaches that might also be termed hermeneutical. In our estimation, hermeneutic methods quite likely evolved out of the obvious connection between the linguistic constitution of human understanding and the linguistic constitution of written texts, as representations of that understanding. If we accept that language guides all facets of human being (even if less completely than Gadamer claims), and therefore that human existence is fundamentally defined by linguistic meaning making, including the representation of existence through writing, then it seems reasonable that methods used for the interpretation of written texts and of human action in general would reflect those meaning-making processes. In this regard, hermeneutic methods would appear to be most appropriate for capturing the hermeneutic nature of human being.

SHAPING THE DEBATE THROUGH WORK WITH YOUTH

Working from the perspective that hermeneutic methods are well-matched for the understanding of human being, our framework incorporates and builds on textual approaches that draw from each era of the method/being debate. In the sections that follow, we briefly highlight specific characteristics of work with youth that stem from the debate, or more specifically, from the various contributions of the debating theorists. These contributions are more fully developed throughout the remainder of the book.

The Text-Making Method

Our methodological model is indebted in part to Schleiermacher's ([1819] 1977) methods for interpreting sacred or historically important texts. Applied developmentalists trained within our hermeneutic framework construct written texts based on interpretive syntheses that are designed to capture the stories of their work. These syntheses, exemplified in Chapters Five through Eight, Ten through Thirteen, and Fifteen through Eighteen, pull together extensive notes taken on each aspect of the trainees' experiences, including their relationships with clients, supervisors, and colleagues, and on the systems in which their work occurred. In a fundamental sense these written works become the sacred texts of the writers' training experiences. They are as critical to professional development as academic texts read for skill development and theoretical understanding. These trainee-generated texts are meant to capture what is most important in the writers' professional development and in the progress of their work with youth. It is in this sense that the texts are sacred—they represent once-in-a-lifetime perceptions of personal and professional development.

Even though interpretations of these texts are conducted by the trainees themselves, their analyses must be historically based. Every subsequent experience in an intern's training revises the interpretation of previous experiences. Therefore, to read early contributions to a training text as "fact" would be to miss the evolutionary or historical nature of the training process, the process of becoming an applied developmentalist.

The written texts are representations of human action, and in that sense our work draws from Dilthey's ([1900] 1976) early contributions. The human experiences captured by these texts are interpreted in a manner that reflects Dilthey's use of the hermeneutic circle for understanding human interactions: the written texts allow their authors to examine critically the various ways in which individual, seemingly disconnected pieces of experience contribute to the whole of the counseling or youth development gestalt, and how that gestalt is reunderstood over time in response to the emergence of new experiential pieces. In addition, the ongoing development and revision process of text construction and interpretation affords new youth service providers an opportunity to appreciate the historical context in which their stories live and grow. As they gain some distance from the events themselves, as the events become historicized (captured in time) through writing, the trainees experience firsthand how the same story is interpreted differently after multiple readings at various points in time.

Horizons of Prejudice and Misunderstanding in Applied Development

The emphasis on time in this methodology leads to our utilization of Heidegger's contributions. His conceptualization of humanness as "our interpretations of our connectedness to the world over time" (Nakkula and Selman, 1991, p. 190) serves as the guiding definition of human development within our hermeneutic framework. Heidegger's focus on the expansion of horizons through uncovering alternative ways of being in and understanding the world is a natural fit for work with youth. Much of adolescent development is about expanding horizons; the applied developmentalist's job is to help reveal productive possibilities for the expansion process by co-creating meaningful modes of connectedness to the worlds we help uncover. Each uncovering leads to at least slightly new revelations that change, to varying degrees, our perceptions of that which came before (our past), our ideas for functioning in the moment (our present), and our expectations for the next steps forward (our future). In this regard, every uncovering and interpretation contributes to the incessant revision of our personal histories, including the historical development of our future. All being is being-in-time; no meaning of being applies beyond time, beyond the revision process that necessarily alters meaning as life's consequences unfold. In working with youth, particularly those with troubled histories, the revising nature of time is an immensely powerful tool.

The tool of time, particularly the utilization of time to revise and reinforce prejudices, is central to the incorporation of Gadamer's work in our model. Prejudice and misunderstanding, two of Gadamer's organizing concepts, have been invaluable to our perspectives on human disconnectedness and interpersonal conflict. The written texts created by our youth development trainees typically emphasize the evolution of their prejudicial views—their prejudgments or preconceptions stemming from previous life experiences—and the contribution of these prejudices to their misunderstanding of the youth they serve and the colleagues with whom they sometimes struggle to collaborate. By writing about their interactions, interventions, and interpretations over time, the trainees uncover intersections of prejudice and misunderstanding that prompt a deepened acknowledgment that any position, however staunchly held, is open to eventual revision and is therefore only temporarily valid at best. This acknowledgment, when internalized, serves as personal prevention against a prevalent form of self-indoctrination: the self-serving and unintentionally self-limiting indoctrination into particular truths, specifically those misguided truths that convince us that our versions of reality are more real and correct than alternative versions that appear unfamiliar, alien, and not readily beneficial. The hermeneutical process of de-alienation, of making the alien progressively more familiar and approachable, is an important goal of applied developmentalists in the effort to help youth move into a largely unknown and often unwelcoming future.

Communication and Power

To assist in our encounters with prejudice and misunderstanding, we draw on Habermas's notions of communicative competence and action. His emphasis on ideal speech contexts is emphasized in our model as well, although in less idealized form. The arenas in which youth development work occurs, for example, such as schools and community health centers, are generally laden with oppressive barriers to open communication, including overly busy class and counseling schedules and rigidly cast role distinctions regarding power and authority. In these various arenas, youth are typically viewed as needing something they lack, such as educational competence or appropriate behavior, or as possessing something destructive, such as a flawed character or a propensity toward violence. Rarely are they perceived as having something valuable to offer, including interesting opinions and uniquely developing worldviews.

When youth feel disempowered within their homes, schools, and communities, they often devise creative methods for circumventing or coping with existing power structures. Such methods include dissociating from educational discourses (school lessons) from which they feel alienated, adopting inflated social images of strength and beauty to compensate for deflated personal images of worth and efficacy, and learning not to share intimate truths for fear of being violated, patronized or disrespected.

Our approach is designed to encourage what Habermas would term ideal "speech situations" for countering oppressive communication. This is a complicated task, given that applied developmentalists enter their work typically representing the very authority structures that youth attempt to circumvent. Consequently, much of clinical and developmental work becomes a matter of addressing the circumvention process. The undertaking begins with the youth developmentalist's acknowledgment of the client's power to largely define, or at least co-define, the terms of the relationship. In many cases, this acknowledgment marks the first time that youth are presented with such an opportunity in a relationship with an adult who holds a position of authority.

Rather than being reprimanded for one impropriety or another, a student or client is recognized for her or his role in deciding whether to share and withhold information, and in co-selecting the topics around which to structure the relationship. Through these acknowledgments, a redressing of the initial power imbalance is under way, and possibilities for something at least approximating consensual dialogue begin to open up. The youth worker brings interest, respect, and expertise of a particular sort; the client brings primary control of discourse content and personal accessibility, among other qualities. Within these various contributions, an ongoing negotiation of collaborative authority emerges. This authority is used to coauthor a new story, or at least to begin a new chapter, one featuring a revised communication role for the protagonist and for the developing interactions that lie ahead.

Undeniably, a large power differential remains even within the most balanced therapeutic and educational relationships. Nonetheless, participation in a relationship with less coercive communication practices creates a model for more ideal speech contexts. It is this model of spoken and experienced text, which youth help to create, that becomes the successful outcome, or more appropriately, the continuing outgrowth, of a hermeneutically based developmental process. The model becomes an internalized script to be further developed and revised through future opportunities for consensual communication.

Spoken Versus Written Texts

Finally, our work draws from multiple aspects of Ricoeur's conceptualizations of hermeneutics. Using the extensive note-taking process referred to earlier, trainees review the written texts of their notebooks searching for signs and symbols that point to and represent deeper meaning than might be indicated by the surface structure of their documents. Documentation is critical to Ricoeur's understanding of the human text metaphor. He argues that speech and writing have discriminating functions within the linguistic traditions of human history and individual life. Spoken language is temporary in important respects; it creates and communicates meaning in the moment, allows people to move forward, then is partially forgotten, distorted, and transformed. Its function is largely immediate. This is not to say that storied legends are not passed down verbally from generation to generation in a manner that helps to create the very soul of culture for many peoples. But even the medium of the spoken word is open to dramatic transformation based on the workings of memory.

Written language, conversely, leaves a permanent mark on history, according to Ricoeur. Written words that mark the page represent thoughts that mark time—that mark our thinking at particular points in time. In a sense these historical markings become fixed. They become permanent fixtures of historical movement that are captured on paper for all to see, and to interpret as they deem appropriate. As such, once written, our thoughts are no longer exclusively our own; they are laid open for others to use and manipulate within their various historical contexts long after we are gone and available for clarification and, in some cases, self-defense.

In applied development work, spoken and written language have an essential relationship with each other in the construction of the therapeutic text. As Ricoeur's position would imply, the spoken word allows us to move the counseling or educational story forward flexibly, to co-construct linguistically the counselor-client, teacher-student text. But the very movement of that relationship, the history of the developing text, is dramatically lost, or reshaped in memory, if the integration of themes and subthemes are not fixed in writing along the way. Marking the relationship in writing does not, of course, fix it in meaning. The written word does not guarantee or strive for an objective historical account. It does, however, provide a lasting account that the reader—generally the applied developmentalist and her professional colleagues—can make sense of in multiple ways as the story continues, even after the historical actions have been completed.

In our training experience, nothing has been more enlightening to new youth development workers than rereading the written accounts of their work at different points in time. Although it is often astonishing to see how our thinking changes over time, it is even more astonishing to learn how much we forget as we create our training texts and move forward. In what Gadamer (1962) has termed the *forgetfulness of being*, once we learn well, we internalize our lessons and move on. This forgetfulness is quite functional in ordinary life, but for youth development trainees it is important not to forget the essential processes of successful work and professional development, including interventions that fall flat and seem disappointing in the moment. By fixing their progress in writing, applied developmentalists create the opportunity to relearn, remember, and critically reread the important markers of their growth.

In summary, the method/being debate has been a fertile dialogue for the hermeneutic approach we have developed. Each iteration of the debate has added more texture to the evolution of hermeneutics as a methodological approach and as a description of being itself. We refer to hermeneutics as a description of being rather than as a metaphor for being because human existence is rooted in interpretation from birth through death, in work, love, and play. Hermeneutics is not only a text metaphor that captures the essence of being; more fundamentally it is a linguistic effort to communicate what being is. Hermeneutic methods, then, are those designed to uncover (research), understand (theory), and facilitate (practice) hermeneutic development.

THE IDEAL FIT OF HERMENEUTICS AND YOUTH DEVELOPMENT WORK

Because of the nature of applied development work, with its emphasis on interpreting the meaning of human action for the purpose of revising both actions and their subsequent meanings, we view hermeneutics as an ideal way of being an applied developmentalist. We hold this view because counselors and educators work both explicitly and implicitly from guiding theories of human being (human thought, feeling, and action and the meaning that integrates them). More than virtually any other profession, the mental health professions are oriented toward understanding and influencing the human condition. Succeeding in this endeavor requires the ability to anticipate the likely consequences of one's ways of being, and the meaning of alternative modes of functioning and ways of being. In a most fundamental sense, human development work is grounded in guiding theories of how humans are on an everyday basis.

But informed youth service work is also grounded in research, specifically inquiry into the process of growth or change. We imagine particular readers proclaiming: "Hold on, I view myself as an outstanding practitioner, but I don't know anything about research. Research is fine for people who like statistics and live in their ivory towers. My passions are with the people, with real people I work with every day."

Several of the contributors to the chapters that follow uttered similar sentiments as they entered their training process. And many still have an aversion to statistical analyses conducted in ivory towers. But their conception of research has changed. They have learned that research is sys-

tematic inquiry into important concerns. All conscientious interventionists are interested in whether their interventions are working, how they
are working, what their relationships mean to their clients, and what
they might be missing that would be important to address. We propose
that being a researcher is an important part of being an applied developmentalist, and we provide methods for conducting phenomenological
research as part and parcel of applied developmental practice.

Hermeneutic methods of counseling and educational practice do
not, however, entail simply integrating theory and research into youth
development work. Hermeneutic practice utilizes particular skills,
those that encourage the construction and interpretation of life stories;
that promote the understanding of thoughts, feelings, actions, and personal meaning within both broad and specific contexts; and that focus
on relationship development as the primary activity of being human.
Hermeneutic practice not only emphasizes applied developmentalists'
interpretations of their clients' stories; it also emphasizes the clients'
roles as creators and interpreters of their own stories (including the
story of the developing therapeutic relationship).

Central to the overall interpretive process in hermeneutic youth
work is the focus on *everydayness,* on the ordinary events of everyday
life that define people as more than the problems or dramatic incidents
that often initially bring students and other clients to the counseling
process. By explicitly addressing everyday life rather than implicitly
viewing it as the taken-for-granted background of the "presenting
problems," applied developmentalists can provide a context for facilitating the ongoing transformation of ordinary being rather than narrowly emphasizing the remediation of problems and the resolution of
conflicts.

Applied development work within our hermeneutic framework,
then, is a simultaneous venture into the workings of theory, research,
and practice. Although in an effort to differentiate contributions to
each facet of the framework we will discuss the parts of this multifaceted endeavor individually, hermeneutics in action is a unification of
theory, research, and practice, an interactive whole. Hermeneutic
development work, too, is a way of being—of being an applied developmentalist—that is rooted in the engaged activity of understanding
and conceptualizing how people are and how applied youth development works (theory); of uncovering and making sense of the ways in
which people change and grow, and determining the manner and extent to which one's practice is effective in altering and promoting
change and growth (inquiry or research); and of interacting with

people to help them construct, interpret, share, and revise their life stories (practice). Each facet of this multifaceted framework directly informs the others, and as one progressively uncovers and further utilizes this mutually informing process, not only does the work of applied youth development become more expansive and holistic, but the very meaning of being an applied developmentalist is transformed.

APPLIED DEVELOPMENTALIST AS THEORIST

The primary goal of theoretical training within the hermeneutic framework is to set in motion the applied developmentalist's recognition that she has guiding theories of human development, of health and pathology, and for conducting her practice. We have made this goal primary in response to the common assertion made by practitioners-in-training and by those already in the field that they have no theoretical leaning, or that they are atheoretical by choice. It is not unusual to hear trainees state, "I don't want theory; I want skills." A question we ask in response to such statements is, What skills do you want, and why those skills as opposed to others? There are, of course, an infinite number of skills that can be selected for development. An informed choice of skills to develop depends on what aspects of client functioning one believes are important to address, and why particular skills would be effective for addressing those issues. Such decisions are rooted in either an implicit or an explicit understanding of human functioning, and as such they are based on theory, or within the language of hermeneutics, they are conceptual prejudices or biases.

Although all applied development work, and human action of any sort, is guided by our biases toward what we believe in, these biases often exist beyond our conscious awareness. Lack of awareness of the motives behind our actions can be momentary—as in the case of fully absorbed, nonreflective involvement in our work—or it can be ongoing—such as when our actions are informed by biases that have been covered either through forgetting or because they have developed gradually, outside of our awareness, and therefore have not been reflected upon. The second step in theoretical training for hermeneutic counselors, following the recognition that one has guiding theories or theoretical concepts, is to uncover how those theories and concepts are embedded in personal biases, how they contribute to the development of further biases, and how they affect one's work with colleagues and youth.

The concepts of bias and prejudice have been brought into hermeneutical work most prominently by Gadamer, who suggests that prejudices represent our unique perspectives on the world, and the manner in which we filter in and out the stimuli we encounter. As noted previously, for Gadamer prejudices are prejudgments. They are the judgments developed on the basis of previous experience and subsequent reflection on that experience. Such judgments open us up to seeing the world in particular ways, and close us off from seeing it in other ways. But most importantly, these judgments form prejudices, preformed judgments that guide us into every action and help to shape the meaning of these actions and our assessment of their consequences. In this sense, prejudices simultaneously create opportunities for functioning and restrict possibilities for alternative modes of functioning.

Gadamer's notions of prejudice and bias can seem oppressive and a bit fatalistic. One might ask: Am I destined to be held captive by prejudices that limit my functioning? Our answer is an unequivocal yes, and an equally unequivocal no. Within the hermeneutic framework, prejudices are inescapable, but they are also transformable. The prejudices we hold can be altered through critical reflection. They can also be blindly reinforced through a lifetime of repetition if critical reflection is not practiced.

Why are prejudices central to the hermeneutic approach to applied development work? Because whether made explicit or not they influence every aspect of theory building, and even help to define what we mean by the word *theory* itself. If we accept that all applied developmentalists operate according to internalized theories or theoretical concepts, then a necessary training step and critical component of ongoing practice is the uncovering and articulation of those theories and concepts in order to be conscious of their influence on our work. How does this uncovering occur? It occurs through multiple modes of dialogue.

Writing About Where One Comes from

In the hermeneutic framework, the dialogical process of theory building is set in motion early in training when students are informed of our bias that internalized theory guides practice, that conscious and unconscious ways of viewing the world inform every act of youth development practice, sometimes subtly and at other times dramatically. Through the Risk and Prevention Adolescent Practicum Course that spawned this book, students trained in the hermeneutic model are initiated into their work with a thinking and writing assignment entitled "Where We Come from, What We Bring." The assignment is presented as a first step toward examining how life experiences and prior educational and professional training have prepared them to view themselves, other people, and the world in their own idiosyncratic ways, and how these ways of knowing influence what they come to view as effective practice.

These unique ways of knowing, we argue, create the individualized starting point for further theoretical development. They create the prejudices that youth development practitioners must uncover, and perhaps revise, in order to see the world more broadly and do their work more flexibly. Students are often astonished by what they uncover in a short writing assignment of five to seven pages that explicitly focuses on the links between their experiences, their views of the world, and their developing work as professionals. By sharing with their classmates aspects of what has been uncovered, the students are able to compare the range of biases that exist within their training group.

This process of sharing aspects of personal history can be both validating and disconcerting. It can be validating, for example, to learn that our peers have experienced similar hardships, and that they come to the work with similar missions of helping others to transcend those hardships. It can be disconcerting, however, to feel misunderstood when, upon sharing our historical contributions to our work, our biases are not received as acceptable or legitimate by another, which sometimes occurs when differing biases are generated from similar experiences. A hypothetical example of this scenario is the case of two trainees who come from backgrounds of family trauma. Because of differences in intervention experiences, one of the trainees may have developed a bias toward aggressively removing children of abuse from their families at the earliest possibility, whereas the other might be a staunch supporter of maintaining the family unit and working through the problems with the children in the home. Depending on the lasting impact of these experiences, such differences of opinion can be intense and expressed with a wide range of emotion. But whatever one's stance on the issue, it becomes an initial bias that guides the development of one's theoretical orientation toward intervention. And sharing that bias with another creates the opportunity for viewing it more clearly and from an alternative point of view.

Reading and Rereading as Forms of Dialogue

Another step in the dialogical process of uncovering and revising the biases that contribute to theory development is the guiding of students toward a critical approach to reading. It is quite common for trainees who are interested in learning new skills to approach their reading with a desire to find answers or directions. Within the hermeneutic framework, readings are presented as texts designed to generate ideas rather than to provide answers. We encourage students to read themselves and their experiences into these texts, to read their questions into them, and to make connections that open up new possibilities for thinking about things and conducting practice. We frame this approach as a shift from "reading for answers" to "reading for meaning and the opening up of possibilities." In this sense, we view reading as another form of dialogue: the reader interacts with the text to generate multiple interpretations of it and to generate new interpretations for her work.

Just as editing and revising are important to writing, rereading is essential to reading for meaning and the opening up of possibilities. As part of the theory-building dialogue, our students read exceptionally dense material, including philosophical works by Ricoeur (1981) and Gadamer (1976), for example. These readings plunge them into abstract theoretical realms that often feel impenetrable, irrelevant to their work, alienating, and frustrating. But as they gradually build an intellectual context for this material by learning and internalizing new vocabulary, including concepts like *fundamental ontology, hermeneutic phenomenology,* and *postmodern epistemology,* their forestructures for understanding complex theory are developed—the ground is prepared for the planting and growth of new ideas.

Thus, rereading the same material at multiple points in time proves to be an enlightening exercise in exemplifying the workings of the hermeneutic circle. Each new piece of information revises the forestructure of understanding at least a little; the cumulative effect of this revisionary process makes it possible for students eventually to comprehend the majority of what they initially experienced as impenetrable texts. More importantly, our students not only reach a point of feeling that they have an approximate understanding of an author's intent, but many also move to a place of critical rereading in which they critique the value of the author's argument and consider its implications for their own theoretical development.

From Theoretical Dialogue to Dialogue in Practice

On the basis of their dialogues with instructors, peers, and the written words of authors, students take evolving views of their work to the field and to critical dialogue with clients, colleagues, and their clinical supervisors. As students immerse themselves in their work with clients, following initial exposure to theory building through early self-reflection, classroom discussion, and course readings, their work takes on a more reflective edge than it would have had they approached it from a strictly intuitive position. Clients' comments are heard in a manner influenced by the prereflected-upon theoretical dialogues, just as counselors' responses are biased by them. Initially this intrusion of theoretical overlay can serve as an obstruction to spontaneous discourse and lead to an anxiety-provoking second-guessing of one's responses and of the sense one makes of clients' comments. But as applied developmentalists become progressively more practiced in listening and responding from a theoretically informed position, they become more comfortable with the nature of second-guessing and learn to use it as a tool for accessing what we refer to as alternative interpretations, points of view, or perspectives. As we discuss in the practice section that follows, this solicitation of alternative perspectives is a core skill in our approach to hermeneutic applied development work.

Perhaps the most intense component of the dialogical theory-building process is the trainee's relationship with her supervisor. The supervision forum ideally allows for the testing of developing theory. Perspectives on readings as they relate to work with particular clients can be shared in supervision, where alternative interpretations of reading implications might be generated and appropriate intervention strategies developed. Just as new trainees often view their readings as a place to find rules for their work, they frequently view supervision as the place to get "expert" advice. And indeed, acting as advisor is an important component of a supervisor's role. But ultimately, we believe, supervision is a central place where trainees learn to be professionals. From our hermeneutic perspective, this includes the ongoing revision of human development and counseling theories, which will serve as essential guides for the enhancement of skills and their application through reflective practice.

Self-reflection, critical reading, reflective writing, discussions with peers, interactions with clients, and summarizing and critiquing one's thoughts and actions in supervision all serve as essential components to the dialogical process of theory building. Each of these contexts for dialogue, when viewed associatively and critically, informs the others. One goes from supervision back to her reading assignments, for example, with at least slightly revised views of her work, which will lead to differences in what she looks for, finds, makes of, and takes from her readings. Lessons from the readings will be taken back to discussions with her peers and the ongoing work with her clients. In an endless cycle of critical interactions, the engaged trainee finds herself fully involved in the hermeneutic circle, the process of understanding in which her views or biases toward herself and the world undergo constant revision; the more intense the process of critical reflection on her activities, the more thoroughly her interpretation of those activities will be revised.

APPLIED DEVELOPMENTALIST AS RESEARCHER

How will I know if my intervention and prevention approaches are working? How can I realistically measure change in my clients? Questions such as these are asked by virtually every new youth development worker as he begins his training. Within our hermeneutic framework, such questions are treated quite formally. Rather than relegating them strictly to the domain of academic discussion and perhaps supervisory discourse, we require that new trainees treat them as research questions, that is, as questions to be pursued rigorously through systematic inquiry. But rather than separating the research requirements of hermeneutic training from those of practice and theory building, we present trainees with a methodology that incorporates systematic inquiry into the larger process of *being* a counselor.

Phenomenological Investigation

Heidegger referred to his major work *Being and Time* as a phenomenological investigation into the meaning of being. He labeled his inquiry *phenomenological* because it sought to uncover the essence of the experience of being human. The essence found by Heidegger, as discussed previously, was that human being is primarily a matter of making meaning of our own being, specifically our ways of being in the world. Phenomenology since the work of Husserl ([1900] 1976) has generally been defined as a research approach that targets the understanding or interpretation of human meaning, the essence of how humans make meaning of real-world phenomena, primarily phenomena related to human action or interactions. The fundamental characteristics of any phenomenon, according to this perspective, are the essential meanings humans make of the phenomenon in question. As previously discussed, Husserl's early work argued that we could reduce complex phenomena to essential meanings that would be universally agreed upon if our methods of observation were adequately developed.

In Heidegger's adaptation of Husserl's phenomenological methods, he essentially reversed the notion of "reduction" through his notion of the "expansion of horizons." He argued that everything found leads to an expanded or altered view of the world, which in turn leads to possibilities for new findings, for seeing the same phenomena from different angles; therefore no finding is essential, that is, complete or final. Although Heidegger agreed with his mentor that careful observation could reduce seemingly disparate thoughts and action to deeper core meanings, he went a step further by articulating the situation of the observer as critical to the meaning that gets uncovered. This latter step had profound implications for phenomenological research, and if considered carefully it holds meaningful implications for all research. Situating the observer within a personal and historical context, and agreeing that this context will influence what is found and interpreted, suggests that common methods lead to different outcomes.

Ricoeur refers to Heidegger's process of inquiry, and to most of phenomenology that follows Heidegger, as the "grafting of hermeneutics onto phenomenology." By this he means that phenomenology, with its emphasis on the uncovering of underlying core meanings, is joined by hermeneutics, with its emphasis on interpreting that which is uncovered from the unique perspective of the interpreter. The grafting of the two concepts might be termed the "relativizing of essential meaning." To make an essence relative sounds like a contradiction of terms, but we would argue that this is precisely what we do every day. We attempt to get down to what is "most important" to us. What is essential to our understanding has everything to do with who we are and how we are situated in the world at a particular point in time.

The relativity of essential meaning is also at the core of applied development work. Although standard methods of interaction, observation, and analysis are available to applied developmentalists, each individual practices these methods somewhat idiosyncratically, and every therapeutic relationship yields its own unique application process. What gets uncovered as essential by one youth service provider might be very different from that which gets uncovered by another. From the perspective of Husserl's early work, this would indicate a problematic application of method. From the perspective of Heidegger's hermeneutic phenomenology, the different findings would represent variations in the historical situations of the applied developmentalists as they interact with the situations of their clients, and these variations would be based on differences in training and other life experiences. Such differences not only would be viewed as legitimate, but also would be expected and even considered necessary, given that no two people approach an interpretive encounter from the same position.

STRUCTURE AND FUNCTION OF THE PHENOMENOLOGICAL INVESTIGATION. Because we consider applied development work to be a classic example of hermeneutic phenomenology in action, research training within our framework is guided by prescribed hermeneutic phenomenological principles or guidelines. These principles are presented and organized for trainees through a year-long research project called the *phenomenological investigation,* or PI. The PI is designed to teach phenomenological methods of observation as part of the everyday work of the hermeneutic counselor, and to frame what is uncovered by these methods as an artifact of the intersecting life experiences of the applied developmentalist and her clients.

The Role of Research Questions

As with other approaches to research, the PI begins with orienting concerns. But consistent with Husserl's emphasis on tangible, real-world investigation as opposed to abstract, distanced reflection, the orienting concerns of our students are connected with the everyday, engaged activity of their practice. This engaged activity leads to the initial research questions that guide the beginning of the phenomenological investigation.

We emphasize initial research questions at this point because within the hermeneutic framework these questions serve as a starting point for inquiry, not necessarily as the ultimate, central focus of the investigation. As such, initial questions function as guides for our inquiries, propelling and sustaining the ongoing process of further uncovering and interpretation. But each uncovering and subsequent interpretation may lead to new questions that serve to direct the next steps of the inquiry. Many counseling trainees begin with a question similar to Heidegger's questioning of the meaning of being. They ask, What is the meaning of being a counselor? Although they begin with a preliminary answer to this question, based on the prejudices or prejudgments they bring to their work, there are deeper underlying meanings that they know must be uncovered. The original question generally leads to more focused questions, such as, How can I be more effective? How will I know my approach is working? How can I measure change? How should I choose among alternative approaches to intervention? These more focused questions guide the next steps in the uncovering or discovery process.

Research questions also function to perform the reduction that Husserl sought. They organize our focus by helping us to sift through the infinite phenomena within our vision for the purpose of selecting what we deem is most important in the moment and in our current work context. As important as these questions are to the systematic and rigorous nature of our work, they become problematic if they are adhered to in an overly rigid manner. In hermeneutic phenomenological inquiry, questions guide the direction of the project; they do not place mandates on it. They serve to open up ways and directions for looking, and they reduce what we are looking for into manageable categories. If the reducing function of question utilization inhibits the function of expanding the view of our work, then the questioning process is being misapplied. This is not to say that research questions should be altered at every whim of the investigator, but they should be thoughtfully revised in response to incoming data. An outcome of successful inquiry is the framing of new questions for the next step in our work.

Reframing Data

What exactly are the data to be analyzed via the phenomenological investigation? They are the actions, interactions, observations, perceptions, thoughts, and feelings that relate to our guiding concerns and organizing research questions. They are also the personal meaning (Selman and Schultz, 1990) of these human phenomena, meaning that becomes integrated into interpretations of how we are growing and how our work is proceeding. Note that *growing* and *proceeding* are active and evolving concepts. Hermeneutic interpretations of phenomenological data focus on movement, or *change over time.* The essential meanings of this data collection and analytical method are change and growth. Change observed in a client, for example, might be primarily a matter of change in the counselor's perspective. This is the sense in which Heidegger addressed the concept of *time.* Human being, for him, is being-in-time; the world around us is always known differently as new angles for experiencing are uncovered over time.

How are the data for the investigation collected? Here we return to the text-making process discussed earlier. Data collected by any method represent a larger reality; they symbolize the phenomena to be examined by concretely manifesting a sample of those phenomena. In the case of applied development work, changes in actions, interactions, and perceptions are symbolized by words that constitute the applied developmentalists' written texts, which are constructed with the intent of capturing the essential processes and meanings of their training experience. This text-making method can be complicated and arduous. It is complicated in that everything one reads potentially informs the revision of perceptions that influence the counseling relationship. The connection between reading and revision should be documented in the written text, which we refer to as phenomenological notes or process notes. Every conversation with a colleague and supervisor can also influence the ongoing work; these influences should also be captured in writing to maximize their benefit.

But the complications do not end with the connections one makes in the moment. Larger patterns of change are generally found gradually through layered interpretations of the written text. Layered interpretation is the iterative process of making meaning of the text in a particular way at a given point in time, revising that meaning, or parts of it, in response to the unfolding of new information, and continuing the process in an ongoing cycle of interpretation and revision. This enactment of the hermeneutic circle of interpretation is unsettling in that it constantly shifts what would traditionally be regarded as the foundation for one's developing analysis. Hermeneutic phenomenology, however, is explicitly antifoundational. The concept of a foundation is replaced by the forestructure of understanding. This forestructure represents where we stand as we enter the next encounter; it is assumed that the encounter will in some way revise the forestructure rather than simply build upon it. From this perspective, growth is not cumulative, it is transformational. It occurs through interactive revising rather than through linear or even nonlinear building or constructing.

Because this data collection and interpretation process is potentially endless, reduction of the data through written text making is vitally important. The text represents the evolution of our research endeavor. It captures observations and insights from particular moments throughout the history of our work and incorporates ongoing summaries and layers of interpretation generated along the way. The text is our concrete representation of where we have been and where our study is headed. But the whole story of the text has an arbitrary endpoint. Even after a counseling relationship has been completed, the meaning of that relationship could continue to evolve indefinitely. We assume, then, as consumers as well as creators of such data, that the written results represent *a* meaningful story, not *the* final story, that the findings are carefully selected words but not the final word. We assume this not as a compromise but as a realistic portrayal of human action and meaning making. Findings presented as static, established truths would strike us as invalid and inappropriate for the subject matter under investigation—the matter of human interpretation.

FROM TEXT MAKING TO TEXTUAL ANALYSIS. In a certain sense, the distinction between data collection and data analysis is artificial within the framework of the PI. The text-building process itself is an ongoing interpretive activity. Multiple levels of analysis are involved in every decision to record a particular observation or interaction. Specific phenomena are chosen for recording based on our preconceptions and judgments about the importance of those phenomena to the developing story; they are made sense of in a preliminary way at the time of recording, and in a more thorough way following reflection and the emergence of future data. The ongoing revisions of the developing text become part of the text itself. In this sense, data analysis cannot be cleanly separated from data collection.

Nonetheless, there are specific approaches to interpreting and reorganizing the written texts of one's work that we consider primarily data analysis tasks rather than the collection of new data. These approaches are essentially interpretive summaries of the developing text, designed to organize and synthesize connections across and within the various domains of data collection—for example, syntheses of written dialogues with clients and supervisors and of documented connections between readings and one's understanding of practice. The interpretive summaries are formulated into what qualitative researchers of various strands call *memos*. We use several different types of memos, each one designed to synthesize a different type of data.

Reflective Memos

Reflective memos summarize the critical reflections on one's written texts. These memos represent the return arc of reflection in Gadamer's conception of the hermeneutic circle. That is, the written text of observations, interactions, and even preliminary interpretations mark different points along the forward arc of projection: they capture the applied developmentalists' experiences of being thrown into the engaged activity of our everyday work at different points in time. Reflective memos represent our efforts to step back from experiences and critically reflect on them for the purpose of revising our understanding. Gadamer refers to the return arc of reflection as objectifying our experience for the explicit purpose of self-examination. This opportunity to take our experiences, our self-in-action, and our self-in-relationship as "objects" of study allows for an interpretation of the developing counseling text that places the applied developmentalists' own biases, actions, and understanding at the center of the story. Placing the applied developmentalist in this position, rather than reserving it exclusively for clients or the system, for example, is critical because it is the individual's selective data collection decisions and interpretive stances that largely determine the content of the written texts.

As summaries of written text, the reflective memos are constructed and reviewed at various intervals. Some youth developmentalists find that weekly reflective memos are beneficial to their progress, whereas others find that biweekly or even monthly memos are more productive because they allow the database to develop further between summaries.

Actual construction of reflective memos occurs through the following steps:

1. Interns read the process notes generated from their work; initially this includes the entire body of notes, but as the text expands, more recent entries are emphasized.

2. In the manner of other qualitative researchers, the interns note themes that emerge from this reading, particularly themes that capture change—in client behavior, in their own behavior, and in the developing perspectives on their work.

3. They summarize their understanding of these themes and the connections among them, leading to updated syntheses of the larger story of the text to this point.

4. They close with an overall summary of the reflective process—what the reflective memo accomplished, what it uncovered, and what it means for the work at hand.

Reflective memos tend to range from two to five pages in length. They should be succinct analyses rather than lengthy rehashings of the process notes.

Integrative Memos

Integrative memos are similar to reflective memos, but they are explicitly designed to make connections across different domains. Rather than openly reflecting on the written text in a freely associative manner, integrative memos direct applied developmentalists back to their readings and ask them to make links between the readings and the development of their work. In this manner, theoretical learning serves as more than a background guide; it is made directly applicable to one's real-world concerns. A similar process is implemented for critical dialogues. As part of integrative memoing, trainees are asked to reflect on supervision, peer dialogues, and classroom discussions, and to make connections between these interactions and the texts of their intervention experiences. This explicit focus on connections across the domains of learning is designed to uncover new interpretations of the developing text, and to generate alternative strategies for future intervention and dialogue.

Existential or Self-Reflective Memos

Existential or self-reflective memos place the emphasis of reflection squarely on the experiential quality of applied development training. Authentic applied development work of all sorts comes with a good degree of anxiety and a host of related feelings. Existential memos are designed to capture the quality of these feelings, particularly as they shift over time. Initial anxiety tends to be centered around questions of ability and competence. As trainees gain confidence, a reduction in anxiety typically follows. By capturing connections between experiences in practice and shifts in affect, applied developmentalists are able to gain a fuller appreciation of their own professional development.

Because the work of counselor training is so affect laden, it is not difficult to document and summarize the existential quality of the experience. Unfortunately, however, anxiety and related feelings are generally viewed as problems to overcome. In our model, these feelings are viewed as guideposts and markers that, if attended to respectfully, will lead the applied developmentalist to a deeper engagement in the learning and developmental process. As such, existential memos serve to focus directly on the value of one's felt experience.

Analytic Memos

Analytic memos pull everything together. Their function is to synthesize the main themes of the story and to summarize as succinctly as possible that which is being uncovered and learned. As such, they can connect the felt experience captured in the existential memos with the substantive links made across domains of experience captured in the integrative memos. Analytic memos respond directly to one's research questions and pull responses from each aspect of the developing text. In response to a global question like, How is my counseling work progressing? analytic memos would summarize relevant information from the reflective, integrative, and existential memos, and from other insights that might be generated in the moment. Analytic memos must be especially systematic; that is, the responses to research questions must be clearly and succinctly supported by references back to the larger text of process notes and previous memos.

Because of their central function within the PI, analytic memos require an especially thorough approach to their construction. The need to systematically support analytic summaries takes a fair amount of time. As such, these memos are written less frequently and in more depth than the others. In general, analytic memos are written approximately once per month. If, however, reflective, integrative, and existential memos are written on a regular basis, it might be more manageable to synthesize their findings through analytic memos less frequently, perhaps every two months. The time-consuming nature of this holistic memoing process can seem quite daunting and perhaps overdone. But if it becomes systematized and made part of the essential work of youth development practice, memoing can be an organizing activity that actually reduces the anxiety that trainees typically feel about the progress they are making in their training and in their delivery of services.

The final analysis of a PI is essentially a lengthy analytic memo. Main themes from the text are identified and supported by reference to the overall text-making process. The themes are organized according to the initial research questions and those questions that evolved during the course of inquiry. Findings, or the story of the ongoing text, are presented through a new text—an overall phenomenological account that summarizes the questioning, uncovering, and interpretation processes. The student papers presented in this book provide case examples of completed inquiries presented as phenomenological accounts.

VALIDITY, OR THE ACCURACY OF INTERPRETIVE FINDINGS. To what extent are the analyses of the PI "valid" representations of the data? To respond to this question, we borrow directly from the work of Packer and Addison (1989), who have provided a succinct and helpful summary of the literature on validity for interpretive research. Packer and Addison list four criteria for assessing interpretive validity that we find applicable to the PI: coherence, external evidence (including interpretations of the participants being studied or worked with), consensus, and practical implications. As the authors suggest, whether used alone or in some combination, these criteria do not guarantee the accuracy of an interpretive account. We have found, however, that when used together they enhance the believability, or convincibility, of an interpretation rather than achieving validity in an objective sense. This reframed notion of and method for achieving validity—that is, getting closer to the meaning but still not fully apprehending it—is the core of what hermeneutic interpretation seeks.

Coherence

Coherence applies to the internal structure of the interpretive findings. For hermeneutic applied developmentalists attempting to understand processes of change and growth, coherence is accomplished by the reconstruction of interpretations of client functioning, or by the counselor's interpretations of her own effectiveness. Rather than simply asserting or loosely formulating an argument that group counseling has been helpful to a particular client, for example, a coherent interpretation of "helpful" might articulate specific changes in the client's functioning that seemed to coincide with participation in the group; it might also capture particular responses to group activities that seem related to larger changes in behavior; and it might include comments from the client that the counseling experience has been valuable. More importantly, however, a coherent interpretation would capture the subtlety of change; it would depict particular moments or events, and the evolution of moments and events, in a manner that convinces one that the group was helpful to the client. It is this subtle specificity of findings to which coherence is addressed. The more subtly coherent an interpretive argument is, the more believable and convincing the interpretive findings will be.

External Evidence

A convincing and believably coherent interpretation does not guarantee validity. There may be competing interpretations that are equally convincing and believable. Which of these interpretations are true or most accurate? Although from our perspective there are no "true" interpretations, the relative value of competing options can be assessed in part through the use of external evidence, or evidence that exists beyond the text one has analyzed. Referring back to the example, internal evidence to support the success of group counseling might have been captured through process notes and memoing, which become the text of one's analysis. Going beyond that text to support one's interpretation might include checking with teachers, parents, and peers on the functioning of a client (if that is appropriate). It might also include reviewing changes in school grades or attendance. Depending on the issues of concern, it would be useful to go beyond the data used to construct an interpretive argument to get a sense of whether that argument is supported by external indicators in the client's life.

A primary source of external evidence is the client or research participant himself. The counselor could ask the client direct questions about the impact of the group. If the client's response is consistent with other external evidence and supportive of the counselor's original interpretation, it would seem that the counselor might be onto something. The counselor is left, however, with the question of competing interpretations.

Consensus

Consensus building is one means of addressing alternative views of the data. Within hermeneutic parlance, consensus is interpretive agreement. Packer and Addison are careful to point out the difference between agreement through consensus and the establishment of *inter-rater reliability,* which is commonly sought in more mainstream qualitative research. Inter-rater reliability is a matter of independent raters sharing their perceptions of observed phenomena, or their judgments of the meaning of interview texts. Consensus building is more a matter of bringing different interpretations into dialogue.

Perhaps the client whom the counselor feels was helped through group counseling is viewed very differently by a teacher. The teacher might see a deterioration in behavior where the counselor sees improvement, or she might see similar improvement but attribute the growth to different contributions. The goal of sharing the details of contrasting perspectives is to arrive at an interpretation that the differing participants can support. Such a consensus-building process typically results in modified interpretations due to additional data being brought to bear on the issues. The modified interpretations are not viewed as "the truth," or as the most accurate point of view; rather, they are viewed as a reminder that the more perspectives that are brought to bear on any interpretation, the richer and more representative the interpretation will be. Any consensus reached is simply the most current and most feasible one, given the available evidence and the ability to take perspective without critical distance.

Practical Implications

For hermeneutic applied developmentalists, perhaps the most important indicators for supporting an interpretive assessment are what Packer and Addison refer to as the practical implications. To what extent is it important that an interpretation be considered believable or valid? To the extent that real implications are at stake.

Because of the practical implications of youth development work, the validity of youth developmentalists' interpretations are of critical importance. Although it is unreasonable to suggest that all applied developmentalists should carry out hermeneutical research projects that frame questions related to the progress of each of their clients, and that they should respond to those questions with a systematic note-taking and memoing procedure such as that outlined earlier, we believe it is feasible for applied developmentalists to conduct what might be termed *isolated research projects* on specific aspects of their work. These projects would require youth care providers to challenge the veracity of their interpretations and interpretation-building processes. Systematic inquiry into one's own work affords the opportunity to sharpen one's interpretive skills and to uncover the taken-for-granted power of one's decisions. Active engagement in the research component of hermeneutic applied development work allows the practitioner to go beyond the assessment of validity in her interpretive findings and move toward the construction of more valid or productive intervention interpretations. Therein lies the purpose of phenomenological inquiry for hermeneutic youth developmentalists: to uncover more options for effective practice. If practice is improved, one's research findings have been valid.

RELIABILITY OR THE REPLICABILITY OF INTERPRETIVE FINDINGS. If one is convinced that findings from an interpretive inquiry are valid or meaningful, is it important to be able to replicate those findings, or to reach similar interpretations if one is presented with a similar set of data? This is a tough question. We believe that for youth development work, replicability of method is more important than replicability of findings. That is, there are certain processes for responding to research questions and to questions stemming from hermeneutic youth development work in general that should be reliably implemented. Note taking, memoing, soliciting alternative points of view, and other strategies discussed earlier ought to be utilized in any effort to attain believable and meaningful findings. The less rigorous and systematic the data-gathering and data-analysis process is, the more random one's interpretations are likely to be.

Reliability is essentially accountability. One can count on findings that have been gleaned from a rigorous dialogical process of interpretive research more securely than on findings that have evolved more exclusively from intuition or single points of view. Within the hermeneutical model, any finding is considered temporary and context-specific. Interpretations constantly change as people move and grow. Therefore, it is less important to emphasize the particular findings from a phenomenological inquiry than to develop a reliable or accountable method of uncovering new findings on an ongoing basis. Because human being is largely a process of uncovering and interpreting meaning, hermeneutical research requires reliable methods for capturing the uncovering and interpreting process. The methods discussed here have been designed with that goal in mind.

HERMENEUTIC APPLIED DEVELOPMENTALIST AS PRACTITIONER

Although we have referred to applied developmental practice from our hermeneutic framework throughout much of this chapter, it is important to conclude this methodological overview with a clear statement on the centrality of practice for this work. It is youth development practice that brings the theory and research implications into the world in a meaningful way. Interpretive theory and interpretive methods of research are simply attempts to capture the interpretive core of human being. Interpretive practice is an attempt to understand and help develop the interpretive activities of youth. It is through this process that hermeneutics as a way of being and hermeneutics as a practical method of enhancing human being come together as an obvious and productive pair.

The Subjectivity of Truth

The most recognizable tenet of our hermeneutic approach to applied developmental practice is our emphasis on the subjectivity of truth, particularly as this subjectivity is manifested through interpersonal relations. Individual views of reality, or worldviews, become the focal point of youth development practice. The intersection of worldviews, as manifested through connection and confrontations in peer groups, in teacher-student relations, and through cross-cultural encounters, become the working arenas for hermeneutical practice. The uniqueness of individual interpretations of the world are difficult enough to uncover and understand; the confrontation of interpretations as they emerge through social contact further multiply that difficulty. Whether trainees are working with individual students, pairs, or groups, their emphasis is on the subjectivity of the participants' stories.

How is the emphasis on subjectivity actualized? By treating children and youth as philosophers—that is, as meaning makers contemplating responses to the world's most important question: the meaning of their own being. It sounds simplistic to suggest that children and youth should be treated as philosophers or meaning makers, because, after all, is that not what all approaches to child and youth development emphasize? Unfortunately, in our experience most approaches treat young people, and particularly those deemed "at risk," as anything but philosophers. They are more likely to treat them as actors, and mostly as bad actors or as actors doing bad things, such as failing in school, getting in fights, getting pregnant, or taking drugs. In this scenario, the goal of intervention is to make them better actors. We are not thoroughly opposed to the action approach on principle, but in practice we believe it is frequently ineffective and even cruel.

Hermeneutic applied developmentalists work with children to help them create possibilities for changing their own behavior. We do this by focusing on what is most meaningful to the children at particular points in time and in particular contexts. If a fourth grade boy is referred for counseling because he is fighting in school, for example, we will work with him to understand the meaning of fighting for him, rather than only implementing strategies to make him stop fighting. His original responses to our questions about why he fights are likely to be fairly superficial, disguised answers—such as "I just do it because other people act stupid," or "I don't know; I just get an attitude sometimes"—which are designed to keep us at a distance. Fighting might be something he learned on the streets or in his family, and he might not trust us with his genuine motivations. And why should he? We are still strangers to him. And if he wants to distance us, for whatever reasons, why would he be receptive to strategies to help him stop fighting?

If, however, we engage the boy in response to his seemingly simple answers with genuine queries like, "Hmm, I've never seen you get an attitude. What kinds of things make you get one?" he might choose to take us another step into dialogue rather than feel the need to defend himself. If we can "go there" with him, on his terms, at his pace, we are more likely to move closer to the deeper meanings of fighting for him. As fighting becomes an object of exploration in the counseling relationship, it also becomes an activity over which the boy has more control. In the developmental meaning-making framework of Robert Kegan (1982), the ability to make a subjective experience an object for discussion or examination gives children control of that experience; it renders children less subjected to it. In the case of fighting, the fourth grader's ability to examine his fighting for its deeper meaning allows him to choose fighting rather than simply being a fighter. Greater access to the choice typically leads to access to alternative choices as well.

More importantly, the search for the meaning of fighting establishes a model for the search for meaning in general. In our intervention model, the counselor rarely stays on the fight track or the track of other presenting problems for long. There are a multitude of issues that children and youth find meaningful that adults never ask about. Grown-ups tend to ask questions of youth when problems arise. We do not, however, tend to investigate interests that do not in some way intersect or interfere with our own functioning. And when they do investigate such interests, we typically do so at a level below which children and youth are often grappling to make meaning.

In an opening session of an eighth grade boys' discussion group, we asked participants to share what is most interesting and important to them. One boy said, "I'm interested in getting a job." After discussing with him and other members of the group the types of jobs available to eighth graders, of which the options were few, we asked what types of work they would like to do in the future, when they are older. Various professional and semiprofessional job options were listed. But the heart of the conversation emerged when the boys discussed why they want good jobs in the future—the meaning of this to them: "I want to raise my family in a safe neighborhood," "I want money so my kids don't have to be on welfare," "I want a good-looking wife to do things with—you need money to do things, you need a job."

The eighth grade boys in this group had aspirations similar to those of older teens and young adults. Where do the meanings of these aspirations get discussed and explored in depth? Where are these dreams—realistic dreams—taken seriously? Sometimes at home, but often not. Sometimes in school, but rarely. For many young people, there is no context in which they can count on having their deepest ideas and hopes received and genuinely appreciated. When they get into trouble in school, their fights and failures are sure to be addressed in the most serious fashion. Yet their deeper truths are expected to flourish unacknowledged—if, that is, they are believed to hold such truths. This is grossly unfortunate and painfully unfair. Young people, specifically those educated in low-income urban, small town, and rural schools, are commonly neglected at the level of their deepest truth—the truth of what is most important to them now and in the future.

Hermeneutic applied development work attempts to uncover and develop the subjective truths of youth. Rather than just exploring the availability of jobs and the training and education necessary to become employed, for example, hermeneutic applied developmentalists explore the meaning of work and education. Without this foothold in meaning, education and career-path development remains abstract and seemingly unreachable. The same holds with relationship concerns and interpersonal conflicts. Until the meaning of relationship is explored with youth, strategies for relationship building and conflict resolution are fairly meaningless.

Subjectivity and Everydayness

Heidegger's notion of everydayness suggests that the core of human being is experienced through everyday participation in the activities that define our culture, our ways of being, or the world as we uniquely and prereflectively know it. By *prereflectively* Heidegger means our intuitive, instinctive, and visceral experience of being in the world versus knowing through abstract or distanced thought and reflection. Our emphasis on exploring the subjectivity of what is most important to children and youth is not meant to contradict Heidegger's perspective on everydayness. In fact, we attempt to counter the problem orientation of many counseling and other intervention approaches precisely because those approaches address what stands out as problematic in a person's life.

Our working model goes beyond what stands out to the life context from which problems emerge. Hermeneutic youth developmentalists ask youth about the activities of their everyday lives. What do they do after school? Who are their friends? What do they do together? Do they have hobbies? How much time do they spend with family? In what capacity? What TV shows do they like? Until the counselor knows what youth do, he or she cannot work with them on what daily life means for them and how it relates to the way they hope to live in the future. In addition, understanding the experience of everydayness allows the counselor to understand better the meaning of problems. Problems exist within an everyday context, and everydayness creates the context in which meaning and choices are made. Unfortunately, problems are too frequently the only part of that context to get seriously addressed. When that occurs, the problems are magnified and come to represent a larger part of everyday being; they become the one part of that being to receive reflective emphasis. Problems move out of the larger prereflective context and receive reflective priority. The goal of hermeneutic youth development work is to reprioritize the activities that receive reflective attention. By attending to the actions, interests, and possibilities of everyday life, hermeneutic youth developmentalists hope to magnify those aspects of ordinary being around which youth can build productive and gratifying lives. We do this by taking the details of youths' everyday lives seriously, thereby validating the value of their larger life contexts and the meaning they make of those contexts.

Because practitioners often are not accustomed to addressing the everydayness of youth development, it can be difficult to uncover it and keep it at the center of their work. The note-taking and memoing processes previously discussed are crucial tools here. It is worth noticing whether one's notes and memos are marked by dramatic events or ordinary ones. For example, we encourage counselors to consciously incorporate information on the daily lives of their clients—how they feel about coming to school, being in school, going home, and being at home. As these everyday experiences are built into the note-taking process, they are more likely to be further explored in subsequent sessions.

By keeping ordinary activities and feelings at the center of the note-taking process and ongoing work, it is possible to encourage growth and change in everyday functioning. An approach that emphasizes problem resolution is particularly inadequate in schools where large percentages of students are underproductive. Growth in everyday productivity is required here. As the daily actions of ordinary functioning are uncovered, reflected upon, and better understood, realistic changes in that functioning can be addressed as well. Such changes are not addressed within a paradigm of "problem resolution," but rather by an approach to "getting more of what you want." Everyday life must be respectfully uncovered and validated in order to implement strategies for building on it.

Assessing Everyday Change

The emphasis on systematic note taking and reflection on everyday events is the direct result of our trainees requesting tangible skills to counter the feeling of not accomplishing enough in their work. In response to such requests, we encourage conscious recognition of the everyday interactions trainees are having with their clients, rather than looking beyond these interactions to more dramatic disclosures, insights, or behavioral changes. As a result, the note-taking process allows trainees to capture small, incremental changes in communication patterns, in gestures of trust, and in other emotional and behavioral expressions.

When our trainees summarize the results of their phenomenological inquiries, they begin to see that many important and dramatic changes or shifts have occurred through their work, and that these changes would likely have gone unrecognized if not documented for interpretation. Through this process, they also begin to appreciate how their own understanding of their clients had grown incrementally, and how they themselves have changed as youth service providers. This method of uncovering patterns of incremental change over time allows the student-practitioners to realize the powerful and meaningful effects of their work, both for their clients and for themselves. This realization is among the most powerful tools in hermeneutic applied development work; it reinforces the value of fostering small, in-the-moment connections that lead to ongoing, incremental growth.

Promoting Everyday Change Through Cultural Development

It should not be surprising that applied developmentalists often seek out the dramatic in their work. There is an attraction to drama in this society, including the drama of extraordinary success and failure, of romantic happiness and painful suffering. This societal flair for the dramatic quite likely contributes to practitioners and social policy-makers emphasizing prevention and intervention for gang violence, drug abuse, suicide, and school dropout, while often paying less attention to the everyday experiences that contribute to these concerns. If service providers of all sorts could recondition themselves to attend to the ordinary "culture of childhood," as the educator and youth worker Karen VanderVen (1996) argues, they would be more likely to promote "normal" growth rather than responding to "abnormal" or "pathological" reactions that stem from extraordinary deprivation.

Childhood culture is developed through, among other things, the repetition of rituals. Just as adult culture is centered around such activities as lighting Sabbath candles, wearing a pink triangle, or daily meditation, childhood culture also has ritualistic regularities. Relationships with and between children are developed through repetitive rituals such as walking to the cafeteria, playing basketball, and drawing together. These everyday, seemingly uncomplicated activities make up a significant amount of the exchanges that go into building trust. Among the most important of these activities are everyday forms of play. The use of play to develop a culture of childhood, or a counselor-youth cul-ture, is central to hermeneutic applied development work; it is through playfully engaged activity that children and adolescents are best able to "lose themselves" in their world, thereby finding a meaningful place within it, a place of comfort and connectedness.

Something as mundane as playing checkers, if it occurs repeatedly over time, can become the foundation for a mutually engaged thera-peutic alliance. In Project IF (Inventing the Future), explicitly designed from our hermeneutic framework, activities constitute the center of counselor interactions with students. Relationships in Project IF are built in a variety of ways, including weekly games of checkers, chess, and cards, or through drawing, sewing, and the writing of songs, poetry, and life stories. Because Project IF relationships are given time to grow through activities in which students feel comfortable and in which simple strengths are developed, there is an opportunity for adult-youth relationships to develop within a culture that the adult and youth co-construct. As this culture evolves, exploration and interpreta-tion that reach beyond the games and activities become possible and even welcomed as part of the counseling cultural norms.

Culture and Relationship-Based Perspective Taking

As stated at the beginning of this section, hermeneutic youth develop-ment work addresses children as philosophers or meaning makers. Issues of subjectivity, everydayness, play, culture, and relationships are elements of the perspective-taking tasks that mark the daily lives of children and youth, just as they orient the work of hermeneutic coun-selors and applied developmentalists. Our focus on perspective taking owes much to Robert Selman's work on the development of interper-sonal understanding (1980) and childhood friendship (Selman and Schultz, 1990). Selman's developmental schema helps us to organize our conceptualization of the meaning-making process for children and youth, particularly meaning making in developing relationships.

Selman argues that children move from an initial inability to take perspective on their own needs and interests to more advanced levels of perspective-taking capacities. In a best-case scenario, by adolescence youth develop the capacity not only to take perspective on their own social agenda but also on the agendas of others with whom they are closely involved. At its best, this perspective-taking ability is translated into actions that are assertive, respectful, flexible, and caring. When perspective taking does not develop so fully, youth become stuck in social ways of being marked by self-centeredness, rigid judgmentalism, unhealthy prejudices, and abusiveness. Between the poles of limited and advanced perspective taking and related actions are intermediate levels of development, with a movement from self-centeredness toward more mutually oriented insight and action.

Our hermeneutic approach to social perspective taking emphasizes the interpretation of contrasting or alternative ways of being. In building a counselor-youth culture through game playing, for example, whether in groups or through individual counseling, hermeneutic counselors seek opportunities to differentiate the interests and wishes of the various participants. In so doing, they create contexts for highlighting multiple wishes, competing interests, and varying perspectives. Learning to defer self-interests to those of a peer out of fairness or caring is a step toward acting on an expanded view of one's social world.

The differentiation of perspectives for older youth can be highly complex. As youth mature, they inhabit progressively more expansive cultures. They move between life at home, in the neighborhood, in school, and at work, and between relationships with family, teachers, employers, friends, boyfriends, and girlfriends. In many urban communities, the social world also includes turf struggles between neighboring groups or gangs, struggles that often include the negotiation of personal safety, even life and death. How are all of these worlds made sense of within one internal culture—the extended conception of culture or society held in one's mind? This question becomes a focal point of hermeneutically based practice.

Because youth move so swiftly from one context to another, and often do so in a taken-for-granted manner, the shifting is generally done instinctively or prereflectively. In individual or group counseling, and in other modes of applied development work such as leadership training, this complex social task is uncovered and analyzed. An early and important step in such work is to recognize, define, and validate the process of culture shifting or code switching (Anderson, 1990). It is an extraordinary accomplishment to navigate successfully through the multiple demands of today's multifaceted youth cultures. Even partial accomplishment should be recognized as an important milestone.

After acknowledging the existence of culture shifting, youth development work can focus on different approaches to this task. What are alternative approaches to negotiating with parents and friends when differences of opinion arise? What are the language shifts that various youth use when moving from one culture to another? How can one save face in the midst of conflict? There are strategic responses to questions such as these. There are also meaning-based responses to support or reject the given strategies. It is the differences in personal meaning (Selman and others, 1992) that the hermeneutic approach emphasizes. These differences represent the multiple interpretations that youth make as they develop into more sophisticated social philosophers.

From perspective taking in the social world, our hermeneutic approach moves toward perspectives on the future. Heidegger and other existential and hermeneutic theorists, including Salvatore Maddi (1988), argue that present activities are primarily guided by future expectations. High-risk or self-destructive activities, from this perspective, are often guided by a relatively hopeless view of the future, whereas healthier behavior is guided by a more optimistic view. At Project IF, we help youth to connect explicitly their behavioral and social choices of today with their hopes and expectations for the future. Often this can be a difficult task. Many youth cannot articulate a realistically gratifying future. They feel stuck in a life filled with inordinate challenges and obstacles, and live only to survive. When asked to articulate future plans, they communicate vague fantasies at best. Even by late high school, many such students view the future as an extension of today, not as something toward which to dream, plan, and work.

In both group and individual work, hermeneutic practitioners focus on helping students to define clearly their possible futures. This step is necessary in the effort to help youth differentiate past and present behavior from a future toward which they are striving. If there is not a future to be developed or compromised, the past and present lose an essential part of their context. In this sense, hermeneutic youth development work is essentially future oriented. It is about taking perspective on one's world for the purpose of growing productively within it, and for the purpose of changing one's being in certain contexts of the world in order to survive, transcend, or help change those contexts.

The specific approaches to helping youth take and share perspectives on the future, and to creating strategies for productively moving into it, are virtually infinite. Prepared applied developmentalists need not approach their work with predetermined or preplanned strategies. The methodological core of hermeneutically based practice is to uncover everyday ways of being in the present and to connect those ways with possibilities for the future. Each youth and relationship will present different challenges for this method. The applied developmentalist's task is to honor the idiosyncrasies of those challenges, and in doing so to validate the youth who present them. Through the process of validation, uncovering and interpretation evolve. Through that evolution, both the youth and the applied developmentalist can come to see each other and their possibilities for connecting and moving forward in an expanded light.

We move now from this methodological thesis on what we do and where it comes from to the core of hermeneutic methodology in action—who we are and where we come from. However abstract hermeneutic theory, research, and practice can seem at times, interpretation is a profoundly personal activity. Our prejudices, biases, and misunderstandings arise from our experiences. Any abstract layerings placed on this experience are influenced by the lives we have already lived. Accordingly, the next chapter presents our personal contributions to this work. What we have written in this book stems from how we have lived. How we practice professionally is heavily biased by what we have practiced in our personal lives. In this vein, the following chapter serves as an essential link between the abstraction of methodological discourse presented here and the practical work presented for interpretation in Parts Two, Three, and Four of the book.

3

WHERE WE COME FROM, WHAT WE BRING

The Historical and Relational Underpinnings of the Hermeneutic Framework

---

THE AUTHORS OF THE PHENOMENOLOGICAL CASE STUDIES presented in this book began their training experiences with an assignment to clarify a conscious starting point for their prevention and intervention activities and for their interpretations of those activities. The assignment, as discussed in Chapter Two, is called "Where We Come from, What We Bring." Its purpose is to help trainees in the hermeneutic framework to begin cultivating an ethos of looking inward as well as outward in their work with youth. It is designed to begin a dialogue about the ongoing process of uncovering the prejudices, biases, and already-internalized theoretical concepts that guide their work. As important as anything new they will learn, we argue, is what they have already learned, internalized, and in many cases forgotten. If it remains concealed, the already-learned-and-forgotten plays a hidden or unrecognized role in shaping action and interpretation; if unconcealed or revealed, its power can be acknowledged and worked with more flexibly.

It would not be feasible to include each student-author's "Where We Come from, What We Bring" assignment in this book; yet it seemed important for us to provide readers with a sample of this essential starting point for the sort of inquiry we are presenting. Accordingly, we have chosen to share and interpret parts of our own histories—familial, cultural, and individual—in a manner that parallels what we ask from the students who conduct their training through the Risk and Prevention Adolescent Practicum Course. In this chapter we make meaning of our histories in both a retrospective context (what our experiences have meant to our previous development) and an emergent context (what those experiences came to mean to us subsequently). We offer these historical portraits not only as examples of the type of self-reflection in which our students engage, but also as a potential model for the reciprocal sharing of experiences between instructors and students, supervisors and trainees.

PORTRAIT: MICHAEL NAKKULA

Where I Come from: Roots of the Hermeneutic Framework

On August 29, 1981, Vicky and I got married. We had each just graduated from large public colleges in Michigan and were prepared to take our plunge into the real world. Vicky received a job offer as a special education teacher at the Cobb Elementary School in Duluth, Minnesota, so we packed the car (didn't need a U-Haul), found an apartment, and I went out to look for work. I went armed with two bachelor's degrees, one in psychology, the other in communications, although my passions, and the majority of my undergraduate coursework, were in literature and religious studies. In addition to my paper credentials, I had several years of experience as a residential treatment counselor for developmentally delayed adolescents and adults. I was, I thought, quite prepared for the job market.

And indeed I was right. After a good bit of searching, interviewing, and turning down jobs selling everything from vacuum cleaners to life insurance (pay by commission, of course), I found the plum. I got a job as a paperboy. The *Grit* (weekly rural newspaper) route my brother Tim and I had as kids nailed it for me; I didn't tell them we eventually lost the route for lack of payment and the call of baseball. Well, my new job wasn't exactly a paper route. I was hired as a circulation manager for the *Duluth Herald and News Tribune*. My job was to recruit and train paperboys and papergirls, and to watch over their accounts (this is why I didn't tell them Tim and I had lost the *Grit* route). The local newspaper in my hometown of Hancock, Michigan, made the job sound even better when they reported, in the notice of my marriage to Vicky, that I was taking a post as "the Manager of Circulation for. . . ."

Not bad for a first job out of college. In my later forays into hermeneutics, I found it interesting that this little twist of language could lead to a large change of meaning. Language and misunderstanding: once linked, you see the connections everywhere.

Except for the fact that Duluth's climate rivals that of Siberia—and paperboys and papergirls delivering their bundles in the dark, frigid early morning (we're talking 6:00 A.M. here) must have felt like former Soviets being punished for crimes against the state—the job wasn't bad. After all, it got me into the newspaper building where real writers worked. And being a writer was really what I wanted to do when I grew up. But beyond that, the job had other attributes that clearly anticipated the work presented in this book.

First, I didn't have to arrive at work until 10:00 in the morning, but Vicky's job started at 7:00 or 7:30. This gave me several hours of alone time, which I used to cultivate my interest in the history of psychology. Always one to lean toward the dramatic, while simultaneously being driven by a ferociously ambitious and disciplined Finnish Lutheran upbringing,[1] I developed a pattern of waking up at 5:00 in the morning and reading books on the history of psychology, along with the primary philosophical works to which the psychology historians referred. During the first year of this routine, I poured over two history of psychology books from a class I had taken during my final year at Michigan State. That class had whetted my appetite for such reading by making me aware of all I hadn't (and of course, couldn't have) learned during my education to that point. I also read and took detailed notes on Kant's *Critique of Pure Reason,* and read minor BOOK pieces by Sartre that would eventually serve as my entry point into Heidegger and hermeneutics.

I was twenty-three years old at the time, having stayed at Michigan State an extra year to earn my second degree, which had fortunately led to my taking the history of psychology class. At that age, if all I had been doing was reading dense philosophical works and attending graduate school, the rest of the story would have been much different and, for me, less gratifying and interesting. But at 10:00 I was getting out and going to work. I was going into the office to call disgruntled newspaper customers, going out to deliver undelivered papers, and perhaps bowling a few lines at lunch with my colleagues Tim, Gary, and Arnie. At about 3:00 in the afternoon, I'd go out to meet with the children who were picking up their afternoon bundles and talk with those who were mismanaging their accounts; given my own shady history as a childhood paper-carrying accounts manager, there was no tricking me on this score. In short, I was in the world doing real-world work with youth. But I was taking Kant and Sartre with me. I was motivating children to deliver papers, working on an out-of-control hook on my bowling release, and spinning inside with matters of truth and authenticity.

This era marked the professional start of my interest in linking the most abstract of abstract thought with the most practical of real-world work. It began to highlight the dialectic that has served me in much of my career and life. But there are family and religious ties that preceded this and that are equally relevant to the work presented in this book.

The Legends of My Youth

I grew up among legends. My father, Arvid Nakkula, was the strongest man in the world. He could work harder than anybody, beat anybody up if he had to—but only if he had to—drink more and better than anybody, and still, despite all the toughness, he'd be the first to cry at funerals and weddings. This is how I saw him as a child. As I grew a little older, I came to see him as a practical man, a copper miner, coal shoveler, and construction laborer. He was the person doing the "bull work," as he called it, because he didn't have an education. The oldest of fourteen children, he had quit school in the fifth grade to help raise his family. Work, hard work, was what he knew. When I was born and became his oldest son, it was what he taught me. But there was a theoretical part of my father that I came to appreciate only much later and that has been immensely important to the course of my life and work.

With only his fifth grade education, my father was still a man of the book—not the Bible, but another book of principles. He was a man of his small, black AFL-CIO laborers manual. As the union steward, he was the voice of the workers, always out there on the front line debating pay, work policy, fairness issues, and above all, safety. Being a union steward was about turning policy into practice and principles into action, and about interpreting quality through productivity. It was, as this book is, about the links between theory, practice, and research (or the outcome of practice). Unfortunately for my father, he left his union job on construction for a safer one as a maintenance worker with less bull work. This was unfortunate in that an unsafe work practice led to his slipping down a flight of freshly waxed stairs and becoming permanently disabled. Principles that guide work are not just for thought; they're critical to responsible practice.

My mother, Joyce Nakkula, also was a legend of my youth. Like my father, she too was one of fourteen siblings, but she fell in the middle somewhere, which perhaps explains how she became so adept at seeing things from different angles and accepting cruel twists of fate that would have baffled and destroyed a person of less vision and faith. Part of my mother's legacy was her ability to create legends. She was always the storyteller, always the dramatist. With her there was a blurring of realities, a merging of fact and fiction. She was, in a sense, a person of multiple realities. Around her the world seemed larger than was possible to contain. It seemed filled with life and possibility beyond what was tangibly available. I grew up feeling that I could have and be anything, even though there was no material evidence to support that feeling. Her stories provided access to other-worldliness; they provided transcendence beyond the here and now to possibilities not quite envisioned but clearly felt, experienced even, on another level of awareness.

Being aware of the unknown, having faith that you're getting somewhere important even if you're not quite sure where that might be or what it might bring—this I got from my mother. And this I try to pass on to my students and the children and youth with whom I work. Project IF (Inventing the Future), which is described in this book, comes almost directly out of my mother's stories, my mother's essence. And my attraction to hermeneutics as a philosophy and practice of multiple truths and infinite possibilities is, quite obviously, connected to a childhood of storytelling.

There were other legends in my family, many more, and in retrospect I can see how they all play a critical role in this book, in how I got here, in what I bring to my work. With parents from such large families, my childhood and youth were filled with color, personality, difference, love—lots of love—and almost infinite variations of role modeling. There also was a great deal of loss, pain, and sorrow, of people dying or just going through their idiosyncratic versions of hard times— divorce, alcoholism, neurosis, depression—the stuff of ordinary families, only there was more of it in mine because we had more people to share in it. It all makes for a huge family album or two. In fact, there are so many scenes, so many pictures, we couldn't hang them all from a family tree; we're more like a family forest: old trees, new plants, vegetation everywhere, always something else growing wild, blossoming, decaying, and dying.

The point is, I was prepared early for my line of work. I grew up among people, lots of people! There were so many stories going around; there was so much to interpret. I had to create myths to keep it all together, to keep it all in perspective, to have it all make sense somehow, even the contradictions. The legends of my youth became the metaphors for my life. I developed complex, internal working models of relationship and functioning. I became an associative thinker, because there was so much to connect. All of this I bring to my work, and much of it I find represented in the writing of my students.

Difficult Texts, Being Mentored, and Learning to Give Back

Professionally, I come from another place that contributes centrally to my interest in hermeneutics and my approach to my work. Following my year of solitary philosophical reading and working with the newspaper, I began a master's program in counseling at the University of Minnesota–Duluth. Two things happened there that dramatically influenced my career. First, my year of intensive reading made graduate study seem simple, simplistic even. And this is not a statement on the quality of Duluth's program, which I thought was superb. I learned solid skills, and was exposed to a wide range of psychological reading, but I hungered for the depth of theoretical understanding that I had been attaining on my own. Whereas I was an average student in high school and college (a 3.0 GPA in both places), I felt like an extraordinary graduate student. It all came so easily. I liken it to basketball, in which practicing shots just out of one's range makes the normally difficult ones seem suddenly easier.

My students at Harvard are benefiting from this lesson. They are required to read demanding philosophical texts by Ricoeur, Gadamer, and Habermas that have little obvious connection to their work. Initially, many see this as Harvard esoterica; they want hands-on skills for immediate use in their fieldwork. It's hard to explain Duluth to them, and 5:00 in the morning, and why I think this abstract reading is the most practical thing they can do for themselves and their work. But I try, and they listen, and soon they write papers like the ones you will read here. And I wonder, how did they get this so fast? And near the end of the year they say, "I wish it hadn't taken me so long to make these connections." I can only grin with an immensely warmed heart.

This confrontation of difficult texts is an ethical issue for me, connected with growing up in a working class family devoid of such readings. We had few books in the house; the collection of stories my mother told was our version of literacy. Many of my students in the Risk and Prevention Program come from similar backgrounds. I feel it is necessary to communicate that they, like me, deserve access to all the ideas that shape our world, not just those that are readily available. Learning to read is an ongoing process. At all points along the way, it should be challenging and capable of opening up depths of understanding not previously envisioned. I pass this lesson on to my students. They, I expect, pass it on to the children and youth they meet in their practice.

The second thing that influenced my career in Duluth was meeting Joe Morris, my advisor. Joe is an African American man of tremendous intellectual and personal power. He took me under his wing, brought me into the relatively small African American community in Duluth, and opened me up to cross-cultural youth counseling and development. Just as important, he befriended and mentored me and opened his home to my wife and my younger brothers. All of these acts touched my soul and shaped my view of what was possible in counseling, youth work, and academia. In short, they empowered me and expanded the horizons for my work to a degree that I could not recognize at the time. Only upon reflection could the magnitude of that time, of that historical moment, stand out for me in the fullness of its current meaning.

Vicky and I left Duluth after I graduated with my master's degree, as I followed her for a second time. This move took us to New York, where she began her graduate studies in developmental psychology at Columbia University Teachers College. I again hit the pavement (and found much more of it in New York than in Duluth) looking for work, this time armed with one more piece of paper and a good deal more experience. I landed a job as an addiction counselor in the Bedford Stuyvesant community of Brooklyn. Maybe I'd read Kant and Sartre, had a master's degree, and experienced the mentoring of Joe Morris, but when I got to Bed Stuy, I was still a country bumpkin. This was another world and I was a childlike visitor.

But soon enough the connections began falling into place. I was sitting, hour after hour, mostly with African American, Latino, and Haitian clients, listening to stories of addiction, childhood trauma, negative self-perception, and relationship problems. I was also connecting with my clients as people, not just as addicts in need of help, and I began looking forward to our sessions. I was coming to realize that the people in front of me were telling stories that could have been told in my family—in fact, were telling stories similar to those I had heard in my family and in my community. I also came to realize that I would not have been listening to those stories had Joe not provided access through our relationship. I was learning and thinking about power in mentoring, in counseling—specifically, cross-cultural counseling—and I was thinking about giving back, about passing on what had been provided to me.

Perhaps mostly, though, Bed Stuy made me think about my family, about friends left behind, and it shaped my thinking about the children and youth with whom I would work in Boston. These thoughts were all tied together by the dialectical tension between pathology and possibility. The stories of alcoholism were commonly stories of tragically underdeveloped potential—of wrecked or miserable lives in which there was little hope early on of a decent outcome. This reminded me of the miseries my parents and other family members suffered due to limited opportunities for an easier life, a life of less bull work. Why, I began to ask, did I have it as I did, when family and friends who were equally talented had it much tougher? It's a question with many valid answers, and it drives my efforts to develop programs that promote opportunity development for children and youth from low-income and working-class families.

In addition to my work in Bed Stuy, our stay in New York was important for another reason. Vicky brought us into the Ivy League from our public school educations in the Midwest. This exposed us to another brand of intelligence: book-learned intelligence. Most of her classmates came from private school backgrounds, and we got our first taste of the advantages and disadvantages that provides. We could not help but compare what we knew with what "they" knew. The upshot, for me, of this thoroughly biased comparison, was further verification that my independent reading, which I picked up again in New York after completing the required readings of graduate school, had served me well. I felt at least as informed, and educated in a focused sense, as the graduate-level Ivy Leaguers I was meeting. When it was time to apply to doctoral programs, I dared apply to those at Columbia and Harvard, among others, and was accepted at both. How was this possible for someone who had been a high school and college student with very ordinary grades and consequently mediocre SAT and GRE scores? Some obvious answers: relational support from Vicky and Joe, and the willingness to read beyond my range. Life support, mentoring, and academic challenge: I owe a lot to these contributions. I try to give them back where I can.

Matters of Religious Interpretation

I owe a lot to something else as well, something that has everything to do with hermeneutics, with meaning making, with the construction of guiding myths, or as others might have it, with sacred truths. I owe a lot to my religious background, to the Finnish Lutheranism mentioned at the outset of this chapter. My adolescence, including my early college years, was marked by a devout belief in a Christian God, and a fairly careful practice of my faith. I attended church regularly, read the Bible compulsively, prayed obsessively, and neither drank, smoked, nor used drugs. There were other sins too plentiful to name that wore heavily on my conscience, but by and large, religion served as my protection against the risks of the world and as my cautious guide into it. As with my mother's stories, religion served as transcendence beyond material and temporal limitations. It served as assurance that ultimate success could be achieved through faith.

Without knowing it, I began at that time what I would now call early hermeneutic investigations of the Bible. I scoured the gospels for meaning, tried to make sense of contradictions where I found them, and eventually tried coming to terms with the sacred truth of my faith and the messages I was hearing in my religion classes. To further complicate these matters of religious interpretation, I married Vicky, a Catholic, and did so in a Catholic ceremony. Because the minister of my conservative parish would have found such an act blasphemous, I hired a stand-in minister from a more liberal protestant church where Tim, Dad, and I used to work as part-time janitors to participate in the marrying ritual. Obviously the sacredness of my belief system was beginning to crack. Truth and goodness seemed more flexible than I'd originally thought. Christianity was beginning to look like one of many roads to peace and understanding. But it was the road that got me through adolescence and the one that first led me to in-depth examinations of truth.

So, how does all this relate to counselor training, the practicum course, and to this book? In every way. I bring to counselor education and youth development work a deep belief in the construction and interpretation of stories, of myths, of legends. I bring to it a belief in the impact of powerful relationships that serve to provide those connections to the world that help us uncover alternative and expanded possibilities for being. I bring an applied belief in the connections between theory and practice—applied in the sense that I live that belief through my ongoing reading and development of theoretical positions that I take consciously into practice. I bring my history to this work because that is how I understand my being here, given where I come from. And understanding, revising, and using personal history is what counseling and much of youth development work are about. To me, more than anything, this work is about interpreting history for the purpose of making it.

PORTRAIT: SHARON RAVITCH

Interpreting Connections: Revisiting and Reframing My Personal and Cultural History

I make deep connections between my familial and cultural history, connections that continually shape and reshape my worldview. I begin this portrait with a story of a moment that reaches back decades and centuries: back through ages of learning and flight, to shtetls in Russia and voyages to America, to places and events and choices that have shaped and transformed the individual psyches of generations and the legacy of my family and my people.

Two years ago, my mother told me this story:

> As you marched across the stage to receive your degree from Harvard, I felt moved beyond speech—you and your sister are the first two women in our family to go to college, and then to graduate school! As the choir began singing, I heard a whisper in my ear. It was a low whisper, in Yiddish, and the voice kept saying "Mummashanah [dear one], teach me an English word. . . ." It was my Bubbie [grandmother] Sadie, and her whisper brought me back to the room we shared on Eighth Street in Logan. My grandmother, an immigrant, did not speak a word of English, but would ask me to teach her the English words I was learning in the first grade—not for the sake of prosperity or prestige, for she was already an old woman, but for her desire to learn.

This moment reaches back, touching the lives and building from the stories of many, and as I interpret it, it is about barriers and possibilities, about a yearning for personal development, and most of all about the resonance of voices and connection. One connection I make between this story and my formal education relates to the concept of possibility and its relationship to education. Growing up in my family, learning of many sorts—cultural, emotional, creative, religious, academic—was modeled by my parents, Carl and Arline Ravitch, through the ways they chose to live their lives. Together they made sure that our home life was focused on our community, on commitment to family and community service, on philanthropy, and on a profound appreciation for what we had. My parents repeatedly told my brother Frank, my sister Elizabeth, and me about what it was like for them growing up (my father grew up on welfare and my mother with little more). Linking their pasts to our futures, my parents implored us not only to recognize and "count our blessings" but also to use what we have been given to work toward helping others and achieving *tikkun olam*—healing the world.

My parents created an environment in which relationships were valued, patience was nurtured, and the consideration of others' perspectives could be realized. In addition, they are each a role model for me of the value of curiosity and learning, both formal and informal, relational and academic. Both of them have shown me, through example, the power that education, combined with support, can have to change and improve one's life, and therefore the lives of others. I think of my mother, who has dedicated her life to learning and teaching by leading and participating in study groups at our synagogue (which my parents helped to found so there would be one in our community), by learning Hebrew as her children did in school, by taking classes and studying rigorously on her own, as well as by collecting an extensive library that she and our whole community can use as a resource. Throughout my childhood my mother was, as she still is, passionate about learning and dedicated to communicating what she learns to others. In addition to enriching our family with her wisdom, she has worked for many years as a volunteer and community educator, and is always teaching and learning from others—be it history and religion or empathy and kindness.

By watching the ways in which my mother interacts with others, I have learned what it means to live profoundly—with a generous spirit and a receptive sensibility. My mother embodies, for me, the reciprocal relationship between learning and teaching, as well as the importance of placing relationships at the center of one's life. Hers is a unique and dynamic combination of scholarly and intuitive learning that is based in the intense strength and wisdom that come from her deeply held faith and her love of humanity.

Equally as powerfully, my father's life has framed education for me as possibility. Born an only child into a financially disadvantaged family, my father devoted himself to study and excelled in school, becoming the first and only person in his family to attend college. My father's desire to educate himself, combined with familial support, helped him to transcend his circumstances and to create opportunities for himself (and later for his children) where there were once only barriers. But even with his success, my father did not end his diligent pursuit of knowledge—he reads two newspapers and several magazines a day and often two books at a time—nor did he leave his roots. Dedicated to his family, my father supported them throughout his own education, early married life, and tenuous beginnings in the then unfamiliar world of business. And later, after he was able, he returned with my mother to his never-forgotten Jewish and communal roots; they have given their time, money, and ideas to many charities and foundations so they could create possibilities for others.

My father's is a quiet and unassuming form of teaching. He loves with strength and consistency, affection and tears, laughter and unwavering support. He loves with patience and energy, with the kind of tenderness that too many men of his generation (and mine) have been socialized out of. He has been able, in a culture that often separates people from their families for the sake of earning material success, to negotiate his desire for this form of success with his value of prosperity at home. I continually learn by watching him, listening to him, and observing him interact with others. He is, as he has always been, a role model of proactive living, humility, and resolve.

Each of my parents teaches me, continually, to reach higher and to go deeper. And this model of my parents actively working side by side to raise their own levels of education, to teach their children, and to remain with their people and in the world community is more than anything else what has implanted in me the value of learning not only for the sake of learning but also for the sake of transcendence—both my own and others'.

I embrace this generous, loving, committed, and passionate background, which my parents and my grandparents worked so hard to give me, as the foundation of who I am and what I bring to my work with youth. Even though I feel intense appreciation and gratitude for the wonderful ways in which I was able to grow within my family, as a result of my study of and experiences with critical hermeneutics I have learned that this proud legacy must be placed within the context of the larger, oppressive societal forces that have shaped my experience in the world. For me, this means that I must learn to embrace tensions and profound contradictions.

Throughout the past four years of focused study I have come to realize that as an educator I must challenge my perspective by being critical of where it comes from, as well as conscious of how it can create blind spots and assumptions about myself and others. I must locate the source of my strength and ideals as well as my weaknesses and naivete, in order to engage with youth from backgrounds different from my own, across racial, socioeconomic, ethnic, religious, and national lines, in relationships that are honest and empowering.

(Re)Locating Myself: Looking Back to Now

I want to describe some of the profound changes I have experienced over the past few years, changes that I feel are directly linked to the reflective practices of hermeneutics. Throughout each season of my education at Harvard I remained connected to the Risk and Prevention Adolescent Practicum Course. This connection began in the fall of 1993, when I arrived at Harvard, freshly graduated from Temple University, to begin the master's program in Risk and Prevention and decided to enroll in the practicum course from which this book has evolved. This point in time, when I was an intern, student, and researcher of hermeneutics, marks the beginning of a focused struggle to examine aspects of myself and revise my perspective. This process has meant, among other things, embracing the ambiguity of a perspective that uncovers the subjectivity of human thoughts and feelings, and how these are embedded in and shaped by larger societal forces.

A second wave of examination commenced in the fall of 1994, when I began working towards a degree in Human Development and Psychology. During this period, Michael Nakkula and I continued to engage in research together and I became a participant-observer and evaluator of the practicum course. By observing others work through their experiences in the course, and because I began working as a counselor at Project IF (described in Chapter Two), I was able to deepen my understanding of both the substantive and the experiential components of the course.

The following year I began doctoral studies at Harvard, which offered a third year of involvement with the hermeneutic framework for applied development. I worked as a teaching fellow for the practicum course and was responsible for facilitating weekly group discussions as well as for supporting and working with master's students as they strived to concretize their ideas and questions and articulate them in their written work. During this time my primary role was threefold: to help teach the hermeneutic framework of theory, research, and practice to new students; to coordinate Project IF, which works explicitly within a hermeneutic framework; and to continue my ongoing investigations into hermeneutically grounded theory, research, and practice with Michael Nakkula.

As a master's student, I had a strong sense early on that the practicum course would be emancipatory in terms of my growth and professional development. It became clear to me that the course lectures, readings, and debates were causing a dramatic shift in my thinking. When I entered graduate school, I had already begun to think critically about texts I read, in the sense that I knew to consider a variety of contexts in any piece of writing. However, I did not see that such "academic" practices—that is, textual analysis—could be applied to the realm of human interaction. I did not yet fully conceptualize how interactions and communications are affected by the contexts of both speaker and listener, and that there is a need to contextualize continually any communication within the multiple and simultaneously interacting subtexts of both individual and shared evolving contexts. Realizing the subjectivity and fluidity of interpretation and the implications this has for my work with youth was a powerful experience. This shift, while seemingly small, has had lasting effects on the way I view and conduct myself, my relationships, and my professional life.

This newly held understanding brought with it a realization that I, like everyone else, work from a guiding perspective that is informed by biases about "the way things are." I consequently realized that it is an ethical consideration both in research and practice to explore in depth these biases and prejudices. The powerful concept that biases and prejudices need to be reframed—not as inherently pejorative but, when they are acknowledged and reckoned with, as openings for better self-understanding and the understanding of others—has become a central lens through which I view myself and my work.

Learning these concepts and their practical and ethical implications as a young graduate student in the intersecting fields of education and psychology felt revolutionary. I clearly remember thinking that I had just stumbled upon a way of seeing things that would help me to understand more by being sure of less. This was a seemingly paradoxical perspective, but it was the first time I could articulate, and in the process build on, my intuitive sense of some of the themes taught in the course: the need to consider others' differing perspectives, the importance of contextualizing communications more broadly and deeply, and the value of looking at changes and patterns of connection in relationships over time. Because I grew up in a culturally, intellectually, and spiritually Jewish home in which the Talmudic tradition of questioning was encouraged and internalized, the value of interpretation and critical questioning was not foreign to me. Still, I did not conceive of them as active and conscious aspects of my daily life beyond this Jewish context. It is the active reflection, self-consciousness, and link to action of the hermeneutic framework that awakened in me the need to look within and then work out into the world from there.

Many significant shifts have occurred in my thinking over the past few years that are the result of my research and work in hermeneutics and psychology. Most importantly, my desire and ability to challenge myself to feel uncomfortable and vulnerable in order to allow others' perspectives, when they do not bolster my own or when they challenge me, to teach me. My willingness to revise my interpretations based on what I learn from others has certainly been developed and refined over time. However, I can directly locate the impetus to integrate this point of view more fully into my life within the first year of the course, when I began to realize that I am often "wrong," in the sense that I misunderstand others and appropriate the meaning of what they are saying (or not saying). I remember feeling surprised by the realization that all communications are a matter of interpretation, and that as I misunderstand others, they misunderstand me. In my work with young people, and in the dialogue we had in the practicum course about issues of race, class, culture, and power in the realms of youth service and research, the realization of my potential for appropriating others' meanings and the consequent questioning of my assumptions frightened me. This was the first time I was forced to confront my biases and preconceived notions about others—both individuals and groups. It was also the first time I felt compelled to look at the socioeconomic privileges and taken-for-granted lifestyle that my social class and whiteness afford me because of the way American society is set up.

At first, this experience was painful—I had to reckon with the forces of guilt, regret, and fear, to see beyond them and to move myself past them. I believe that had I not experienced the high level of anxiety that I did in the course, I would not have felt challenged to really check myself on the ways in which I have internalized the racism and classism that are so pervasive in society. As my phenomenological investigation (see Chapter Five) chronicles, this was an arduous process. I was forced to look at myself and not only to dislike some of what I saw but to make changes that felt radical and threatening, while at the same time exhilarating and enormously important.

This process of feeling alienated from myself had many stages. I recall at first feeling angry that I was being placed in a situation in which I had to take a good, hard look at myself. I remember complaining to a friend that "I didn't come to Harvard to be made to feel guilty about growing up the way I did." I remember telling this same friend that "I just want to learn counseling skills. After all, I'm in a practicum course—let's get practical." These statements say so much to me now. First, they remind me about how I artificially separated my personal self from my professional self (which seems impossible for me to conceive of now). Second, they call my attention to the degree to which I used to dichotomize theory and practice. Today I believe there is nothing as practical or as central to counseling and education skills as the ability to look at personal biases and how they can potentially disempower others. These statements also tell me a lot about the development of my desire to live mindfully (through reflection) and about the shift I have made from an aversion to self-criticism to an acceptance of this as my responsibility.

I recall experiencing this time of my life with mixed emotions because I began to feel deeply ashamed about having grown up in a nurturing and financially prosperous white family. Before this, I had never felt anything but appreciative and proud of how I grew up. Coming to graduate school with this perspective, I felt angry that I was being unfairly asked to question my values and upbringing. Looking back, I can see that while I *was* questioning my background, there is something extremely fair about that—personally and societally—both for myself and for the students with whom I work. Since this initial shift, I have continued to work through the issues and feelings entwined with the realization (and all the new ones that keep emerging now that I am open to them) that my experience must be problematized by seeing it in relation to a larger societal context of severe racism and inequality of many sorts. Moreover, I now know that I must not only acknowledge my privileges but I must use them to work toward raising consciousness, effecting empowerment, and fomenting change.

The transformation of my perspective and worldview has occurred in stages: doubting myself because of where I came from, feeling my background was a liability in working with youths placed at risk, realizing that my comfort is sustained by others' discomfort and the oppression that keeps our societal system firmly founded, and negotiating my realizations and new understanding with my desire to still enjoy and honor my heritage. This was, as I look back, a process of learning to embrace contradictions, or as Goldner (1992) termed it, a both/and rather than an either/or perspective.

Through challenge and with support, I have been able to reframe my life history in a way that empowers me to engage in this work. My goal is to connect with youths in order to help them think of ways to reframe their histories in order to uncover and develop their strengths and, like my father, to create possibilities where there once seemed to be only barriers.

From Connection to Respectful Tentativeness

I now enter interactions expecting to be misunderstood and to misunderstand. This hermeneutic concept has moved from feeling daunting, from wondering how anyone can communicate if we only misunderstand each other, to feeling empowering, because I now realize that there is something infinitely liberating about maintaining a respectful tentativeness about others. I have learned that it is much too easy to be overly confident that I understand what someone means with only a small amount of information. I believe I must embrace what I do not know or cannot know about people, and in realizing this I can work to become a more generous person, allowing others more freedom to explain their meanings to me rather than assuming I already know or understand them.

As a researcher and practitioner (and as a friend, daughter, sister, student, and colleague), my goal has shifted from "getting the facts" of a person's experience to trying to understand what those facts mean to her or him. This helps me to develop my humility and, I hope, to become a more ethical researcher and a more respectful and empowering educator. In the context of my relationships with youth, this realization shapes my understanding that I must truly give the same weight to youths' interpretations of their experiences and the meanings their actions and relationships hold for them that I give to my own "expert" interpretations. I have internalized the belief that kids are experts of their own experiences (Delpit, 1995) and that I must listen carefully to make sure I genuinely hear them. There is a tension that exists here: while I must work to maintain a respectfully tentative stance, particularly about what I believe youths should prioritize or resist, I also want to help reframe aspects of their lives that cause them pain or limit their possibilities. The tension resides in the negotiation of hearing and honoring youths' interpretations while discerning which ones I feel need to be reframed in a way that is emancipatory. It also resides in negotiating the pain I feel when I actually hear their stories, without trying to smooth things over.

I have internalized much of the vocabulary of hermeneutics and the meaning complex that is inextricably linked to this vocabulary. It has become a part of my consciousness, partly shaped by it, partly shaping it. As I tell these pieces of my story, I am aware that while my goal is to explicate the shifts that have occurred in the ways I frame things, it is difficult, if not impossible (and altogether undesirable), to go back to a point when this intellectual, emotional, and experiential framework was not a central part of my being. What I can say about the transformation I have experienced is that I continually feel myself growing as I work to acknowledge where I am, where I am not, where I am in relation to others, and what biases I carry with me. Most of all, I believe I am better able to remain cognizant of all that eludes me as I grapple with what I know all too well.

FROM PERSONAL HISTORY TO INTERPERSONAL TRANSFORMATION

As our portraits suggest, we come to this work from very different backgrounds. We have found, as is often the case, that our differences act as counterpoints for our approaches to working in youth development. What we bring individually to this work—from Nakkula's Finnish Lutheran faith, working class family roots, and training in cross-racial counseling to Ravitch's grounding in Jewish culture, focus on gender issues in psychosocial development, and background in feminist hermeneutics—helps us to see and understand it from different perspectives.

In addition to differences in where each of us comes from, we have experienced changes in our relationship within a variety of contexts over time. Our collaboration began as student and professor, then moved to co-researchers as part of a Faculty Research and Innovation Fund grant from Harvard, which led to the further development of the hermeneutic framework. Next we began working together at Project IF as counselors, administrators, and evaluators. Over the years we continued our research, practice, and evaluation of Project IF, while continuing our general research into the applicability of the hermeneutic framework for applied development. Finally, we began working together in the teaching of the practicum course and in the eventual writing of this book.

As we discussed various aspects of the practicum course, the hermeneutic framework, our work with middle school students, human development, politics, and philosophy, we realized the differences in our interpretive frameworks and how these point to the larger issue of how different and even competing or opposing worldviews get played out in communications and interactions. This realization—that even between two people who share a commitment to help empower youth through a grounding in hermeneutics there exist infinite differences in how we understand and make use of this theory—exemplifies the hermeneutic tenet that understanding of all forms is contingent upon our experiences historically, ideologically, philosophically, politically, and personally.

NOTE

1. *Sisu* is the word that Finns and, in my case, Finnish Americans use to define our character. It means guts, determination, and stamina, and is associated with getting things done without regard for personal cost or energy.

PART TWO

THE TRANSFORMATIONAL ROLE OF INTERPRETATION

4

SELF-REFLECTION AND MUTUAL TRANSFORMATION

TO AN OUTSIDE OBSERVER, the relentless focus on self-reflection at the center of the hermeneutic framework can appear to be no more than an esoteric exercise in self-indulgence. At worst, it might be seen as the sort of "work" that privileged Ivy League students do in the security of their ivory tower. But paradoxically, self-reflection in the hermeneutical sense is designed to lead the interpreter beyond the trappings of the self, beyond the hold her concealed prejudices have on her possibilities for understanding and interacting with others. For applied developmentalists working with youth, particularly youth characterized as "at risk," "learning disabled," or "hyperactive," for example, self-reflection is especially important. It is all too easy for the practitioner to see problems, including those that emerge within a professional relationship, as residing exclusively inside the other and outside the self, and therefore to place the burden of responsibility for those problems "out there" with the "problem holder."

Placing "identified problems" within the other is especially common where relational power differences are most obvious, as in the case of counselor and client, particularly adult counselor and child or youth client. Typically, a counselor helps to define what the problems are, both within and outside the counseling relationship, then implicitly or explicitly places responsibility on the client for resolving them. The applied developmentalist's role in this scenario is to help uncover and clarify problems, and to provide support and strategies for their resolution. However, the responsibility for change remains with the client. For example, when relationship conflicts occur in school-based counseling, the locus of those difficulties tends to be identified in the "resistance," "pathology," or "antisocial behavior" of the "disturbed youth," or in the "irresponsibility," "bad parenting skills," or other "dysfunction" of a student's family. Our intent is not to argue that youth come to school or to counseling without their own, already developed problems, or that their families have not, in some cases, painfully contributed to these difficulties. Rather, our aim is to show that applied developmentalists also bring their own, already developed histories into relationship with the histories and behavioral manifestations of their clients. Counselors' histories, like those of our clients, are filled with struggle, prejudiced perspectives, hope, and fear. This intersection of histories, we argue, ought to be the locus of problem identification and change. By focusing on and changing interaction patterns, transformation is viewed more as a mutual process of client and counselor development than as a unidirectional, intrapersonal concern.

We have found that counselors and other youth development practitioners generally enter their work with notions about changing others in need of help. Yet, with accumulating experience, practitioners commonly find that their motivations for helping others change are rooted in their own histories, in their desire for self-change or at least deeper self-understanding. By turning their focus inward as they look out toward the concerns of clients, the hermeneutic process not only allows for self-change and the deepening of self-understanding, it also requires it. From a hermeneutic perspective, the facilitation of another person's growth, a client's growth, must be accompanied by the practitioner's own self-development. But although the concept of mutual transformation through meaningful engagement with clients, including children and youth, may sound reasonable, exciting, or even obvious, therapeutic models tend to look almost exclusively at client change, with counselor responses to the therapeutic relationship viewed as "countertransferential," perhaps overly involved, and generally as something to remedy. Such responses are seen at best as important "data" for understanding one's client; rarely are they viewed as important contributions to the development of one's self, or the development of self-understanding.

Most of us in the broader counseling and development field view ourselves as caregivers, not as recipients of or participants in a change process. As such, we find that using a multidirectional lens with one part facing inward—revealing, in part, the influences of our clients—is often uncomfortable, particularly in cases where the lens begins to focus on concealments, those hidden parts of ourselves that have become isolated barriers to genuine growth. Unidirectional caregiving, conversely, is pseudo–self-comforting because it creates the illusion of placing and keeping us in charge. Mutual transformation requires letting go and becoming vulnerable.

SYMBIOTIC DEVELOPMENT AND THE ACCEPTANCE OF DIFFERENCE

Messer, Sass, and Woolfolk (1988), in their collection of papers on hermeneutics and psychotherapy, refer to the therapist/patient or counselor/client relationship as a *dialectic of mutual influence*. In their view, any change in the therapeutic process is a mutual construction, a synthesis of differing positions. Growth, in this sense, is a symbiotic growing together. It is not common growth toward a similar end, but individualized growth through mutual influence. This view does not suggest that counselor and client will come to see the world similarly, but that they will necessarily see the world differently, in essential ways, than they did prior to engaging with each other. A central assumption of this model is that counselor engagement necessitates counselor change—not a comforting assumption for those of us with set prescriptions for treatment, for those of us who believe that our training is complete.

As the chapters in this part of the book indicate, the potential for such symbiotic development depends, in part, on the acceptance of and interaction with difference, and on the welcoming of misunderstanding and discomfort as part of the practitioner's raison d'être. Difference is at the heart of dialectical growth. Differences of opinion, worldview, cultural background, and life experience all serve as fuel for the dialogical process. But to recognize and engage with difference requires the willingness to acknowledge misunderstanding and to be misunderstood. This, too, can be uncomfortable for counselors who commonly view their work as a practice of increasing understanding. Genuine empathy, however, cannot be achieved without an authentic willingness to misunderstand, to strive to connect only to miss the point, and as such to feel disengaged. All too frequently, false connections are maintained in order to salve the discomfort of disconnection. A productive synthesis of differences requires a grappling with discomfort, a clear recognition of disjunctions. Willingness to reach toward understanding in the midst of such discomforting misconnections is, from a hermeneutic perspective, a healthy prognosis for mutual growth.

This process of growth through the acknowledgment and respectful working through of difference and discomfort is ideally not only accepted by the applied developmentalist but also explicitly addressed with clients as a natural and healthy part of building relationships and self-understanding. In this way, the therapeutic relationship becomes a space for the explicit working through of difference and disconnection for relationships in general. To reframe relationships through a mutual engagement in the articulation of difference and discomfort is a powerful way to promote skills for authentic communication in children's and youths' relationships. In this sense, the applied developmentalist can normalize children's often hidden feelings of difference and disconnection in a way that paradoxically may be comforting, especially for youth who experience so much pain and discomfort in their lives already. The ability to become conscious of, and to learn to constructively communicate, their feelings and needs can help young people create alternative ways for dealing with interpersonal difference and conflict. As that happens, there is a transformation in their capacity to feel ill at ease, to appreciate that growth for self and in relationship is not always about feeling comfortable as quickly as possible. This is a transformed understanding of difference and discomfort and therefore of self and relationships.

The student-written chapters in this first cluster are organized around the hermeneutical notion of transformation. We lead into the entire collection of chapters with a discussion of the concept of transformation because for all practitioners, and most importantly for those in the training stage of their careers, learning to promote and recognize growth is at the heart of successful practice. But as we have suggested earlier, applied developmentalists generally are not trained to assess or value the changes that occur in themselves through their relationships with clients. The studies in this cluster exemplify the dramatic impact that recognizing self-change can have on one's training experience, on the quality of one's interpersonal and professional interactions, and on one's view of the counseling and youth development profession in general.

TRANSFORMATION THROUGH PREJUDICE AND MISUNDERSTANDING

Although human transformation or substantial shifts in some aspect of our existence might, in general terms, occur through any number of encounters, transformation in the hermeneutic framework used here is specifically related to the confrontation with misunderstanding. According to this view, we are particularly opened up to possibilities for change through our recognition of and reflection on our prejudices or biases toward the world, which most clearly come to light through confronting our misunderstanding of others and our feelings of being misunderstood by them. The experience of misunderstanding can lead to feelings of alienation from ourselves, from others, and in some cases, from a general sense of connectedness in the world.

[handwritten margin note: assumption of "good"]

But when misunderstanding occurs, it creates the opportunity for our worldview, which is generally held firm and taken for granted, to become shaken, knocked off center in a manner that requires a recentering or, perhaps more accurately, a revising. If there is a genuine attempt to understand incidents of misunderstanding—that is, to attempt painstakingly to see the various contributions to it—a revised view of the perspectives of both self and others is almost certainly required. If this new view is clarified rigorously enough, the prejudices that contribute to misunderstanding have room to emerge. This emergence or unconcealment is at the core of hermeneutic transformation. In a fundamental sense, all hermeneutic inquiry is a study of prejudice, an uncovering and interpreting of prejudged realities. These prejudgments reflect our experiences, and in that sense are not negative. They are, however, parameters for engagement—that is, they establish guidelines for how and what we take in, and how we make meaning of that input. Such prejudgments represent both opportunities and limitations for understanding and human interaction.

Self-Understanding and the Transformation of Worldviews

According to Gadamer ([1962] 1976), openings for transformation are revealed through every meaningful interaction. From his perspective, self-understanding is always *on the way;* it is never complete, only modified, with every modification merely a preparation for further development through the next meaningful encounter. Within Gadamer's schema, the more critically reflective one is, the more self-understanding and awareness of others become possible. Gadamer's definition of self-understanding is a natural extension of the Heideggerian notion that every meaningful action uncovers expanded ways of seeing the world, particularly one's participation in it.

In *Being and Time,* Heidegger ([1927] 1962) argued for a recasting of Western philosophy's focus on the meaning of external reality to emphasize what he deemed to be the most pressing question of all knowing: the question of "the meaning of being"—in particular, the meaning-making essence of being human. He responded to this question with his argument that human being—human growth, change, and existential experience—is fundamentally the ongoing activity of uncovering and interpreting our experience in the world. "Truth," in this Heideggerian sense, foreshadows Gadamer's view of self-understanding: truth is our individualized understanding of the world as determined by our involvement in it. Although from this perspective all individually held truths inherently contain their own semblance of validity, such truths also inherently contain their own limitations. We are opened to possibilities and restricted in our actualization of them by virtue of our worldviews, our notions of truth. Just as importantly, we do not derive our truths in a vacuum. They are constructed through meaningful relationships in and with the world—relationships with work, with play, and most importantly, with those people with whom we engage in mutually caring interactions. These various relationships with the world provide the connections, the life data, that become our own to uncover and interpret, and thereby to develop into our own worldview, our essential understanding of ourselves in the world. This, in short, is the hermeneutic view of human development.

In the work presented in this cluster, the authors go beyond the general hermeneutic notion of uncovering possibilities to the very specific and ethical importance of this phenomenon when working with low-income children and youth. Many such children are exposed to fewer opportunities and possibilities for development compared to their peers from more privileged backgrounds, at least in the educational and career development arenas. For this reason, the hermeneutic framework is especially fitting for youth counseling and applied development work.

Although much attention in the field of prevention is paid to concerns about substance abuse, gang violence, teen pregnancy, and school failure, another epidemic, from our perspective, is the everyday lack of genuine opportunities available to many young people. But opportunity development must reach beyond provision of better textbooks and new computers, even though these would be invaluable contributions. Genuine opportunity development must promote possibilities for making connections to people and engaging in the world—possibilities that allow for the productive revision of self-understanding. Productivity of this sort is a matter of interpretation, a matter of viewing one's self as an important contributor to any productive outcome. This view is difficult to cultivate without adequate relational contexts for its development.

Self-Transformation as an Ethical Act of Service to Youth

The contributors to this cluster, in addition to presenting contexts for child and youth development, the primary contexts of their relationships with children, present portraits of self-transformation, which ultimately serve as a transformational context for their future work in the field. That is, if we agree that adults grow through their relationships with children just as children grow through their relationships with adults, then the process of practitioner self-transformation is an act of service to children. Our own growth as youth service providers is anything but a self-centered endeavor; it is a revising of the people with whom children will interact and through whom they will uncover possibilities for their own growth and development. For this reason, explicit efforts toward the development of self-understanding are an ethical responsibility for youth development practitioners. To remain ignorant of our prejudices, to remain satisfied with the status quo of our current self-awareness, is to choose limited effectiveness and to risk transmitting unexamined and potentially harmful biases onto the youths with whom we work. To actively confront prejudice and misunderstanding, however, requires the knowledge that they exist. The chapters in this cluster help to provide that knowledge. Reading them should be viewed not only as an exercise in understanding the authors and the concepts they describe, but also as an exercise in self-understanding.

THE CONCEPTUAL ROADMAP

Within the overarching theme of transformation, each investigation in this cluster presents subthemes that are of particular meaning and importance to the authors. Because many of these themes overlap, we have organized them to create a conceptual roadmap that should help guide readers through what is at times relatively dense and challenging material. While there are many more guiding themes within each individual chapter than are presented here, the subthemes that emerged across inquiries have been used for our roadmap. We hope this map will make readers better able to traverse the conceptual terrain of this cluster in a manner that encourages more than a casual visit or brief encounter with each author. The map is intended to promote a deeper, more welcoming dialogue, one that we hope will lead readers to discover the utility of this framework for their own lives and work.

The Ethical Importance of Self-Reflection

To reiterate our argument, self-reflection is not just an academic exercise; it is at the heart of responsible and ethical practice. In each of the phenomenological investigations presented in this cluster, the importance of self-reflection and its connection to improved work with youth serve as organizing themes.

Sharon M. Ravitch's study, "Becoming Uncomfortable: Transforming My Praxis," captures the movement from the place of her newly found desire for critical self-reflection to the application of introspective insights in her work with children. Central in Ravitch's work is the shift to understanding the inextricable connections between her personal and professional perspectives. This is a transition many students experience through their training in the hermeneutic model. Ravitch's progression, from the discovery of a need for self-reflection to the feelings of alienation from herself and her work that this causes, depicts a growth trajectory rooted in what she terms "concerned engagement." The hermeneutic model is centered in concerned engagement; it argues that genuine understanding can only develop when one is authentically concerned with the questions or persons present. In Ravitch's case, concern for her school counseling work is present throughout; it is the manner in which she engages with her concerns that is transformed quite dramatically. For example, upon uncovering a number of disconcerting biases and prejudices that she initially wants to disavow, she is able to confront them head-on rather than circumventing them to avoid discomfort. This move toward the confrontation of her class- and race-based prejudices allows her to make shifts in practice that accompany those made in self-awareness: as she personally experiences "radical transformation," so does her practice.

In his chapter, "The Flight of a Black Butterfly: A Hermeneutic Investigation of Metamorphosis," Gregory Seaton poignantly discloses the discovery of his preoccupation with others' influences on his own perceptions of his work and well-being, and the discovery of his belief that he lacked the reflection necessary to realize his effects on others. Specifically, Seaton discusses his acute awareness, as a black man, of the effects that colleagues' thoughts and actions have on him: on his thoughts, behaviors, and sense of self in a hegemonic white society. As Seaton makes clear, hermeneutic self-reflection was not necessary for him to recognize the feeling of being judged; growing-up black in urban America provided recognition of this reality. What self-reflection did uncover, however, was a deepened awareness of the range of influences his actions have on those around him. This realization became the thread that weaves together the whole of Seaton's experience as a middle school counselor with the Urban Youth Connection, a prevention-oriented counseling program for early adolescents.

Seaton centers much of his discussion on "the return arc of reflection," the part of the circle of interpretation that looks back on those experiences into which one previously was thrown or projected. Through the benefit of productive hindsight, the return arc of reflection allows one to retrace the tracks of prior understanding. In critically looking back, Seaton concedes that he had not taken adequate responsibility—because he had not recognized that it was his to take—for many of the actions in which he had engaged that negatively affected his counselor-training experience. Consequently, he was fairly oblivious to their effects on his site placement and on the youth he was counseling. Based on this revised view of himself and of the potential influence of his actions, Seaton consciously altered his approach to his work.

This alteration led to functional shifts in a variety of relationships. Seaton became more assertive in his supervisory relationship, which included taking a more active role in co-determining the direction of the supervision discourse and the quality of clinical dialogue. More specifically, Seaton assumed his share of responsibility for conflicts of interpretation, as well as for clashes of personality that had previously arisen in supervision. Rather than viewing conflicts of perspective as problematic, he came to see them as important differences to address, and therefore as the core of the supervisory relationship. Seaton's relationships with school personnel, primarily teachers, also shifted as he came to a clearer understanding of his influence on their perceptions and of their influence on his. By uncovering what he perceived as gross misunderstandings in the teachers' perceptions of his work, and of counseling work in general, Seaton prepared for a confrontation with these misunderstandings that would eventually solidify his view of himself as a developing professional and strengthen his commitment to his work with youth. For Seaton, critically reflecting on his experiences with conflict as a school counselor, and on his own identity as a professional black male who is both a part of (and to his surprise and dismay) apart from, the world of the students he counsels, moved him toward deeper and sometimes more painful levels of self-understanding.

Through an interactive process of personal/professional and systemic/ societal critique and reflection, Karin E. Liiv, in her investigation, "Another Backward Arc: Further Reflections on 'Expert' and 'Problem,' " makes significant changes in her views about youth and youth service, and therefore in her approach to working with students within Project Success, an in-school suspension program. Her year-long process of deepening self-reflection for the purpose of providing fuller services and enhancing her own and her students' self-respect is made painfully evident in Liiv's investigation. Through reflecting on her fears as both a person and a practitioner—fears related to issues of authority, expertise, and conflict—Liiv is able to acknowledge missed opportunities for supporting her students, and in so doing learn alternative methods for creating new opportunities in her relationships with them. Liiv's sometimes resistant but always genuine struggle to understand herself and the system of Project Success led to productive transformations both in her life and in her work. Throughout her investigation, Liiv reflects on her transformations: in her sense of who the experts are, in her understanding of how the systems of school and society shape and define youth and pathologize their resistance and autonomy, and in her reflection on and realization of her own internalization of power, authority, and hegemony. These changes in her worldview allowed Liiv to respect her students more fully and ultimately made it possible for her to collaborate with them in strengthening their perspective-taking skills.

Kristin M. Carvill's chapter, "Fear and Courage: Interpretations from Beyond a Life Half-Lived," is a vivid portrayal of the roles that emotional turmoil and traumatic life history play in psychoeducational practice and hermeneutic inquiry. In her chapter, Carvill uncovers the intensity of personal suffering that so centrally influences the conduct of her work in every conceivable domain. In reading her account, one is compelled to ask, Can we leave our feelings and histories at the door when we enter the counseling session and the classroom? Upon reading further, however, it becomes clear that a better question might be, Would we *want* to leave our feelings and histories at the door, even if we could? Carvill's story convincingly depicts the inevitability of past experience as intrusion and guide for our current work, and the value of engaging in reflection on it. Through her reflection on her past and on the current implications of her experiences of trauma, Carvill is able to uncover meaning for herself and in her relationships with students. This uncovering holds within it the promise of a transformation of the very truths by which she and her students live.

Similar to Liiv, Carvill examines her own fears as she steps into her training experience at the James Elementary School. She traces the movement of her feelings about herself and her competencies, and the impact of these feelings on her capacity to connect with students. In particular, Carvill examines and graphically shares her experience of being relentlessly haunted by traumatic memories. These memories, which terrify her at night, translate during the day into her modes of functioning and relating with others, including the children with whom she works. Naming the frustration that stems from the compromises her history has imposed, Carvill refers to her life as one only partially experienced: a life half-lived. As she grapples with the impact of this life on her work with children at the James School, Carvill uncovers the centrality of courage in her existence and in the functioning of the children. This common recognition, made through critical self-reflection and increased self-understanding, becomes the momentum for her ongoing efforts toward living and serving young people more fully.

Discomfort and Alienation

Although the concepts of discomfort and alienation ring of existentialist notions of suffering, our emphasis on them in the hermeneutic framework does not stem from a desire to promote angst as a means to achieving some idealized notion of genuineness or authenticity. Rather, these concepts serve to highlight those aspects of one's life experience that clash with others' beliefs, values, and ways of being. Discomfort, in particular, can viscerally direct one to important differences between one's self and others, and to the distances between different points of view. Such divergences between people and their beliefs are among the most important human experiences that applied developmentalists must uncover and address in therapeutic relationships. Costly errors and missed connections occur when such differences are avoided either out of indifference or out of the misguided, although quite common, perception that discomfort is the mark of a flawed counseling relationship or an underskilled counselor. Self-conscious examination and addressing of discomfort affords us an opportunity to become closer to our clients by disrupting the unproductively comfortable, often casual distance that can enable a lack of depth in our relationships.

Alienation may be related to discomfort, although the experience of being alienated need not feel uncomfortable. Alienation, in the hermeneutic framework, is characterized by feelings of disconnection or "outsiderness." It is the feeling of being clearly separated, for reasons such as rejection, lack of information, or irreconcilable differences. We can be alienated from ourselves as well as from others, as is the case when we cannot "get into" what we are trying to do, think, or feel, or when we cannot cross over to that sense of peace or security that connects us to who we are. Whether uncomfortable or not, alienation highlights important separations, those aspects of our own or others' experience that are, at least temporarily, alien to us. In doing so, alienation, like discomfort, directs us to the fundamental disconnections that need to be addressed in our work. The paradox of alienation is that it can facilitate connection if we use it to move toward the distancing separation it represents.

As Ravitch's paper suggests, the willingness to feel alienated from others, to feel uncomfortable with ourselves, and to sustain these feelings rather than prematurely glossing over them is ultimately the path toward more genuine connection, with both ourselves and others. Through the process of opening ourselves up to feeling discomfort and alienation, we move toward more clearly identifying who we are and who we are not; but beyond this, we move toward expanding and revising who and how we want to be, both with others and within ourselves. In essence, discomfort and alienation are central to the ongoing reorganization of our identity and worldview: by highlighting differences to traverse or transcend, transformation is given its direction.

Reframing discomfort and alienation, then, is a necessary step within the hermeneutic framework. By bringing distance and disconnection into view, we make them available for discussion and for the larger work of counseling and applied development. Rather than viewing disconnection and alienation as barriers to growth, the hermeneutic framework casts them as possibilities for change.

Seaton's inquiry clearly exemplifies the hermeneutic precept that discomfort and alienation promote growth. By placing these concepts within the larger themes of identity and professional role confusion, he links discomfort and alienation with growth in a number of different settings. In his work as a counselor at the Urban Youth Connection and as a graduate student at Harvard, Seaton fights with himself and the systems surrounding him to determine the sources and implications of his struggle to feel successful and appreciated. To what extent, he questions, is he struggling because he is a young black man from an urban neighborhood resembling those where many of his Boston middle school students live? Furthermore, he questions whether he feels alienated from some of the teachers because he looks, due to both age and race, more similar to many of the African American students than to the adult staff? Although Seaton wants to identify with his student clients in order to reach them more deeply, in practice he feels the world of difference that separates his experiences from theirs.

Seaton uses each of his questions and positions to better understand himself, his students, and the inevitably complicated process of transformation that still awaits him. Perhaps most complicated and painful is the separation he feels developing between himself and his home (broadly defined as family and roots) as he continuously grows into someone different from the young boy who "went on," who moved forward to create a "better" life for himself and a proud legacy for his family. In essence Seaton shows that growth is not an additive process, but one of change. As we change we become less alienated from that which was once so different and foreign, and in some respects more alienated from the ways of being that were once so familiar and self-defining. When the butterfly takes his wings, the caterpillar is forever left behind.

Liiv's study approaches discomfort and alienation from several vantage points: the system of Project Success, the overarching public school environment, society at large, and her fit within these and other contexts. Whereas Seaton places discomfort and alienation within the larger themes of identity and role confusion, Liiv locates them within her struggles with power and authority. Following initial attempts to cope with her struggles by avoiding them or by placing the locus of responsibility in the hands of others, Liiv progressively moves toward seeing herself, along with her students, as experts. While this shift in locus of control is uncomfortable because it requires her to take on more responsibility, Liiv comes to see the place of expertise in the interactions among individuals and systems rather than in the hands and minds of isolated experts. This recognition is transformative for herself and her students because it opens up possibilities for uncovering and utilizing the internal talents and resources, or power and expertise, that are available in each person. Important to Liiv's inquiry is the phenomenological method itself: had she not documented her struggle, it seems unlikely that she would have been as available to it and as able to recognize the specific places where change could be promoted.

Carvill's inquiry not only uncovers and depicts discomfort and alienation, it thrusts these experiences upon the reader. The degree of suffering communicated through her work demands empathy and respect not only for her but for the many children who share similar childhood experiences. Carvill bravely merges her personal history with her current issues as a counselor. As we read her story it becomes clear that the personal prose included is a carefully selected slice of historical data that allows us to sample and learn from the role of personal history in our work. Carvill's discomfort with herself, rooted in a long history of childhood trauma, makes it initially difficult for her to comfortably engage with her elementary school clients. Her discomfort is located in fear, and is at times manifested in alienation from her work, particularly from her creativity and ability to spontaneously function as an effective counselor. But essential to Carvill's portrayal is the graphic depiction of discomfort and the relentless pursuit of courage to overcome or, perhaps more accurately, to respond to it.

(Dis)Connectedness over Time

As with discomfort and alienation, and prejudice and misunderstanding, a hermeneutic framework calls for a reframing of the balance between connectedness and disconnectedness in everyday life, and in our counseling relationships. A rule of thumb for applied developmentalists is that the closer the connection between counselor and client, the more productive the work. In general, we support this assumption, but with critical caveats. Just as discomfort and alienation can assertively point us toward areas for growth due to the feelings these issues arouse, a less emotionally charged, safely-distanced relationship can comfortably allow for conscious and unconscious assessments of growth opportunities. Why, we might ask, should an elementary or middle school student—any such student, not just one with a history of neglect or trauma—trust an adult stranger who has recently come into her life to provide support services? Too frequently this question is not asked. We simply assume that the child should trust. Unfortunately, such assumptions blind us to opportunities for working with healthy resistance and other versions of the "checking out" stage of everyday relationship building.

While new applied developmentalists often feel anxious when thinking about or experiencing distance or disconnection from important others, including their clients and clinical supervisors, granting distance its natural position within relationship development is crucial to authentically reaching deeper layers of relating. In fact, the very process of moving from distanced positions to more connected ones is arguably as important to therapeutic growth as the work that occurs after trust and intimacy are firmly established. This argument points once more to the organizing concept of time in the hermeneutic framework. Matters of interpretation are matters of time. A static assessment or achievement of closeness is not as important to understanding counseling relationships as the assessment of movement, of relationship building, of traversing the distance from disconnection to connection that is a natural developmental stage in a growing relationship. If we recognize and internalize this perspective of time, we can more fully appreciate disconnection and the value it has for the future of our working relationships: its value as an essential marker of movement—ideally movement toward the closeness one seeks, a closeness that will benefit our clients.

In therapeutic relationships, which ideally are safe-enough contexts in which clients can experience and work through conflictual feelings, there must be an understanding, at least on the part of the professional, that there will be times of disconnection and a need for space. These time and space concerns need to be framed, however, within a larger holding environment of connectedness. That is, one can safely experience distance and a full range of feelings when there are clear messages that a secure undercarriage of faith and care are constantly present. From this perspective, connection and disconnection coexist; they are not either/or positions. This co-existence may be referred to as the yin and yang of relationship: each part is necessary for the other to exist; the two parts interactively define the whole. Apart from each other and without the appreciation of the crucial role of time in relationship, connection and disconnection have little meaning.

Each of the authors in this cluster of chapters interprets shifts in connection and disconnection through a range of counseling and related professional relationships, such as those with supervisors, teachers, and colleagues. Liiv interprets such shifts in a variety of interacting contexts. A guiding theme throughout her inquiry is the fluctuating sense of connection and distance she feels toward Project Success, and the implications this holds for her provision of youth services. By consciously linking her feelings of disconnectedness within the project to the quality of her work with students, Liiv was able to assume more authority in the general domain of collaborative relationship building; seeing the practical and ethical risks of remaining disconnected motivated her to develop closer relationships with colleagues, supervisors, and ultimately the students.

Liiv captures the relationship between herself and her students by communicating the parallel between her own feelings of helplessness and disconnection at her site, her seeming inability to empower and connect with her students, and the students' own inability to feel empowered and connected in their educations. Perhaps most compelling in Liiv's work is her ability to interpret connections and disconnections carefully from multiple perspectives. At different points in time, she interprets her feelings of disconnection as fear of inadequacy

as a counselor, as resistance to authority, as an overestimation of external "experts," and as a lack of faith in the system in which she works.
These multiple interpretations of disconnection, however, ultimately
allow Liiv to identify strategies for moving closer: closer to herself and
her internal sense of competence, the students of Project Success, to her
supervisors, and even to the larger system. Each of these strategies are
located in a recognition of the possibilities and limitations that she can
help define.

Ravitch, like Liiv, explicitly frames experiences of connection and
disconnection as guiding themes in her investigation. She looks within
herself, her site system, her relationships with students, and her general
learning process as she attempts to make meaning of connection and
disconnection in multiple, interrelated contexts. Through the careful
construction and analysis of her textual database of process notes,
Ravitch begins to notice positive shifts in her relationships with students that seem linked to insights she develops through her training. In
this sense, her inquiry is exemplary of the role theoretical reading plays
in practical training. By becoming progressively more receptive to and
familiar with the theoretical principles underlying her training, Ravitch
creates new ways of understanding her work, and of interpreting and
eventually reducing the distance between herself and her students.

An important finding that emerges from Ravitch's analysis of her
process notes is a clear recognition of the "not there," of connections
not being made. Uncomfortable with what she perceives as a pro-
longed absence of meaningful connection with many of her students,
Ravitch begins to work toward the development of explicit relationship building. This change, instigated by the integration of theoretical
readings with her experience in the field, profoundly reshapes the
direction of her training experience, including her self-perception as a
developing counselor.

For Seaton, experiences of disconnection in his training are clearly
related to the feelings of discomfort and alienation discussed earlier. He
experiences disconnection in virtually every aspect of his work, from
the culture of the site placement, to the school in which the site is
located, and to his relationships with his supervisor, the school teachers
and administrators, and ultimately the students themselves. But by
documenting these feelings in his process notes over the course of his
work, Seaton is able to determine where and how he wants to make
efforts to reduce the distance he experiences. And although he acknowledges the ongoing separateness that remains a part of his training, he
is able to make shifts that bring him closer to his student clients and his
colleagues, and to a better understanding of himself.

Carvill's inquiry uncovers the relationship between confronting her fears and developing connections with her students. Initially she presents a parallel between her feelings of frustration and disconnectedness in her work and her personal history. She locates her anxiety in her fear, which she knows must be confronted if her life and work are to move forward. She captures the intersecting evolution of her personal and professional connectedness through the story of her own and her students' growth. By carefully articulating her growing sense of ease in working with the children in her groups, Carvill discovers more than a talent for connecting with children; she reveals for herself the possibility of living a life that is not based in fear. Particularly through her work with children of divorce, which takes her back to the trials of her own family history, Carvill begins to recognize real possibilities for a freer life. These possibilities, however, remain slippery at best. For as thoroughly as Carvill wants to transcend her past, she will not pretend that it is behind her: through both connection and disconnection with her students, she courageously moves with her past as an everpresent guide.

In all four chapters it is clear that becoming aware of disconnection, when the goal is to move towards engagement, allows for connection to more honestly and naturally develop.

Power and Authority

The forces of power and authority in interpretation generally, and in youth work particularly, are central to the hermeneutic framework. While we discuss these issues in greater depth within the context of the third cluster of phenomenological investigations (Chapter Fourteen), transformations in concepts of power and authority are central to the investigations included here.

Each author in this cluster takes a reflective stance—personally, professionally, and politically—with respect to issues of power and authority in their service provision and relationships with students and in the systems in which they work. For all four authors, power and authority are guiding themes of their practicum experience working in schools.

Seaton explores several overlapping issues of power and authority in his phenomenological investigation. The author grapples with issues of imposed authority from teachers, administrators, and his clinical supervisor. By looking at himself as both subject and object of power differentials, Seaton is able not only to locate himself within these crucial societal and youth service issues, but also to wrestle with the complex nature of both implicit and explicit power issues that impinge on his movement and work. Seaton frames his observations of, feelings about, and issues with power and authority within his struggle as a black man living and working within the larger societal context of racism and inequality. Through his careful analysis and articulation of how he navigates (and gets lost) in this rough terrain, Seaton is able to reposition himself and claim the authority that is both crucial for his youth work and for a painful departure from his initial view of himself as a contemporary of his student clients. His position within issues of power and authority, which he painfully refers to as his "enemy within," reflects forces that Seaton wrestles with—from his experience with the caterpillar on the street to his realization that he has changed into the butterfly. Seaton struggles with his own authority and with the pain it provokes in his relationships. Further, he locates his struggle within the school system and the society that have shaped and will continue to influence his identity.

In her investigation, Liiv traces her process of reflection on her views about power and authority and explicitly addresses the interrelationship of shifts in her personal views and in her professional performance with students. Liiv invites readers into her painful and exhilarating process of reckoning with power and authority as they relate to working across issues of race, gender, and ethnicity. Through her examination of herself, her views, and her practice, Liiv learns (and then teaches) that intervention work needs to flow from genuine collaboration and reciprocity, that practitioners must help students to learn faith through connectedness and increased perspective-taking skills, and that students should be provided with opportunities to question, rather than simply given lectures or directives for change. Liiv moves from a place of profound ambivalence about the meaning and implications of her power and authority to an empowered position in which she locates herself, shares her authority, and facilitates explicit dialogue with her students around power differentials in their work and in the students' lives in general. Liiv's is a moving account of transformation through critical reflection on herself and the society within which she has been socialized.

Carvill's investigation deals with issues of power and authority within the context of working with students from backgrounds of divorce. By virtue of the changes in their families, many of the children, like Carvill, have dealt with power and authority through having their lifestyles dictated by situations out of their control. The author discovers that she can empower her students, as she empowers herself, through their connection; and through the process of writing about their experiences, they come to feel more control over themselves and their own lives. The process of coempowerment that is evident in Carvill's chapter is unique in its clear articulation of the mutual influence between counselor and client on intimacy development, and of the healing power of transformation. There is a poignant parallel between Carvill's increased ability to be her own voice of authority, with power to claim and hold her truths, and the increased ability she co-creates with her students to write their truths and thus uncover meaning in them.

Through the course of her investigation, Ravitch uncovers important issues of authority and power in her role as a counselor. She simultaneously reflects on and problematizes the power and authority she had previously taken for granted. Through her engagement in critical questioning, Ravitch struggles with the reality that it is not only because she is a counselor and adult working with young people that she wields power and authority, but also because she is a white person who comes from a privileged class background. These realizations, because they are uncomfortable for her, cause her to radically revision her role with youth from different socioeconomic, cultural, and racial backgrounds.

Ravitch begins what she acknowledges as "an ongoing and arduous process" of working through some of these critical societal and therapeutic issues by making them explicit in her process notes and investigations. Although she is aware that she will need to explore these issues over time and in relationships in order to sustain the changes she is making, she has begun to revise some of her views and her approach to youth work. Some of the practical implications she communicates are an increased desire and ability to more fully open herself up to hearing students' opinions (including those about her); to consider her language and the way it both shapes and is shaped by her biases; to focus in her work with students on the fostering of an increased sense of self within the schools' "culture of power"; and most importantly, to commit herself to the process of uncovering deeper layers of her own prejudice and misunderstanding and the ways these can disempower youth.

THE STRUCTURE AND EDITING OF THE PHENOMENOLOGICAL CASE STUDIES

As stated previously, this book is centered around twelve phenomenological investigations, written over the past three years by students involved in the Harvard Risk and Prevention Program's Adolescent

Practicum Course. Each of the chapters included here has been significantly condensed from its original incarnation. In some cases we have combined two investigations (a mid-year and end-of-year piece) into one text. In other cases we have shortened one longer text that was written for only one of the two semester assignments. In addition, most of these studies had lengthy and very clearly articulated methodology sections (as per the assignment). These sections have been edited out (with some regret) because the methodology is clearly articulated in Chapter Three. Finally, several of the studies had more intensive sections devoted to the theoretical framework, which we have shortened because the theoretical framework is laid out in several places throughout the book. All of these abridgments have been made to allow room in the book for a broader sample of investigations. By condensing these texts, we are able to represent twelve different cases, thereby giving readers a chance to sample more perspectives on the hermeneutic framework—its theory and practice connections—and on applied development work more generally.

In addition to the edits for length and clarity, we have also, for ethical reasons of confidentiality, altered the names of children and disguised certain information about the children and their communities, supervisors, and the schools in which some of the programs are located. In a few cases we have kept program names intact, with permission from the people who work there.

5

BECOMING UNCOMFORTABLE

Transforming My Praxis

Sharon M. Ravitch

IN SEPTEMBER 1993, I BEGAN a year-long internship with an urban public school system's conflict resolution and peer mediation program as part of Harvard University's Risk and Prevention Program's Adolescent Practicum Course. The mediation program serves many of the system's schools and is based in violence prevention, peer mediation, and conflict resolution curricula. My roles in these schools are as diverse as the placement itself. I am cofacilitator of a seventh and eighth grade peer mediation group, of two eighth grade girls psychoeducational discussion and writing groups, and of a classroom group focused on violence prevention.

This phenomenological investigation is grounded in my training experiences and in interpretations of them that have been uncovered during the past four months. I will try to articulate the development of and changes in my interpretations of systems, texts, thoughts, and interactions with students, and of myself and my roles, using the process notes I have taken throughout this term. These notes serve as the primary framework for this further investigation into, and reflection on, the meaning of the interpretive data that my work and relationships with students have generated.

ENTERING A NEW CIRCLE

My involvement in the practicum course is marked by the continuous interplay between concrete experiences and abstract theories. I believe there is a powerful interaction between the background I bring to the readings, the lectures, and my work in the schools, and the nature and design of the course. A brief examination of my educational background will help to illuminate some of the reasons these readings and discussions have been such essential fuel for my work in the schools.

I came to Harvard with an academic background in religion and women's studies. I had previously separated my work in the realm of critical theory and textual exegesis as theoretical and my work in schools as practical, not seeing direct points for connection between the two. Abandoning plans for doctoral study in religion and going into education, which had always been a side-line passion, left me feeling a certain tension—that I would be unable to both participate in experiential learning (teaching/counseling) and hold onto my desire to engage in the realm of theory.

The structure of our practicum course—focusing on an integration of theory, research, and practice—has served several important functions for me. First, it has provided a framework (critical hermeneutics) for making connections and building bridges between theory and practice by giving me a way to articulate ideas that were previously intuitive and seemingly too abstract to translate into my practice. For me, this marked a redefinition and reframing of theory to include practice.

Second, the course reading and dialogue have helped me to realize that I work directly from my interpretations of past experiences, and they therefore have allowed me to reshape my intervention work in the schools in a way that feels more respectful of the students with whom I work. I recall feeling at the beginning of the course that the readings and class discussions, both because of the theoretical framework and because of my own new context (entering a new field, making a shift from working in high school to middle school, and encountering new experiences on many levels), were liberating and even revolutionary. I began to think about myself in challenging ways and to push myself to question different areas of educational theory and practice, including my role in each.

Third, as a result of engaging with hermeneutic concepts of critical questioning, the driving force for my work in this course and in my practicum placement has been the desire to question and challenge myself on issues and concerns that are emerging for me as a counselor, as a part of several school systems, and as an individual engaging in dialogue and activities with youth. I have learned much from Gadamer ([1966] 1976), who states that "the real power of hermeneutical consciousness is our ability to see what is questionable" (p. 13). I have, since studying hermeneutics, begun to focus on what is questionable. Some of the questions that have guided my work this semester are:

1. How do my biases, prejudices, and preconceptions affect my work and relationships with students? (Implicit in this question is that I now accept that they do.)

2. How can I better understand, in a respectful and appropriately tentative way, students' interpretations of themselves in terms of the meaning they make of experiences in school and in their sociocultural worlds?

3. What does it mean for my practice to realize that there is a power differential between myself and the students with whom I work?

4. How do I use the phenomenological data I generate from working with students to move toward engendering positive changes in their lives?

I hope to chart my emerging answers to these questions in this investigation, and to continue with my search for answers and new questions throughout the rest of the year (and beyond).

EXPANDING MY CIRCLE: A BRIEF REVIEW OF INFLUENTIAL READINGS

"There is always a world already interpreted, already organized in its basic relations, into which experience steps as something new, upsetting what has led our expectations and undergoing reorganization itself in the upheaval" (Gadamer, [1966] 1976, p. 15). This quote captures the essence of my experiences this semester. The gestalt of this course— the readings coupled with analysis of them, which gets challenged through discussion and practice—has entered my world and upset the equilibrium to which I formerly clung. This chapter is one step in my reorganization amidst the upheaval this framework has caused in my understanding of society, interactions, and myself.

The past four months of involvement in my practicum site can be best described in terms of movement and change. I believe that the movements and changes themselves, as well as my ability and desire to be cognizant of them, would be critically different were it not for my involvement in the course and with the texts I have read, reread, and discussed in our class. I begin this investigation by including my interpretations of the readings and lectures that have shaped my self-understanding, in order to convey the impact they have already had on my overall perspective and my approach to youth service work.

Everydayness and the Circularity of Understanding

Woolfolk, Sass, and Messer's *Introduction to Hermeneutics* (1988) has helped me to realize that I am better able to understand and relate with students when I pay more attention to "small" aspects of their daily lives. The authors' review of Heidegger's concept of "everyday being-in-the-world," or the role that ordinary, seemingly minute things play in the development of relationships and in the shaping and reshaping of children's self-interpretations, has shifted my view of counseling and youth work. In terms of my own daily interpretations, I am learning to more fully realize and appreciate the profound simplicity of everyday events—a child's glance, smile, or silences—and the meaning and significance these have when they are contemplated over time and in the context of our relationships. This shift from looking only at dramatic events to seeing children's daily experiences as meaningful allows me to better appreciate the complexity of nuance in relationships.

Woolfolk, Sass, and Messer also expand on Geertz's (1973) description of "the circularity of understanding" as "a continuous dialectical tacking between the most local of local detail and the most global of global structure in such a way as to bring both into view simultaneously" (p. 239). This concept has helped me to conceptualize and pay attention to the multiple societal contexts (such as political and economic systems) in which students make meaning of their lives, and to the particular contexts (such as family, neighborhood, appearance, culture, religion, and temperament) that factor into each student's life. The concept of the circularity of understanding holds implications for considering my own multiple and guiding contexts as well, because it helps me to place myself and my professional decisions into a larger context (family background, culture, race, class, and professional objectives), and so facilitates a deconstruction of my perspective on, and communications with, youth. In the same way that the concept of everydayness has shaped my understanding of the implications of even small actions (or inactions) for therapeutic alliances, the notion of the circularity of understanding has shaped my conception of the larger context from which we step into our counseling sessions. Thus I am

challenged not only to contextualize seemingly small events and interactions within the larger context of our relationships, but I am further
challenged to place these relationships within the broader contexts of
school, race, culture, societal inequality, and power differentials. The
awareness that there is a need to strive continually to contextualize
people and interactions is one hermeneutic innovation in my worldview and perspective on human service work. Further, to conceptualize
processes of understanding as circular, with a crucial reflection component that helps me to make sense of things retrospectively, allows me to
be more patient with myself and my students in the moment because I
know that I cannot possibly understand the multiple influences on any
present situation. This working concept of continually emerging understanding inspires me to be more persevering, knowing that I must
always work to become increasingly aware of myself and more
involved in the pursuit of understanding youth.

Most powerful for me among the messages in Woolfolk, Sass, and
Messer's chapter, is the concept of the subjectivity of our *lives as interpretations*. This concept suggests that our lives are constituted by an
accumulation and interaction of complex interpretations, which then
guide current decisions, actions, and subsequent interpretations. It also
suggests that because this process is highly individualized and fluid,
"our understanding of life is only a constant approximation; that life
reveals quite different sides to us according to the point of view from
which we consider its course in time is due to the nature of both understanding and life" (1988, p. 7). The working concept that our lives are
guided by the interpretations we make, and that these interpretations
are subjective and revisable, feels revolutionary. It also feels frightening, because it forces me to acknowledge that I do not *absolutely* know
anything. Although this understanding is uncomfortable to hold, it is
also liberating, both personally and professionally. It is liberating
because I believe people are socialized into believing that our truths
and ways of living are "right"; and because I now realize that I am constantly only approximating the meaning of situations, I am more committed to allowing room in my interpretations for others' truths and
ways of being, even when they challenge my own.

De-Dichotomizing Theory and Practice

Reading Packer and Addison's (1989) book *Entering the Circle* has
helped me to conceptualize the interrelationship within myself of individual and practitioner. In the same way that I dichotomized theory

and practice, I polarized the personal and professional aspects of myself. After engaging in the course lectures and readings throughout the first semester, I am amazed that I could conceptualize these as two discrete and distinct parts of myself. The implications of my realization that who I am necessarily shapes what I do professionally is a central aspect of my year. For example, this study focuses on the investigation of my interpretations of myself and my practice, and on the role that my personal biases have in my youth work. Before this course I spent reflection time focusing solely on the students, feeling that my being there was enough to facilitate my own growth as a counselor.

In the introduction of their book, Packer and Addison write: "Interpretive inquiry begins not from an absolute origin of unquestionable data or totally consistent logic, but at a place delineated by our everyday participatory understanding of people and events" (p. 23). The awareness that I enter relationships with students with a preliminary understanding of many aspects of our encounters based on my own history—expectations of who they are, how they view me, of how we will interact—and that this is at once an understanding and a misunderstanding, both of which guide our interactions, has been essential to how I understand communication and approach these exchanges. Further, the idea that we all work from our preconceived notions builds on my growing sense of the value of viewing our lives as interpretations and thus reinforces the need for me to take in and consider multiple perspectives. Increased perspective taking has become a focus in both my personal and professional development, and an explicit agenda in my counseling work with students.

Uncovering and Working with Prejudice

Another concept from our readings that has contributed to a radical shift in my perspective is Gadamer's concern that "any attempt to dispense with prejudices would lead not to their eradication but to their deeper concealment" ([1962] 1976, p. 18). This concept, that by claiming not to have prejudices I am in fact embedding them deeper into my psyche, has become a powerful motivation for more conscientiously looking at my biases. Embracing this approach has led me to grapple with my previously set ways of thinking, hearing, communicating, and interacting. Gadamer's notion of prejudice as an unavoidable aspect of human consciousness has had a profound impact on me; I have worked for years to convince myself that I have no prejudices and have been forced to confront this naivete.

Upon first reading and making sense of Gadamer's notion of prejudice, I struggled, as I still do, to excavate my unconscious prejudices as well as ones I had worked so diligently to cover over. I am still in the process of uncovering these prejudices and I believe that this is an unending and arduous task; yet the notion that uncovering prejudice is a starting point for self-understanding, which is always necessary for understanding others, rather than the mark of a flawed character is itself a realization that has been empowering for me.

Gadamer revealed the world of prejudice in a new and critically different way for me. His article brought into focus several concerns about the biases I bring to my relationships with students. In particular, it is clear to me now that the fact that I come from a different cultural, racial, and economic background than the majority of my students has major implications for our work together. Not only am I reckoning with the implications of this realization ethically, but it has become central to my counseling and intervention approach. I am beginning to facilitate explicit discussions of interracial and intercultural relations as well as prejudice and stereotypes in my counseling groups and relationships with students. I am finding that centralizing the subtexts of racism, sexism, homophobia, and economic inequality—for myself and with my students—though it can be uncomfortable and anxiety-provoking, is empowering because it opens doors to connection, change, and growth through developing relational and social consciousness. That I am able to address these subtexts despite the tensions that emerge points out, I believe, that my threshold for anxiety has been raised through the practicum course dialogue, and that I have begun both to desire a more reciprocal vulnerability and to accept that engaging with discomfort can facilitate change.

Additionally, the discussion of language in Gadamer's article was an important introduction to intervention work for me. I have begun to consider more fully how students may internalize messages and define themselves negatively in the face of languages that often exclude or devalue their own dialects. I have realized that I not only need to structure sessions around building the students' repertoires of skills for dealing with interpersonal conflict, but I also need to build my own repertoire of skills and language to engage effectively with youth in their everyday lives. This realization refocused my attention on the need to create an environment and shared language that is respectful, authentic, and comfortable for the students and myself.

Language Barriers and Other Walls

Entering several new youth service systems in quick succession—the Risk and Prevention Program, the Cambridge Public School System, and my larger practicum placement—Margonis's (1992) article "The Cooptation of 'At-Risk'" was invaluable for me. In this article, Margonis problematizes the very notion of "at risk," showing how it marginalizes and stigmatizes certain students who diverge from a set norm, which has been defined in large part by white middle-class standards. With Gadamer's discussion of the power of language as a foundation, Margonis's article about the implications of risk language for youth forced me to question what I mean by "at risk," as well as how I may generalize students' various "risks" as sharing commonalities when in fact they are highly individualized.

Margonis's article is an excellent example of the power of language on a macro (policy) level, and it also has an impact on how I approach each student on a micro (developmental) level. Because I now realize the extent to which language generates meaning, I am able to reflect on how the language of risk and its underlying assumptions can be stigmatizing and pathologizing for many students of color and low-income students, who generally are the recipients of these diagnoses. As a result, I have been able to become more critical of the preconceived notions I carry with me about these populations, of the language I use when speaking about groups of people and specific developmental difficulties in various individuals, and of how these notions affected the ways I interacted with my former students in Philadelphia. I now realize how important it is not to take language for granted and to examine the biases inherent in my language and working model.

Patricia Lawrence Wehmiller's (1992) article "When the Walls Come Tumbling Down" provided me with critical insight into the barriers (in addition to language) that some students face in their school environments. Building on Margonis's discussion of the power of language, Wehmiller's article helped me to think about some of the other walls that can constrict the interpretations students bring to and take from school. The following is an excerpt I frequently consider as I go to school:

> Today I want educators to think hard about the traditions and assumptions that live on inside the walls of our schools. . . . I want us to dare to ask what we really mean by inclusiveness and diversity. Do we mean that we want to take the walls down? Those walls

[handwritten margin note: act of interpretation through language]

protect our institutions. They protect the assumptions that have been made for generations about what is best for students. . . . Once inside the school, there are little walls everywhere—rituals and symbols and language and habits that represent the way it has always been. Do we mean we want to look at these, carefully dismantle them brick by brick, and discard the ones that aren't relevant or that actually offend [p. 376]?

Wehmiller helped to prepare me not only to consider the implications of working inside a system with walls built into it, such as teachers and professionals whose views are not conducive to ameliorating the risks and challenges that some of their students face, but also to think about the walls in my own emerging orientation to working with students. Reading this article also helped me to understand how the walls that students perceive and internalize necessarily come into play throughout our relationships. I wondered what walls they face, how I can help to dismantle them, and how I can detect what they perceive as walls. Will I be able to do any of this? What new walls do I create?

Reading Texts and Human Development

I have become conscious of the fact that my interactions with youth exist in the medium of a mutual relationship, or what Woolfolk, Sass, and Messer (1988) refer to as a *dialectic of mutual influence.* Michael Nakkula uses this concept to describe the process of development work as a mutual coauthoring: I coauthor students' lives as they coauthor mine. This notion is embedded in Ricoeur's metaphor of *human life as a text.* In "The Model of the Text," Ricoeur (1981) writes that the metaphor of text as human life is fluid in meaning, ever-changing, always in revision. His conceptualization of meaningful action as text has important implications for the ways I think about my interactions with students. This metaphor helps me to understand human development from a more textual and textured perspective in which there is much room to help revise the texts of children's lives. Considering that the texts many students have written about themselves (with the help of parents, teachers, friends, and society at large) are often rigid and extremely self-critical, this view highlights opportunities for restorying their life texts in healthier and more generous ways.

I have thought a great deal about the nature of text and how each reader brings her own meaning to it, meaning that may differ from the initial text itself. According to Ricoeur (1981, p. 206), "In the same way that a text is detached from its author, an action is detached from its agent and develops consequences of its own." My awareness that I speak from a specific context to others who hear from a different one reminds me of the infinite possibilities for misunderstanding in the ways I hear and am heard, and has profound implications for how I speak and listen. For my work and relationships with youth, Ricoeur reminds me that I must not assume how students hear me, and that I must constantly be critical of how I hear (and mis-hear) them.

Ricoeur's article holds four interconnected lessons for me. The first is that the students with whom I work write their life histories based on how they interpret themselves, that this is shaped in part by their school experiences ("I am stupid," "I am intelligent," "I can't achieve"), and that these interpretations and the patterns of behavior that stem from them can be moved or interrupted by new experiences. The second lesson is that I realize my role as coauthor is not neutral, that it reflects my biased interpretation of students' school experiences and their worlds outside of school, and that I need to remain cognizant of this as I try to reframe students' experiences with them. Third, the realization that my record of the changes within each individual and in our relationships can have profound implications for the quality and texture of our work together holds implications for how carefully I document my interpretations of our experiences together over time. The fourth lesson is that I realize that my words, as a text, are in many ways subject to having their meaning fixed in time—interpreted by students in ways I may not intend. This is a caveat for me to be mindful of the messages, implicit or explicit, that I convey.

Gadamer might argue that many of the lessons from our readings and class discussions, which have contributed to my vocabulary of hermeneutics, have been forgotten in the sense that they have become part of my working interpretation. Through reading my process notes I realize how new these concepts were to me only a few months ago. Gadamer articulates this phenomenon: "Every determination of word meaning grows, as it were, in playful fashion from the value of the word in the concrete situation. . . . A new word usage comes into play and, equally unnoticed and unintended, the old words die" ([1960] 1993, p. 56). This passage holds two critical and interrelated points for understanding the work I have done this semester. First, it articulates my belief that once we encounter and truly engage in the meaning and implications of a new language and then take this a step further and act from our understanding of this language, we internalize the language, thereby in some sense fusing it with our reality (and shaping our reality in its wake). In hermeneutic terms, the theories have become part of the biases through which I understand my interactions with students, and they simultaneously act as a counterpoint to the biases with which I entered into these different capacities. Second, it points to the value of applying theory in concrete situations. Clearly the real challenge of theory comes when I must act on it. Through my relationships with students, new challenges, questions, and concerns have surfaced that have formed what Gergen (1988) terms my *emergent context*—the context that follows prior interactions and integrations. This emerging context leads to the next part of this investigation, which grounds my initial reflections on myself and my objectives in an inquiry of·my work within an urban public school system.

BECOMING UNCOMFORTABLE: MOVING FORWARD WHILE EMBRACING DOUBT

Writing the assignment "Where I Come from, What I Bring" was an excellent way to self-consciously examine my background and what I brought to my work with students. Rereading Gadamer's ([1962] 1976) discussion about the need to revise the stigma attached to prejudice helped me to critique that paper after I had completed it. I wrote at length in my journal: "I just wrote a paper about what I bring to my work. I bring so much. I grappled to excavate, as truthfully as possible, the biases and preconceived notions I have by virtue of my background and experiences. This helped me to clarify where I am and where *I am not* in terms of my growth. I need to move forward by working on my prejudices or all of this work and my relationships with students has the potential to be oppressive. That is an unpalatable possibility" (Nov. 4, 1993).

In rereading my process notes, I found that at that time (November 6 to 23) I began to work through questions about the degree to which my own interpretations had come to limit my relationships with students. At the same time I began to question how to bring about changes in the students from my groups in terms of how negatively they seemed to define themselves. This marked a period of dealing with a parallel struggle: to find the meaning and implications of my interpretations and to connect with the students in order to work with their often damaging self-interpretations. As time passed, I began to feel somewhat more reconciled with my prejudices (in the sense that I was trying to combat them honestly) and to move beyond just *being interested in* the students toward *being engaged with* them (Lecture Notes, Oct. 1, 1993).

Transforming My Praxis

I will now evaluate my interpretations of the movement within two of the three groups that Beth Moughty (my co-intern) and I lead together. During our third month with these groups we were met with tremendous resistance from the students. All three groups seemed to fall into a slump and we did not understand the reasons for this. Amidst my confusion and frustration I returned to several of the readings and to my class notes in an attempt to make sense of my role within the groups and to clarify my interpretations of the group dynamics.

Packer and Addison's (1989) discussion of the Heideggerian concept of the *circularity of understanding* helped me to realize that I had created expectations for these groups that were not attainable in such a short period of time. I realized that I needed to work towards co-creating authentic relationships with the students by reflecting separately on each group, each child, and myself in each situation. This helped me to find a direction for all of the groups that was more connected to where each individual and each group was coming from. As Packer and Addison have taught me:

> When we try to study some new phenomenon we are always thrown forward into it. . . . We will have some preliminary understanding of what kind of phenomenon it is, and of what possible things might happen to it. This means that we both understand it and at the same time misunderstand it; we inevitably shape the phenomenon to fit a "fore-structure" that has been shaped by expectations and preconceptions, and by our lifestyle, culture and tradition. If we are persevering and open, our attention will be drawn to the projective character of our understanding and—in the backward arc, the movement of return—we gain an increased appreciation of what the fore-structure involves, and where it might best be changed" [pp. 33–34].

Reading and reflecting on the concepts in this chapter was a catalyst for my decision to restructure my approach based on a better (that is, more reflected-upon) understanding of the students in each group.

In order to write a site evaluation, I began to analyze my process notes beginning with the week of December 5, 1993. After reviewing my finished evaluation, I realized there was little mention of individual students, of specific interactions, or of the groups as separate, self-contained units in either my process notes or the evaluation. Noticing and examining what was *not* in my notes or in my site evaluation was uncomfortable because I realized that I lacked feelings of connection with the students, and that they seemed to feel distant as well. Because of this process of reinterpretation, I was able to spend some time figuring out how to revise my approach to better meet the students where they were, and as a result, to more fully connect with them and engage in our work. Writing consistent and thorough notes proved essential to this process of reflection, realization, and change, because I was able to uncover patterns of everyday connection and disconnection and move in new directions based on a better understanding of those patterns.

The first group I will discuss is the girls group at the Elysha School. By the end of November, the girls had become increasingly disruptive in our meetings. When Beth and I began our sessions, the students made it clear that they did not want to be there and seemed to be doing everything they could to make the experience unpleasant (possibly with the hope of driving us away). After several sessions, Beth and I realized that we were not doing much to understand their discontent or to change the situation. Instead, we were expressing our dissatisfaction to each other and to the students in inadvertent ways during our weekly meetings. This felt unproductive and potentially damaging to the girls, so we decided to restructure the meetings and our approach to the material we wanted to cover.

We decided that if we could get to know each other better we would be able to create a relationship from which meaningful interaction could flow more naturally. A major turning point occurred when Beth and I agreed that we should stop bringing in highly structured activities and try to, as Nakkula teaches, "just be" with the girls to figure out where they were coming from and to give them insight into where we were coming from. The sessions following this shift were wonderful! We talked without any formal agenda, laughed, shared stories, and listened to each other. The girls were much more open and warm, they shared food (this had previously been a problem) and listened to each other. After observing this shift I realized that I needed to relinquish my cherished role as leader and transmitter of knowledge and allow us to co-create a more reciprocal relationship based on mutual and appropriate levels of sharing.

This period of restructuring (or destructuring) my approach and the group sessions marked the beginning of changes in the way our group interacts. I believe that this is how we should have "structured" all of our groups from the beginning. I now realize, because of the course lectures, the readings, and my experiences in these groups, that it is often the unstructuredness and idiosyncratic nature of counseling sessions that creates the possibility for concerned engagement, which I now see as the key to prevention and intervention programs. I am finding that there is an incredible freedom in realizing the important meaning of everyday events. When more importance is placed on everyday interactions, there is less pressure to create, force, or dictate meaning because the meaning flows from the relationship itself. Trust, connection, and the modeling of reciprocal behavior—between Beth and I and between each of us and the girls—is necessary if we are to expect to improve the students' interpersonal, collaboration, and perspective-taking skills. This period of reconstruction also marks my acceptance of these girls as genuinely important to me on a personal level, as well as my ability to integrate theory and practice more fully.

Experiencing Change over Time

I will now examine the change and growth in another of our groups. At the beginning of this second girls group, Beth and I mainly played the role of disciplinarians. Over time, however, we formed relationships with the girls, and we are now able to understand one another on a deeper, more mutual level. The most telling example of change in this group is reflected in Nikki, who had been very disruptive and hostile throughout the first two months of our work. During a session one month ago, Nikki was about to punch another girl in the face when I broke up the fight and asked her to walk out of the room with me. As I closed the door she seemed prepared for me to yell at her, so when I asked "What's going on?" she began to answer in an angry tone: "Nothin', she was makin' me mad." When I said "No, I mean how are you feeling?" trying to communicate that I was concerned about her rather than wanting to attack her, we were able to begin discussing why she disliked school and our group. For the next hour we walked up and down the hallways together as we talked. Looking back, I feel that this interaction precipitated an opening for us to connect. I made myself vulnerable by asking Nikki to critique me and our group and I feel she began to sense that I did not intend to be another figure of authority yelling at her or trivializing her feelings of anger.

Since this incident, Nikki and I have been spending more time together. I want to understand her, to allow her to ask me questions, and to just hang out together, because I believe that building a comfortable and safe relationship is the intervention she needs most. Over time Nikki has slowly begun to participate in group discussions. She has been consistently warm and receptive to me and much more friendly to the rest of the students (though her teacher tells me that this still seems isolated to our group). Nikki has begun to talk about herself and to ask questions about our lives.

This experience marks a shift in my practice—from simply assessing students' behaviors to trying to figure out the underlying meaning of their actions. One thing I have learned from this experience is that without a genuinely reciprocal relationship we are no more to children than two more staff members expecting them to open up and change without giving anything of ourselves. My desire to share parts of my own life with Nikki and the rest of our girls group stems in part from reflections on the notion put forth in Packer and Addison's (1989) chapter "Evaluating an Interpretive Account" concerning careful interpretive research: "as inquiry that seeks reciprocity; that calls for interactive, dialogic interviews that require self-disclosure on the part of the researcher; that involves negotiation of meaning" (p. 277). Bringing this notion into the realm of interpretive youth work, I am reminded that in the context of building relationships with students it is important to share appropriate parts of my life with them if I expect them to share parts of their lives with me. Particularly as a woman working with girls, I find that this meeting at the crossroads between women and girls, as Carol Gilligan (Brown and Gilligan, 1992) teaches, is a powerful developmental exchange for myself and for my female students.

Even with the many positive changes and developments throughout the semester, I have experienced periods of intense frustration. In the schools, I am frustrated and at times angry at the harsh treatment of the students and at the criticism expressed about their ways of dressing and speaking. Reading Delpit's (1988) article "The Silenced Dialogue" provided me with an explicit framework for dealing with my own feelings of helplessness within the system as I tried to help students better understand the systems in which they learn and live. Placing our interactions within what Delpit terms the *culture of power* in schools and classrooms enables me to better support students to resist internalizing the often negative images of themselves that some of their teachers and school administrators reinforce daily. It also helps me to see how I reinforce my own values, priorities, and beliefs when working with students. As Delpit writes, "We must believe that people are rational beings, and therefore always act rationally. We may not understand their rationales, but that in no way militates against the existence of these rationales or reduces our responsibility to attempt to apprehend them. And finally, we must learn to be vulnerable enough to allow our world to turn upside down in order to allow the realities of others to edge themselves into our consciousness. In other words, we must become ethnographers in the true sense" (p. 297).

Delpit's discussion of the need to make the implicit power structure of institutions explicit as a way to create avenues for self-understanding is becoming a vital part of my youth service philosophy. Reading her article through a hermeneutic lens, through a lens of self- and other-interpretation, has allowed me to see myself as part of this culture of power, and I take this quite seriously. I am conscious of understanding our co-construction of meaning as a function for the students and not for anyone else (for example, my work with students is not intended to make them complacent and quiet in their classrooms). I want to help foster an understanding that the school, teachers, and our society at large can be oppressive, and that students need to know how to view themselves as part of these sometimes-oppressive structures, yet as distinct from them. To uncover this power structure in a manner that will be constructive for students is essential. I do not view this effort as creating an adversarial relationship between the students and the teachers and administration, but rather as an uncovering of forces that can negatively define students—definitions they often internalize. I feel that this effort is about teaching youth, as I learn myself, to think critically about these things, to effectively communicate needs without being disrespectful, and to know and understand the differences and implications of each of these functions. My aim is to help students to see how they can bring their own powers and ways of being into school, to validate their feelings of frustration, and to work with them to figure out strategies for dealing with rules that can be unfair and denigrating. To do this I must critically examine my own agenda, my unacknowledged prejudices and assumptions. As an upper-middle-class white woman, I question my ability to speak against the power structure, and wonder how I can deal with the ways in which I both symbolize and reinforce it.

PRELIMINARY CONCLUSION: BETWEEN THE ARCS OF PROJECTION AND REFLECTION

Over the past four months I have come to more of an understanding that in order to truly learn and expand my frame of reference, to really question the effects of societal forces such as race, class, and culture on cross-cultural youth service work, the theories I am learning about and my reactions to them need to be challenged in multiple settings and in a variety of relationships. I have learned how important it is for me to allow myself to feel vulnerable in a way that can allow me to be more receptive to learning (from the students) about what I can improve. I hope to be able to actualize this learning over time. Through continued reflection and self-conscious interaction with students, new questions concerning my biases and prejudices are emerging. I am finding that transforming my praxis is far from a one-semester enterprise: "I have *a lot* more work to do. I need to sustain my feelings of discomfort in order to continue to facilitate change" (Process Notes, Dec. 20, 1993). Over the course of this semester I have become acutely aware that as a youth service provider I have an ethical responsibility to engage in an active and ongoing process of self-reflection and a continual reinterpretation of where I am in order to move in a direction that is more firmly grounded in social realities and therefore more emancipatory for my students.

I end this investigation and usher in the New Year with Gadamer's ([1962] 1976) idea that through every interaction we are changed permanently. He writes, "Through every dialogue something different comes to be" (p. 58). This statement embodies my experience this semester. I am different now than I was only four months ago. As a result of this systematic process of uncovering, I have made changes in myself and shifts in my practice. Our groups, the students in them, myself, and our relationships will continue to change, and I hope that at the end of this year I will look back to this point as one step in a direction toward better self-understanding and being-with-others, and as movement towards my larger vision of equity, empowerment, and possibility.

6

THE FLIGHT OF A BLACK BUTTERFLY

A Hermeneutic Investigation of Metamorphosis

Gregory Seaton

A GENTLE BREEZE CARESSED THE YOUNG BOYS as they stooped at the base of the tree. The sun beamed down on their faces and the peace was interrupted only by the rhythmic roll of cars down the cobblestone street. A green caterpillar was the object of their attention. During that time of year, caterpillars making their pilgrimage from the concrete to the shrubbery were a common sight. The boys, with Popsicle sticks in hand, teased, taunted, and tried to impede the pilgrimage and process of metamorphosis. They were amused by the determination of their subject to reach the solitude of the shrubbery. Repeatedly, the caterpillar climbed one Popsicle stick after another. It seemed undaunted by the obstacles the environment threw in its way; it persevered. The caterpillar eventually proved to be unworthy entertainment, for it no longer amused us. We turned our attention to the more exciting prospect of football. And so the caterpillar made its pilgrimage to the shrubbery and completed another stage in the process of being and becoming. Days later, the only memento of the metamorphosis was a hollow brown sack that dangled from the branch of a shrub. And a single black butterfly.

The caterpillar seems so minuscule in such a large world, yet the prophetic message of its life cycle has proven invaluable to me. At the time I could not see the prophecy of the caterpillar; I was a little kid passing time on a spring day. Now I realize that the caterpillar is a fitting symbol for the discourse of hermeneutics and for my experience this year, because it symbolizes change and metamorphosis over time. The example of the caterpillar will serve as a metaphor for my examination of change and "connectedness" over time.

Connectedness, for this chapter, will be operationally defined as the type and quality of relationship between individuals. Language will serve as the vehicle of facilitation and revelation of connectedness. Through language we are able to access and relay our connectedness over time. Through the examination of connectedness, meaning is realized in such a way that it invites metamorphosis. In short, when we examine connectedness, we are compelled to view "variables" in context. Connectedness transforms abstract numbers into people, places, situations, emotions, and contextual background information.

A primary tenet of the hermeneutic process is to obtain knowledge, via the interaction of the specific with the global as they relate to a particular context. In short, hermeneutics attempts to uncover truth, through an examination of individual (self) and group (nonself) interaction. Unlike other methodological pursuits of "truth," hermeneutics does not encourage the investigator to control his biases. This approach demands that the investigator recognize his biases and understand the effects they have on the phenomena being observed. Thus the investigator not only gains a better understanding of that which is being observed, but he is simultaneously afforded a more thorough understanding of self. The acknowledgment and use of biases as data affords one a more holistic understanding of people and phenomena. The investigator is not given the luxury of a false sense of security that he is able to control for all possible "data contaminants," but is forced instead to deal with the data and biases as they are in the "real world"—inextricably united.

The primary purpose of this paper is to examine changes in my "connectedness to the world" using daily field notes, Assignment One, an explication of my biases, and readings presented in the practicum course. The constituents of the world that I will examine include the Toffler Middle School, the Urban Youth Connection, Harvard, my peers, and my perpetually evolving self.

THE TOFFLER CONNECTION

The Toffler Middle School is an inner-city school in Boston. As a part of the practicum course, I spent fifteen hours per week as a counselor for the Urban Youth Connection (UYC). The UYC is a school-based counseling and drug intervention/prevention program that is a collaboration between the middle school, a community health center, and the Harvard Graduate School of Education. My experience at Toffler is influenced by a host of players: UYC staff, teachers, administrators, and the students I serve. Someone once wrote that change is inevitable; that has certainly been the case as I relate to Toffler. There have been dramatic shifts in my relationships with the students. I will use my data from the year to illustrate these changes.

In the first assignment, rather than employing higher-order perspective-taking skills as described by Nakkula and Selman (1991), I paid an inordinate amount of attention to my perceptions of others. Because I was too preoccupied with my own perceptions, thoughts, and feelings, I neglected to explicate what I perceived others were thinking of me. Some may argue that by noting exchanges with others their perceptions are implicitly acknowledged. I contend that exclusively noting exchanges from one's own perspective limits the meaning-making process. Consequently, this chapter will include my perceptions of others' perspectives as a means of enriching the data and offering another lens to examine phenomena.

The philosophical core of hermeneutics is based on meaning. Packer and Addison (1989) introduce Heidegger's metaphor of the hermeneutic circle as a perspective on how meaning is constructed. They divide the circle of meaning into two arcs: the forward arc of projection and the return arc of reflection. Writing this chapter has revealed that I had been limiting myself to an overly generalized construction of meaning. I have yet to experience the full 360 degrees of the circle. The 180 degrees of forward projection is the arc with which I am most familiar. By exclusively walking the line of projection, self is exonerated from any type of scrutiny or analysis because issues are always others', and not one's own. Whether conscious or unconscious, posing general questions about meaning afforded me some degree of safety. Because my questions remained general, there was no need to travel on the reflective arc of the hermeneutic circle. For me it has always seemed easier to project than to reflect. And it has been easier to project at a depth far greater than the depth from which I reflect. Due to this imbalance, my understanding of myself, and of others, was skewed.

Reflection on changes in my experience *over time* with Toffler's case supervisor has allowed me to realize and experience the theoretical transformation from crescent to circle. During the beginning of my internship at the UYC, I felt that Maria, my clinical supervisor, played the role of drill sergeant for my coworkers and me. I experienced her as difficult, unapproachable, and oppressive. An excerpt from my first paper reads:

> Ideally, supervision should be a forum where new and inexperienced counselors (such as myself) are trained and aided through counseling procedures. I find it to be more of an ordeal than an assistance. Under the impression that I have an inability to relate to non-blacks, she gave me a white client. Before meeting with the client, and having only read his file, I thought that Ted, my co-intern, would be better able to serve him. Ted has experienced many situations that this young man is going through. I mentioned this to Maria. In an accusatory fashion she suggested that I did not want to work with the individual because he was white (when I did not know he was white until that point). Another example is that she recently gave me a "compliment": "I was scared when you told me you are an Afrocentrist. I thought you were going to be a Khalid Muhammad—kill the white people! I just want to commend you on how well you get along with your coworkers: a white male and female and a Latino woman." Did she expect me to kill them? Not wanting to be misunderstood, I began to withdraw and withhold from supervision [Process Notes, Nov. 17, 1994].

This excerpt is indicative of my initial line of inquiry. My first question was, What is meaningful to me? This question allowed me to avoid reaching deeper levels of analysis and therefore afforded me only a lop-sided experience of the hermeneutic circle. Until now, I had never concerned myself with the question, What does the presence of an African American male mean for the students and for the program? As I projected onto others, I avoided reflecting on how I was affecting them. Now my line of questioning has evolved to include, How do I construct meaning? and Why are certain things meaningful? The reader might construe this as a minute shift, but I contend that it is an important one. My focus is no longer solely on the object of meaning, because I realize that answers lie within the interactions between myself and the object of meaning. This personal paradigmatic shift has allowed me to view Maria in a new light, in addition to accepting some responsibility for the outcome of our interactions.

An essential factor in my epiphany is *time*—in particular, the freezing of thoughts, feelings, experiences, and connectedness at different points in time. Through analysis, reinterpretation, and the reevaluation of what Gergen (1988) has termed "moments frozen in time,"[1] I have been able to work toward creating an equilibrium between my arcs of projection and reflection. Equilibrium is important because it provides the opportunity to reflect and to view each individual's contribution to situational dynamics, and thus prevents one from assuming that feelings and issues are the sole property of others.

Returning to the story of the caterpillar, I now realize that at first I only understood how the world was affecting me. There were factors in my environment that introduced barriers to impede my progress. I never thought about the impact I had on those little boys or on the caterpillar itself. I never stopped to consider how I was affecting the world around me. What was it like to meet me in various states: as the caterpillar who only projected, as the cocooned one who needed time and space to learn to reflect, and now, as the black butterfly who has struck a balance between projection and reflection?

Reflection and I were once intimate strangers. Over this year we have become more familiar as I have learned about myself through reviewing my notes concerning Maria. Two excerpts, when juxtaposed, demonstrate this change over time:

> Can life get any worse? I never really wanted to kill a kid before. I could not believe it. It was like I was right back around the way again. Me, the civil intellectual, the counselor from Harvard. Jesus, help me! I was walking Damion to class today. He reeked of weed and I did not want him to get into trouble—the teachers be hawkin' him. It was him, Al, and Bill—three of the most ostracized brothers in the school. We were walkin' down the hall, I had an arm on Damion's shoulder as I whispered to him that I could smell the herb and that he should get to class before he gets in trouble in the hallways. The others were following closely behind. Damion began to engage in some type of ritualized game—"To the fifty, the forty." He assumed the posture as if he were playing football. He was a running back using my arm as the football. Then he began to pick up speed with my arm! I gently kicked his foot and caught him as he lost his balance. I told him he did not make a first down so he had to go to class. He and the others laughed. Then it began. Al and Bill began to joke with Damion, "Ah, you got clipped; he stopped you." It was like Dr. Jekyl and Mr. Hyde—he musta' been smokin' turbs—the smile quickly left his face. He was angry! "Why you tried to trip me man!" I tried to explain, "I wasn't tryin' to

hurt you man, you were playin,' right. . . . C'mon and go to class man." He pulled away and began to yell, "I'm tired of you teachers always f-ckin' with me." Bill, Al, and I looked at each other bewildered. Damion pushed me! I pushed him back. Automatically I began to think of a plan for how to take him out—fake a left jab, stiff right, left upper cut, then a right uppercut, if he was still standing. [My brother was the 1990 Philly Golden Gloves Champ and tried out for the Olympic Boxing Team; I was his stand-in sparring partner.] I could not believe what I was thinking, and I was disturbed at how hard-wired fighting is in me. I looked at my fists and they were clenched tight. Damion charged at me again, he pushed me against the wall as he hollered, "You can't beat me, teach! You can't beat me." Bill and Al began to grab him. To be honest, I wanted to mop his face up and down the hall. What would my mother say? What would it mean for my academic career? Would the UYC get kicked out of the school? What would I tell my other kids? Me, a twenty-two-year-old Harvard graduate student beat up a fourteen-year-old middle school student" [Process Notes, Jan. 8, 1995].

The "good guy" always finishes last. I went downstairs for supervision. I really didn't want to talk to her for fear that she would say that this proved I was incompetent. Just what I need, another reason for her to scold me—talk about power and silencing. Maria shocked me. "O.K. We will go up there right now and take care of it. He is high and that is why he acted like that. I'll go up there and talk to him and the principal. It's really good to get on top of these things before they get blown out of proportion. . . . You did not hit him did you? How are you feeling? Are you O.K.?" I could not believe it. She said: "You never know what a kid might do when he is high." Was this the same woman who made me out to be a racist? She is now sensitive, she listens? What is going on here? [Process Notes, January 12, 1995].

As these entries suggest, from my perspective Maria changed significantly. It meant a lot to me to see the level of confidence she had in my ability, especially at a point when I was doubting myself. This event marked a turning point in our relationship. Maria would continue to make a concerted effort to be supportive. And because of her change in behavior, as well as realizations I was making as a result of learning about hermeneutics, I was able to get in touch with some of my own issues. Maria's initial approach made it easy for me to hold her accountable for my own insecurities.

Upon reflection, I am able to admit that I was terrified to sit in a room alone with a kid I did not know. I found the novelty of the counseling relationship difficult to handle, so I deferred my baggage to Maria. I am not suggesting that Maria was the perfect supervisor or that it was my insecurity alone that made the supervisory relationship problematic. Maria changed in response to a lot of complaining and discussion. Once she began to confront her issues, with the help of others, I was able to confront my fears and insecurities about counseling. To be sure, we are now better able to meet the needs of the students. This experience has tremendous implications for those who work in schools, and for the students they serve. It suggests that when we are able to adequately project *and reflect,* students are provided with a higher quality of service because services are less tainted by our unacknowledged biases and/or fears.

IDENTITY

In this section I examine my identity from two different perspectives: my role at Toffler and my personal history as it relates to this role. These two perspectives speak to the uncertainty I have felt toward my experience at the UYC.

Role Ambiguity

As a counselor at the UYC I have encountered many conflicts that revolve around identity. A large majority of my internship was marked by my own role ambiguity: I was not a teacher, but some students perceived me as one; some teachers perceived me as a student; and I was a counselor, but the teachers wanted me to function as a teacher.

One teacher who readily comes to mind is Mrs. Brown. Mrs. Brown is a short, stern black woman whose presence commands respect. I have the utmost respect and admiration for her as a teacher because she has a way of reaching the kids, and they really learn in her classroom. Still, as colleagues our relationship has been strained. Mrs. Brown, like many of the other teachers at Toffler, has, I believe, a distorted view of counseling and the effects that it should have on the students. I often feel as if teachers expect us to work miracles with students. Their idea of counseling is that they can send students with chronic behavioral problems to counseling once or twice and the students will be transformed into studious angels.

I was walking John to his classroom. John is an extremely intelligent African American male who gives minimal effort toward working to the best of his ability. If John decided to be at least half-motivated about school, he could easily become a straight-A student (the same would be true if the school was more motivated about encouraging John to learn). This was my second time meeting with John. Two weeks earlier I had introduced myself to him in the lunchroom and persuaded him to refer himself to the UYC. I was excited by his potential, and it encouraged me to work extra hard on his intervention. We had just finished an intense session in which we discussed the effects of marijuana on the body and the importance of coming to school.

> John asked me to go into the classroom with him because he did not think his teacher would believe he was with me. I complied. Mrs. Brown was sitting at her desk and the students were working quietly when we entered. John took a seat and asked a friend what he was doing. I walked over to Mrs. Brown and began to explain that John was late because he was in counseling. "John was" was all I was able to say before she said in a stern tone, "Can I talk to you outside?" She was speaking to me as if I were one of her students. "John is a very smart kid, but he has a lot of problems. . . . He can be doing a lot better but he never comes to school on time." I tried to speak, but she would not let me. "What are you doing in counseling? He still is not coming to school on time and he is not completing his work." I fought to be heard. "John just started counseling. How could we begin to even think about changing his behavior in just a few meetings?" She continued: "Maybe he does not need to be in counseling if it is not working for him. You guys are taking these kids out of class and bringing them back the same way they left. . . . I have seen y'all with the kids laughing, smiling. . . ." "I am not a magician," I retorted as she slammed the door in my face. I was pissed. The teachers at Toffler need to find out the real deal, counseling does not work like that. Neither does dialogue [Process Notes, Nov. 17, 1995].

Mrs. Brown has some definite misconceptions about counseling and the role of UYC counselors. I, too, am learning that counseling is a process of incremental change. Very seldom does one see very dramatic changes in a student's behavior over such a short period. How did she expect me to erase a lifetime of reinforced negative behavior over the course of two forty-five-minute counseling sessions? It simply cannot be done. Counselors do not say a magic incantation and the students are then placed on the honor roll. It is a long and hard process.

I believe that Mrs. Brown, in addition to not understanding counseling as a process, did not understand the need for the counselors' relationships with the students to be different. In turn, she confronted me in an effort to make me comply with the established norms of the teachers. A prime example of this tension occurred in mid-January. It was the repercussions from the incident with Damion.

> I feel like I'm being closed in here. Two teachers tried to straight-up play me. The cluster-leader said the teachers were concerned about my "inappropriate behavior with students." What? What? What the hell was going on here? They're trying to get rid of a brother. I know the deal! I was nervous and mad all at the same time. It turns out that my "problematic behavior with students" was laughing with them in the hallways. What, we cannot laugh? This was only the beginning—I was going "beyond the boundary of teacher" (I am not a damn teacher). "I do not think that it is appropriate for you to give the kids handshakes, high-fives, or whatever it is that you do. And all that 'yo man' slang that you talk with the kids. We are trying to teach them proper English, not that street stuff." That street stuff is who I am. Why won't Boston just let me be me? [Process Notes, Jan. 15, 1995].

In this segment, the way teachers envisioned the counselor-student relationship is readily apparent. As counselors we did not draw the lines of authority and power dark enough to satisfy the teachers. Counselors were not supposed to be friendly with students. How could I create a safe forum for students to discuss personal issues if I was not friendly? As counselors, it is imperative that we be able to validate students and relate with them. The means to achieving this end are very different from those employed by teachers. I talk to the students in a manner they can understand. In addition, this mode of talk-Ebonics (Asante, 1991) is authentic for me. It is not my job to teach the students English. I am the counselor. My objective is to relate to students and to assist them in making well-informed decisions. The teachers' suggestion that I relate to students in a manner that is not authentic also suggested that my culture, which is consistent with that of most of the students, was not wanted or appreciated at the school.

As I reflect on the identity crisis of Toffler, I am afforded a deeper understanding of what it takes to create change in an institution that may be resistant to it. My understanding is rather paradoxical. To create institutional change, one must be clear about one's own identity. Identity, as I am describing it, is the aggregate of personal experience, institutional role, and institutional agenda. I now realize that identity confusion or ambiguity is a prerequisite to identity solidification and clarity. I think we gain insight into our actual identity through identity conflict. My conflict reacquainted me with the pressure to conform, the same pressure that many students are faced with from other peers and teachers. The conflict allowed me to become a more effective counselor. I understood how many black students felt alienated from the school, which is largely Hispanic. I understood my objective with much more clarity. My role, as I came to see it, was to prepare students for the inevitable alienation they would experience, while simultaneously relaying to them the importance of the education provided by the alienating institution: their school.

No Illusions of Inclusion

When posed the question, What biases or prejudgments do I bring to Toffler? one assumption readily comes to mind. I assume that most blacks, if not all, will have similar life experiences because we exist within a racist society. I recognize that experiences vary due to variables such as economics, location, and factors related to individual personalities. But I also believe that this variation in experience does not discount the fact that the meaning of the experience, for the most part, is communal. In general, blacks have different experiences but arrive at similar conclusions. Our experiences often translate to mean that this is a white world and there is no place here for nonwhites. As I wrote in my "Where I Come from, What I Bring" paper:

> I was first made aware of "my difference" when I was about fourteen years old. I lived in a semi-integrated working class neighborhood in Gainesville, Florida. Most of the neighborhood kids were white and we all would get together and play football and other games. During play, no mention of race had ever occurred (I suffered from what I now call "illusion of inclusion"). I thought I was a white kid in a black body. On the way home from school it was a common practice for the children to walk through the woods as a short cut. One day as I walked through the woods I met one of my "friends." He was an older white guy who usually played with the younger kids. I said "Hi" as I approached him. He did not respond. The situation did not feel right. He pulled out a knife from his back pocket. The long sharp blade glistened in the sun's rays. Like a deer caught in traffic, I was paralyzed: I could not move. He hollered as he began to approach me, "I'm going to kill you nigger!"

The baggage I bring from this experience suggests that my presence is so despised that there are individuals who are eager and willing to inflict physical harm upon me. This statement could hold true for any individual anywhere, but placed in a historical context, it holds especially true for African Americans. I feel obligated to warn and counsel the students of color at Toffler about this being inevitable. By warning them, I am attempting to provide black youth with a better understanding of the system they live in, what Delpit (1988) refers to as the *culture of power*. I consider this preparing them for the realities of racism: preparation is often the best prevention.

Toffler was not the only place where I experienced role ambiguity and conflict. Numerous dialectical tensions have evolved as a result of my enrollment at Harvard—tensions that relate to differences in personality and class. Each time I return home I am reminded that I am no longer the same Gregg who left the ghetto of North Philadelphia. I feel guilty when I cannot relate to family and friends in the same manner I did before I left. We have all changed. Having no other means to relate, I resort to my old, now outdated states of being, which no longer feel authentic. Feelings of silence are overwhelming, for I cannot explain to my family what I study or do at Harvard. Upon attempting, I am often misconstrued as arrogant, or my audience is lost in the perceived irrelevance of the subject matter to their lives. It is difficult to have a joy and passion and not be able to share it with those you love.

Moreover, my potential economic reality has changed drastically. At the same time, the economic reality of my family has also changed—for the worse. This makes it extremely difficult to share my joy with those who are experiencing so much pain. How can I rejoice over numerous job offers when my cousins cannot find a job and my father is scarcely making more than the minimum wage? My victories are often private ones that cannot be shared. I have resolved that I will never be fully accepted in the white academic community, and I work hard to prove my allegiance to the black community with which I identify. I am stuck between two worlds, concurrently despised and revered by both.

BIAS, EMPOWERMENT, RESISTANCE

At both the conscious and unconscious levels, the phenomenon of guilt has had a large impact on my interaction with students, in particular black students at the UYC. I make a conscious effort to target black students, because I am aware of the issues they face or will face.

Reasonably in touch with my own pain and issues, I try to provide them with the means to confront theirs. As a black male it is my responsibility and duty to educate and model empowering behaviors for other blacks, particularly males. My sense of duty has been created by my acknowledgment of the impact that other black males have had on my life, rather than by an absolution of guilt. I realize that my feet rest on the shoulders of many and that I, too, must make my shoulders strong if the race is to be uplifted. As a result, I have actively sought out black males to be a part of the UYC and have started an intervention group that consists of ten black males.

Admittedly, I entered Toffler with a definite bias—a personal need to intervene specifically in the lives of black boys. They were the individuals I viewed as I do myself—as the primary target of America's racism. Following Packer and Addison's (1989) model, this bias was used as data in interpreting my experience at Toffler. Working with black males this year has brought up numerous questions and concerns about my effectiveness and willingness to work in a system.

Numerous black males were assigned to me for counseling and I desperately wanted to make a difference in their lives. My passion, my existence, was predicated on empowering them to make wise decisions. The boys in my group and I connected, or at least I thought we did. One of my favorite students stated before he went to a class he dislikes that "the only reason I'm goin' in here is because of you. . . . I'ma do my work today." Two weeks later he was expelled from school for punching a substitute teacher. About a month before that, another black male, whom I thought I was reaching, was expelled for possession of a firearm and crack; I turned him in. Throughout the year, numerous other black and Hispanic males with whom I considered myself to be connecting would be suspended or transferred to other schools for disciplinary reasons. Moments of truth emerged in our work together, yet the boys were unable to make correct decisions in important moments, which has cast serious doubts on the impact I have had on these young men.

Paradoxically, I have been empowered through my alleged inability to perform. As the result of reflection, I can now see how I have internalized the outlook for which I once scolded teachers. I must remind myself that counseling is indeed a process of incremental change and that behaviors do not miraculously change overnight. This is a concept that is very easy to forget, particularly when I become attached to students. Although students continue to behave negatively, it does not necessarily mean that the interventions and/or I were ineffective.

Another variation of the guilt or identity confusion that I have experienced at Toffler relates to the parts of me I see in the kids. Although thousands of miles away, I have walked the same streets my counselees have and I have operated by a code that is very similar to theirs. Elijah Anderson (1990) refers to this as the "code of the street." The code demands "an eye for an eye and a tooth for tooth." If you hit me, I am going to hit you back harder and more frequently, for in the street, survival is only promised to the fittest. And fitness is based on the ability to get props (proper respect) or a rep (reputation) at the expense of others.

I was forced to confront pieces of "the code" that I had internalized when a student brought a firearm to school. The group session started pretty smoothly. The trouble began when we returned to the room for discussion. One of the black students (James) poured apple juice on a Latino student (Jose) by "accident." Clearly, it was not an accident. "Oops, I'm sorry man. My b[ad]," he said as he laughed hysterically. Jose smiled momentarily, grabbed the bottle and doused James with juice. A fight was brewing, but Bill (the co-leader) and I broke it up before any actual blows were thrown. Later, two other group members came to me and said, "Gregg, man, he got a gun. I saw it man, it was in his pants. He's going to shoot Jose after school." I did not know what to do. I believed the claim of the two other group members; I remembered that before the basketball game James was secretive about placing some items in his bookbag. I reported my suspicions to numerous school officials. Later that day James was escorted from school, screaming, kicking, and crying, by five police officers and in handcuffs. In my notes that day I reflected on my inner conflict with this situation:

> As I watched James being put in the car, I could not help thinking about my friends in Philly. When we walked the streets, went to a party, and sometimes school, someone almost always had a gun. How was I any different from James? I feel like an old Baptist minister who preaches on a Sunday morn' about the immorality of adultery and fornication. He preaches the message with passion, fervor, and conviction, aware that two of the married women in the congregation are carrying his child. Neither of them is his wife. Hypocrite! [Process Notes, Feb. 25, 1995].

This incident has caused me to explore the "factors of environment" that compelled me to ask the question, Was there a better way of handling the situation? A large portion of my first paper was devoted to a discussion of race, racism, and systems. What prompted my inquiry about alternative methods for handling situations was my discomfort with the system to which I reported James. I consider my role as preparing kids to deal with a system that places them "at risk" in a larger societal context. Nonetheless, I acted as an agent of the system. Seeing him being escorted out of the building by white cops, I made an association with the Rodney King episode. I realized that the officers did not care about him, nor did the judicial system he would now become a part of. Should I have approached him and gotten the gun from him on my own? I am not sure. But I do know that six or seven years ago it could have been me being escorted out of the school. This is just one example of the many bouts I have had with the enemy within.

CONCLUSION

This year I have experienced the joys of growth, accomplishment, and change. As I examine my process through the lens of hermeneutics, it begins to make sense. Meaning is constructed and understood at deeper depths. The mission of my journey began, simply stated, as a desire to help as many kids at Toffler as possible. I discovered, in my migration from the concrete of North Philadelphia to the shrubbery of Harvard, that change is indeed inevitable. It is up to me/us to make hermeneutically derived meaning of those changes and to change our environment based on that meaning. It is through the production of meaning and understanding that I have gained tremendous insight into myself. Through reflection I have learned that I not only influence but am influenced.

For a long time I was preoccupied with how I was going to change the world, but I never realized how the world was changing me. In relation to the UYC, I have been teased and taunted by the Popsicle sticks of identity, hopelessness, conflict, and maturation. This has led me to new discoveries. I no longer perceive myself as just an agent of change. I am also an agent changing.

The flight of this black butterfly has been painful, exciting, and contradictory. At various stages of metamorphosis I have faced conflicts within myself and the world. As I fly into the world after spending time in the cocoon of hermeneutic inquiry, I possess a deepened understanding of myself in relationship with others. It is an understanding based on the certainty that my conceptualization of self is open to constant reevaluation, revision, and reinterpretation. And like the caterpillar struggling toward the shrubbery, there are many obstacles in my path, but my resolve is deep.

LOVE !

NOTE

1. Gergen suggests that language enables one to freeze a moment in time. The frozen moment is reinterpreted and processed differently each time it is revisited. Changed interpretations of revisited text are primarily due to the addition of new experiences and reflections to meaning-making faculties.

7

ANOTHER BACKWARD ARC

Further Reflections on "Expert" and "Problem"

Karin E. Liiv

THE PURPOSE OF THIS INVESTIGATION is to examine my practicum placement at Manitou High School in conjunction with the Harvard Graduate School of Education's Risk and Prevention Program's Adolescent Practicum Course. I examine my own movement through this year-long course in relation to my counseling approach with students sent to Project Success, and most notably, in relation to my interpretation and understanding of what constitutes an "expert" and a "problem."

Manitou, a public high school in the greater Boston area, is home to more than 2,300 students representing seventy countries. Project Success is Manitou's in-house suspension program. In terms of disciplinary action, Project Success falls between detention and out-of-school suspension and is assigned for periods ranging from one to three days (one-day "sentences" are the most frequent). The students served by Project Success have committed disciplinary infractions, such as missing detentions, fighting, truancy, absenteeism and/or lateness, being caught off school grounds, or sexual harassment. The stated intention of the program is to provide redirection and/or reintegration of these "at-risk" students into the school community through counseling and referrals to additional services and resources. The students who are sent to Project Success range in age from fourteen to eighteen, are predominantly male, and come from diverse racial and ethnic backgrounds (Asian, Haitian, Puerto Rican, Cape Verdean, African American, Caucasian, and Latino/Latina). During the 1991–1993 school years, Project Success served more than 900 students.

The primary form of documentation for my work at Project Success are case notes on interactions with students. These notes were written at the end of the work day and went into a shared computer file. I believe this diluted their authenticity in that I was aware they could be read by my supervisor and coworkers, and thus sought to document "results" rather than my own feelings and experiences. Other forms of documentation utilized in this study were my personal journal and papers written for concurrent courses and research seminars.

TRACING MOVEMENT OVER TIME: SEPTEMBER TO JANUARY

I began my internship at Project Success proclaiming my defiance and skepticism of authority: "I have a deep distrust of anyone or anything that purports to be the 'right' thing or 'right' way or 'only' way. I have a deep distrust of hierarchical, patriarchal authority" ("Where I Come from, What I Bring," p. 7). However, upon reflection I realize that I was in fact quite awed by the rules and patterns of the Manitou system. Because the system seemed so immense, vast, and endowed with resources, and because it was repeatedly touted as progressive, I initially felt incapacitated, almost incompetent, and ignorant about the complexity and inner workings of the school. I did not believe I could adequately counsel students because I did not feel confident that I could refer them to the proper resources should they need additional help (which surely they would, given the fact that I was so inadequate!). As a result, I spent most of my first month trying to gain knowledge of my new environment through touring, observing, and planning.

So I began my experience at Project Success thinking that I needed to learn and understand the rules, and that I needed access to "experts" if the problems I encountered with my students proved too severe for me to handle or if the students were "resistant" to being "rehabilitated" in the (usually) single day we had together. I thought the Project Success students had problems that needed fixing and I felt that if only I had more "information" I would be able to serve them better. Perhaps I felt that increased knowledge could serve as a buffer between me and my students, between my comfort and their pain.

I also spent my first month at Manitou observing my supervisor in her counseling sessions with students, putting off counseling students on my own until late October. Upon reviewing my first case notes, it seems clear that when I felt uncomfortable or overwhelmed I turned to the rules—either by looking at alternative behavioral options focused exclusively on rule keeping, or by asking the "right" questions about college and career and homework.

On my first day of counseling I encountered two students whose lives outside of school were filled with domestic violence and drug dealing. With one of these students, Karl, the story I heard led me to panic. Karl revealed that he had been "pumping" (dealing drugs) for two or more years, and that he had to continue because of threats made against his younger brother. Karl viewed himself as the sacrificial lamb of his family, eloquently explaining his view of the worlds of light and dark. In his mind, Karl had to carry the dark for the family so that his brother could remain in the light.

While hearing his story, I felt myriad emotions, from joy that Karl felt he could trust and confide in me, to panic at the thought that I had no idea what to advise him to do but knew I needed to do *something,* to fear that Karl could get hurt or that I might get hurt if others knew that I was aware of his illegal activity. Highly agitated, I turned to the "experts"—I confided in my site supervisor and called my practicum advisor, hoping they would guide me to someone even *more* expert who could help Karl. I was then able to give Karl the name of an individual working in gang prevention for him to talk to if he felt he needed more advice from someone who knew the drug-dealing world better.

My first reaction, then, when faced with a situation that made me feel helpless and out of control was to run to the experts, to disempower myself and my own ability to sustain and nurture connection. Since giving Karl the name of the gang prevention expert, I have seen him only in passing. This is in part due to the difficulty on both the students' and my part of finding time for follow-up, but it still can be done, and I did not take the energy or time to find Karl and ask how things were going. It is as if I assumed the problem to be fixed, or at least that it was no longer my responsibility to fix it. I know in my heart that this is a lie. What Karl needs ultimately is not "expert" advice, or even to stop pumping, but ongoing connection and continued concern from as many sources as possible.

The more I work with students, the more I am convinced that it is critical to establish a pair relationship, especially a mentor/mentee relationship. Many of the students who came in seeming despondent or hopeless about their own lives brightened up considerably when discussing the possibility of such a relationship. In noticing the importance of paired or one-on-one relationships in the lives of many Project Success students, and in my own ongoing experience as a Big Sister to my now-twenty-one-year-old Little Sister, I began to appreciate Robert Selman's (1993) interpersonal development model for the possibilities it offers in devising preventive strategies, particularly short-term interventions such as those attempted by Project Success.

Selman has identified various levels of interpersonal action, based on social perspective-taking ability:

> Level 0: physical, flight-or-fight response, such as fighting or withdrawal
>
> Level 1: unilateral, self-centered response, such as commanding or ordering
>
> Level 2: reciprocal strategies, such as bargaining
>
> Level 3: collaborative approaches, such as compromise

Many of the students sent to Project Success operate primarily in either level 0 (fight-or-flight) or level 1 (unilateral) modes, exhibited by verbal or physical aggression, bullying, or other forms of acting out. For these students, it is critical to provide a forum in which level 2 (reciprocal) behavior can be practiced.

Another assumption I brought to Project Success was again the result of my desire to believe in a system that "knows best," or at least "knows better." This view stemmed from my illusion that students who dropped out or broke rules were "bad" or needed "correction." Margonis (1992) would say that it is assumed that these "at-risk" students carry a deficit and, further, that I operated from certain basic assumptions of which I was unaware: "Assuming that the major institutions of school and society are supportive, and that agency lies with individuals, at-risk reformers conclude that something is wrong with the students who choose to leave school" (p. 356). Margonis is right: I did initially believe that any failings were those of the student, not of the system. I assumed the system to be beneficent, so I did not seriously examine my feelings or questions about it.

Over time, I have come to see a picture of Project Success students that is much different than my original snapshot, one that is closer to Michelle Fine's assessment. As Fine describes in Margonis's (1992) article, "The dropout was an adolescent who scored as psychologically healthy. Critical of social and economic injustice, this student was willing to challenge an unfair grade and unwilling to conform mindlessly" (p. 356). Rather than attempting to fit students back into the system, on the assumption that the system operated with their best interests in mind, I began to focus instead on providing them with validation, with encouragement and support for their positions and their stand in relation to the school system. I began to acknowledge the power structure of the school and the fact that it did not always provide students with an accurate picture of the power inequities that exist outside of school, in the world in which the school was ostensibly preparing students to live.

At the end of December, two months after my initial counseling sessions with students and three months into my practicum, I spoke with David, who was "opposed to study hall in theory if he did not have work to do" (Case Notes, Dec. 22, 1993). In my notes I described David as "incredibly well-motivated, doing very well academically, already applying to colleges for environmental science, in which he has been interested since he was nine or ten. He basically follows the beat of his own drum. . . ." David clearly told me that "he gets in-house [suspension] about once a term and that we will see him again because he will not go to study hall if there is no need" (Case Notes, Dec. 22, 1993).

I remember David specifically because my session with him marked the first time I found myself unable to push rule following. There seemed to be no need to force this bright young man to sit in a room and do nothing if he had no work to do. Any attempt to convince him that this was a productive experience, or that study hall merited attendance because it was the rule, would have seemed false to him, because I myself saw no point in it. He wasn't getting into fights, skipping school, or being disruptive while out of study hall, so why not let him continue following his own beat? While I told him I looked forward to seeing him again, I was still aware that others' eyes would be on my notes, so I felt obliged to write the following, halfheartedly: "I suggested that David could work on his college applications during study halls and maybe avoid in-house next term" (Case Notes, Dec. 22, 1993).

But something in me had shifted, and about Lili, the next student I met, I wrote: "I encouraged her to continue to use her strong voice to state her opinions and feelings whether or not she was listened to or validated—we need powerful, committed women in the world! She says she is sometimes told that she is loud and I told her to keep on speaking!" (Case Notes, Dec. 23, 1993).

My view of the students was changing from seeing them as "problems" to seeing them as "resisters." The next logical step for me was to question the role of the Manitou system, to examine the nature of the system and its impact on the effectiveness of Project Success in achieving its mission.

Using Selman's model briefly described earlier, I began a developmental analysis of the system. What I found was a system that operated primarily from a level 1, unilateral "commanding" perspective. In addition, the two program directors had very different approaches. One director fluctuated between level 0 and level 1 perspectives, acting either indifferently or unilaterally, and firmly believed that the Project Success students needed only more knowledge (such as math skills and college admissions requirements), that the students and system would essentially never change, and that life at Manitou was about politics and territory. The other director emphasized reciprocal communication and collaboration (levels 2 and 3) as keys to system change; however, she had little or no support in pursuing goals collaboratively, and she lacked the level 1 (unilateral) ability to firmly and unequivocally state her needs.

WHERE IS THE EXPERT? MOVING FROM THE OUTSIDE IN

From a starting point of faith in "the system" and in the "experts," I have moved to a stance of examining the limitations that the system imposed both on the development of students and on Project Success. Because I could no longer go outside myself for answers, I had to start looking within.

Over the course of this year my whole idea of what constitutes an expert has shifted. In beginning to think of myself in that capacity, and in giving the students back their own "expertness" in running their own lives, I have had to examine many of my deepest fears. First among these is my unwillingness to take responsibility for my own actions, to deem myself the expert, because I still want someone else to give me the answers, to take on the ultimate responsibility for success and/or failure. But just as I fear control, I *want* it. I want *my* point of view to be *the* point of view; that is, I want my reality to be the "right" reality. There have been times when I have wanted this enough to force my opinions on others, to discount theirs completely or think less of them, because I've been unwilling to experience the anxiety of free-floating in a universe where each individual's reality is as valid as my own. I have strongly ambivalent feelings about both control and authority.

My ambivalence about authority has shaken my faith in meritocracy, particularly my belief that I have earned my right to be comfortable and to live in privilege, that this comfort and privilege have been earned by dint of my own hard work and initiative. I see again how difficult the system makes life for those who dare to challenge its rules and regulations, and how easy it is, in the face of it, to slip into quiet, unilateral obedience, to state unequivocally that it is the system that is at fault and that the system cannot change. There have been many days when I do just the bare minimum with a student, when I do not go the extra mile and then blame the student for being tuned out, nonresponsive, apathetic, or hopeless. It is hard work to be continually engaged! Delpit (1988) beautifully describes the difficulty of maintaining a reciprocal relationship, of letting go of our cherished notion of *ourselves at the center,* which reciprocity requires: "To put our beliefs on hold is to cease to exist as ourselves for a moment—and that is not easy. It is painful as well, because it means turning yourself inside out, giving up your own sense of who you are, and being willing to see yourself in the unflattering light of another's angry gaze" (p. 296).

While I initially approached my work with the students at Project Success with the primary purpose of fitting them back into the system, I now emphasize finding alternatives and options. If the student seems stuck in a role, I try to make sure that she does not remain stuck in that role. As I learned in Linda Powell's class (Groups in Schools), it is not taking on a role that is dangerous or destructive, but getting stuck in the same role again and again. Delpit (1988) speaks of the "need to help students to establish their own voices, [and] to coach those voices to produce notes that will be heard clearly in the larger society" (p. 296). I am no longer invested in making sure that the students' voices blend into the single note struck by the system; rather, I encourage them to enhance or harmonize with that note, always careful that the student's note is not so jarring as to be ignored or dismissed.

I think that the first step in developing resiliency is to affirm students' experiences in the here and now—to ask the question, How is the behavior of a student adaptive given the conditions leading to his or her suspension? By affirming to the student that his behavior seems reasonable based on what he knew and felt at the time, one can begin to examine alternatives and options without making him feel he made a wrong choice. Making a wrong choice implies that there is a right one, and that seems oversimplified to me. There are thousands of choices available along a continuum—but it is not a continuum of right-wrong; rather, it is a continuum of increased perspective taking. How can we maximize the number of people in any situation who are getting their needs met? And how can we realistically assess the situation in terms of conditions that can and cannot be changed, with the goal of moving conditions from facticity (unchangeable givens) to possibility? (Maddi, 1988).

The "serenity prayer" discussed by Maddi (1988) has a great deal of personal meaning for me and is a tool that I have used on a daily basis for years. To bring this into use with the students with whom I work had not occurred to me prior to reading Maddi's article. I find that the questions I most consistently ask myself are as useful for the students at Project Success: Is this situation one that can be changed, or is it one that needs to be accepted? If it can be changed, how can I go about changing it? What are the steps I need to take to change or accept these circumstances? These questions apply as readily to a disciplinary infraction as they do to more difficult personal situations a student may be experiencing.

The basic difference I have with Maddi concerns the issues of powerlessness and control, and faith. I am not sure whether I agree with him that an increased sense of control is always the key to resiliency or hardiness; it is certainly not the key to serenity. Control can merely mask the feeling of powerlessness, which still needs to be addressed. In my experience, the more powerless I feel, the more I need to control, and the more stubborn I become. For me, it is dangerous territory when I feel I am running the show, that everything is my responsibility. There are some things over which I just have no control, that need to be accepted: if I cannot see this, then I become frustrated and my energies are misdirected and wasted. It is here that, like Kierkegaard (cited in Maddi), the concept of faith comes in for me—the faith that there is an order to the universe, that the natural cycles are still in sync, that I can relax and let the grand rhythm wash away my fear and frustration.

It is when I feel this connection, this connectedness, this being a part of, that I am most free and joyful. It is in these moments that I can think to myself, when some rude driver has cut me off and stuck me at a red light: there's some reason to all of this, something I may never understand, but perhaps if I had made it through this light I'd be in the path of the drunk driver around the corner, or I'd get flagged down by the cop who saw me speed through the light, or I would have missed the beauty of seeing a small boy holding his mother's hand as they cross the street in front of me, giving her a kiss in the snow. I can't see the big picture, the larger perspective, but I need to know it is there, and I also need to know that my perspective matters, that it's impor- FEAR tant. My life contributes to the life of the community, and the country, and the world, just as the little bits and moments of my life contribute to my whole life, to the large pattern that I weave and create. To convey this to students is a critical challenge, and one that, as a counselor, I must face every day at Project Success.

So, back to Maddi, who says that control, challenge, and commitment are components of, and prerequisites to, hardiness: I would question whether a sense of control is absolutely necessary to achieve hardiness or resiliency. Certainly when you look at the lives of most Project Success students, you do not often see great opportunity for control. They live in a primarily unilateral school system, and many experience even less control at home in family situations that are often chaotic. Challenge these students have, and plenty of it. Commitment, yes, to the extent that many are fighting the system, fighting for their own perspectives, their own ideas and ways of doing things. We have to acknowledge and celebrate that, even if it does go "against the rules." But control is something most of them will not get at this point in their lives.

So what can we give them instead of control? I would say we need to provide faith. What I call faith is nothing more than perspective, getting out of my own little sense of self and realizing that not only are there millions of other people in the world with their own problems and interpretations, but there is a much bigger story going on, one in which I play only a very small part. But this requires the ability to take a perspective (ultimately a third-person perspective). I believe that first and foremost we need to teach youth increased perspective taking. Only through this can we hope to generate the faith that can serve as an antidote to powerlessness and helplessness, which many of the students feel acutely. I agree with Maddi that we can find alternate areas in which students can find mastery, but the main point is to teach faith through perspective. And while I work to increase my students' ability to take others' perspectives, I also aim to cultivate healthy resistance among them, to keep their spirits strong and questioning. I do this by continuing to question and challenge my own spirit, by activating my voice and seeking reciprocity and collaboration in my own relationships.

So where am I now? My work stems from a base of critical hermeneutics: it is not just about "fixing the problem" so that the status quo remains the same; it is about validating the youth who see the problems and helping them find ways to create positive change. It is about acknowledging power differentials and helping students see what power they *do* have and how to use it, without relinquishing the responsibility that lies with me as an educator and counselor. It is not the students' fault if they do not see their power; that is why I am a *teacher:* "It is those with the most power . . . who must take the greater responsibility for initiating the process" (Delpit, 1988, p. 297). Most importantly, "to act as if power does not exist is to ensure that the power status quo remains the same" (p. 292).

ANOTHER BACKWARDS ARC: FEBRUARY TO JUNE

One of the key ideas discussed in my first phenomenological investigation was the lack of support for Project Success by the larger school system. Given Manitou's lack of support, both financially and systemically, it is not surprising that the primary theme of my work in the Spring of 1994 has been confusion, based on wondering who has the "ultimate authority." Although I began in the Fall of 1993 to question the role of the expert (and my eager willingness to confer this status to others) and to realize that this role was largely illusory, I seemed to regress for a time in February. I again began to question who was at the center of it all, believing that someone other than me had the whole picture. When I could not find this person, I became increasingly angry with "the system" and "the way things have always been done." I reacted by minimizing my time at Project Success, alternately wondering if anyone would notice my absence and feeling angry at my advisors because none of them were addressing our funding and staffing problems. Did they not see the problems? Who was really in charge? Who had the power to make change?

During February 1994 I also did not take a single note on my site, nor did I write in my journal. I had many conversations with different program managers, but nothing seemed to hold for me, to make sense, to give me the sense of grounding for which I longed. I still believed that all the stories, all the versions of the story called Project Success, should somehow all fit nicely together to make one unified jigsaw puzzle. Perhaps by removing myself from the site in February I was trying to prevent what I knew ultimately would occur: the understanding that there is no unified puzzle. Until I accepted this, I avoided taking responsibility for my own version and for working from my vision.

In many ways I was struggling to come to terms with what might be termed a "postmodernist" view of the world. In her course "Family

Narratives," Meg Turner introduced me to the idea of multiple versions of reality, and the notion that reality is selectively constructed from bits and pieces of our memory in accordance with a narrative structure of our own choosing. This seemed commonsensical, and it certainly tied in with the hermeneutic philosophies in which I had been grounded over the first semester. I came to understand how my own biases colored what I saw, and that everyone had their own biases based on their experience of being in the world. As Parry (1991, p. 42) wrote, "Hermeneutics . . . is the logical response to the realization that there is no single truth, only different perspectives, each one a 'true' or valid perception of the world from that vantage point."

During February I also understood firsthand what Frank and Frank (1991) note in their discussion of an individual's assumptive world: "The human mind abhors a vacuum of meaning. All human behavior reflects the need to make sense of the world. . . . Our need to create a meaningful world is manifested by the automatic formation of certain assumptive systems or schemata (Goleman, 1985) about ourselves, other persons, and the non-human environment. The totality of each person's assumptions may be conveniently termed his or her assumptive world" (p. 24).

I also certainly "tend[ed] to attribute [my] behavior to external circumstances and the behavior of others to their internal motivations" (Frank and Frank, 1991, p. 25). It seemed very clear to me that the reason I was not doing my work at Project Success was because of the external lack of system support: I was rebelling, in fact, against *other* people's lack of commitment to Project Success, their laziness, their deceit, their lack of vision.

I remember reading the Frank and Frank article in February almost with a vengeance, as if it proved me "right" somehow. What is difficult for me to see now, in looking back at that month and in rereading the article, is my own lack of commitment to my own vision and, most sadly, to the students themselves. As I railed against the system that seemed to care least of all for the students, I inadvertently abandoned the students in order to "make a point" to the system, as if "the system" itself had ears and a heart. Further, I denied myself the opportunity of any "corrective learning experiences" that might challenge my assumptions—in the case of Project Success, the notions (1) that the students were good and right (victims) and the system was bad and wrong (oppressor) and (2) that someone other than myself was responsible for making things different and working towards change. All my readings indicated that the possibilities for change were limited to the extent that I could tolerate the emotions associated with changes in my assumptive world.

In the second semester, I found my approach to "working with" students to be quite different from the first semester. By the close of the second semester I felt little compunction to tell students anything (either reminding them of rules or trying to get them "back on track"). I also found myself resistant to writing anything about my interactions with the students for the project record. Their experiences seemed too complex to be captured in a paragraph or two, and it was futile to pretend that I know anything about the life of a student after a one-hour encounter.

I had come to a new understanding of my role with the Project Success students: that it involved, first and foremost, *careful listening,* which requires constant work to stay aware of my biases and my desire to fill in the plot with narrative structure, and to *resist* doing so; and that I had a great deal more to learn about what it meant to "co-construct" reality. I was reminded of this by Packer and Addison (1989), through their observation that "we would be better employed working to open up new perspectives, rather than trying to justify whatever perspective we currently hold" (p. 291). Again, my job is to learn from the students, to be open to their (new) perspectives. This is not to say that the students' perspectives are always more valuable than those held by me or the school ("I can come to school at whatever time I want"), but neither can I hold my or the school's perspective as paramount ("I've had to take care of my sister's baby because no one else is home, so I come to school at whatever time I can").

The sessions I had with students at Project Success during the second semester became about listening to them, creating a space in which they felt safe and validated, and creating an environment that would permit them to express what they felt a need to. More importantly, it became critical for me to acknowledge power differentials and to give students the chance to explore these differences. This decision, this understanding, came about because of my readings in hermeneutic theory, because of my experiences at a Tavistock conference, and because of continuing questions I brought to my work across cultures, questions well articulated by Mio and Iwamasa (1993).

Mio and Iwamasa reminded me of my obligation to act, and that nonaction was also an act of choosing: "If one were to continue to ignore what is right, one relinquishes one's duties as a human being" (p. 206). They also raised key issues for me concerning my ability and willingness to counsel or advocate for students across cultures—whether that culture is racial or ethnic, class-related, or based on gender or sexual preference. I had begun to doubt whether I could really reach across certain boundaries, and I had become acutely aware of the power differentials between the students and me: when I called them into the back room, they *had* to come in. Was it really possible to establish an equitable, reciprocal relationship given this power differential? Did acknowledging the differential diminish its power? As I thought back to my experiences, I listened closely to Mio and Iwamasa's questions: "Can those White researchers with awareness of the importance of [multicultural research] possibly exist without doing something about it? Can they not act? No. Will they receive criticisms from various sources, including the very individuals whom they would otherwise feel are advocates? Of course. Should this prevent them, from continuing their pursuits? Of course not" (p. 207). I consider myself a researcher in the sense that I believe I can learn from any encounter, especially ones across cultures. I think that anytime you "counsel" or "teach" across boundaries, you are doing multicultural research.

In mid-March I had an experience with two students that was a turning point for me. For the first time I felt I had created an environment in which differences could be explored and conflict and tension could be tolerated. Throughout this hour-long exchange, which took place after the viewing of a video on racism entitled "Shades of a Single Protein," both students looked to me as if simultaneously fearing and wishing that I would intervene and stop their "conflict." Instead, I encouraged them to continue, only intervening to provide a larger perspective when I felt things were becoming too personal or potentially hurtful:

> Bayla is West Indian; Lou, a black American. In the heated discussion that follows the video, they examine the differences between their cultures, berate the monolithic approach to "blackness" that pervades American culture, and determine that cultural differences probably also exist among white Americans. Lou expresses his desire to exterminate the white race, stating that this is one way to alleviate the huge power differentials that whites enjoy and that he has experienced. Bayla responds that there are rifts within the black community that need healing before beginning to tackle other problems of oppression; Lou agrees, but believes that one way to get together is to unite against a common enemy. Bayla counters: "Exactly, we need to learn to get together, but we can't even do *that* yet." Lou nods in agreement, and Bayla quietly continues: "but if we could figure out how to get together, maybe we wouldn't need to

get rid of whites but could instead get together with everyone."
Both are silenced by the wisdom of this statement [Case Notes,
March 1994].

What struck me after this session was that my behavior as facilitator
had changed in several key ways from the last time I had led Project
Success students in a group discussion, more than two months earlier.
First, I acknowledged that oppression as "power over" existed (in this
case, in the form of racism), both by showing the video and by making
direct statements. I did not say, as I might have previously, "Oh, that's
terrible" or "Oh, that shouldn't happen" but rather, "Yes, racism
exists." Second, I acknowledged that as a white person I enjoy certain
privileges in society simply by virtue of being white. Third, I acknowledged what I did not know, as well as my fears: "I know nothing about
West Indian culture, nor of the differences between it and what Leo
termed 'Black American' culture, and I fear that others will read this
ignorance as racism on my part." Fourth, I let the students lead and
direct the discussion, raise their voices, disagree with one another, and
become passionate about what they were saying. Fifth, I was clear
about both physical and emotional boundaries, from the amount of
time allowed for discussion to intervening when the conversation
turned to "cracking" and stating clearly that this was not tolerated, so
that there was a "container" for the discussion. Sixth, I acknowledged
what I had learned from each student and thanked them.

After this day at Project Success, I became fascinated by the possibilities provided by an environment in which youth felt safe and
respected, and by my role as an adult (and subsequently the role of all
adults) in providing for, and being part of, that environment. Again, I
continued my move away from viewing youth as "problems" that
needed "fixing," toward focusing on the work (emotional, psychic, and
intellectual) that *I* needed to do.

I also began to trust that the student herself would know exactly
what she needed to tell me in our sessions. One student, Sarni, had
been sent to us for fighting with another girl. I called her into the back
room and began by telling her that just because I had called her in did
not mean that she had to share anything with me, that there was nothing she was *supposed* to do, but that I was curious about what had
happened because, to my knowledge, this was her first fight and I
imagined that things must have gotten pretty complicated for her to
have to resort to physical violence. For the next hour Sarni told me a
beautiful and complex story about her relational world:

The intricacies of relationship that this young girl holds and weaves together are astounding. Her memory for the details and nuances of relationship is acute: she shared with me tones of voice, hand movements, exact bits of phrases, issues of territory and conspiracy—a complex world in which she saw fighting as a matter of honor and something that she resorted to only when all other options had been exhausted. How could I "scold" her for what she had done? We talked for a while about the aftermath of the fight. . . . She told me that while she had been asked about the fight by many different people—school administrators, guidance counselors, parents—no one had given her the space to really tell her story. How many times am I going to have to hear this? [Case Notes, March 29, 1994).

At about this time I read Michael Karcher's work-in-progress "Engendering Affect" (later published as "From Perspective-Taking to Emotion-Making in a Middle School Pair," 1997), which crystallized for me many disparate theories and notions from the year. The idea that children communicated through nonverbal means when other means were not available to them coincided with work I was doing in O'Keefe and Barr's course "Engaging with Resistance." Together, the ideas of "delinquent" behavior (that is, acting out, aggression, lying, stealing) as modes of communication and, more importantly, as expressions of the desire for understanding and communicating other perspectives were revolutionary for me. Karcher's notion of "engendered affect" gives a greater locus of agency to children by positing that their behavior is designed to engender in me feelings that they themselves are experiencing. Children want, perhaps unconsciously, to share their experiences with me and also, by provoking feelings in me that *they* experience, to get a sense of what life is like for their parents (or whoever is producing those feelings). In any case, youth are expressing a need and desire for a perspective other than their own, as well as a need and desire to share their perspectives. In examining the feelings they engender in me, I gain a greater understanding of their experience.

So, again I am brought back to the theme that students are not the ones who are at fault or problematic: it is I, as an adult, who needs to continue to learn about how to understand and interpret their experiences. The more questions I ask, the more questions I uncover and the less time I have to blame or invalidate others.

8

FEAR AND COURAGE

Interpretations from Beyond a Life Half-Lived

Kristin M. Carvill

IN MY FIRST INVESTIGATION, "Interpreting a Life Half-Lived," I described my life and counseling practice at the James Elementary School as a life lived in fear and therefore half-lived. I introduced the concept of fear as one that shaped my inquiry because it has shaped my life. I am an adult child of divorce and an abusive remarriage, and I have defined these experiences as my culture—a culture that creates a risk for self-stigma and the potential for a lifetime of entrapment within an experience from which I once hoped to escape. As a child and adolescent, I began the search for an absolute truth about myself— specifically, my place within this culture of broken family. Negativity surrounded me, it permeated my soul, it destroyed any hope I held for finding a delicate balance between my external and internal worlds. My external world consisted of a brutal conflict between battling parents and the presence of a raging stepfather, and my internal world consisted of distortion born out of denigration.

In my first investigation, I wrote that for many years, as a child and adolescent, I lived my life in fear, and I explained that while in my previous papers I had described fears precipitated by trauma, I had not captured the essence of their consequences, which I now face as an adult. I felt these consequences as I faced the task of reflecting on my experience at the James School in order to uncover questions most important for investigation. I confronted the difficulty of this process as I looked through my field notes in search of patterns of change over time. Although I found paragraphs and pages filled with promise for interpretation, I was drawn to a compelling and permeating theme: fear. I wrote that for the previous three months I had been faced with numerous questions, most left unanswered, about my work with urban youth. None of these questions felt more important for my learning, however, than uncovering and investigating the question, How do I find the courage to sustain this work?

Inherent in this question was the notion of fear; not only has it shaped my life, but it had shaped my work at the James School as well. *A life lived in fear is a life half-lived.* My life at the James School felt like it was a life half-lived; my initial fear had paralyzed me, it seemed, from head to toe. It was a life half-lived because I had been frightened to speak, act, and engage with myself, as well as with the children. Although I realized the value of capturing the movement of relationships between myself and the students, I could not escape my personal, lived experience. Just as Nakkula and Selman (1991) delineated the movement of a relationship in their article *How People 'Treat' Each Other,* I also felt compelled to understand the movement of a relationship—my relationship with myself. I found it important first to address how my sense of self had changed over time, and then to propose that it was only through the process of self-understanding, interpreting my life half-lived, and uncovering my courage that I could proceed to focus directly on the movement of my relationship with the children, as well as on their relationships with one another.

By entering the hermeneutic circle I embarked on the process of facing my fears by drawing on the possibilities presented by my traditions, the process of projecting onto this fear of the unknown the "known" of my successes as a scholar and athlete. The projection made possible an uncovering of courage and, in doing so, became a self-healing process, although, as I am realizing, a temporary one. I concluded the first investigation with a conviction of being "armed with courage" (Phenomenological Investigation I, 1996, p. 17), and a commitment to help the children uncover their own courage: "It is now my time to show them [the children] courage" (pp. 17–18). I had not, however, defined the meaning of courage. I cannot seem to find this courage, which leads me to believe that I do not yet know its meaning, nor the meaning of my truths. This ignorance has implications for my practice, given my claim that courage is necessary if I am to engage meaningfully in a relationship with the children at the James School.

In my first phenomenological investigation I wrote the following:

> My forestructure not only opens up an inquiry based on fear, but also guides my interpretation of it. Interpreting the change in my sense of self comes less from recognizing the beauty and power that seemingly mundane events have in giving rise to feelings of worthiness, and more from understanding my readiness to accept them, to face the fear; it comes from understanding how my traditions and individual sources of facticity, that is, how "settled beliefs about my characteristics, worth, requirements, strengths, and weaknesses," contribute to a reticence in pursuing possibility (Maddi, 1988, p. 188). I once described my sense of self as being torn between two worlds, two families, two sets of expectations, struggling to mend the tear in my fragile, developing identity. For years, I have internalized a negative sense of self, and have just recently become aware of how, through development, understanding important relationships and my internalizations of them, as well as understanding the manner in which new interactions between the self and others, creates opportunities for restructuring my self-understanding.
>
> For example, I believe that my recurring life themes—low self-esteem, self-blame, rejection, fear, disappointment, and anger—are what Maddi (1988) describes as individual sources of experience that contribute to limitations and force a sense of complacency on me. A fear of the unknown coupled with a belief that I am "unworthy and incompetent" to perform this work has initially prevented me from engaging in the pursuit of possibility—the possibility that my strengths will resonate, that I can succeed. Implicit in my words is the notion that I am moving from accepting facticity toward pursuing possibility. I must question how this movement in relationship with myself has occurred, what factors have motivated me to face my fears and relinquish the past as given. How have I found the courage to sustain this work?
>
> In my first investigation, I uncovered courage, only to be projected into the circle again to question its meaning, what my truths are, and how this doubt plagues me. I have since reconciled this "viciousness" to be merely self-understanding incomplete, but not lost.

I am wakened to the realization that I presupposed my life story to be a fully transparent text. Although I revisited how my painful life experiences of divorce and trauma shaped my understanding of fear and my need for courage to combat the feelings those experiences caused, I failed to consider the full complexity of how those experiences shape my understanding of the *personal meaning* I make in my life, of the truths I hold, and in turn, how these values shape my interpretation of the children's self-understandings. Acknowledgment of this failure prompted me to read and reread hermeneutic concepts, to reflect critically on how I make meaning in order to emancipate myself from the burdens of personal dilemmas, and to consider what I believe meaning and transformation look like in practice.

If practice means "the actuation of life" (Gadamer, 1981, p. 90), then I find it important to no longer interpret my life or practice as half-lived, but instead to interpret how I have and will make it whole. As Packer points out, "It is always possible that a little more work will uncover a hitherto unsuspected perspective on things. In this way interpretive inquiry resembles the rest of life" (Packer and Addison, 1989, p. 113). This "little more work" is precisely the impetus for this second phenomenological investigation.

The motivation for this inquiry is more than a practical *concern;* it is a necessity. For if, as Heidegger proposes, the "truth of an interpretation . . . is a matter of uncovering [in order to] get to a new understanding of what the truth is" (Packer and Addison, 1989, p. 278), then it seems necessary to trace my forestructure for understanding what truths shape my current context. In particular, I am most interested in investigating and uncovering understanding in response to the following interpretive questions: (1) What do I hold to be my truths? (2) How can I explain the manner in which these truths shape what I deem as "evidence" of a student's construction of meaning? and (3) How can I explain the manner in which these truths shape my ability to trace development of meaningful relationships and transformation in children of divorce?

UNCOVERING

The process of uncovering, central to the hermeneutic method, began with a revisitation of my previously written text, and subsequent questioning of meaning, both in my life and in my practice. By tracing the motivation behind my current research questions, I employed a philosophical hermeneutic approach that generates a need to reflect critically on truths I prematurely believed to be self-evident, in order to uncover deeper self-understanding and a new understanding of the students at the James School. Reflection entails my engagement with what Packer terms my "record of fixed action," to be read as "an unfolding drama, regaining a sense of its openness and surprises" (Packer and Addison,

1989, p. 102). This record comprises the process notes written two days per week after my interactions with an eighth grade language/arts class, seventh and eighth grade peer mediators, a fourth and fifth grade girls psychoeducational group, and four children of divorce in group counseling. Indeed, I do read this record as an unfolding drama, and together with the reading and teaching of hermeneutic concepts such as textualism and explication as application (Gallagher, 1992), I am gaining a new sense of openness and an element of surprise unrecognized in my last inquiry. This process also entails a reflection on the sense of completeness I feel through my writing, a reflection that allows me to introduce the writing of two students as "evidence" of meaning being made.

Method of Uncovering

Writing, or my style of writing, deserves special attention, for it shapes my approach to, or method of, uncovering an answer to the first and second interpretive questions.

To trace a truth is to trace a prejudice; the power of writing is that it produces new meaning. Because I have not been consciously aware of this bias, I did not do what Gadamer (1981, p. 111) asserts: "We have to acknowledge what is, and so we cannot change the fact that unacknowledged presuppositions are always at work in our understanding." I have always acknowledged the "what is" as a tradition shaped by a culture of divorce and remarriage that "in living through it, has produced frightening insight, an incessant need for reassurance, heightened insecurities, and fear" (Phenomenological Investigation I, 1996, p. 8). However, I had not been attentive to the manner in which I make meaning of my experiences, nor to how they affect my awareness of others who share this background. As I engage with students this semester, I trace through process notes how this lack of acknowledgment moves into view as I begin to question my meaning-making process:

> I am panicking. I am realizing that with each passing day there is one day less that I will spend with these kids. I only have six weeks left with them. What has been accomplished? How do I measure this accomplishment? Why do I feel scared, angry, sad, all at the same time? . . . I want our time together to be creative, productive, transformative, meaningful . . . all of these things, all at once. But how? What is my role with them? Do we offer our curriculum or do we just throw it out the window and simply spend time with

them? This is so difficult for me to negotiate. When I think about the issues we are facing in hermeneutics—such as reproduction versus transformation, explication and application, and emancipation—I am struggling inside to make meaning of them in relation to my work. How can I do this with and for the children and for myself? [Process Notes, March 12, 1996].

Explication as Application

"Explication as application" is one concept that has shed light on my struggle to locate meaning in myself and with the children. Being introduced to this concept through Gallagher's (1992) critique of textualism heightens my awareness of my held truth about, or prejudice toward, the power of writing. I believe, as Gallagher contends, that "there is no learning (understanding) without explication and application" (p. 331), and I propose that learning and understanding, for those of us who find comfort and strength in silence and through writing, has occurred.

I now realize that I am engaged in a process of uncovering possibilities given that "interpretation, working out the possibilities projected in understanding, shows entities explicitly, often for the first time . . . the entities [which] have been hidden from our awareness" (Packer and Addison, 1989, p. 278). As seen in my previous investigation, I made meaning by interpreting my own life story, my life lived in fear, and did so not through explicated words, but through passionate writing. I introduced a journal entry to capture the struggle I faced in finding peace within myself. In my first investigation I wrote:

> To give my words vitality and my reader an opportunity to understand the origins of my fear, as well as a context from which to understand future interpretation, I share a journal entry written three years ago. While at Harvard, and especially at the James School, I have read it for the first time since it was written. I believe it makes painfully clear the fourteen-year battle I had in finding peace within, as well as in facing the pain and fear precipitated by familial drama.
>
>> It is so hard to keep smiling, to keep my head held high; goodness, it is even hard to get out of bed in the morning, sometimes harder to stay in bed with my eyes closed because those are the times when the nightmares are alive. Sometimes I just lay there with my eyes open. That seems to be the most secure—with my eyes open, that is. That way if I see something that scares me, like the truth of my past, I can close them real quick before the

tears start to build, and reopen them again before the devil begins to scream.

I know, though, that there is more to my life and my soul than hiding behind my fears and hiding behind open and closed eyes. Not one person deserves to feel this ambivalent; it is torture. Even the loudest screams and the most silent tears can't seem to ease the pain.

What is this pain? That is probably one of the easier questions to answer. Some may think pain is physical—it isn't. Rather, it hurts much more. It is being deprived of what so many others take for granted.

Pain is never spending a day at the beach with your family, or

Spending a day at the beach with your family, but not being able to remember it.

Pain is having to teach yourself to swim.

Never going to the circus . . . never going to Yankee Stadium with your Dad.

Never having vivid memories of your Dad . . . good or bad.

Never seeing your parents smile at each other,

For that matter, never seeing your parents smile,

Still yet, never seeing your parents together.

Pain is spending most of your childhood with a baby-sitter.

Empty promises. No promises.

Scraping your knee on the sidewalk

Without a strong hand to pick you up and kiss the hurt away.

Arguing, fighting, screaming. . . . Silence can be worse.

Being scared of the people who are supposed to protect you.

Losing confidence. Never having it.

Trusting the ones you love only to realize that they have never trusted you.

Pain is fear.

Pain is the fear that at that one moment you are smiling,

You wake up from your dream.

Pain is fearing who you are, Who you are not.

Pain is the fear of knowing exactly where you have been . . .

And hating all of it.

Pain is the fear of being a parent.

It is the fear of loving and being loved.

What is happiness then? I wish I knew. I often wonder whether or not I'm better off not knowing. It is one less thing that I may be robbed of if I had it. Sure, I smile, I laugh, I appear healthy, vibrant. To those who don't know me, I have everything. A major part of me feels as if I have nothing.

It's a shame, isn't it? So much sadness inside fighting to be released. I want more than anything to have the strength to tear the demons from my heart, to knock them down, to kill them. I will, I know I will—eventually. When I am ready. I'm not ready.

My pain has been my enemy, but it has also been my best friend. It has shaped me into the individual I am today. If it dies before I am prepared, it will only come back to haunt me. I haven't let it exercise too much control; I am doomed the minute it suffocates me, so I always try my best to keep my head above my heart. So far my best has been good enough.

I am alive. Fortunate to be.

There is so much still yet to be given to me,

So much to be given by me.

This passage, reread three years later, holds meaning quite different from the meaning in which it was written. Although I was aware as a twenty-year-old that "it [pain] has shaped me into the individual I am today," I do not believe that I was aware that the "it" is my tradition, my culture, that which shapes my forestructure for understanding my existence in this world, and at the James School in particular. Gallagher (1992) asserts that "traditions shape what we are and how we understand the world" (p. 87). Mine is a tradition that, in living through it, has produced frightening insight, an incessant need for reassurance, heightened insecurities, and fear. Establishing this perspective, this forestructure, opens up a place from which to establish courage; it projects me into the circle of understanding (Phenomenological Investigation I, 1996, pp. 5–8).

Healing occurs for me through writing. If my forestructure for understanding the embodiment of meaning lies in passionate narrative experience, then I project this "known" onto the "unknown" of what meaning appears to embody for the students with whom I engage. This projection uncovers "evidence" I deem to be constitutive of meaning and deep self-understanding—such as passionate poems written by one eighth grade student:

ISOLATED HOPE

Leave Me Alone
Let me be what I want to be

Let me rest and have
My peace and harmony.

Frustration runs through my head
Like a madman never stopping for a breath of air.
Anger runs through my veins
As thick as blood.

I'm suffocating, choking in a world of no peace.
I dream of breaking through your overbearing chains
And soaring free, Like an eagle.

Hear my final plea for a solitary life.
I only ask to be left alone.
Is that too much to ask for?

When I wrote, "I can only speculate as to the fear these children live with" (Phenomenological Investigation I, 1996, p. 17), my relationships with the students were much more tenuous than they are today. Although to state that this poem illustrates implicit fear in their lives is also speculative, given that I "can only understand an author's intention in terms of [my] own culture and time, and so the character of that intention will always remain open to interpretation" (Packer and Addison, 1989, p. 283), I nonetheless believe that meaning was made in its drafting. Again, although we never know the full extent of another individual's meaningful experience, I suggest that had I not asked for a copy of their art, I would not have been able to make this interpretation. I strongly believe that their willingness to share their inner thoughts with me through writing conveys more meaning than explication ever could. One way to validate this interpretation, as posited by Packer and Addison, is "to ask the author or agent whether we have understood what they meant" (1989, p. 282). The validation I received for this interpretation was written when the author of *Isolated Hope,* whom I will call Xiomara, "said hello to me for the first time ever. Last week when I had asked her for a copy of her beautiful poems, her eyes lit up, yet she remained silent. Today, the first time I have seen her since my request, is so special. Today, she looked me in the eye and with a smile and spoke. Perhaps I validated her as a genuine human being, showing concern and an interest in her life. Has she made meaning of her life through poetry?" (Process Notes, Apr. 26, 1996).

I have uncovered writing as one solution to the practical concern or difficulty I had in understanding how meaning is made in my life and how it shapes what I search for in my interactions with students. To end here, however, would be to end prematurely, for I am faced with a separate concern that also requires interpretation.

Tracing Meaning and Transformation over Time

To give voice to my experience through the many stages of the divorce group, I introduce a series of process notes that together delineate movement and trace meaning. Each entry signifies a progression toward the transformed awareness and self-reflection and toward a deeper understanding of how I am to make and trace meaning:

> There is such anxiety and excitement inside about this group; so much that I fear I will be disappointed. No one can understand the need to have something I call my own—something I can feel confident about in delivering and learning from [March 12, 1996].

> Most important to me today was the beginning of our divorce group with four kids all varying in age and grade. . . . I honestly never believed that this would be happening [March 19, 1996].

> It is too soon to tell how this group will develop, whether or not they will grow from and with one another. Too common are the effects and themes stemming from the divorce experience, yet too uncommonly are individuals' experiences and feelings about that experience spoken. When we talk about difference, we welcome such potential for healing, as well as potential for harm. What seems somewhat clear to me after this first session together is that Aleida and I together need to create a space that is comfortable enough (not necessarily tension free) for both of us, as well as for them. Time will unfold deeper understanding [March 19, 1996].

> We need to create a relationship, though, so I cannot expect simply to familiarize myself briefly with their pain and then jump right in to help them make meaning of it. I still am trying to make meaning of my own experience. This is what Gadamer meant by uncovering the questions to the answers—the questions that were asked based on a personal interest in uncovering. I am still in the process of uncovering myself. Confusion, anger, sadness—they still haunt me. I am entering into a relationship with these children that, no matter how much time is left, will become a relationship that is healing to some degree for all of us—whether we are conscious of it or not [April 12, 1996].

> I spoke to Aleida afterward and shared with her my feeling that although it is important for them to voice their feelings, we need to do more; we can't just invite them to speak and then leave their

words out on the table. We need to try to make sense with them of
the painful events in their lives, to help them define their "philosophy for life," as Mike lectured about. Voicing their feelings is of
first importance, but it needs to be followed by more—hopefully
with them we can find meaning [April 9, 1996].

As I reflect on these writings, it is clear that I *am* finding meaning. It
is a pleasure to realize and report that despite my initial fear and doubt
that I would not be able to trace meaning being made and transformation in the children, a strong development of relationships within and
outside the development of the group relationship is occurring.
Important factors in this development are my situatedness, my participation, and the reciprocity I elicit within the group. I engage in a practice and "inquiry that seeks reciprocity; that calls for interactive,
dialogical interviews that require self-disclosure on the part of the
researcher" (Packer and Addison, 1989, p. 277). I am much more than
a researcher, however. I am one of them:

Toward the end of the session, we each shared something that we
miss as a result of our parents no longer being together. I shared
that I missed my brother. It was amazing to see their attentiveness,
their seeming interest in my story. I proceeded: "I really miss my
brother. You see, like so many of you, I too have grown up with a
dad, a stepdad, who wasn't so nice to me. He wasn't so nice to my
brother either. My brother left one day and has never come back.
And so I miss him a lot." They responded with questions like,
"Where did he go? What's his name? Are you the same age?"—
questions I did not expect, but welcomed all the same [Process
Notes, April 9, 1996].

In tandem with the movement I traced within myself during the earliest stages of the divorce group, I am able to trace movement of my
relationship with Pammy, a fifth grader to whom I have become especially attached. This child has been, and continues to be, a significant
influence on my work at the James School and on my daily thoughts. In
a short time I have witnessed her growing attachment to me, and by
bringing myself more fully to her, I believe we were able to move into
more meaningful relationship together. Through a careful note-taking
process I was able to capture this powerful movement and, upon reflection, uncover a world of possibility—healing for both of us. I begin
with a series of notes written about Pammy and the change I witnessed
in her as she and I came into relationship:

Pammy, a fifth grader, is the only female student. I observed her as much as possible. She sat in her chair, legs crossed, and looked away from the group over her left shoulder for a significant part of the time. She told us that she was in fifth grade but wasn't sure if she belonged with us. I asked her why and she replied, "Because my mommy and daddy were never married." I can only speculate as to whether her demeanor was trying to "tell us" that she felt different and inadequate because her parents aren't divorced because they had never been married. It is possible, in my opinion, that children of divorce feel different within the mainstream, and to have a place to come together instills some sense of worthiness and specialty. However, for Pammy, possibly, her sense of differentness may have been compounded by hearing how different the three boys' stories were from hers. Different, yes, but not alien [March 19, 1996].

More on this change I'm seeing with Pammy. She was also the first to put out her feelings today, without being questioned first. "I hate my daddy." "Why do you hate your daddy, Pammy?" I asked. "Because he hit my mommy and made her cry." For Pammy to tell this, given her demeanor and shyness during the first couple of sessions, this telling, for me anyway, marked something major. Pammy is becoming increasingly comfortable with us, with me in particular [April 9, 1996].

I was approached by Pammy—something she has never done before outside of the group. "How come you only see me once a week Kristin?" This question hit me directly in the heart. "Pammy, would you like to see me more than just on Tuesdays?" "Yes," she responded, and then walked away [April 12, 1996].

"Kristin, can't you see me more?" As we walked down the hall together after our group session, Pammy, the young girl who just weeks ago could not look me in the face, reached for my hand [April 23, 1996].

I read and reread each of these entries in search of words to describe the meaning I find in them.

Immediately, I trace Pammy's words, "How come you only see me once a week Kristin? Kristin, can't you see me more?" Her simple action of reaching for my hand, and her words, as captured in our dialogue, are signs that indicate the formation of trust and meaning in our relationship. While I can interpret this awareness directly by *what* she says, it is "lit up" (Packer and Addison, 1989) by *how* her words speak to me. This child, by nature of the frequency of her questions, seems to value our time together and places trust in our relationship. I interpret these signs as reflections of a nurturing relationship in development because of the forestructure I hold in defining them as such. Just as I hold the therapeutic effects of writing as a truth, I hold as another truth the importance of supportive, trusting, protective relationships for all children, and for children of divorce in particular.

CONTEXTUALIZING ENDINGS

As a child of divorce, this belief in protective relationships shapes my life, and certainly the termination with my children in the divorce group. How can I possibly rob them of the support, trust, and protection we have developed together, knowing how painful doing so can be? Granted, I must be honest with myself by asking, "Who will it be more painful for—you, Kristin, or the children?" While I cannot find words to answer this question, I can provide reflection in my thoughts about termination:

> I want to just reach out to these kids and tell them that they will always be with me, wherever I am. I never expected such attachment so soon. I can already see that termination will be difficult. Today when Aaron was talking about letters, I had a very difficult time restraining myself from saying that writing letters would be okay. I realize the discussion we had in class about the termination issue, but frankly, I don't agree in full. To have someone who supports them, someone they feel safe, happy, and comfortable with is crucial for children of divorce at this point in their lives. Divorced children are so special to me; if the mentor I had when I was their age decided to write me out of her life, I'm not so sure where I would be right now. I still write letters and she writes back—I thank God that she didn't tell me that we couldn't keep corresponding. I see so much hope and strength in these two children, they want me to be a part of their life, and I want the same [Process Notes, April 23, 1996].

Termination with the children remains a vital, discomforting concern in these remaining weeks. Although its complexity warrants a separate investigative inquiry, the concept serves as an appropriate segue into closure of a different sort—termination of the current inquiry. In this second investigation, I projected myself into the hermeneutic circle to reflect on my truths, on how they shape self-understanding, on my vision of meaning made by the children, and on the transformations I have seen them go through. I uncovered the possibilities for narrative in the formation of trusting relationships, and for bringing myself and the students more fully to one another and to ourselves. Most importantly, this investigation uncovered truths that, prior to critical reflection, I held to be self-evident, yet paradoxically unrecognizable. To uncover a knowledge about one's self that had been hidden from awareness is quintessential to any meaningful experience. To uncover truth is to discover meaning.

This year has been one of personal growth and critique, one that has reopened scars once believed to be healed. Above all, in light of its tumultuous nature, this year, and the interpretive process in particular, has been one of profound learning. Packer and Addison (1989) assert that "interpretive inquiry has an emancipatory interest; an interpretive account has the potential to emancipate people, to free them from practical troubles" (p. 287). Has this inquiry emancipated me from practical troubles? In terms of validating the meaning and healing that I find in writing, yes. Writing and relationships are at the core of my being, and I believe they exist at the center of others' as well. In terms of feeling that my healing is complete, no. However, to know that "self-understanding is always on-the-way" (Gadamer, 1981, p. 104) gives me hope.

PART THREE

INTERPRETATIONS OF THE MISSING

9

CRITICAL ABSENCES AND HIDDEN INFLUENCES IN INTERPRETATION

THE CONCEALED holds a central place within hermeneutic tradition, just as it does within the history of psychology and applied human development work more generally. According to ancient myth, the original missions of Hermes entailed the delivery and translation of essential messages from his fellow gods and goddesses. The Greek and Roman citizenry depended on the divine wisdom of sages such as Zeus, Athena, and Ares for guidance through the struggles and mysteries of daily life. But the guiding messages of the sages were often complicated and indecipherable, thereby compounding the very problems they were called upon to rectify, and further concealing ordinary access to the vital information necessary for survival and prosperity. Life for this ancient citizenry, as for us today, was ripe with challenges and barriers. There was prosperity to be had, and critical information to map one's progress, but gaining clear access to that information could be tricky, even deadly. Although the truth of happiness and prosperity seemed close at hand, the reality was, as it is today, that barriers to this truth existed at every turn and at each step along the way. To further complicate matters, Hermes, the beguiling trickster of translation, was enlisted and relied on to clarify this morass.

It might seem irrelevant, this brief visit to Hermes in his work and time. But the connection between his efforts and those of applied developmentalists in our time is compelling, at least on the level of metaphor or symbolic teaching. While the sources of "the truth" are different, the need for guidance today is at least as profound as it was in ancient times. Applied developmentalists, wherever and however we work, are cultivators of access to the truth—that is, to vital information and the personalized meaning of that information for the purpose of enhancing lives. And although as educators and service providers we tend not to perceive ourselves in the beguiling light of Hermes, we too can distort the truth and further complicate the matters of others (even if unconsciously) by virtue of our own histories and our deeply held investments in what we perceive as "right" and "good." As specialists in interpretation, counselors and educators have been granted a power not dissimilar to that of Hermes. If not recognized and honored, that power can lead us, and those we serve, into roadblocks and distortions similar to those that befell the ancient recipients of early hermeneutic interpretation.

Hermes, also known as Mercury for his cunning and mobility, in addition to being anointed the deliverer and translator of the sacred word, was the mythical god of commerce and science—the overseer of daily business and the study of truth. This interesting combination of responsibilities is one that, in our day as well as in Hermes' time, might be a formula for distortion. Ever facile in negotiating obstacles in his path, Hermes delivered the desperately anticipated words of wisdom and guidance. But much was lost and gained en route. More than a carrier and translator, Hermes became a transformer of messages, at times distorting "the truth" to fit his own needs and desires. Through his dual responsibilities for science and commerce, he commercialized the truth, packaging and selling messages that promoted his own interests, and in the process concealed from others their rightful access to what became, through distortion and disguise, the "secrets of success."

Hermes, as carrier, translator, transformer, and distorter, symbolizes much that is inherent to interpretation. It is, in some respects, a tricky business. And in many cases, it is a business plagued by roadblocks and self-interest. It is also, in one form or another, the business of every aspect of everyday life. The well-being of others is frequently dependent on our delivery of important messages. And our well-being is often dependent on the interpretive receipt of those messages. To ensure a favorable reception upon delivery, we often disguise parts of the information; as more and more parts become disguised, forgotten, and lost along the way, initial messages become dramatically transformed, and everyday truths are fundamentally reshaped. Much of hermeneutics is about uncovering and revising processes of distortion. Early hermeneutical work in theology, for example, was undertaken to reverse the distorting influences of Hermes, to uncover and fill in what had been concealed and lost through partial delivery.

Each of the four investigations in this section points to the need for an ongoing process of uncovering in contemporary counseling and applied development work. Themes of loss, silence, disappearance, and hiddenness are at the center of these inquiries. The unseen, the not-said, the covered over, the distorted: these influences play as central a role in interpretation and human development as do the more obvious contributions of direct support, empathy, clear and caring communication, and opportunities made readily apparent and available.

A THREE-FOLD CONCEALING PROCESS

In essence, the counselors who contributed their work to this section confronted a threefold concealing process similar to that encountered and exacerbated by Hermes. The three concealments are presented as a process because of their interactive, compounding influence. First, there is the hidden, unseen, or inaccessible truth: the basic information all children and adolescents need to pursue a healthy and prosperous life. For multiple reasons, this information is not readily available to all children. This problem is compounded by the second concealment: the saturating, everyday influence of media sales, marked by the overaccessibility of potentially destructive messages that insidiously substitute for those truths that are absent. Third, counselors and educators confront these prior concealments with the distorting influences of our own messages. Given the socializing influences of human development, we cannot help but insert, often implicitly, value-laden biases into every aspect of our work. Although we view this phenomenon as natural and potentially helpful, it is problematic to the extent that our biases go unexamined, particularly as they influence the well-being of others.

The First Concealment: Basic Information

For reasons personal, familial, educational, and perhaps most important, societal, essential information for growth is covered over by multiple barriers and walls for many children, especially for low-income and working-class youth. Many such youth, for example, will be less prepared for college than their middle- and upper-middle class peers, even though they may be similar in intelligence and motivation. This is due, in part, to dramatic differences in the messages the two groups receive. Youth who are educated in large public schools, particularly if they come from low-income and working-class families, are frequently ill-informed of the possibilities for attaining a college education.

Because their talents are often underdeveloped in overcrowded schools, teachers and guidance counselors lose sight of their potential, thus contributing to a cycle of academic disappearance.

The chapters in this cluster address this first concealment from a number of angles. In her investigation, "Meaning, Purpose, and Hope: The Case of the Disappearance," Shuna Keenan examines the role of hope—for both the students and the adults responsible for their development—in making students available for learning and for attaining the basic information they need for their lives. Deborah H. Cheng, in her chapter, "Treading Softly: A Critical Phenomenological Investigation of the Voiceless in the Hermeneutic Circle," addresses the pervasive problem of silence and shyness, which can serve to passively remove students from academic discourse and social interaction. In his study, "The Concealed Influence and Power of Nondirective Counselors," Hugh McDonough presents fewer direct implications of the first concealment than the works of his fellow contributors, but his analysis of "nondirective" counseling clearly raises questions about basic messages that get delivered, ignored, and reinforced. Anna Mackey's investigation, "The Dance of Interpretation: The Dialectic of Loss and Connectedness," looks at the depleting effects of multiple losses, including absences from school, death of family members, and the ultimate loss of interest in learning.

The Second Concealment: Disguised Messages

Modern-day counterparts of the pagan gods and goddesses from Hermes' time, those icons who hold the keys to success, often impart their messages through equally confusing jargon. Depending on the gods of which we speak, today's "word" can be overly abstract, ambiguous, uninteresting, irrelevant, and otherwise indecipherable. It can also be overstimulating, intentionally misleading, and packaged to sell rather than to guide or teach. Parents, teachers, politicians, and religious leaders, the obvious sages and scapegoats, have been joined, and sometimes superseded or replaced, by MTV, the World Wide Web, rap and grunge music, *Penthouse* and *Cosmopolitan* magazines, and the larger advertising industry as contemporary purveyors of the "right way to be." "Just Say No!" has been joined by the equally simplistic, if not more exciting, "Just Do It!" as guiding slogans for the young. So what does one just say no to? And what is the "it" that one should "just do"? It depends on which truth one seeks, or perhaps more appropriately for our time, "buys into." This second concealment that must be confronted by applied developmentalists might be termed the "packaging of information."

Today's youth face multiply packaged messages, the meanings of which must be disentangled, unwrapped, compared, and deciphered, and they face them on a day-to-day, sometimes minute-by-minute, basis. They are confronted with a literal and unprecedented onslaught of overt and covert messages about how to look, act, and eat in order to create and sustain the seductive images being sold. Marketers in our technological era are able to reach youth at progressively younger ages and our children are saturated from their youngest years with sales messages via television, movies, magazines, overstimulating video games, music, and various other forms of marketed sexuality. It is arguable, in fact, that the worlds of many young people are defined more by the media than by any other social influence, including family and school. For these youth, every aspect of their lives is permeated with marketing messages in a taken-for-granted manner. Without a place in which to dissect and critically examine this steady diet of marketing, children internalize these messages without understanding that they are being manipulated for the economic benefit of others.

Examples of the media's hidden influence can be seen in young girls and women who internalize images of emaciated, oversexualized, and disembodied models who, through the hidden benefit of airbrushing, are free from blemishes, imperfect hair days, and other human shortcomings. Similar influences captivate young boys and men who emulate images of "manliness" culled from repeated exposure to the emotionally detached, violently reactive superheroes featured in our movies, music, and magazines, and at times in our political offices and on our sports pages. The disguised yet pervasive nature of the media's influence, coupled with the frequent absence of adults to help children reflect on the messages they ingest, disallows youth the opportunity to examine critically this influence on their behavior and developing identities. Contexts for such examination are necessary if youth are to understand and respond articulately to the plethora of messages that target and shape their culture.

But contexts for critical reflection rarely exist in environments such as schools and youth clubs, which might otherwise foster a healthy critique of media images. In-school discussion groups for males and females can serve as excellent contexts for critical reflection, but they are conducted far too infrequently and are generally made available only to students deemed to be "at risk" for one problem or another. For example, in female discussion groups, girls can explicitly examine the models being imposed on them as ideals of female beauty. By critiquing these ideals with the help of a counselor or a counselor-teacher team, and by assessing the extent to which they have bought into unrealistic and unhealthy standards, girls can learn to construct alternative models of femaleness, models that embody the natural blemishes of everyday life and that resemble real women they know and admire, such as sisters, aunts, mothers, friends, and teachers.

In male discussion groups, boys and young men can be exposed to alternative models for maleness in a forum centered on interpreting and critically examining the connections (or disconnections) between their beliefs, feelings, and actions. Such groups can provide a safe space in which boys can explore the myriad of emotions they experience, such as sadness, grief, affection, hopelessness, disappointment, and insecurity. These emotions often have no outlet for private or public expression and so are suppressed and experienced together as anger. Not only is this anger potentially acted out behaviorally in a manner that is difficult for others to understand, but it can also be turned inward in ways that are punitive or destructive. This emotional and relational reframing of their experiences can free young men from their sometimes stifled communication styles, by opening up their experience to a fuller range of emotions than are typically expressed in many public arenas of society. For all youth, such reconstructions can lead to more functional self-images and serve as buffers against the multiple exploitations of marketed youth culture.

Discussion groups can be expressly designed to address the behavioral and psychological influences of advertising not only on one's self but also on one's community and family members. Examining the proliferation of cigarette and malt liquor advertisements in predominantly black and low-income neighborhoods, for example, can dramatically raise the consciousness of many students who walk by those advertisements on a daily basis. Lively debate and personal disclosures often follow the framing of such basic questions as Who benefits from the cigarette and liquor sales? and Who pays the price? In response to these questions, it is common for youth to reveal, often emotionally, the impact of tobacco and alcohol use on siblings, parents, and other family members. Heightening awareness in this manner makes students more sensitive interpreters of their environments and more critical consumers of the media.

Hans-Georg Gadamer (1981) has long been among the more insightful critics of technology in our postmodern age. According to Gadamer, life conditions in the age of technology make it substantially easier, for both ethical and technological reasons, to dehumanize others for one's own benefit. As human connections become briefer and more efficient, there is a natural reduction in the fostering of human care and concern. Consequently, it becomes easier to circumvent human ethics in the exchange of goods and services; as products are mass produced, the recipients of those products are viewed abstractly as a market rather than as people. Within this framework, it makes good sense that the guiding ethic would be profit margins rather than human relations.

Compounding the problem, from Gadamer's point of view, is that the technologically aided pace of modern life leaves little time to reflect on how one lives. Busy parents have less time for their children and almost none for their neighbors. Consequently, the traditional infrastructures of family and community have deteriorated. Technology, while it makes life easier and more convenient in many respects, also encourages isolationism. Some of us work at individualized computer terminals and on mechanized assembly lines, buy gasoline with a magnetized Mobil card, thereby avoiding the attendant, and close the day by relaxing with televised images of our media families. While this scenario does not hold for everyone, it approximates aspects of daily reality for many of us, and exemplifies the conditions of vulnerability placed on youth. The flip side of progress is societal neglect: the technical prowess of our time has created a largely unchecked epidemic of media child abuse.

It is critical for applied developmentalists to *unconceal* these hidden influences on our own biases and communications, as well as to bring this discussion explicitly into our work with youth. By doing so, we can help to mitigate the damaging internalizations of this morass and the painful legacy it leaves for children.

The Third Concealment: Developmental and Therapeutic Biases

In tandem with the hidden influences of inaccessible and manipulative messages, counselors and educators face a third concealment: the distorting influence of our own communication. Hermes' distortion of information from his fellow gods and goddesses symbolizes the manner in which applied developmentalists' own investments, our own multiple, sometimes competing agendas, interfere with our work as interpreters. As the chapters in this section depict, the distorting process need not be conscious nor malicious, it need not be driven by obvious self-interest or selfish motives. More commonly, twists of interpretation are carved out through internalized directives, such as our values, our personal struggles, and forgotten messages embedded deeply in our life histories.

In helping youth to make sense of the messages they receive, counselors—all of us—infuse our own necessarily biased understanding of those messages. This infusion process can be minimal, as in the case of reinforcing clearly understandable directives from parents or teachers, or it might be dramatic, such as when a counselor confronts what she perceives as a child's misunderstanding of that child's own thoughts and feelings—what some cognitively oriented therapists refer to as "crooked thinking."

In the language of hermeneutics, it is impossible to preclude our prejudices, or prejudgments, from our interpretations. Not only impossible, but in fact, undesirable. Clarification in therapeutic processes is more a matter of sharing judgments and bringing biases into the light of inspection than it is an uncovering of objectively existing messages, beliefs, or other "dis-coverable" truths. Recognizing the existence of multiple, perhaps equally valid, viewpoints is a core therapeutic principal. Healthy flexibility of thought, feeling, and action is believed to stem from this recognition.

In *Being and Time,* Martin Heidegger ([1927] 1962) offers an important view of clarification: that everything revealed conceals something else. Clarification, from this perspective, is a matter of shining light on a hidden phenomenon from a particular angle; more specifically, it is a clearing of the brush so that light can shine through. Where and how we clear determines what comes into focus, and although some of us have greater peripheral vision than others, any visual lens can grasp only so much of even the widest clearance. Other ways of seeing, from other angles, through alternative clearings, become blocked once we set our gaze.

From this perspective, when applied developmentalists clarify with clients, or help to clear the view, we do so from our own particular vantage points, thereby shielding other ways of looking, other points of view. Our own socialization influences not only what we see and attempt to share with our clients, but also *how* we see (the methods), how we clear away the obstacles. Although an outstanding clearance may have been co-constructed, it is only one. And by looking from the selected angle, we might miss what others have seen and tried to communicate. By attempting to understand other peoples' views from our own angle, we always distort their meaning to a certain extent; and depending on the difference in angles and the context of the vision quest, we are capable, even with the best intentions, of distorting their messages dramatically.

THE CONCEALED IN MAINSTREAM PSYCHOLOGY

Mainstream psychology has also placed a great deal of emphasis on uncovering and understanding that which has been hidden, lost, denied, and distorted. Psychoanalysis, of course, delineates the powerful, natural, and destructive processes of forgetting and covering over life history as central to the development of the human psyche. "Defense mechanisms," in this analytic model, might be viewed as internalized psychological gatekeepers of one's experience. They exist, largely, to defend and protect us from our own interpretations. Through such processes as "repression," "denial," "avoidance," and "projection," our defensive system conceals and disguises our experiences for the alleged purpose of making them more manageable; direct access to the raw truth of our existence would be too much for our egos to bear. For the human condition to thrive, raw and untamed instincts must be transformed, or sublimated, into messages we can handle.

Healthy development, in the psychoanalytic model, is in part a function of the defense mechanisms becoming flexible gatekeepers to our archives of experience. Such gatekeeping must allow for selective access to our histories of instinctual desire, interpersonal experience, and unconsciously stored interpretations of life. Appropriate access makes possible the interpretive application of our histories to present experiences, thereby shaping possibilities for a healthy future. Pathology, in this model, develops when the gatekeepers become overly rigid or protective, thus limiting the angles from which we can view ourselves and our potential for interaction with others. It also develops when the gatekeepers become underprotective, leaving us vulnerable to and overwhelmed by our experiences and desires. In short, pathology occurs when our experiences are either overconcealed or underconcealed, overdisguised or underdisguised, resulting in interpretations of ourselves and the world that are functionally distorted. Treatment, in psychoanalysis and the derivative psychodynamic models, entails some combination of uncovering, reexperiencing, reinterpreting, and reshaping, for contemporary use, those experiences and consequent messages that had been improperly concealed and distorted for reasons of earlier self-defense.

But although psychoanalysis comes to mind immediately as the psychology of the concealed, other approaches place primary emphasis on the "not seen" as well. Behavioral approaches address the often unrecognized role of habituation in human development. Because, from this perspective, habits can dictate what we can and cannot do, how we come and do not come to be, there are options for living that become blocked; certain pathways become deeply entrenched, guiding us, often against our will, in the usual direction and fashion, thereby blinding us from seeing options that exist on either side in various forms.

Many cognitive approaches to psychology also address blocks and distortions—blocks and distortions in thinking that in turn influence feelings and behavior. By having certain ways of thinking about life reinforced at both local and societal levels, thoughts about one's self and others, thoughts about the world, become routinized, patterned, and restricted. None of this is inherently problematic or dysfunctional—in fact, it is quite natural—but it is all potentially limiting. When thinking becomes overly constricted and unhealthily redirected by blocks, distortions, and manipulative reinforcements, the likelihood of harm to self and others is increased. Treatment entails uncovering patterns and consequences of distorted thinking; it involves opening up, broadening, and revising new ways of thinking that are constructed to facilitate healthier functioning.

Finally, humanistic approaches to psychology, to which hermeneutics is sometimes linked, also address the unseen. Carl Rogers's (1965) client-centered approach to counseling and human development suggests that each person has, within herself and within conscious access, the answers required for relieving pain and promoting growth. Those answers, however, have been covered over by unsupportive life circumstances. The applied developmentalist's role is to provide support and validation, thereby freeing the person to "dis-cover" more ideal ways of being, and particularly, of seeing herself. For the client-centered and many other humanistic approaches, the counselor is less translator and messenger of "truth" and more facilitator of support for the individual's own dis-covery and interpretive process. In his contribution to the cluster of chapters that follow, however, McDonough portrays the often unexamined influences that client-centered counselors have on their clients' processes of self-discovery.

PHENOMENOLOGICAL INVESTIGATIONS OF THE UNSEEN

In this cluster of chapters, Keenan, Cheng, McDonough, and Mackey each address the "not seen" or the "not there" of interpretation. They address the roles of concealing, disengaging, alienating, disappearing, and loss from a variety of angles and on a number of levels.

The Slow Fade and Everyday Loss

Keenan's chapter, "Meaning, Purpose, and Hope: The Case of the Disappearance," highlights the necessity of meaning, purpose, and hope for healthy development, and examines how the weakening of these experiences can lead to both literal and figurative disappearances. Keenan's study uncovers what is arguably the single most critical absence underlying the epidemic levels of disappearance that plague our schools and communities today: the loss of everyday meaningful connection. Although more dramatic losses such as school dropout and academic failure are easier to see, they do not, as Keenan suggests, "happen all at once." They are, rather, endpoints—or more accurately, further developed points within a cycle of loss—that were reached through a "slow fade" of disconnection, or an incremental process of disappearance.

As a phenomenological investigation, Keenan's study does an outstanding job of uncovering and interpreting the process and potential meaning of what might be termed the *fade cycle*. She begins the investigation where most service providers, and particularly, service-providers-in-training, initiate their work: in the presence of her clearly stated, and firmly held, ideals. By reviewing the clear presence of meaning, purpose, and hope in her own life (and the consequences of their absence in the lives of others close to her), she sets out to instill these cognitive and emotional experiences in the youth with whom she works. Keenan refers to the development of healthy ideals and dispositions in youth as *prosilience,* a proactive parallel she coined in response to the more common notion of resilience, which is generally defined as the development of strength in the face of adversity. Keenan's argument is that adversity should not be a prerequisite for the development of such strengths.

In initiating her work, Keenan comes to recognize that service, in whatever form it is envisioned, cannot simply be provided for another; it must be jointly created through meaningful relationship building. More importantly, Keenan also recognizes what many service providers (teachers as well as counselors) miss: that loss, disconnection, and failure are also co-constructed, that mutual disengagement—the joint disengagement of students and their counselors and teachers—is central to the fade cycle and the ultimate losses experienced by children.

What is perhaps most painful about Keenan's study is the tension she captures between presence and absence, between connecting and disconnecting. Every presence highlighted is accompanied by an equally powerful absence. Keenan's own success is presented within the context of the struggle and loss experienced by a sibling. Why, she asks, must success be experienced as the "exception" in the black community? Why are barriers so high that achievement is the exception rather than the norm? We might ask ourselves, as educators and service providers, whether, when we view success, we see the exceptional figure as one standing out from a background of ordinary failure or mediocrity. The exceptional student is a symbol, a symbol of accomplishment, hard work, connectedness, and light; she might also symbolize the larger absence of these very same qualities. To "appear" as "exceptional"—which is sometimes a tokenizing term attributed to people of color who "beat the odds"—is to highlight the unapparent norm: the background of family and community from which the "exception" emerged, a background stigmatized as somehow inadequate or "less than."

Significant Findings: Uncovering the Unseen

The case of Cherise in Keenan's chapter "signifies" two additional interrelated examples of the presence/absence dialectic: Cherise's strongly connected presence and eventual disappearance, and Keenan's own strong presence and later disappearance in her work. We use the word *signify* here for a specific reason. "Significant findings," in traditional research approaches, generally indicate the strong correlation between two or more phenomena or variables, or important changes that have been found within a particular group or sample of people. In the hermeneutic phenomenological approach used here, a "finding" is something uncovered that had previously been concealed. Such a finding is "significant" if it lends itself to practical answers to real-world concerns. Within the hermeneutic framework, it might be argued that any finding, any uncovering, is significant given that it constitutes one part of an integrated whole or constellation of interacting parts. But the significance of any part, of any finding, varies according to the practical use that is made of the discovery. We believe that the findings presented by Keenan in this study have significant practical implications for those who are potentially engaged with youth in the fade cycle she articulates.

Signify, then, represents that which must be dis-covered. A significant finding is that which has been found in response to signifying leads—leads taken from that which is already manifest and understood. For Keenan, the fact that Cherise dropped out of working with the theater group signified the larger phenomenon of the slow fade, which had been covered over to that point: "When meaning, purpose, and hope disappeared, so did Cherise." It also signified the figurative disappearance of Cherise through previous disconnections from her work with Keenan, and it signified Keenan's own cumulative experience of the decline in meaning, purpose, and hope, the very ideals by which she purportedly functioned and that she set out to instill in Cherise and her peers. What is poignant here is that both Cherise's and Keenan's losses are disappearances; that is, they represent the gradual fading away of that which strongly existed. It is the loss of "what was" rather than the lack of something "never there" that marks Keenan's discovery as particularly significant. And indeed, this is the very tragedy behind much of the loss in our schools and communities: children often begin from a place of meaning, purpose, and hope, or at least reach that place at some point in their early lives, only to have these ideals dashed or slowly eroded, either through repeated traumas or chronic disconnection.

Losing What Was, What Was Not, and What Never Can Be

Mackey's paper approaches loss through disappearance from another angle. On virtually every page, she reveals compelling and often emotionally jarring examples of intersecting histories of loss through disappearance—the disappearance of loved ones through death and other departures. But being especially attuned to the power of loss, the "no longer there," because of her own life experiences, Mackey is also in touch with losing "the never had." Inherent in the sadness of loss is the grieving not only for "what was" but also for "what was not," and for what "never can be." This grieving is reminiscent of the grief that high school students feel as they approach graduation and recognize that the tomorrows of their educational planning have suddenly become yesterdays, and that those yesterdays are not marked by realized plans for improved grades, strengthened friendships, and the taking of intended risks.

Appropriately, Mackey's story begins with a "termination scene." In what eventually turns into, in many respects, a painful thesis on the role of death in human development, Mackey's story begins with a relatively more benign grieving. Like many of her peers, she is grieving the end of the school year. But there is a poignancy to her grief, an insight into lost possibilities that makes her experience unique.

The role of ordinary, everyday loss is revealed through Mackey's chapter within a broader context of more traumatic departures. She presents her insights into the relational dynamics of loss through an analysis of her work as a pair counselor with two fourth grade girls, Kiana and Leticia. These two young girls, like Mackey herself, come to the pair work having lost their mothers and other important family members. As is often the case, the girls are referred to pair counseling because of difficulties they are experiencing with peer relationships in school. It comes as little surprise that profound loss would be associated with difficulties in connecting, not only with people but with education, fun, and life in general.

For children repeatedly groomed in loss, there seems to be little benefit in exposing one's self to the risk of further replication by developing new relationships that once again can be taken away. Yet we know that if children are to survive painful losses and ultimately thrive in life, they must somehow learn to develop or renew their capacities for human closeness. Pair counseling is designed to encourage just that sort of renewal. Mackey's presentation of herself, Kiana, and Leticia exemplifies how complicated and essential this form of relational rebuilding can be.

How can people come to connect with one another, to understand and accept what each person has to offer, given the tremendous undergirding of loss on which they are attempting to build close, meaningful relationships? This is, perhaps, the central question to which Mackey's findings respond, and the sort of question that all of us, as human service workers and as human beings, must apprehend. Mackey approaches this question through an interesting perspective on writing her chapter, which parallels her attempts to connect with Kiana and Leticia. She approaches the study from the perspective of hoping to lose herself in it, as a means, paradoxically, of finding herself more fully. This process parallels her work with the pair of girls, except that unlike her feelings of success in losing herself in her writing, Mackey felt blocked from losing herself in her counseling work; she was not able to find an "un-self-conscious" rhythm for the work due to breaks and inconsistencies in schedule, to illness, and ultimately to Leticia's removal from the school for personal reasons.

Gadamer's Notions of Loss, Alienation, and Self-Understanding

Mackey's chapter provides a helpful example for considering the utility to the human service professions of Gadamer's ([1962] 1976) dialectical description of losing and finding one's self. Building on Heidegger's conception of human development as entailing the loss of one's self—the loss of scrutinizing self-awareness—through wholehearted connectedness to meaningful activities in the world, whether they be activities of work, play, or relationship, Gadamer outlines his model for self-understanding. According to this model, the more thoroughly one is absorbed in various acts of living, the less self-conscious one is of the micromovements and discrete thought processes that make up those acts. Genuine actors are lost in the play, genuine players are lost in the game, and genuine partners are interdependently lost in relationship. But genuineness does not come easily in this model; it comes through the gradual establishment of task-specific and larger genre-specific rhythms.

The genre of pair counseling, for example, is composed of multiple specific tasks or acts, which in turn compose the rhythm of the triadic pair counseling relationship. The girls' relationship with each other and each of their relationships with Mackey form the relational triad that comes to define the core of the "pairs world." The primary acts in the pairs world, as in the world at large, revolve around the development of relationships. Because Mackey, Leticia, and Kiana all bring painful pre-pairs histories of loss to their relationships with one another, each act of relationship building is ridden with the complexities of multilayered self- and other-scrutiny. Each partner is far from losing herself in the rhythm of relating, due to the losses and critical absences of consistent meeting space and time for their work. Self-understanding, or finding themselves, through loss in the pair relationship will be especially difficult in this case.

How difficult is it to learn the requisite emotional and behavioral skills necessary for the act of trusting, after one has been repeatedly abandoned and traumatized by loss? We would argue that it is significantly more challenging than learning the more ordinary, and even extraordinary, skills necessary for such high-level acts as school achievement, athletic prowess, and career success. Mackey is faced with the immensity of this challenge in her efforts to bond with Kiana and Leticia, and to help them bond with each other. Riding on her potential success is the possibility that the girls will revise, to some extent, their internal working models of relationship—revise them from models marked by fear, distrust, and anxiety to ones that include some semblance of joy, trust, and positive anticipation.

Most applied developmentalists bring to their work with children expectations similar to those exemplified by Mackey in her work with the girls in her pair, and they sometimes bring those expectations from histories of extreme childhood loss and hurt. Consequently, a tremendous amount of stock is placed in their efforts to help others, to provide better care than they themselves might have received. The weight of their expectations makes it difficult, then, to lose themselves in their work, to be less self-conscious, less self-scrutinizing as counselors. In addition, new counselors worry that their mistakes will cost others dearly, might inflict further pain, and might even be life threatening. Although these concerns are based in a legitimate sense of ethical responsibility, they can also be debilitating, and make it extremely difficult to find one's rhythm as a developing counselor.

Mackey's attempts to reach the girls in her pair, and to understand herself as a developing pair counselor, were influenced not only by her work conditions (inadequate meeting space and systemic underappreciation of her efforts) but also by her personalized expectations and hopes for success, which were rooted in her own history of loss, and by the particularly complicated case of Kiana and Leticia. These factors, and others, made it difficult for Mackey to move beyond the micro-acts of pair counseling and into a less self-conscious rhythm. Within Gadamer's model of self-understanding, the inability to lose one's self in such a rhythm results in a particular form of alienation. That is, one remains separate from one's own acts, distanced from them and looking in rather than connected to them from within. Alienated acts are experienced as "acting," as unreal or less than genuine, whereas rhythmically engaged action is experienced as authentic, as essential and ordinary to one's being.

Gadamer does not suggest that healthy living and profound self-understanding require constant existence in a state of blissful authenticity. He argues, rather, that self-understanding emerges through a dialectic of authentic and alienated states of being. Authentic being in his model is experienced as fairly un-self-conscious immersion into the daily flow of activities, with alienation being represented by the conscious and critical reflection on the meaning of participation in these everyday acts. According to Gadamer, alienation in and of itself is not negative; in fact, it is necessary to making sense of the authenticity in our existence. But without authenticity, without the ability to lose ourselves in our daily activities, alienation becomes a lonely separation; it becomes vigilant consciousness without meaningful connection.

Although Mackey regrets the frequently felt disconnection to her work, she utilizes her alienated state of reflection to uncover the insidious power of loss and disconnection in the lives of Kiana, Leticia, and herself. And paradoxically, in uncovering the pervasiveness of these losses, she loses herself in the very act of uncovering. She loses herself in the writing of her investigation, thereby revealing in the final analysis (to this point) the quality of self-understanding she previously experienced as absent.

Silent Absences

Cheng's investigation approaches the critical nature of absence from yet another angle. Whereas Keenan reveals the disappearance of that which was clearly visible, and Mackey uncovers the hidden influences of one loss on another, Cheng presents the struggle to be seen and heard at all. In her presentation of the "model minority"—Asian students who do their work, who make no "scene," who neither fight nor fume—Cheng loudly cries out for recognition of the painful losses the "model" signifies for many students like herself. She draws poignant parallels between her struggle to express herself and be heard as a Harvard graduate student and the struggles for connection and recognition experienced by her Asian middle school students, many of whom are first-generation immigrants.

As a teaching tool, Cheng's chapter alerts us to the "not said" but not unimportant in everyday educational discourse. The contrast between the depth of her writing and her struggle to be heard as an essential voice in the classroom painfully highlights the lost contributions that exist in our schools and in our society. To worsen matters, these lost contributions can be mistaken for outstanding performance. In large public school classrooms, quiet students who cause little trouble, although perhaps experiencing plenty of it within themselves, typically are rewarded as good students, model students even. For those with language barriers who feel particularly ostracized from mainstream peer culture, academic success becomes an especially important forum for connection. But connection at what cost? For some, according to Cheng, at the cost of a persistent and tormenting loss of voice.

From the perspective of our hermeneutic applied development model, Cheng's insights are profoundly important. Growth within this model requires the exchange of perspectives. While students who do not speak in class nonetheless contribute through their presence, body language, and written work, silent perspectives in the classroom or the counseling group can restrict the breadth of exchange. This can be felt particularly, as Cheng suggests, by the silent students themselves when they view their lack of verbal participation as inhibiting a consensus or resolution that a group of students might otherwise reach. In addition, silent students often feel less responsible for decisions made and less ownership over material learned.

For many quiet students, hermeneutically oriented counseling must emphasize the sharing of opinions and feelings, and encourage practice in feeling uncomfortable, as Ravitch discusses in Chapter Five of this book. Reaching the point of feeling authentically connected to public discussion will require intensive practice in feeling inauthentic, nervous, even terrified. From our perspective, while all communication and learning styles must be respected, honored, and contextualized, both culturally and individually, no student should be enabled, or worse still, encouraged, in what might be experienced as an "unspoken compromise."

Cheng's investigation makes the loss of silent voices audible, making this absence present by framing this phenomenon as unacceptable. Her study amplifies the silences that many counselors and educators do not hear. In doing so, she makes possible a critical questioning of what it means to be quiet and to speak, to verbally engage and disengage, to listen honestly to one's self and to make one's self heard. Cheng's is a strong voice that makes what was once an easily missed, and commonly dismissed, presence into a glaring and resounding omission.

From Silent Absences to Hidden Influences

Power, as the author Lisa Delpit (1995) argues, is least recognized by those who have it, and most recognized by those who do not. McDonough's investigation exemplifies Delpit's argument. As a white, male, middle-class, Harvard-educated counselor for an urban high school composed predominantly of low-income students of color, McDonough is placed in a position to exercise a great deal of authority. But given mainstream, white middle-class liberal biases, he initially deems it most appropriate to "share" whatever authority he might possess with the younger clients in his charge. Accordingly, he assumes a "client-centered" approach to his work, which by definition means that he will allow his clients to determine their own agendas (within the realm of school rules, of course). It also means that he will show "unconditional positive regard" (within reason). And first and foremost, he will neutralize his own input and judgmental reactions in order to defuse the power imbalance that would otherwise restrict therapeutic progress.

In a remarkably astute self-critique, and corresponding critique of "nondirective" therapy, McDonough uncovers the multiple ways in which his explicit assumptions shield him from the implicit directiveness of his position and status. Through his efforts to "help" his student client by gaining his trust as a necessary first step in helping the student to access his own insights, McDonough comes to realize that his approach has afforded him an unusually privileged position in this young person's life. Contrary to the stated philosophy of client-centered therapy, McDonough views this position as one that virtually assures a highly directive and bias-imposing role. He comes to this view through a careful analysis of his client's change in language use, which leads him to conclude, "From this position of trust, I could wield great influence by indirectly guiding my clients towards conceptualizing the world in the manner in which I understood it."

Central to McDonough's findings is an awareness of how therapists can manipulate clients' thoughts and behaviors in thoroughly unanticipated ways. This is, of course, not a new finding. Psychoanalytically oriented counselors and therapists, as discussed at the beginning of this chapter, pay a great deal of attention to unconscious influences in the therapy room. But McDonough particularly captures what he terms "the subtle transmission of bias and prejudice." He reveals the imposition of his biases by capturing changes in his client's language structure that mirror his own speaking patterns. This is an interesting reversal of at least two core processes of client-centered therapy: mirroring and empathy. In this case, the client begins to mirror back the therapist's language, and he seems to do so out of his perception that the therapist needed his language mirrored in a particular way. Ordinarily, the client-centered therapist would do precisely what McDonough finds his client doing for him. This reversal provides him with a unique window into the direct influences of nondirective therapy.

Although the student's empathy toward his therapist's situation might be perceived as benign and even healthy, McDonough recognizes that it signifies something more: for him it signifies what Jurgen Habermas (1990) refers to as the potential for language to dominate thought and human interaction, becoming a force of oppression rather than a tool for emancipation. Whereas the client-centered therapy room, at first glance, might be considered a close approximation of the Habermasian "ideal speech context," McDonough uncovers powerful concealments inherent in the unrevealing stance of the client-centered therapist. Whereas Cheng depicts silence as influencing possible interpretations through absence, McDonough depicts values, biases, and individual desires as influencing interpretation and communication through their concealed presence.

CONCLUSION

Silence, disconnection, loss, and hiddenness profoundly influence one's interpretations of the world, precisely because they function beyond the view of ordinary perception. In *Being and Nothingness,* John-Paul Sartre (1956) revealed the everpresent context of "the nothing," the "not there," which serves as the background for understanding everything that is. Each of the investigations in this cluster colors in more of the missing background, highlighting the space between the lines that gives the lines their special meaning, and the space its massive spaciousness—its seemingly endless room to be viewed as something more, as something different, than what appeared to be from the previous view. These investigations uncover more of the ground that upholds the figures we see and understand in a problematically comfortable, taken-for-granted manner. By doing so, they give the figures more contextualized meaning, and they set the context in its rightful place at the center of our work.

For every sentence spoken, there is an unspoken volume many times larger; Cheng reminds us how rich that volume can be. For every appearance of success being applauded, there are disconnections and disappearances into failure being forgotten; Keenan reminds us of our role in that. For every new child born to the world, there are, unfortunately, other children losing parents, friends, and hope; Mackey makes us feel the magnitude of such losses, and the role they play in how children find themselves. And for every overt act of student empowerment facilitated by applied developmentalists, there are matching covert acts of hidden influence; McDonough helps us to see what and how we hide from ourselves.

With these messages in mind, our hope is that the following collection of inquiries will heighten readers' awareness of the texts not yet written, and of the ethical responsibility we have to write them, because the work still to be done holds the most promise for the future and the most possibility for a different outcome.

10

MEANING, PURPOSE, AND HOPE

The Case of the Disappearance

Shuna Keenan

I GOT THE CALL NEAR THE END OF MAY. Something serious was going on over at the Massachusetts Prevention Center and they wanted me to go undercover and investigate. As an intern there, I had a good vantage point to be an informant. I had worked at the center as an intern for the previous eight months and had written an investigative report on my experiences during that time. That report prompted the current investigation. This time, however, things were going to be different. This time I knew that I was on an important case and that I was looking for something: change. I sought to investigate the change or growth that had taken place in me, in the system in which I was immersed, and in the students I encountered. Now, more than four months later, I must once again report my findings.

METHODOLOGY

This was not going to be an easy case to investigate, because the questions before me were complex, and growing even more so as I delved into the issues. For example, as I considered my questions I began to wonder, Is just possessing meaning, purpose, and hope as ideals enough to drive progress, or are they simply the labels given to the progress as it is manifested? I did not want to find myself going in circles. Or did I? Given that one of the central principles of hermeneutics is that "all understanding has a circular structure," it could be that the only way I would find any answers would be to enter the circle (Gallagher, 1992, p. 58). To do this, I was going to have to muster all of the skills I had acquired during my days as a cadet at the Academy of Hermeneutic Inquiry. In those days, I didn't even have enough experience to qualify as a rookie. I still had much training before me to become a P.H.I.: a Private Hermeneutic Investigator. However, the Academy of Herme- neutic Inquiry is where all of the great hermeneutic investigators started out, and I've come a long way since my days as a young cadet. I've become both more confident and more competent in the work I do with youth. I've been able to hone my skills through practice and by gaining a better understanding of the art of interpretation. I have incor- porated this understanding into my work with youth by realizing that we all enter into current experiences with the influences and prejudices of the past.

Despite my training, however, I was at a loss for where to begin or what to say about my experiences at my site in this present investigative report. The problem I faced was that there was a wealth of rhetoric but a dearth of material and evidence from my site experiences to help me answer the questions and move my investigation forward. My dilemma was closely related to the issues raised by Spence (1989) in his article, "Rhetoric Versus Evidence as a Source of Persuasion: A Critique of the Case Study Genre." Was my faith in meaning, purpose, and hope based on rhetoric, or on evidence that they could be meaningful tools in one's life? To answer this question, I would have to begin looking not just at my site but at something that I knew much better: myself.

I had been trained well enough to know that there were reasons for why I could not find what I was looking for in my site experience. These reasons lay somewhere within my prejudices, preconceptions, and personal history.

As a result of the realization that I needed to look more closely within myself and my history, one approach I have chosen to take for this investigation is to reflect on how meaning, purpose, and hope had and had not been actualized in my own life, specifically as they pertain to my experiences at the Prevention Center during the last eight months. The other approach I chose for this investigation was to look at the circumstances and events surrounding the specific case of one student I encountered during my internship, Cherise. Looking at my own case and at the case of one of my students raises different but equally difficult questions that help to guide the investigation: What happened to me and what happened to Cherise? Why did we both, in our own ways, disappear? Investigating our disappearances by looking at change over time in the meaning, purpose, and hope of our experiences will, I hope, shed light on my questions about actualized versus imagined meaning, purpose, and hope.

BACKGROUND AND INVESTIGATIVE QUESTIONS

In my initial report, "The Elastic Circle: A Phenomenological Investigation into My Experience of the Massachusetts Prevention Center" (MPC), I began to question how the MPC fosters meaning, purpose, and hope in the youth it serves. I ended the study by challenging and pushing the parameters of my meaning, purpose, and hope schema. In preparing for the initial report, I laid out a framework for how I want to serve children and youth based on meaning, purpose, and hope:

> Meaning, purpose, and hope embody the essence of my desire to serve children and youth. Because of my personal experiences, I view them as antidotes to the ills of nihilism, selfishness, and hopelessness that permeate our society. Meaning, purpose, and hope convey what many individuals have helped me to discover in my own life, and what I now want to share with others, in particular, young people.
>
> The task of looking closely at the distinct journeys of my and my brother's lives convince me even more strongly of the importance of meaning, purpose, and hope. They help to explain why the year after I graduated from Stanford University, my fourteen-year-old brother was arrested and given a ten-year sentence for armed robbery. I don't know which is more compelling for the work I do, my life experience or my brother's. His experience greatly influences the meaning I make of my own experience, and together they shape who I've become and the work that I want to do. I perceive the strong presence of meaning, purpose, and hope in my life as the foundation of my resilience. While this is enough to convince me of their importance, my perception of the absence of these elements in others' lives, particularly my brother's, is just as compelling.
>
> The protective factors stemming from my experiences came in the form of influential individuals who shaped my life and helped me discover meaning, purpose, and hope. The meaning in my life comes from my religious convictions and membership in a loving,

supportive family. I discovered a purpose by realizing that what I choose to do cannot be solely for myself. The hope in my life is for a future in which I can make a difference by helping others. I now realize that my brother did not experience many of the protective influences that I did. Even though we shared the same single mother and lived under the same economic stresses, my brother and I had very different family, religious, and educational experiences.

One of the reasons I was drawn to the field of education is the profoundly different implications our different encounters with the education system have had for me and my brother. My educational experience was an important protective factor against some of the environmental risks I faced. My brother, who did not have a positive educational experience, faced a double jeopardy. Not only does a good education serve as a protective factor, but a poor education for someone from our background means a great deal of risk. Whereas I excelled in my schoolwork and was singled out by teachers as being "exceptional," my brother did okay in school but was often singled out for negative reasons.

This notion of being considered "exceptional" is something that I have struggled with a great deal and it shapes what I bring to my work with youth. While I feel that I am a unique and exceptional individual, I find it extremely problematic when I am singled out as being an "exceptional black person." The implication seems to be that I am exceptional for someone who is black—as though I have somehow managed to surpass what can be expected of the regular old black folks. This has been a theme that has come up repeatedly in my life, in different forms and in different contexts.

As a result of these experiences, I am conscious of imparting the message to youth that they are all special, unique, and "exceptional" individuals. I will bring this same message and mentality to my work here in Boston ["Where I Come from, What I Bring," pp. 1–2].

As this excerpt conveys, the role and importance of meaning, purpose, and hope in my own life greatly influence how I enter into, experience, and interpret any new system. The systems in which I have been immersed are the MPC and its model of youth development. Specifically, I work with the Peer Leadership Program, one of the MPC's strategies for addressing public health issues through education, outreach, and prevention. Through this program I work with MPC staff to train Boston youth to become peer leaders on alcohol, tobacco, and other drugs, HIV/AIDS, and violence prevention. The peer leaders go through twenty-four hours of training during which curricula developed by the MPC are presented.

The MPC model is built on the belief that youth can empower other youth through engagement, information, and prevention. I view the MPC as fostering the ideals of meaning, purpose, and hope in youth. Meaning is fostered through relationship building and through providing membership in a positive, meaningful group of peer leaders. Purpose comes from helping youth to look beyond themselves to their peers and larger communities and to discover their role in improving the conditions around them. Finally, hope is fostered through the belief that youth can make a difference in their own lives and the lives of others.

While the MPC may foster the ideals of meaning, purpose, and hope, I began to think that simply fostering these ideals is not enough to drive positive change. During my previous investigation, I came to the realization that there must be something more, and in the last report I named it "*pro*silience." With the concept of prosilience I began to realize the limitations of my meaning, purpose, and hope schema. I described this realization in greater detail in the conclusion of my first report:

> As I face the limitations of my meaning, purpose, and hope schema, I begin to formulate such questions as: Are meaning, purpose, and hope enough to help youth overcome the many barriers they face? Are they tangible enough or are they just concepts, too abstract to be useful in everyday life? The investigation of my experiences has led me to different answers than I might have expected at the start of this inquiry.
>
> The new information I am assimilating is the knowledge that meaning, purpose, and hope alone are not enough. This realization both shakes and strengthens the foundation of my mission to serve children and youth by helping them discover the meaning, purpose, and hope in their lives. Meaning, purpose, and hope foster resilience and protect against many of the risk factors that youth confront in their day-to-day lives. Resilience, however, is about surviving the risks and hardships; it does not necessarily drive one towards happiness or success. The need for the concept of prosilience became poignant through my experiences at the MPC and the realization that, like resilience, there also needs to be something accompanying meaning, purpose, and hope that is not only about survival but about moving forward. . . . Instead of seeing the development of meaning, purpose, and hope as an *end* unto itself, I now understand them as only the *means* to achieving something more [Phenomenological Investigation I, p. 14].

Because this investigation begins where the last one ended, I ask not whether the MPC fosters meaning, purpose, and hope in the lives of youth, but whether these ideals are made meaningful and useful in the lives of the youth.

Because of the complexity of the case, I wanted to get a better understanding of and some clarification about the issues I am grappling with in my investigation. The central conflict seems to be between imagined ideals and actualized progress. The 1975 *Random House College Dictionary* has several definitions for the word *ideal,* including "a conception of something in its perfection . . . an ultimate object or aim of endeavor." One definition struck a chord in me: "something that exists only in the imagination . . . not real." These definitions helped to confirm the need to push myself to think more about the ideals of meaning, purpose, and hope at a different level, and also pointed to the necessity of asking the difficult questions driving my investigation: How do we, child service providers, make meaning, purpose, and hope more than ideals that exist solely in our imaginations? How do we make them something that exists tangibly in the lives of youth, and as I wrote in my last report, "drive [youth] toward happiness or success" (Phenomenological Investigation I, p. 14)? Which process is the MPC engaged in: fostering imagined ideals, or driving real change and progress? Finally, what is my specific role in this process?

I could see that this was growing into an increasingly challenging case. There were many critical questions, and when I looked to my experiences at the site for answers, I struggled with the disappointment and dismay that set in when I felt I had found nothing. Did this mean that my investigation would end before it even began? I had to think quickly and come up with leads. Time was running out.

THE CASE

Cherise's literal and my own figurative disappearances were mysteries that warranted investigation. In these mysteries, perhaps, lay the answer to the imagined versus actualized meaning, purpose, and hope dilemma. The causes and implications of our disappearances, though linked, were different for each of us. Cherise's disappearance meant that the opportunity for further developing a relationship that was mutually beneficial had ended. My own disappearance meant that perhaps I was not as capable of fully investing in relationships as I might have been had I not disappeared. More generally, it seems that disappearances of youth and those who work with youth occur with great frequency. Exploring these disappearances in terms of the presence or absence of meaning, purpose, and hope can give us a starting point in our interventions for preventing these "disappearing acts."

Tracing Cherise's Disappearance over Time

I had the privilege of working with Cherise for the entire duration of my internship—well, that is, until she disappeared. Cherise's disappearance did not happen all at once; it was not as though one day she was there and the next day she wasn't. Cherise's disappearance was more like a slow fade; yet as I reflect back on it, I observe that nothing much was really done to stop it, either by me or anyone else. In fact, the way the site is set up, it is possible that only myself and one other person were even aware of her disappearance and the circumstances that surrounded it.

Cherise was one of the participants in the girls theater group Teenage Girls InFormed (TGIF). TGIF is composed of seven high school girls. The piece the girls perform, "No More Cheers," deals with teenage girls and alcohol use and abuse. The TGIF girls perform for other middle school and high school youth, then answer questions and lead discussions on the issues raised in their performances. In my first investigation I described my interactions with the group, to which Cherise belonged: "[One] opportunity for longer-term relationship building is through my year-long involvement with TGIF. Since the first time I met them I have made sure to tell my girls that they are beautiful, to compliment them, to touch them with a hug or pat on the back, to smile at them and ask how they are doing. All of these little things that can seem so unimportant have had an impact on the development of our relationships" (Phenomenological Investigation I, p. 7).

Despite the development of our relationships, Cherise eventually stopped participating in TGIF activities. At one point, before she completely disappeared, she told me that she would probably stop coming because she was beginning to think that TGIF was a waste of her time. Sometime before this, she had also stopped going to school, presumably for the same reason. I was at a loss for how to convince her otherwise about either TGIF or school.

Cherise started out as a very active member of the TGIF troupe. She was one of the few girls who showed up consistently and on time every Monday for rehearsal. She even attended performances in which she was not participating, just to be there and support the rest of the group. In retrospect, I believe that one of the major contributors to

Cherise's gradual disappearance was the decision to allow her not to perform. She decided that she still wanted to be a part of TGIF, but as a writer instead of as an actor.

Throughout the year, we talked about creating a new script for the girls to perform. Cherise wanted to write this new script instead of performing the old one. While this sounded like a great idea at the time, in reality little time or effort was put into creating a new script, so it never materialized. Because of this, I believe, Cherise ended up feeling on the fringes, as though she really had no role in the group. Hence came the conversation previously mentioned, about TGIF becoming a waste of her time. At that point I told Cherise that I understood why she felt this way and tried to convince her that she was an extremely valuable member of the group. I told her of our plans to begin using our regularly scheduled rehearsal time to work on the new script.

Even before this conversation, however, I could see that we were in danger of losing Cherise. Her attendance at rehearsals was becoming sporadic and she had stopped attending performances. I remember sharing this concern with my colleague Rob, who also worked with TGIF. I told him that I felt we were in danger of losing Cherise if we didn't do something soon. Rob agreed and we decided to begin using our meetings to work on the new script.

Cherise's frustration with the group was most evident during two incidents in particular. She was eager to see TGIF move on to something new. During one of our sessions we were discussing the upcoming performance and workshop that TGIF was scheduled to conduct for the Mayor's Youth Summit. Cherise suggested that we use this opportunity to debut the new script, which at that point had yet to be written. The other girls were reluctant, because they felt they would not have enough time to learn new roles in time for the Summit, which was that weekend. Cherise tried to convince the rest of the girls that we would never move forward if they weren't willing to take risks. She offered to spend the next few days writing the script and to meet again later that week to rehearse. The other girls continued to resist and Cherise gave up in what seemed like frustration and defeat. Although she would not be performing, Cherise was supposed to be a part of the workshop presentation. That Saturday, however, she didn't show up at the conference. In the context of TGIF, Cherise had never missed something to which she had committed. When I reached her by phone that Sunday, she said that something had come up but she would be at rehearsal on Monday.

As it turned out, that Monday's meeting would be the last one that Cherise would attend. At that rehearsal, Rob and I tried to initiate a process for writing the new script. It was a frustrating process, but we did make some progress and Cherise played a large role in moving the process forward. When we disbursed that afternoon, it seemed as though we were finally moving toward creating the new script. For the next two weeks, however, TGIF did not meet, for various reasons, such as midterm exams and winter vacation. Consequently, we lost our continuity and momentum in writing the new script. We also lost something else: Cherise.

In thinking about incidents involving Cherise and the events leading up to her disappearance, I can in many ways relate them to meaning, purpose, and hope. Each of these ideals had been an active part of the TGIF experience: meaning through membership and positive relationships, a sense of purpose beyond the self, and a hope for making a difference. Being an active part of the TGIF group and working with the other girls, Rob and I provided the opportunity to discover meaning through positive membership and relationship building. However, when Cherise's role in the group started to feel pointless, some of the meaning gained through membership was lost. In terms of the relationships, I can't say what meaning they provided from her perspective, only from my own. I described how I perceived the relationships within the group in my last investigation. Nothing, however, reflects how close the girls have become as a group better than the events preceding their first performance: "Before the TGIF girls went on we had a very close group moment. . . . We all stood in a circle and held hands to give each other comfort and support. Each girl said comforting and encouraging words to the group. . . . Then we all gave each other hugs and 'it was on.' I felt close to them and I think the girls felt close to each other. I stood right in front as they performed, like a beaming, proud parent" (Phenomenological Investigation I, pp. 7–8).

From my perspective, I felt that I was beginning to develop a special relationship with Cherise, different from my relationships with the other girls. Cherise and I often walked home in the same direction following the TGIF rehearsals and this allowed us more time to talk and get to know each other. As I said, however, I can only speculate about what significance our developing relationship had for Cherise. As for purpose beyond the self, when Cherise stopped performing and the development of the new script went nowhere, her outreach to others as a TGIF member ended. Finally, I can also only speculate about the hope that was or was not being fostered in Cherise through meaning, purpose, and participation in TGIF. I surmise that when the meaning, purpose, and hope disappeared, so did Cherise.

Deliberate reflection and the note-taking process has allowed me to piece together and trace Cherise's history and disappearance. Without this active process, many of the details and the significance of this case may have been lost. Instead, investigating the changes and the disappearance over time sheds light on the case and on the contrast between what happens when the ideals of meaning, purpose, and hope are imagined rather than actualized.

Tracing My Own Disappearance over Time

Just as I can relate Cherise's disappearance to meaning, purpose, and hope, I can do likewise with my own. At the same time that Cherise was physically disappearing from the scene, I felt myself disappearing in a less physical but still very real sense. I found that I was extremely disengaged from my work. I was showing up and still, to my knowledge, giving my best effort to the site and students, but something was different, something had changed. Things at the site, as far as I could tell, seemed the same, so I figured the change must have been within me.

My perceptions of my site and the contributions I was making had gradually changed over the course of the semester. I continued to contribute to projects as needed, but felt that overall my presence and the work I was doing made very little sense or difference. It was time to admit that I did not feel very connected to my students. What caused me to feel this way, I believe, was the brevity of many of the encounters I had with the youth. There was little time to develop relationships that would last beyond the duration of an encounter. I would show up and they would (usually) show up for events, but I often felt that there was no meaningful bond between us. I realized, of course, that I could not really know the impact I was having on the students from their perspectives, but from my perspective I felt that I was having very little.

The exception to these feelings of disconnection, at one time, had been the work I was doing with the girls involved in TGIF. However, Cherise's disappearance and other events changed even how I felt about this group. Upon reflection and in retrospect I am positive that Cherise's disappearance greatly contributed to my sense of failure and incompetence. Even with the understanding that I knew very little about what else was going on for Cherise, I could not help but feel a sense of responsibility for what happened. Here was one of the most intelligent, articulate, and talented students that I had met and I could not even convince her that it was worthwhile for her to obtain her high school diploma. I was especially upset because of the relationship that I felt I had established with Cherise and because of the value that I personally place on educational attainment. I felt hurt, and concerned for Cherise, and I began to question my own abilities to be a positive influence. I was also beginning to question and doubt the connections that I had (or had not) formed with all of the girls in TGIF.

My questioning and doubts are reflected in the following excerpt from my notes: "I feel like I'm losing the girls in some way, like we're no longer coming together. I feel like I've failed the girls as far as helping them through school. Things move so rapidly and I'm spread so thin all the time that there doesn't seem to be a space for this, or at least I haven't created one" (Phenomenological Notes). These notes mark a major change in the way I looked at my work with the MPC, especially in regard to the work I was doing with TGIF. Not only was I questioning my relationships with the girls and the outcomes to which I had or had not contributed, I was also questioning the amount of effort I had put into shaping these relationships and outcomes. Whereas I had once felt very confident and positive about the work at my site, I now felt insecure about my contributions and unsure of the value of the work itself because I had no clear sense of the outcomes I was affecting.

For example, I was responsible for training a group of peer leaders in the alcohol and drug prevention curriculum. This group had received a full training the previous year in the AIDS/HIV curriculum and therefore were only due to receive a partial training this year. I was conducting the training by myself and felt very competent and confident about the work I was doing with the group. Apparently, however, the students felt otherwise. At one point during the training, the opportunity arose for the students to prepare and conduct a workshop for their peers at a youth conference. Much to my surprise the students immediately rejected the idea, saying that they did not feel prepared to present the material we had been discussing for the past several weeks.

This incident opened my eyes to something that I must have previously been ignoring: the possibility that the work and time put into the peer leader trainings was not as productive as we at the MPC may have wanted it to be.

Because of my growing feelings of doubt, I found myself questioning, much more than I ever had before, the point of the whole endeavor, and more generally, the point of the MPC. Did the MPC actually make a difference? In retrospect I realize that what I was really questioning was the very presence or absence of the meaning, purpose, and hope in my site experience. The many questions and doubts that I was experiencing must have contributed to my disenchantment, disengagement, and eventual disappearance from my site.

Closing the Case

"Only when I have first understood the motivating meaning of the question can I even begin to look for an answer" (Gadamer, 1981, p. 107). Gadamer maintains that there are motives and presuppositions at the root of all questions, and that an understanding of, or at least reflection on, the questions is necessary for a fully informed answer. At the root of my questions about how to activate ideals in myself and the students with whom I work, rather than just imagine them, was a desire to know if we were making enough of a difference in the lives of youth, and more important, if I was. Of course, what constitutes "enough of a difference" is open to interpretation. What I wanted to know was if I was really affecting positive change through the notions of meaning, purpose, and hope, or was it another case of theory separate from practice, of rhetoric outweighing evidence, or simply put, of "all talk and no action."

The change in my questions over time represents a marked change in the "motivating meaning" of the questions explored in my first report. Previously, my question was about how meaning, purpose, and hope are fostered at the MPC. This question was based on the fact that I felt they had played a significant role in my own development. Coming from this perspective and framing my question in this way, I was sure to find meaning, purpose, and hope, or at least to interpret phenomena as meaningful, purposeful, and hopeful. In the present investigation, my concern was not with whether the ideals were present but with how they were activated toward positive change.

Meaning, purpose, and hope are nice words and admirable ideals, but what "significant" difference was being made? By realizing that how students interpret what is significant may be different from how I would, I was looking for change that was significant in my own terms. Because I did not find it, I began to feel that maybe there was nothing to be found, and I struggled with where to look for answers.

Just as many investigators find that their cases take them places they never expected to go, my own year-long investigation has brought me to a new place in my approach to working with youth. I now know of not only the importance of the presence of meaning, purpose, and hope in fostering resilience, but also of the critical importance of their activation in fostering prosilience. Furthermore, through the experience of and reflection on disappearance, I have also learned to look for answers in the absence of these ideals or their activation. Recognizing the absence or disappearance of meaning, purpose, and hope creates an agenda for how to make connectedness reappear.

What I found through this phenomenological investigation is the circular relationship between fostering ideals and actualizing positive change. They work together in "making a difference" and "driving progress." The ideal of meaning is in fact actualized through positive membership and through engagement or connection in relationships with others. A sense of purpose beyond self is actualized by becoming involved in activities that aim to improve the conditions around you. Hope is driven by the activation of meaning and purpose. The significance of each of these in an individual's life is not something that can be imposed by one person, program, or intervention. Significance must be co-constructed. Fostering the ideals of meaning, purpose, and hope drives actualization, and this actualization in turn drives the further development of ideals. The case was closed and my training at the Academy of Hermeneutic Inquiry had not failed me. In the end, understanding ultimately came from within the hermeneutic circle.

11

TREADING SOFTLY

A Critical Phenomenological Investigation of the Voiceless in the Hermeneutic Circle

Deborah H. Cheng

HERMENEUTICS IS DESCRIBED AS CIRCULAR, but in some ways it seems more like a spiral. Throughout the year I have spiraled back again and again to the experiences of my past, and to my "forestructure" of understanding. I find myself nearly touching the past when I see my students at the Joyce Middle School struggling with voicelessness. Yet in all the spiraling back, I never quite return (I hope) to any point where I was before. Rather, I continue to achieve a point somewhere beyond it, close, but distanced enough so I can look at it, consider it, interpret it, and be critical of it. The coils build on each other, but move forward toward new understandings of myself, the children with whom I work, and the "system," which in this phenomenological inquiry will include forces in American society and schools that succeed in silencing and oppressing.

The systems that silence and oppress typically assume asymmetric power over those held to be of inferior class, race, or gender (Gallagher, 1992, Ch. 8). The issue of race is particularly salient to this investigation because it has been a central issue to my practicum experience—which includes the practicum class, my personal life, and the lives of my students, in all of which prejudice, voice, and power have been investigated and discussed extensively. Coming to terms with race and with what race has to do with silencing and oppression is a struggle, but I have realized that this is a necessary process of growth for me, personally and professionally. The better I as a researcher with a particular worldview know myself, the better I am able to help others (Ibrahim, 1985). At the same time, the more I help others, the more enlightened my understanding of myself will be. This reflects the nature of the hermeneutical circle: "All understanding has a circular structure. . . . The meaning of the part is only understood within the context of the whole; but the whole is never given unless through an understanding of the parts" (Gallagher, 1992, pp. 52–59).

The hermeneutic circle reminds me of the symbol of nature and harmony originating in ancient China: yin/yang. The yin/yang concept combines the elements of feminine passive and masculine active, dark and light, cold and heat, wetness and dryness, "to produce all that comes to be" (*Webster's Dictionary,* 1992). The essence of yin/yang is contradictions that combine harmoniously to create a balanced and complete whole.

In contrast, the hermeneutic circle was created in another part of the world. Long ago, Hermes, messenger of the Greek gods, interpreted to mortals the wishes and commands of the divinities. Hermes is celebrated in the term *hermeneutics,* which refers to the affair of interpreting (Packer and Addison, 1989, p. 1). In an overview of hermeneutics, Packer and Addison state: "This century has been a time for special recognition of the importance of messages, of translation and interpretation. . . . We've come to appreciate that misunderstanding is as common as understanding. . . . We've come to see that the past, and cultures foreign to us, can be reappropriated, comprehended and studied only in a partial manner" (p. 1).

THE RESEARCH QUESTIONS

The hermeneutic notion of inherent misunderstanding, prejudice, and irresolution seems to preclude the possibility of real harmony. How much, then, is the hermeneutic circle like the yin/yang? Where do the concepts and models of Western and Eastern philosophies overlap and where do they diverge? How does hermeneutics apply to non-Western cultures and people? The phenomenological framework of this investigation incorporates pieces of all of the above questions, with the specific aim of coming to an understanding of *how the voiceless, the silenced, and the oppressed participate, and can participate, in the hermeneutic circle.*

By referring to "the voiceless, the silenced, and the oppressed" I am first and foremost, I admit, referring to myself. These questions are very important to me, as one who has been voiceless through much of my life, and notably in the practicum class, and as one who works with and wishes to continue to help those who are struggling to find their voices. I have asked myself many times, Why am I voiceless? Why don't I speak in class? How can I participate in this hermeneutic stuff? How can I be of any use to others—including my colleagues and especially my charges, if I am so silent? Am I "the voiceless leading the voiceless," unlikely to get anywhere, like the blind leading the blind? It is a difficult reckoning. I have written about my feelings on this topic:

> I sit in class, my ears burning and my heart beating. I feel convicted, and too paralyzed to redeem myself. Why is it that after so many of our classes I leave hating myself, wanting to bang my head against a wall?
>
> We talk of race, conflict, prejudice, challenge, change. I sit there, silent at my desk while voices rage around me.... Am I a bystander? Passive? I fight to recognize my own experience as a true experience, even though very few people would suspect its existence. I have struggled, with myself, with my site, with ubiquitous problems of race and hate and misunderstanding [Reflective Memo, May 7, 1996].

I bear these feelings in silence, finding no strength in my voice, no confidence in what I know. I want to speak, I do not want to speak; I cannot speak; I am voiceless—silenced by myself and the fear that I will not really be heard or understood as I want to be. Some of this has to do with experiences that are uniquely my own, but much, I believe, has to do with being Asian American. Therefore, in this chapter I am referring in particular to Asian Americans when I discuss the voiceless, because I think there is an important connection between being voiceless and being Asian American.

In writing this chapter, I hope to take advantage of this ideal opportunity for me to do a hermeneutical inquiry into an area that may be helpful to me and to my work with the Asian American students. As Michael Nakkula suggested in a class lecture, an important approach to doing this investigation should be to address the questions that are most outstanding, meaningful, and central for the researcher.

Grappling to answer these questions about voicelessness, and attempting to interpret their significance and power to "transform researcher, participants, and setting in a widening of horizons" (Addison, 1989, p. 42) is what I hope to engage in throughout my study.

METHODOLOGY

The data for this investigation consist of notes taken throughout the year: lecture notes, notes on what Dr. Nakkula and my fellow students have shared in class and on my (silent but existent) reactions to them; notes on my practicum site, including the nature of my interactions and my observations and feelings about the students; and readings for the class and analytic memos written in their margins.

The notes I have taken over the year are a combination of "conservative" and "critical" hermeneutic writings (see Gallagher, 1992). I believe that both methods are valuable and necessary for me to conduct an investigation of how the voiceless participate in the hermeneutic circle. Determining *how* requires an attempt toward the objective and neutral recording of events (conservative hermeneutics), but it also requires an effort at understanding what meaning these events hold for the purpose of promoting change (critical hermeneutics). I believe that there are benefits of a balance between reproduction and transformation—the respective aims of conservative and critical hermeneutical processes (Nakkula Lecture, Mar. 12, 1996).

A faithful reproduction of a text (or experience) is useful for several reasons. Reproduction strives for objectivity and attempts to sidestep misinterpretation: "the case of reading something into a text because of one's own bias" (Gallagher, 1992, p. 209). The notes that are conservative and reproductive were written in order to keep a formal historical record of the activities I engaged in with the students. They provided me with raw, uninterpreted data that I could go back to over and again, in a critical fashion, to gain new perspectives and understandings.

I will be interpreting the data I have gathered in a critical hermeneutic framework, which is the framework in which most of my reflective notes were originally written. Concerned with the silent and oppressed, especially in relation to Asian Americans in educational settings—the middle school students in their school, and myself in the practicum class—this approach is imperative for several reasons: the principles of critical hermeneutics explicitly address reproduction, hegemony, critical reflection, and application, which are all central to this phenomenological investigation of the voiceless (Gallagher, 1992).

A CRITICAL INVESTIGATION

Reproduction

Although I have defended a place for conservative hermeneutics in note taking, I believe that a movement away from it must be made in order to conduct a successful investigation of how the voiceless and oppressed participate in hermeneutical processes and how they can be transformed by them. According to Gallagher, a "noncritical understanding simply continues, reiterates, and reproduces tradition, cultural values, ideology, and power structures" (1992, p. 241). To me, this means perpetuating stereotypes—both those we hold about "others" (for example, people of color and those of various classes, religions, or sexual orientations) and those in which we trap ourselves (that is, saying to ourselves, "my experience is so different from yours, there is no way we can come to an understanding of one another").

According to Habermas, hermeneutics is "designed to guarantee, within cultural traditions, the possible action-orienting self-understanding of individuals and groups as well as reciprocal understanding between different individual groups. It makes possible the form of unconstrained consensus and the type of open intersubjectivity on which communication action depends" (Habermas, 1971, p. 176). If we were able to apply the tenets of this quote to our class, to be more hermeneutical by making our aim one of really listening to and understanding each others' perspectives rather than being mainly concerned with telling our own stories, perhaps we would have experienced greater communication and achieved a more heightened consciousness than we did when our voices crossed over each other in our efforts to be heard.

On a personal level, I have spent a surprisingly extensive amount of time trying to gain self-understanding, which has been important for my growth this year. However, I am guilty, by virtue of not speaking out in class, of not contributing to the promotion of "reciprocal understanding between groups." I still feel convicted on the occasions when someone in class says something to the effect of "Why don't representatives of other minority groups speak up and share their perspective? Why is the burden always on us [the black students]?" I think this is a very good question, and one that I will address throughout this investigation.

At the Joyce Middle School, which has a student population that is equally Asian, white, black and Latino/Latina, I also see a lack of communication between the different racial groups. I have never seen the Asian students I work with talk with anyone other than Asian students. I realize that a shared native language that is not English is largely responsible for this phenomenon. However, I worry that this inability to communicate prevents the Asian students from participating in a very important hermeneutic process. The practice of keeping to themselves increases misunderstanding between Asian and other groups and limits possibilities for connections, the broadening of perspectives, and the forming of friendships. This language barrier creates misunderstanding and suspicion, as well as a wall between ethnic groups that have difficulty communicating.

Hegemony

"An established monopoly will not only make it difficult for another voice to be heard, but will also make it seem proper that it should not be heard: it is convicted in advance as irrelevant. . . . Conversation in reality is hegemonic, and this is a constant" (Gallagher, 1992, pp. 308–309). The application of critical hermeneutics to voiceless populations brings to awareness the existence and power of hegemonic systems such as the authority and traditional power structures discussed earlier. This awareness creates the possibility of recognizing and confronting the silencing and oppressing that occurs in society and in schools.

Critical Reflection

A critical awareness of the constraints of reproduction and hegemony can be "lifted or at least loosened by reflection. . . . The purpose of critical reflection is to assist in the achievement of emancipation" (Gallagher, 1992, pp. 243–244). Therefore, by engaging in critical reflection, a voiceless person still has a way of participating in the hermeneutical process. She or he does not necessarily have to "speak out."

It is through writing my process and reflective notes and papers that I have found entry points into the hermeneutic circle. Others also find an outlet and their place for critical thought in pen and paper. For example, when trying to fill out the Joyce intake form with Ellis, I found that he only began to answer the questions when he could write or draw his answers. He was able to engage in the hermeneutical process of reflection and make meaning of his experience, just not verbally. According to Gallagher, some authors exclude explication as a necessary aspect of the hermeneutical process, emphasizing "the interior work of understanding" and asserting that "someone can understand something without necessarily communicating it to an external audience" (1992, p. 324). I would have liked Ellis to share his thoughts, but I do not take his silence as an indication that nothing is happening.

Application

However, while there is an argument that says articulation is not necessary for hermeneutical understanding, there is not surprisingly an alternate view: "Practically speaking, critical interpretation moves us closer to hermeneutical situations in which the interpreter enjoys the possibility of unconstrained communication and autonomous action" (Gallagher, 1992, p. 245). I think that unconstrained communication would be ideal, but it is not a likely possibility for me or my students. I know that for me, communication is usually constrained and my voice is bound.

What is the verdict about which of the two views is better? Should the voiceless be excused from speaking if it is difficult and anxiety producing? As fellow Asian American, classmate, and friend Grace Kim said: "It is not OK for me to just listen. Unless I speak out, I am only getting half an education." I tend to agree with Grace, particularly if one is being silenced as opposed to being silent. I believe it is all right to be silent of one's own volition and still be engaged and learning, but I also believe there is a danger of becoming so lax and comfortable as to stunt the learning and growing process. According to Gallagher (1992), Johann Martin Chladenius, an eighteenth-century scholar of interpretation theory, defined interpretation as "explication leading toward understanding," placing priority on explication over understanding: "Without explication there would be no understanding, since understanding is produced by explication" (p. 325). Chladenius asserted that one cannot learn or understand until one voices herself or himself. According to this argument, the voiceless must "enjoy unconstrained communication" in order to enter the hermeneutical circle and participate in interpretation and understanding.

THE ASIAN AMERICAN EXPERIENCE

I am not sure to what extent my experience as an Asian American is the same as that of other Asian Americans, nor am I sure what about their experiences is true of mine. According to Optimal Theory, the world-view and "being" of each person, of any race, is a combination of human universality, cultural specificity, and individual uniqueness (Speight, Myers, Cox, and Highlen, 1991, p. 32). I want to be careful, when speaking about *the* Asian American experience, that I do not unconsciously reproduce or perpetuate stereotypes. However, when talking to fellow Asian Americans, reading Asian American stories such as Hyo-Jung Kim's "Do You Have Eyelashes?" (1991) or Maxine Hong Kingston's *The Woman Warrior* (1976), and referring to texts on counseling minorities (especially Sue and Sue, 1990), I must say that I do see similarities among them. These descriptions of Asian Americans' experiences are often reflective of my own life as well as of what I think might be the experiences of the students with whom I work. To experience myself as more fully engaged in this chapter, I will use the unifying term *we* when talking about my—our—experiences.

Silence

There are many reasons for the silence that is prevalent among Asian Americans. This is an issue of growing concern to educators who work with this population. Voiceless, silenced, and oppressed, how can Asian Americans, like myself, enter into a critical hermeneutical process that requires articulation, conflict, the challenging of authorities, and asking questions? And why should we enter the circle? Who would want to hear Asian American voices anyway? Who wants to hear about our plight and struggle? Certainly not the hegemonic systems that benefit from oppressing us. It is more comfortable to sustain a false consciousness, believing that all is well with the "model minority."

Asian Americans are considered the model minority in the United States because, despite racism, stereotypes, and discrimination, we have become the example of success for other minorities to emulate (Sue and Sue, 1990). Through quiet and persistent hard work, Asian Americans have achieved a status of "success": educated, rarely delinquent, and never stirring up a commotion. A very well-behaved group, acting just as any nation would want their minority populations to behave. Hegemonic systems encourage the silence of Asian Americans by awarding us the title of "model minority" and touting Asian American "success" as proof that the system is working just fine. Asian Americans do not protest or scream of injustice. We work with silent persistence.

Stereotypes of Asian Americans, however, are not all positive. In the not too distant past, anti-Asian sentiment prevailed; during the

Depression and World War II, Asians were seen as a "yellow peril" with slanted, shifty eyes and strange habits. A resurgence of anti-Asian sentiment occurred during the U.S. involvement in Vietnam. It is no wonder that Asians in America would try not to attract attention to ourselves. It is better to remain silent and invisible, out of the way of ridicule and shame. Even the stereotype of "model minority" is hurtful. It denies the difficulties that Asian Americans experience and sometimes provokes the resentment of other minorities who are chastised for not being "more like them."

Remnants of this fear of ridicule and shame persist. While growing up, I often hid behind a veil of silence to protect myself, and I see the Asian students at Joyce Middle School doing the same. I believe it has been the experience of every Asian child in America to have someone come up to them with the edges of their eyes pulled up at a slant and say something like "Ching-chong-ching, ah-so!" Against this taunting, what defense do we have? We cannot change our appearance and language, and it is thrown back at us like a dirty joke. It seems all we can do is hide and not speak.

Limited English language ability is another major barrier to "reciprocal understanding" and "unconstrained communication," which are key aspects of engaging in a critical hermeneutics that attempts to confront hegemony. Critical theories of education state that "the reception of information by students depends upon their linguistic competence, which in turn is determined to some extent by their social class. . . . The academic use of language is simply one part of—perhaps an essential part of—the propagation of extralinguistic constraints upon educational experience" (Gallagher, 1992, p. 253). Uncomfortable with English, most of my students are marginalized at school, where nearly everything—from textbooks to announcements, from teachers to students—disregards their native language and renders them powerless. One of the girls I counsel has been in America for only five months. She is more willing to take risks speaking in English within our small, supportive group than in the larger community, where failed attempts bring about embarrassment and shame and ridicule. For her, school is still like "a new territory of land mines to traverse" (Kim, 1991, p. 201). So she treads softly, carefully, and quietly, placing her steps with caution.

Even students who have gained a mastery over English are still shy about using it; it is difficult to break the silence. Old insecurity still hampers them, and others, used to their silence, do not hear them when they do speak. The expectation is that these Asian American students are quiet and inhibited, and Asian Americans tend to collude in this relationship, unless a conscious effort is made otherwise.

It is also possible that Asian Americans do not have the tradition of speaking out against the systems that silence and oppress us. Many aspects of Asian culture collude with American culture in imposing silence on Asian Americans. Americans admire independence, assertiveness, informality, creativity, individuality, and free expression. Asian cultures tend to value interdependence, reserve, and the preservation of harmony at all cost. For example, there is a common saying in Japanese about "hammering down the nail that sticks up," which is an adage about enforcing conformity and not allowing any individual to stand out. I suppose the thinking is that if nails are allowed to stick up, things will fall apart. Contrast this with the popular American saying, "The squeaky wheel gets the grease," which underscores the fact that assertiveness is rewarded.

Traditional Asian values can become oppressive when transplanted in America, but they can also be very valuable. The harmonizing of opposites, as in yin/yang, can be paralleled to the harmonizing of Eastern and Western values that Asian Americans must accomplish. There is a tradition and desire to achieve this harmony; however, it is an extremely difficult task. The process really requires a critical hermeneutic model, but this is arguably not the traditional Asian way.

Emancipation and Anger

If Asian Americans hope to end the silencing and oppression that render us voiceless, then we must consider the possibilities of critical hermeneutics to transform and emancipate, and we must step into the hermeneutic circle.

But how do Asian Americans make the step and "transform silence into language and action?" (Lorde, 1984). One way to begin is to engage in the critical thinking, articulation, and application that Habermas ([1983] 1990) claims will culminate in transformation and emancipation. But I believe there is one key ingredient missing to make all this happen: anger. In Lorde's (1984) chapter "The Uses of Anger: Women Responding to Racism," I see how the anger of women, especially black women, has fueled the processes that bring about emancipation.

I find it difficult, however, to envision the same sort of liberating anger for Asian Americans. Anger is not an option that is encouraged. In fact, remaining humble and showing gratitude seems to be more our way. The following are my thoughts on this, written in a reflective memo after a class on May 7, 1996:

> Anger. Constructive uses of anger. I had a thought today on why it was that blacks have taken on the burden of leading the movement of minorities among white supremacy that Asian Americans have not. It's because they are angry. Passionately and rightly enraged. I heard so much anger today in class, loudest from the black members of the class: Randy, Ayanna, Dorothy. The anger came from the past, but still has its place in today. Captured, imprisoned, shipped, sold, traded, enslaved—this was the black experience of coming to America. Not the land of the free. The Constitution did not protect them, the Bill of Rights did not apply. Blacks were dealt a grave and terrible injustice. And it is the fight against such an obvious (at least now recognized as such) wrong that gives blacks every right and reason to be angry, to make noise, and to rally together against a clear enemy. But what about other minorities? As our classmate Claudia reminded us, Latinos/Latinas did not come to America of their own free will either. It was by force. By war. Texas, Arizona, among other regions, and their peoples, were Mexican. They lost in the war and were annexed. These people have a right to be angry. They, like the Native American tribes, really have a reason to scream and rage and fight.
>
> But what of other minorities, like Asian Americans? We were not dragged over here. We were not captured like prisoners of war. We come to America—of our own volition? Sometimes. But often it is as an escape from a home that we would rather not leave but must, the situation, political or otherwise, giving us no option. Often it is a matter of life or death. Escaping to America, we run for our lives. We are indebted to America. America has saved us and given us at least some opportunity. If language were not an obstacle, it is conceivable that great intellects from China could possibly be the great doctors, professors, or politicians they were before they came to America and sweated in the family laundromat. America is still the "land of opportunity." We then, give ourselves up to the mercy of this great country. America is our refuge.
>
> How, then, can we raise our voices and scream of injustice? How can we speak out against the white men who made it possible for us to live in America? That is ingratitude. That is biting the hand that feeds. I realize that using this metaphor is like comparing ourselves to dogs dependent on our masters, but we have reason to be humble.
>
> Yes, we face injustices, discrimination, prejudices, stereotypes, and are treated as second-class citizens. But unlike blacks, we

accept it, grateful that we can be citizens at all, or at least residents, even if "alien." Besides, we are taught, by our families, our ancestors, to forbear, to work hard, to let ourselves be swallowed up in harmony. "Swallowed up in harmony." I just made that up. I don't know if it's a Chinese saying but I suspect that there is one of a similar sentiment. To American ears, that probably does not sound admirable. Being "swallowed up" sounds too passive. Like victims. But in other contexts and other cultures, being consumed by a greater force or state, especially one such as "harmony" or "love," could be quite desirable. There is a oneness, I suppose like "giving one's self up to God," that approaches nirvana, that leaves the fragmentation and contestation, typical of mortals, behind. Perhaps it is not so bad?

Does this theory help explain why Asian Americans do not lead the march against discrimination the way blacks have for the minority populations of this country? Does it explain why we do not speak out in class about our experiences of silencing?

And does it excuse us from being silent and oppressed? No, it helps us to understand where we come from and what we bring as we enter the hermeneutic circle and seek transformation and emancipation.

A FUTURE OF POSSIBILITIES

What does it mean to "enter the hermeneutic circle?" If it is like entering Longfellow 319 (our practicum classroom) on Tuesday evenings, then it means taking risks, speaking out, facing misunderstanding and racism, dealing with silence and anger, making meaning and interpretations, and trying to understand our understandings. But this large, open, vociferous, and confrontational environment proved to be very difficult for those of us who are voiceless, feeling silenced or oppressed.

What are the options for those who cannot speak out in class? Is it all right to use these options, and are they hermeneutical? I believe that my notes and papers allowed me, as well as others who were silent, to participate in the hermeneutical process, but I also am conscious of the fact that my notes and papers are of no use to others in my class who will never read them. Hermeneutics cannot exist in a vacuum; it depends on the sharing of interpretations and understandings, even prejudices and misunderstandings. Can I still consider myself part of the hermeneutic circle?

Why should a person struggle to enter the hermeneutic circle? Why should I, and why should I encourage my students to do so? Many people probably go through life without entering it, at least not consciously or deliberately. One answer is: transformation and emancipation—of myself, of my students, of oppressed peoples. I cannot remain silent if speaking can save someone, including myself, from suffering unnecessarily. There is a price to be paid: Martin Luther King Jr. was assassinated. But it seems necessary if the world, a nation, or even one child is to be transformed. In the case of Asian Americans, even more attention needs to be paid, because as a "model minority," our concerns are often denied. This silencing and oppression can lead to depression, and depression to suicide. In fact, the suicide rate among Asian American youth is three times that of the national average (Sue and Sue, 1990). For those who would benefit, it is worth entering the hermeneutic circle, no matter how great the challenge.

12

THE CONCEALED INFLUENCE AND POWER OF NONDIRECTIVE THERAPISTS

Hugh McDonough

LIKE MOST NONDIRECTIVE THERAPISTS, I previously believed that I was playing a relatively noninvasive role in my clients' belief systems. My main goal in therapy was to allow clients to reflect on their own thoughts while minimizing my own personal voice and beliefs. After giving each individual the "space to open up," I would then use techniques such as empathic language, mirroring, clarifications, and interpretations to help him or her more fully experience and understand his or her feelings. Although I understood that these manipulations affected my clients, I believed that by drawing only from the material my clients presented and by weighing my language carefully I could effectively remove my biases and prejudices. In short, I saw myself as a catalyst, precipitating change but leaving the final product uncontaminated.

My belief in my own therapeutic neutrality began to unravel shortly into my study of the hermeneutic debate. While reading Shaun Gallagher's book *Hermeneutics and Education* (1992) I began to realize how my beliefs are part of a larger tradition in Western thought. While discussing the Enlightenment philosophers' attempts to develop a knowledge system free from all biases and unfounded tradition, Gallagher refers to Hans-Georg Gadamer's position that the prejudice of the Enlightenment was a "prejudice against prejudice" (p. 87). Philosophers such as Descartes, wishing to free their arguments and ideas of unwarranted assumptions, began rigorously deconstructing their own intellectual traditions. However, in attempting this deconstruction, they created a new assumption that implicitly stated that the reasonable observer could potentially escape his or her own prejudices. Gallagher describes how this belief in objectivity has become an almost unquestioned tradition in Western thought, especially in its incarnation as the scientific method: "The belief in the absolute authority of reason manifested in both the natural and the historical sciences is part of the 'basic discrediting of all prejudices.' But this belief that reason stands outside of the process of tradition and thereby offers human understanding a way to escape all prejudices is itself a prejudice" (Gallagher, 1992, p. 88).

Knowing psychology's deep roots in the medical profession, I found myself wondering if perhaps the concept of therapeutic distance was merely another unquestioned expression of the Enlightment's prejudice for objectivity. Upon reflection, I realized that I believed in my own neutral role simply because I had been taught as a counselor to aspire toward it. Perhaps there was no ultimate justification for this belief. Perhaps I was simply another nondirective counselor who had inherited this intellectual tradition.

Once I began to question the actual neutrality of the therapist, I then asked myself what kind of unrecognized effects I could be having on my clients. Again I found the beginning of an answer while reading Gallagher. In his section entitled "Language and Interpretation," Gallagher reports that hermeneuticists hold an "almost unanimous agreement that language plays the role of medium or vehicle by which traditions enter interpretation" (Gallagher, p. 100). In other words, each time an individual "picks up" a new linguistic concept from another individual, he is taking a piece of that person's thinking, thereby altering how he makes sense of the world and entering into a new ideological tradition (Gallagher, pp. 100–110).

As I entered into Gallagher's and the hermeneuticists' discourse on linguistic tradition, I began relating it to my own relationship with clients. It seemed obvious to me that if I were acting as a socializing agent passing on my own ideologies, I would be doing so through my language and expression of ideas. However, limiting my own expression is precisely what my therapy style was designed to accomplish. I was trained to simply mirror my clients' own thoughts. I still could not see how my own ideologies could significantly enter into my clients' belief systems.

Despite this initial reaffirmation of counselor neutrality, I continued to probe my untested assumptions. I read an article by Lisa Delpit (1988) entitled "The Silenced Dialogue: Power and Pedagogy in Educating Other People's Children." While examining the "culture of power" in public schools, Delpit compares African American teachers employing directive teaching methods with white teachers employing nondirective methods. In the course of examining these styles, Delpit points out how the white teachers' linguistic styles tend to deemphasize the explicit use of power while their underlying intent is fundamentally authoritative. To illustrate, Delpit provides the example of a white teacher's nondirect order "Would you like to sit down?" Although this language style tends to deny power, the actual meaning of the statement, from the teacher's cultural perspective, is a command.

Reading Delpit's analysis, I began to contemplate this other Western tradition, the tradition of indirect expressions of power. As a result of our ongoing discussions on race and cross-cultural counseling issues in the practicum course, I was becoming increasingly aware of the unconscious and unexamined ways in which I, as a member of a dominant subculture, participated in oppression. I wondered if my "indirect" therapy style might also contain unexamined power. Perhaps my mirroring, interpretations, and clarifications contained underlying messages of which I was not conscious. Perhaps my nondirect manipulations actually helped me to stretch my influence across cultural barriers.

By the end of my first semester studying hermeneutics, I had only begun to realize the potential influence that my therapy style afforded me with my clients. I did not fully see how my nondirective posture could create a fertile atmosphere for socialization. The last question remained: How did I communicate my ideology even through my sparse linguistic style? Reading over my clinical notes, an idea dawned on me. I realized that perhaps through the very therapeutic manipulations I employed to help clients, I was actually training them to understand their own psychological worlds in the manner in which I envisioned them. I hypothesized that my therapy acted as a kind of Socratic dialogue, in which I never expressly stated my viewpoint but, through subtle verbal and nonverbal clues, steered my clients toward my own conceptualizations of their lives.

METHODOLOGY

In my research, I relied on two sets of data. The first set are case notes in which I attempt to record, in a relatively detached manner, the topics discussed in counseling. Each entry is approximately one page long, which I recorded within a few hours of the session. The notes have the strength of being recorded relatively soon after the event and being kept consistently over time. However, given that each fifty-five minute session is boiled down to a mere page of thought, even thoughts that I selected as important are still highly subjective.

The second set of data are notes that I recorded within a day or two of the sessions. I wrote these notes after reflecting on the first set with the expressed aim of collecting interesting data for my study. The strength of these notes comes from the fact that they are long, ongoing reflections. I was thus able to reflect on my original research question to a great extent. Once again, however, they fall short of being an "objective" report. The very fact that I was creating these notes to answer a predetermined question already created inherent biases in my data collection.

Despite the unavoidable prejudices underlying my inquiry, I set out to capture evidence that my beliefs and cultural traditions were being reproduced in my client's thinking. I searched for changes in my client's vocabulary, such as the use of words I believe he would not have used prior to therapy. I looked for changes in his thought patterns and beliefs that reflected ones I hold, and presumably had modeled. Finally, I studied my notes for evidence that my client had taken action or developed goals that were in concert with my unspoken desires or judgments.

While searching through my written reflections, I made a special effort to look for intrusions that had ethical implications—areas of reproduced thought that involved significant power differentials between myself and my client. I used a method of inventorying individual thought processes created by Farah Ibrahim. In her article "Contributions of Cultural Worldview to Generic Counseling and Development" (1991), Ibrahim decries the negative outcomes of multicultural counseling by proposing a solution for evaluating cultural differences between therapists and clients. She proposes that counselors' and clients' worldviews should be clarified along the lines of "ethnicity, culture, gender, age, life-stage, socio-economic status, education, religion, philosophy of life, beliefs, values and assumptions" (p. 16).

In her review of relevant research, Ibrahim concludes that most models of counseling in the United States rest on the values and beliefs of the majority (that is, the white middle class). She argues that this cultural bias "systematically denies the reality of immigrants, ethnic minorities, women, disabled persons, elderly, and gays and lesbians" (p. 15). In my case, as a thirty-year-old upper-middle-class straight white male born in Boston and nondisabled, I am in danger of denying the reality of each of these groups. In my work at a Boston high school, my background differs from the cultural backgrounds of my students, who are predominantly black and Latino and from low-income environments.

Taking Ibrahim and other critics seriously meant that my most pressing ethical concern was to examine relationships with my clients in which I represented a dominant, oppressive culture. In the case of one of my clients, Sam, I analyzed the dynamics between us: me, a white, upper-middle-class adult, counseling Sam, a lower-income Latino adolescent. Given our differences in race and class, I focused on cross-racial and socioeconomic differences.

SAM'S BACKGROUND

Sam is a seventeen-year-old male whose parents originally came from the Dominican Republic. Sam was first referred to me by his cousin, another participant in the Urban Youth Connection. When he first came to me, Sam complained that he had difficulty sleeping, often felt "depressed," and was having trouble adjusting to a new school.

During the early days of therapy, Sam, despite his self-defined "depression," seemed almost manic in his presentation. His language was highly lyrical, his mannerisms filled with what seemed to be a nervous energy. I found his long descriptions of his history and his personal anecdotes plotless and difficult to follow. He seemed to move without any warning from one topic to another. He often spoke about individuals without naming or making any effort to describe them. Because of the persistence of these and other alarming behaviors, my supervisor and I worried that Sam might be heading toward a psychotic break.

Despite my difficulty following him at times, I quickly developed a very long history on Sam and on the events that I believed precipitated his depression. Five years ago, Sam's family moved from Boston to an outlying town. His father's business had started doing well and, according to Sam, his father wished to improve the family's standard of living by buying them a "nice house in a nice neighborhood."

Sam remembers being very happy in the new neighborhood. He had many friends and a girlfriend. However, at fifteen Sam was involved in a tragic episode. He went to a party against his parents' will and drank. At some point during the party, another boy he knew asked Sam and his friend if they would come down to the street and "back him up." Although Sam knew that the boy was involved in a lot of dangerous business, he convinced his friend to go down. He later told me that he felt "tough" going down. Once on the street, the boy joined a group a short distance away while Sam and his friend watched. An argument broke out and several young men pulled out guns. Sam was hit in the shoulder and his friend was killed.

For Sam, this unfortunate incident marked the end of a happy period in his life. He fell into a year-long depression in which he stayed in his room and smoked pot almost every day. His girlfriend, formerly very supportive, left him, claiming that he would not let her get close to him and his parents and that she could no longer communicate with him. To make matters worse, his father ran into economic trouble at this time. The family left their "beautiful home" and returned to an apartment in Boston.

MY FIRST GOAL

Using psychodynamic theory, my supervisor and I had little difficulty formulating Sam's situation and drawing up treatment goals. We believed that Sam was suffering from posttraumatic stress disorder. He had suffered a tremendous loss under circumstances in which he was not entirely free from blame. Sam's ability to mourn and accept the loss and his ability to process the terror and pain of the experience had been blocked by his own confused feelings of guilt. To free himself from this guilt, Sam would need to be slowly brought in touch with his remorse. As a therapist, I would help Sam discuss his present problems, mirror back the underlying feelings, and tie those feelings to the negative effects left from the accident. We believed that in time Sam would see, or rather experience, these connections, reexperience the original feelings, and successfully mourn the loss.

From the beginning this simple psychodynamic formulation ran into a snag. Underlying the psychodynamic model is an assumption that the client has some idea of what to talk about. Sam, however, did not. Although pleasant and involved, he did not narrate stories in a manner that made sense to me. His stories were disjointed, jumping from one topic to another, introducing new characters with no names or identifying characteristics, and most importantly, lacking any obvious emotional theme.

My supervisor argued convincingly that Sam's manner of discourse was a safe way for him to begin our relationship because it steered clear of any emotional pain. She also hypothesized that he might be heading toward a psychotic break. This diagnosis was borne out by his lyrical, imagistic way of talking and several "visions" he had described. Despite the cogency of this hypothesis, however, I believed that Sam's problematic narrative had less to do with psychological problems than with his lack of familiarity with therapy. The following dialogue is an example:

SAM: So, me and him went down to this place where we used to go hang out.

HUGH: Who?

SAM: Me and my cousin.

HUGH: This is the cousin whose shirt—?

SAM: No, this is my cousin Mark. He's the one from my old town. We went out dancing that night.

HUGH: This is last weekend?

SAM: No, man! Long, long time ago [Case Notes, Nov. 30, 1996].

In exchanges such as this one, I did not see a difficult emotional problem but simply a style of dialogue that was difficult for me to follow. Responding to my need as a counselor to understand my client, I asked Sam simple questions for clarification purposes. However, as time went on I realized that Sam had begun to change the manner in which he told his stories. He began anticipating my needs and changing his discourse:

SAM: Remember I told you about Maria, the girl I was dating? [Case Notes, April 4, 1996].

Although I did not plan to change Sam's narrative style, I found that he became increasingly less difficult to follow. My supervisor suggested that perhaps he was becoming more comfortable with our relationship. However, when Sam developed the habit of summarizing his stories, I was struck by how much these recapitulations resembled the clarifications that I, as a therapist, routinely employed.

SAM: You know what he said to me, Hugh? He tells me some shit about how they're all showered and I look like some fool from playing basketball or whatever. So, I say, fine. You go meet whoever, wherever you're going. You can forget about me. Just drop me off at my crib, you know? And forget about coming over tomorrow or whatever. You got no respect.

HUGH: Geez.

SAM: Yah, so that's it from Mark, man. Can you believe it? I invite him over my house. Treat him good. I mean good, Hugh. I take him over to my cousin's, who doesn't owe him anything, man. I mean he's my cousin, right? So, we sit around and then off they go and tell me I smell or some shit. Can you believe that shit? [Case Notes, April 4, 1996].

I am not claiming that summations are a linguistic form unique to therapists, but Sam did not use this rhetorical device until several months into counseling. Furthermore, his incorporation of this form coincided with an increase in several other stylistic changes. Perhaps most striking are several occasions when Sam actually made reference to his adaptive change. For example, on March 14th, Sam entered into our session excited to tell me some news from his life. He began speaking in a rushed manner but stopped and said, "Wait a second, I have to get my plot together." Since then, Sam has made several references to plots and "getting his story straight." As a former reading teacher, I could not help but be struck by his use of these structural terms.

IMPLICATIONS OF MY POWER

On a superficial level, Sam's adaptation might seem like a harmless, perhaps even beneficial change. After all, his increased ability to communicate with me could translate into more success in other situations, such as job interviews and English classes. In other words, I might have introduced Sam to the language of power that Lisa Delpit speaks about in her book *Other People's Children* (1995). However, with this increased chance for success comes an increased chance that Sam's cultural views will be adulterated by my own.

Although my training of Sam might seem benign on the surface, it takes on a more somber cast when seen in the light of critical hermeneutics. Martin Heidegger was one of the first moderr philosophers to make the assertion that language was not merely a tool for communication but the very medium out of which thought arose. When discussing linguistic forms, Heidegger argued, according to Gallagher (1992), that "we do not so much control language as it controls us" (p. 103). In other words, how an individual thinks, how an individual narrates his life, has a direct effect on that person's beliefs.

Critical hermeneuticists, such as Jurgen Habermas, have taken up Heidegger's definition of language and brought it to its logical conclusions in the realm of social interaction. They argue that specific language forms hold the blueprints that shape a society's worldview. In other words, embedded in linguistic styles are the prejudices and biases that undergird every cultural philosophy, including prejudices that fuel inequalities such as racism, classism, and sexism. Habermas states: "Language is a medium of domination and social power that serves to legitimate relations of organized force" (Habermas, 1977, p. 360).

When I entered into counseling with Sam, I brought with me many of the prejudices of my class and race. I am a white male raised in an affluent background and educated in elite and elitist institutions. Sam is a Dominican male raised in a lower- and middle-economic background and educated in traditional public schools. When Sam begins to emulate my style of discourse and narrate his life along the lines I direct, he is, by necessity, changing the way he values and makes sense out of events in his life. In this way, I am teaching him to value what I value.

RELIGIOUS BELIEFS

When I first began speaking with Sam, he told me on several occasions about incidents that he felt were mystical experiences. For example, on one occasion Sam told me that while lying in bed he imagined that he was in a coffin staring up at a spiritual light. Upon rising, he said, he found that his mother had had the same vision. I gave his story little mystical credence. I took his vision as an unconscious metaphor for his ambivalent feelings as a trauma survivor.

In dismissing the religious import of Sam's experience, I was demonstrating one of my own cultural biases. As a result of my upbringing and education, I have a firm yet ultimately unfounded belief in secular rationalism. According to my worldview, Sam's visions represent a possibly dangerous repression of emotions. In Sam's family, however, visions are respected as otherworldly phenomena, possibly communicating wisdom.

The fact that Sam and I have differing beliefs is not problematic until you realize that my position of authority in society and in our relationship allows for the potential that, even if subtly, I can subvert his religious holdings. Although I never directly challenge the authenticity of his experience—on the contrary, I gain Sam's trust by empathizing with his feelings of awe—my interactions around the issue once again indirectly tip my hand.

HUGH: So how did you feel in the coffin?

SAM: I don't know. It was kind of calm but I wanted to get out too.

HUGH: But you couldn't?

SAM: Yes.

HUGH: You felt trapped.

SAM: Yah [Case Notes, Nov. 6, 1995].

Although this exchange is perhaps a poor demonstration of nondirective technique, it still reveals the ways in which our biases can come across even within the least complex discourse. In this discussion, I create a number of indirect statements. First, I do not acknowledge any spiritual power of the vision; rather I tie it back, as always, to the mundane realm of emotions. Indirectly I am demonstrating my belief that this is essentially a question of human psychology. Second, I am forcing my position that Sam is experiencing ambivalent feelings. Originally Sam states a positive quality to the coffin experience: it is calm. However, with my cultural bias against death, I flip the meaning and turn "calm" into "trapped." Perhaps Sam agrees because he really did feel trapped. More likely, however, Sam took up my suggestion.

Despite my empathic responses to Sam's visions, he eventually stopped bringing them up in therapy. It is possible that Sam began to feel that I did not find them important. If this is the case, then it represents an unfortunate breakdown in communication. However, there is also the possibility that Sam has ceased to have or believe in the visions. Given Sam's increased understanding of therapy, I believe it is likely that his visions have been co-opted by psychological insight:

SAM: Talking to you has really helped me get through a lot of what I was going through.

HUGH: What kind of stuff?

SAM: Like, I don't know. I guess I was kind of still thinking about the "accident." And shit. I was really screwing up my grades and everything. I just couldn't think cuz of it [Case Notes, April 2, 1996].

Despite Sam's feelings of appreciation and the very real possibility that my counseling has helped to ease his pain, I cannot ignore the possibility that I have undermined a more important support in Sam's life. Religion is an important aspect of this young man's family. By training him in secular psychology and dismissing the spiritual world, am I setting him up to experience the same spiritual emptiness plaguing my own culture?

THE VALUE OF FAMILY

By teaching Sam the language of Western psychology, I am also potentially reproducing in his beliefs the Anglo-Saxon rationalist tradition. As Sam learns to identify and articulate unconscious motivations and develops an appreciation for the Western physics of the soul, he is learning a particular value system. He is learning to look for problems rather than solutions. He is learning to isolate his emotional problems rather than tie them into some larger context.

Perhaps chief among these cultural lessons and most inimical to his own culture, Sam has learned the primacy of the individual. When Sam first came to see me, he was frequently concerned about his relationships with his cousins and nuclear family. He often tried to negotiate relationships between his relatives. As a therapist, I often viewed Sam's feelings as "too enmeshed." I viewed Sam at a developmental stage, adolescence, in which he needed to differentiate his own needs and feelings from those around him. With this goal in mind, I attempted to help Sam see where his needs and responsibilities ended and his family's began.

As a result of our discussions, Sam did indeed begin to differentiate himself in the manner I had hoped. For example, when his cousins told him he could not come out with them because he had not showered, he stood up for himself, expressed anger, and went home. Although the situation was unfortunate, as a therapist I viewed it as largely positive. Sam was no longer the plaything of other people's whims.

Once again, however, this result demonstrates a clash between two cultural understandings. As an upper-class white, I have been raised to value the free will and independence of the individual above all else— above the needs of the family, above the sanctity of marriage, above the needs of the environment. In unreflective moments, I rejoice at Sam's supposed emancipation from his family.

In Sam's Dominican culture, from what I have gathered, the family has far more stature than in my world. The individual has loyalties and responsibilities that go beyond anything I understand. In encouraging Sam to step away from these loyalties, even in the interest of his happiness, I am interfering with a system with which I have had little experience. Moreover, although as a white person I can possibly afford to make my way in the world autonomously, I am tampering with a support that Sam, as a disenfranchised person in a racist society, might well need in order to cope and survive.

On April 21st, Sam and I moved into a series of sessions that serve to illustrate the power and dangers of my dominant discourse on family. For several weeks Sam had alluded to family problems and to his emerging understanding of those problems. At one point, when Sam searched for a word to describe his growing psychological insight, I, in an attempt to be helpful, forgot my "neutral" role and contributed my own concept:

SAM: It's like this big thing we never talk about. It's like—

HUGH: An elephant in the living room?

SAM: What?

HUGH: Uh. I just—it's an expression, sort of. It's like if you had an elephant in the living room and everyone walked around it but pretended it wasn't there.

SAM: Yah [Case Notes, April 21, 1996].

Although I had meant the expression purely as a helpful tool for Sam to express himself, I later realized what a value-laden metaphor I had chosen. An elephant is not a neutral description of a family problem. An elephant is a huge, awkward animal that you would not want in your living room. If you had one in your living room, it would be absurd not to talk about it and even more absurd not to get rid of it. Embedded in my image was a clear directive for Sam to follow a particular course, a course wholly informed by my Anglo-Saxon sensibilities about framing and handling family relations.

Whereas in the past Sam had mediated family relations through indirect means—for example, through gift giving, token gestures, and small arguments—following this discussion Sam became focused on having family discussions about ongoing problems. In subsequent sessions, Sam often returned to the metaphor of the elephant and proposed bringing his family in for therapy.

Sam's suggestion that he bring in his parents and siblings at first struck me as a great idea. For quite a while I had been developing the belief that Sam's recovery from trauma would be facilitated by improved communication in his family. When Sam suggested it, I thought it was an excellent sign, that it demonstrated that he was appreciating the efficacy of counseling. Of course, upon further reflection I began to see how I had planted the seeds of my own desired outcome.

IMPLICATIONS FOR CHANGE

In critical hermeneutic discourse, theorists warn that "a non-critical understanding simply continues, reiterates, and reproduces tradition, cultural values, ideology, and power structures" (Gallagher, 1992, p. 241). They also suggest, however, that a critical understanding can redress these reproductions, thus opening up the potential for social reform. In his long debate with Gadamer over this possibility, Habermas (1977) states that "this type of reflection is no longer blinded by the illusion of an absolute, self-grounded autonomy and does not detach itself from the soil of contingency on which it finds itself. But in grasping the genesis of tradition from which it proceeds and on which it turns back, reflection shakes the dogmatism of life-practices" (p. 357).

In other words, the critical hermeneuticists, like Habermas, suggest that critical reflection can liberate us from the blind reproduction of painful or socially harmful traditions. By isolating and articulating our own traditions, we can emancipate ourselves and others from their effects. This is what I have attempted in this research and through therapy this year. I have tried, through critical reflection, to witness the traditions that I bring into therapy and understand how they are being reproduced.

However, having concluded my research, I am left with grave doubts about my ultimate capacity to rise above my traditions. In the end, I am more moved than before by the arguments of theorists such as Gadamer who refute the critical hermeneuticists' suggestions that we can dismantle the very traditions we use to create meaning in the world.

While counseling Sam, I was already relatively steeped in an understanding of the potential for cultural "contamination" in the therapy setting. After all, I had already set up my research to examine it. However, upon reflection, I realized that those few contaminations that I could detect, such as the family and religious values that I highlighted, were embedded in the very nature of my therapy practice. In hindsight, I wonder: If I were to stop communicating my belief in unconscious motivations and individual independence, what would I be saying to Sam?

Perhaps the difficult answer to that question is that I should not be trying to counsel Sam. Perhaps even my most enlightened attempt at aid is ultimately just another expression of cultural hegemony. When I have attempted, as theorists such as Paulo Freire (1970, 1973) suggest, to change the power relationship between myself and my clients, I have run into the paradox that first spurred my research. As I attempt to share visible social power with my clients, I enter further into their trust and affect their beliefs on levels that they cannot often detect. The more I attempt to emancipate them, the more easily they may digest my way of thinking.

I suppose that ultimately it comes down to a matter of practicality. As students in a public high school with a 90 percent white staff, my clients are already being inundated and affected by a dominant cultural discourse. Their worlds are already being crippled by racism, classism, and the other inequalities in our society. Perhaps, as Lisa Delpit suggests, they will be better off equipped with a conscious knowledge of the discourse working against them and the facility to turn it to their benefit.

Ironically, my doubts about my own objectivity have opened up a whole new approach for me with clients. Throughout the year, I became so much more aware of the power differentials and the effects that my language has on individuals that I felt it necessary to become more honest about my positions. With guidance from my clinical supervisor and members of the hermeneutics class, I began opening up conversations about issues such as racism, sexism, and my own position as a member of a dominant culture. These conversations have created a new space for clients to discuss their frustrations and anger over all matters of oppression. Although I still have a great deal of disquiet over my potential role as a socializing agent, I can at least say that my investigation has left each of my clients, as well as myself, with an increased range of expression.

13

THE DANCE OF INTERPRETATION

The Dialectic of Loss and Connectedness

Anna Mackey

AS I BEGIN WRITING my phenomenological investigation, I am aware that May Day is approaching. As I struggle to find a place to begin to make sense of my year at Harvard, I am inexplicably reminded of a Maypole dance I participated in when I was in kindergarten. I was one of the many children who danced round and round the Maypole, in and out of one another, weaving our colorful strands together to produce, in the end, a beautiful design. This image, which I have not thought of in years, exemplifies many aspects of hermeneutic theory that we have studied in the practicum course and that I will attempt to use in order to better understand my experiences this year.

The first aspect is the endless circularity of hermeneutic theory and the lack of one "right" place to start (Packer and Addison, 1989). Next is the weaving together of many strands to produce a whole, which addresses my goal of weaving together my personal history, my work as a pair therapist, hermeneutic theory, and questions I have about my work in order to produce this paper. In addition, another aspect is Gergen's (1988) image of the dance: "We may view the spoken word (in this case) as an invitation to dance. If the dancers succeed in coordinating their actions, understanding has been achieved" (p. 47). I am drawn to this metaphor of the dance as a form of understanding. Finally, I am mindful of Gadamer's ([1962]

1976) notion of "loss of self" as a route to self-understanding. In much the same way as the individual dancer is lost in the dance, I am hoping to lose myself in the writing of this paper, in order to find myself more fully.

As I write this investigation, I look back over the year almost completed and am filled with a profound sense of loss—not only the losses that I brought with me to this experience, or the loss that I suffered in early December, but the loss of opportunities missed, relationships not formed, experiences not experienced. I am thinking specifically about lessons I was unable to learn because of time and energy constraints—in particular, all the opportunities to incorporate at my site what I learned in our course, and all the opportunities for learning from my students. I am thinking about classmates I could not find my way to engage with, whom I will never have the opportunity to know and learn from again.

Although I realize that feelings of loss are quite normal given the approaching termination of the year (LaFarge, 1990), I also believe that based on where I come from and what I bring, loss plays a large part in the work I have been doing at the Nichols School throughout the entire year. This theme of loss is one of the strands that I will weave into the design of my study, along with the many questions that have surfaced throughout this year. I will frame this investigation in the context of my work with Kiana, a second grade girl with whom I am working in pair therapy, tracing her development through pairs along with my own development as her pair therapist.

Any hermeneutic investigation involves an acknowledgment of the context in which interpretations are being made, and this includes the prejudices and experiences of the interpreter. It is important, therefore, to revisit my first paper, "Where I Come from, What I Bring," in order to articulate some of what I bring to my year at Harvard, my work at the Nichols School, and my interpretation of my process notes. As I wrote in that paper:

> The painful experiences of growing up with a mother who had cancer and then as a cancer patient myself combined to deprive me of a "normal" childhood and to isolate me from my peers. My mother's death several years later further deprived me of the essential support of the most important relationship in my life. I believe this childhood deprivation and isolation are the driving forces behind my love of, and desire to work with, children. This seems particularly true in the case of children who experience deprivation and isolation themselves.

INTRODUCTION TO THE NICHOLS SCHOOL

My work at the Nichols School is the focus of my Harvard experience. The Nichols School is an elementary school in the Boston public school system, which serves approximately 690 students from kindergarten through fifth grade.

In my work I have formed relationships with many children in various contexts: teaching a whole class, co-leading a small group, working with two pairs, and working one-on-one with two individuals. I have been challenged in many ways to rethink old assumptions and try new approaches. In some cases I have needed to question my role. Always I have questioned whether what I am doing is helpful or harmful. As the end of the year approaches, my questions clamor ever more loudly: What effect does my history of loss have on my work? Am I getting more out of this than the children? If the problems we are dealing with are really societal rather than individual problems, what is the use of treating individuals? and finally, Why am I here?

I have chosen to discuss my work with Kiana, who I saw in a pair with Leticia, in order to focus my phenomenological investigation of change over time. I will use process notes collected over the course of the year as the data for my investigation.

WALKING INTO THE NICHOLS SCHOOL

On October 14, my first day in the classroom, I wrote: "I was assigned to Mrs. F's class. There were at least five children with pretty serious academic and/or behavioral problems. I felt that I really connected to the children and I really liked Mrs. F a lot. She's very relaxed and accepting of them. Unfortunately, she told me that she has to have two major surgeries and will be leaving next Thursday *(permanently)*."

As soon as I found a place in the school where I felt comfortable, I lost the one person I actually liked. More significantly, the children in the class lost their teacher, who they loved and who was probably one of the most constant adults in their lives. I was concerned about how the children would handle this. The following week there was a substitute.

Toward the end of the week, the new permanent teacher, Mrs. H, introduced herself to the class. I had a chance to talk with her briefly and we really hit it off, which was a relief. I quickly settled into the second grade and began the process of acculturating to the school and learning the names of fifty-four new faces.

The next week Mrs. H started. Then, just as we were beginning our work together, another loss was suffered by the second grade. On Friday, November 4, I wrote: "Mrs. W came to the classroom and Mrs. H left. When she came back in, she told me that Mrs. N, one of last year's first grade teachers had died. She had lupus for six years, but no one knew that she was going to die soon." Many of the children in both classes had been in Mrs. W's class, and all who attended Nichols last year knew her. For the children who knew her and had recently lost Mrs. F, Mrs. W's death was quite a blow.

On the same day I wrote in my notes: "I realized that one of my biases is that children live with parents. I'm finding out that in many cases they don't. There are children in our classes living with grandparents, aunts, uncles, sisters, godparents, and foster parents." I have always known that some children do not live with their parents, but somehow this reality was just beginning to hit me. Perhaps because this knowledge now had a sweet, young face—in fact, many of them—that I was beginning to know and love, it suddenly had new meaning for me.

Throughout the months of October and November, I observed classes and assisted teachers, rotating between the two second grade classrooms. On Wednesdays I was in Mrs. R's room, and on Fridays, Mrs. H's. It was not until the end of November that we decided which children would receive services and managed to obtain signed permission slips from parents or guardians. Consequently, we did not begin any services until the beginning of December. That was when Kiana and Leticia were assigned to me. Because they were both in Mrs. H's class, I would see them on Wednesdays for pairs and then again on Fridays for the ethics and literacy program, Voices of Love and Freedom, and for classroom assistance. This schedule allowed me more time with them to further our relationships, and more opportunities to observe their interactions outside of the pair context.

Kiana and Leticia are both second grade, African American girls. Kiana was referred to pairs because she was having difficulty getting along with classmates, often behaving quite aggressively. Leticia, however, was very withdrawn, with a vague look in her eyes and a large grin plastered on her face. She did not talk very much and often sucked her thumb. It was decided by the second grade team that these two girls, who already knew each other, could benefit from being in a pair together.

Kiana came to pair therapy with a history of loss, both in the context of her larger life and in the pairs context. As she told me on the first day of pairs, her father was killed in a car accident; he had been drinking and driving. For unknown reasons, she does not live with her mother or siblings. She lives in Boston with her aunt and four male cousins. To make matters worse, her pair partner last year moved and had to leave school suddenly and unexpectedly. Coming so soon after the death of her father, the loss of her pair partner was a blow, from which she was unable to recover last year. When working one-on-one with her former pair therapist after her partner had left, Kiana broke down and cried uncontrollably, thereafter refusing to meet with or speak to her therapist ever again. Kiana brought this history with her to pairs this year, in addition to whatever other issues were currently in her life. Knowing her family history and the dangerous area in which she lives, I have no doubt that she had many issues. She is a feisty little "tough guy" who doesn't like to show any feelings or waste time talking.

Leticia also came to pairs with a history of loss. Her mother had died, reportedly from AIDS, and all of her siblings had been separated and placed in different foster homes, except for Leticia and her younger sister Denise, who live with their godmother (their mother's best friend). Leticia and Denise have a very antagonistic relationship. On several occasions, Leticia has told of injuries that Denise has inflicted on her. She has never spoken of a father. However, she has mentioned a brother who died and an older sister who, as she told me at our first and second meetings, has a boyfriend who "kills five-year-old children." Leticia, who has lost both parents, lives in "the projects," a very dangerous area, perhaps even more dangerous than the area in which Kiana lives.

INTERSECTIONS OF LOSS

On Sunday evening, December 11, I received word that my sister-in-law and her fiancé had been killed in a plane crash. This was a traumatic loss in its own right, but it also served to bring up memories and feelings associated with the loss of my mother. It also had implications for my schoolwork, my health, and my living situation (I needed to spend time with my husband in Maine, and I lived with my in-laws, who had just lost their only daughter). These new losses, as well as the old ones, have been woven inextricably throughout my experiences as a student at Harvard and as an intern at the Nichols School.

Wednesday, December 14, was our first pair therapy session. As soon as we sat down, Kiana and Leticia overwhelmed me with information about themselves, talking simultaneously and excitedly at once:

K dominated the conversation and L tried unsuccessfully many times to interrupt. While they were talking, both of them were very serious. This was especially noticeable with L, who completely lost her grin and vague wandering look. She looked so different that I could hardly recognize her. K also seemed different in the sense that she wasn't so angry while she talked about her life. . . . I am encouraged that they talked so much about their lives with no prompting on my part [Process Notes, Dec. 14, 1995].

There is much in just this small excerpt that could be interpreted, but what stands out for me right now is my interpretation that Kiana "wasn't so angry while she talked about her life." Upon further reflection, this seems incomplete. I would now add to my interpretation that she was not as angry because she was being listened to. It seems that there are not many people in Kiana's life who listen to her, and that being listened to allowed her to relax and reveal more of herself to me. I also believe that the initial outpouring of life histories was a way of saying, "This is who I am," which was necessary to their establishing a relationship.

In session two, we made Christmas cards together, and I gave one to each of the girls. Leticia talked more about being separated from her brothers and sisters and about her sister's "drug dealer boyfriend who kills five-year-old children." Kiana did not join in. As I wrote in my notes for that day, "I felt very inadequate. I wasn't sure how I should have handled this." This feeling of inadequacy became an underlying current of tension throughout my work at the Nichols School. I often felt that I did not know what I was doing and I hoped that my affection for the children would compensate for my lack of ability.

The week following session two was Christmas break. The following week I had bronchial pneumonia and was unable to work. Session four, January 18, took place in a different room because our room was taken. Although the girls didn't seem to mind, I did. The new room was huge and smelly, nothing like the small, intimate room we had been using. They had also chosen a new activity: a tennis ball and Velcro mitts. Kiana got really wild, throwing the ball around, climbing up on a chair and table. Later, when another pair therapist asked me if I wanted to stay in that room, "I said no, because it's so big and Kiana sometimes needs to be contained. The other room is better for that. Then she said maybe we can switch off weeks. I felt pressured to say yes" (Process Notes, Jan. 18, 1996).

The week following session four was my vacation. At this point, we had only met twice in a row without missing a week. Although that felt problematic, the vacation was necessary because I was struggling to get caught up with final papers and needed to spend time with my husband in Maine as we both tried to adjust to life without his sister, Lynn.

Session five occurred on Wednesday, February 1. Just prior to a power struggle for Kiana to put down her Gameboy, Leticia had been talking about moving. When Leticia was talking, I was focused on the fact that she said she would be moving in with her "mother." At this point, I had not managed to ascertain whether her mother was still alive. I didn't think she was, so I was surprised by this statement. What I failed to recognize was the significance of Leticia's statement that she was moving. Although I can't be sure, upon reflection I believe this may have had something to do with the incident with Kiana. Less than two weeks before (Process Notes, Jan. 18, 1996), her former therapist had told me about how Kiana had lost her pair partner the previous year, but I didn't realize that at the time. The memory of the loss of her previous pair partner, brought up by Leticia's announcement, may have been what prompted Kiana to withdraw. The fact that Leticia's move might mean she would leave did not even occur to me. Could this be because of my own fear of loss?

Wednesday, February 8, marked the first time that Kiana and Leticia ganged up on me. This is an example of what Selman (1989) calls a "shared experience":

> We played Dominoes the same as last week.... When K realized that I would finish last, she got up and ran to L and whispered to her. Then they both started saying, "Last one's a rotten egg and has to do the Funky Chicken!" A few minutes later, K started saying, "Ms. Mackey's gonna have to do the Funky Chicken!" and L joined in. When I actually did finish last, they screamed and laughed and made me do the FC. I did it for them and they thought that was hysterical. Later they ganged up on me again and started to taunt me, saying, "Ms. Mackey's gonna be the rotten egg! [Process Notes, Feb. 18, 1996].

I interpreted this incident as a positive sign. After only five meetings, Kiana and Leticia's relationship had progressed to a point where they no longer needed me to help them get along. I delighted in their delight at excluding me. I felt it was a good experience for them to realize that there are things I don't know that they can teach me. How often do children get a chance to teach a grown-up?

I also see a change in me as their therapist in this session. For the first time I allowed myself to be vulnerable with them. As it turned out, this seems to have had a positive effect on my relationship with Kiana. Two days later (February 10) I was in Mrs. H's class. I wrote in my Process Notes: "I wanted to hug K, but sensed that I should ask her first. I asked her if she would let me give her a hug and she scrunched up her face and body and said no. I said, 'No? Okay. Maybe someday you'll let me, cause I sure would like to give you a hug.' Later in the afternoon, she rushed up to me and threw her arms around me! I was thrilled." This felt like such a triumph to me. Kiana the "tough guy" had finally decided to let me in. It was quite a step for this child, who has lost so much, to allow me that kind of closeness.

The following week was school vacation. Several interesting things happened during session eight, which took place on Wednesday, March 1. Kiana said she hoped that Leticia would move away so she could have a new pair partner. At the time I couldn't understand where that remark came from. Of course, I am now inclined to think that she believed Leticia was going to leave soon anyway, and this was her way of dealing with this impending loss. I believe this was a sign of her inability to deal with the continuance of a relationship that she knew would soon be over. This may have just been her way of saying, "If you're leaving, then leave and get it over with." The conversation evolved from wanting a new pair partner to wanting to meet in the office instead of the room we were in. When I explained that we could not use that room because a first grade group met in there during our pairs time, Kiana got quite angry: "It's not fair. The first graders always get better stuff than we do. At home, my cousin gets a TV in his room and he's only in first grade and I don't get a TV in my room and I'm in second grade." I said, "It sounds like you got a bad deal," and she immediately said, "It *is* a bad deal, and it's a bad deal here, too!"

This was the first time Kiana had expressed any emotion about her personal life to me. I interpreted this as a good sign. As I write this, I realize one of my biases, that being able to express emotion is a good thing. However, I am forced to consider also how not expressing her emotions has probably been adaptive for her. This leads me to a question that has repeatedly come up over the course of my work at the Nichols School: Are we actually putting children at risk by intervening in their lives in ways that may not be adaptive for them? Is what's good for me good for them? These questions lead to yet another question: Am I really helping these children by creating the expectation that I will be here for them and then leaving? This is of particular concern in the case of children like Kiana who have already experienced so much loss in their lives.

The following week, March 8, was our ninth session. I took the girls outside for the first time. What a different experience that was! "They ran and yelled and shouted, they had so much energy! It made me wonder if they ever get to do things like this. Do they have anywhere they can run around at home? Are they ever allowed to make noise? The atmosphere of the school is so stifling. It was so obvious that they need to be able to do this regularly" (Process Notes, Mar. 8, 1996). Suddenly, I could see that Kiana's energy did not need to be contained as I had expressed earlier. I now understood that she needed to be able to cut loose and run, to use her energy instead of always trying to contain it. She has so much pent-up energy and unexpressed anger that the only way she can express it is to "act out." Why should this surprise me in the least?

After letting them run around and play outside for a while, it was time to go in. "As we walked around the building, L told me her mother had died. K talked about her mother, too. She said that she was in ———, some place she seemed to think I would know about. I couldn't tell whether it was a town, a hospital or a prison. They weren't really talking to each other. In fact, I'm not sure either one of them even heard the other one telling me these things because one or the other kept running ahead of us" (Process Notes, Mar. 8, 1996). It was heartening to see that they felt comfortable talking with me about their mothers. I had told a personal story about my mother's death the previous week. I had not intended to tell, but they asked if she had died and so I told them. This disclosure seemed to have made them feel comfortable enough to talk about their own losses.

During our tenth session, March 15, Kiana and Leticia had their biggest falling out. They had brought the box of dress-up clothes to pairs, and Kiana wanted Leticia to dress up and go outside. Leticia would not agree to this, possibly because Kiana had only shared two small squares of her chocolate bar with her, or possibly because she was tired of always doing what Kiana wanted. Kiana got angry. She said she wanted a new partner because L is "always" embarrassing her. I tried to get them to talk about this. Kiana refused even to consider talking.

At this point, I was interested in pursuing why Kiana felt embarrassed by Leticia. Were other children teasing her? Had her friendship with Leticia become a liability? At the end of this session I was left wondering how much I should be intervening in their squabbles. After reading "Friendship and Fighting" (Selman and others, 1992) I was more aware of how common and even normal conflict is in relationships. I was left wondering about my own discomfort with conflict and the extent to which I try to avoid it. How did that tendency affect my behavior with my pair? As it turned out, the question of how much to intervene became moot because this ended up being our last meeting together.

I could not work the next week because of illness. I was told that Leticia's "mother" had come in that Friday to talk to Mrs. F and our supervisor about how she was doing in school. When I returned to work on Wednesday, March 29, we were informed that Leticia had moved and was withdrawn from the school. This came as quite a shock, particularly knowing that her "mother" had just been in on Friday and had not mentioned moving or taking her out of school. Not only did Leticia leave suddenly and unexpectedly, but I missed my last possible chance to see her because I was sick. I felt devastated. Although I have focused on Kiana in my analysis because she is the one I still work with, Leticia was an integral part of our pair, and her unexpected departure was quite a blow to me.

Not only did Leticia leave before Kiana and I could say good-bye, but our last session ended with the biggest fight they had ever had. This was a difficult way for me to end. I was very upset that whole day and had a tough time dealing with Kiana because of it. Was this because I was unconsciously angry at her for fighting with Leticia the last time we met? When she heard the news, she did not seem upset at all. Maybe she could not allow herself to feel her feelings. Maybe the fight had made it easier for Kiana to let go of Leticia. Maybe the fight was brought on by the fact that Leticia was leaving. Maybe she was not surprised at all. Looking back on the times when Kiana talked about wanting Leticia to move away and wanting a new pair partner, I wonder if they did know, or at least suspect.

I was very concerned with how Kiana was dealing with this most recent loss, so I tried to meet with her to talk about Leticia's leaving. She refused to meet with me alone. After some questioning of how to continue, Kiana and I met with James, a boy from her class. James is an African American boy who has been sick repeatedly all year. The two children had a good time together. In fact they had almost a better time than Kiana and Leticia had ever had together. I was very disheartened by this. It was almost as if Kiana was flaunting how happy she was to be rid of Leticia. I felt completely excluded and alienated from this pair. I was also concerned that Kiana would not talk about Leticia with me.

Upon reflection, I now realize that my own feelings of loss were clouding my perception of Kiana's actions. She was only doing what she needed to do to deal with the situation. She had no responsibility to me or my feelings. I also suspect that she may have been angry at me for not being able to keep Leticia from leaving. She had tried to tell me that she did not want to meet, but I did not listen. I was afraid that if I didn't meet with her, she would feel abandoned by me. I still believe that. Shutting me out was the only way she knew how to take care of herself under the circumstances.

I decided that James should be Kiana's new pair partner, so Kiana, James, and I met again the next week. This new pair ended up being very good for James and he really blossomed in this context. That day, April 5, James and Kiana decided to play Twister. I wrote in my notes: "While they were putting away the game, K said, 'I wish L was here. She was new.' I said, 'I wish she were here too,' and then she said, 'She was new at Nichols this year, and now she's new somewhere else.' That was as far as that went. I was very happy that K had been able to express that she missed L because I was concerned that K was so traumatized that she couldn't deal with it at all."

In this moment I realized how far Kiana had come this year. Here she was, faced with a situation that was in many ways exactly like last year, yet she was able to express herself without falling apart or running away. Was this because of her work in pairs? I do not want to delude myself into thinking that I can take credit for her progress, but I believe that it has been useful for her to go back to the pairs context and have the experience of it being successful. When I think of it that way, it almost seems like a good thing that Leticia left. Repeating the loss of her pair partner has allowed her to rework her previous "failure" to produce a more favorable outcome. On Friday, April 7, I was in Mrs. H's classroom as usual:

> At some point, I was standing in the doorway and K came up to me and took my hands and said in her sweetest voice, "Ms. Mackey, I want to tell you something. . . . I wish L would come back to school here." This was said with great difficulty. I put my arm around her and said, "I know. I wish she would too." Then I had a thought. I said, "Maybe we could make a card to send to her next week." K said, "Yes! On Wednesday!" and ran back to her seat. I was so happy that she was able to talk about missing L [Process Notes, Apr. 7, 1996].

This was the second time that Kiana was able to express her feelings for Leticia spontaneously. I was very excited that she wanted to make a card because I believed it would help her achieve some closure on the loss of their relationship. However, as I had suspected, I was not able to get her interested in making a card for the next several weeks.

Because James was absent the following week, the next time I saw them together was April 26. Unfortunately, this was the day that we (the interns) had decided we would begin the termination process with our children. I had drawn a calendar showing the remaining dates when we would be meeting: "Early on, I tried to talk to them about termination. K immediately burst out, 'It's not fair! Everyone leaves!' to which J added, 'First Ms. F. . . .' K joined in with, 'Yeah, first Ms. F, then Ms. M, and now *you*!' She was very upset. I agreed wholeheartedly with all their complaints because I do think it's unfair that I would be leaving before them. This was tough to explain" (Process Notes, Apr. 26, 1996).

Feeling that I was contributing to a long list of losses was very hard to deal with and brought up questions, mentioned earlier, that I had been wrestling with for some time, particularly, Am I doing more harm than good by creating expectations and then leaving? At the same time, I also felt very gratified: "I must admit that I was touched to find that it mattered to K that I was leaving. All along I had been worried about how hard it would be for her to lose another person, but I hadn't really thought about how she might feel about me. It is good to know that I mean something to her" (Process Notes, Apr. 26).

Wednesday, May 3, was the last session prior to the completion of this chapter. During the session I reintroduced the idea of making the card for Leticia. Kiana was not interested. After a while, I said, "Well, I think I'll make a card for Leticia even if you don't," and then asked her what color paper she thought I should use. After I had gotten the paper and the markers, I asked her what color marker she thought I should use. Before too long, she was working on the card with me. In the end, she wouldn't allow me to do anything except write the words. She drew many multicolored hearts filled with "I Love You" on the front, back, and inside of the card. By the time we were finished, we had a six-page card for Leticia telling her how much we loved her and missed her.

I now feel sure that I have been able to help Kiana. Although we have four more weeks in which anything could still happen, I feel complete in the sense that I was able to help Kiana through her process of dealing with the loss of Leticia. The fact that she was able to express herself at all feels like a triumph. That she was willing to commit her feelings of affection and loss to pictures and words seems like a miracle. This is far more than I ever could have expected from such a wounded little girl, but no less than I had hoped for. I feel very privileged to have played a part in Kiana's development. Although I cannot know what the long-term effects of my intervention in her life might be, I now feel confident that I have done more good than harm.

QUESTIONS LOST AND FOUND

I revisit the Maypole dance described at the beginning of this chapter. To an observer of the dance, the design that would ultimately be produced was not readily apparent. Not until the dance was over and the strands were woven completely together could the whole pattern be distinguished. In addition, as a participant in the dance and a creator of the pattern, I was too close to see the pattern taking form. In much the same way, the outcome of pair therapy was not readily apparent while it was in progress. Similarly, while involved in the events of pair therapy, I was often too close to comprehend their meaning. However, with the benefit of the passage of time and the increasingly emergent context, I was able to situate these incidents in their larger context and arrive at some understanding of their significance.

The paper-writing process has provided me with the opportunity to review my notes and reflect on the events of the past year. The notes have been invaluable in allowing me to revisit many details that would otherwise have been lost. Using hermeneutic theory and my questions to structure my analysis has led to the reinterpretation of many incidents. This reflection and reinterpretation have been essential to the process of unifying my educational and work experiences of this year and integrating them into the larger context of my life.

As I approach the end of my final paper, I complete the hermeneutic circle by returning again to the two most pressing questions raised before: If the problems we are dealing with are really societal rather than individual, then what is the use of treating individuals? And in the face of such huge societal forces, can my work ever make a difference? I share with you a well-known story that illustrates beautifully my answers to these questions.

> As the old woman walked down a Spanish beach at dawn, she saw ahead of her what she thought to be a dancer. The young woman was running across the sand, rhythmically bending down to pick up a stranded starfish and throwing it far into the sea. The old woman gazed in wonder as the young soul threw the small starfish from the sand into the water. The old woman approached her and asked why she spent so much energy doing what seemed a waste of time. The young woman explained that the stranded starfish would die if left

until the morning sun. "But there must be thousands of miles of beach and millions of starfish. How can your effort make any difference?" The young woman looked down at the small starfish in her hand, and as she threw it to safety in the sea she said, "It makes a difference to this one" [source unknown].

And so it is that I will continue to be drawn to helping individuals, in the belief and the hope that it makes a difference to *this one*. As I had hoped, in the writing of this paper I was able to lose myself and thereby come to some understanding. That is not to say that I now have all the answers. In fact, quite the opposite is true. I have raised many questions but have answered only a few, and those few only for the moment. As Packer and Addison (1989, p. 35) have stated, "So although hermeneutic inquiry proceeds from a starting place, a self-consciously interpretive approach to scientific investigation does not seek to come to an end at some final resting place, but works instead to keep discussion open and alive, to keep inquiry under way."

PART FOUR

THE SOCIALIZING INFLUENCE OF LANGUAGE

14

"THE RULES OF THE GAME" APPLIED TO PLAY, POWER, AND POLITICS

INTERPRETATION AND LANGUAGE ARE INEXTRICABLY linked within the tradition of hermeneutics, just as they are within all forms of applied development work. Even nonverbal techniques for promoting healthy development, such as exercise, meditation, and silent forms of play, are mediated by internalized linguistic definitions of these activities. We direct ourselves in exercise and meditation through the language we have developed for each aspect of our participation. To be quiet or silent, for example, means something particular to each of us, based on our association to the words *quiet* and *silent*. Perhaps it means "to be at peace," or "to be removed from the noise and overt chaos of daily life." Whatever it means to the individual, our nonverbal activities are partially guided by our internalized definitions of words that capture what is suggested by not speaking. We do not need to speak or hear to experience the socializing influence of language.

In this cluster of case studies, the function of language is shown in a variety of interpretive contexts. In "Language and Politics: Translating the Rules of the Game—Ayer, AHORA y Mañana," John Ramírez Jr. and Marco Antonio Bravo explicitly address the political influence of language through their work with Latino immigrant students attending a public high school. Their study examines the barriers confronted by immigrant students who cannot functionally "speak the language" of the dominant culture, which in turn prevents them from competitively playing the education game. By helping their students to enhance their English speaking and writing skills, Ramírez and Bravo assist in opening up a broader world of opportunity for youth who might otherwise remain alienated from, and misunderstood by, an educational system with a limited vocabulary of its own.

In "Entering Play: Lessons of Grief, Joy, and Growth," Tara Edelschick provides a very different view of the power of language. Through her grief work with middle school students who have lost loved ones, Edelschick examines the power of creating a safe and even playful space in which children can speak about death and the pain, sorrow, and mystery that surrounds it. Without a safe place for shared expression, Edelschick finds, the weight of loss is magnified. By creating a common language for discussing death, the memory and spirit of deceased loved ones are granted a public space in the ongoing lives of the survivors. In this sense, the socializing influence of language is eternal, continuing beyond the physical existence of individual speakers. Especially poignant in Edelschick's study is the role of play in creating safety, spontaneity, and ordinariness, experiences of particular significance when dealing with an issue as profound and potentially uncomfortable as the topic of death.

From Ramírez and Bravo's discussion of politics to Edelschick's investigation into grief, joy, and loss, Randy B. Hayward takes us, in "What's Love Got to Do with It? Combining the Influences of Race and Love to Create an Effective Black Counselor," into the languages of race and love as they apply to his counseling work with elementary school students. As an African American male who has experienced the pervasive influences of racism on his own development and that of his family, Hayward approaches his work with deeply ingrained assumptions of linguistic barriers between himself and white students, and between black students and white teachers and counselors. Initially Hayward assumes that "talking black" will help him to connect with his black student-clients, which in turn will help him to connect these students to the larger educational process. He comes to find, however, that although the experience and language of racial identification are certainly important parts of counseling and education, there is a language of love and respect that is also powerful, and too frequently absent, in adult efforts to work with youth. As Hayward experiences love and respect crossing racial lines in his work and in the work of a white colleague, he recognizes the limitations placed on applied development work when the power of one's influence becomes too narrowly defined by self-identifying categories such as race and gender.

The cluster concludes with Robert W. Leary's "play on language," entitled "Theatrical Dialogue: A Hermeneutic Analysis of Change in One Act." What appears on the surface to be a much lighter look at language is, on a deeper level, a remarkable synopsis of the contents of this book. Leary turns the concept of the hermeneutic circle into a group of wise, persistent, and overly serious actors in his play on language. He utilizes the structure of the theatrical play (or performance) to exemplify how we become lost in language, lost in the lines that come to define how we think, feel, and interact with one another. As Gadamer, one of the key members of Leary's hermeneutic circle, argues, we become lost in language and then directed by it outside of our awareness. Similarly, a theatrical performance, like other forms of play, is most powerful when its actors become lost in their roles, when they become absorbed to the point that they are no longer acting in a fully self-conscious way but rather are acted upon by the play itself, taken up in the rhythm and purpose of something larger than they themselves dictate.

Although Leary's theatrical dialogue deals most explicitly with the connections between language and play, each of the cases in this cluster addresses that fundamental connection on some level. The "play of language" and the "language of play" are essential concepts for all of development, but they have particular implications for work with youth. As the scholar and youth advocate Karen VanderVen (1996) argues, play is central to the culture of childhood, and a childhood culture lacking in the richness of play compromises opportunities for youth to develop flexible strategies for communication, relationship building, and creativity development. But play shares more with language than simply the context it creates for expression; it shares a common developmental history.

DEVELOPMENTAL COMMONALITIES OF LANGUAGE AND PLAY

Learning to speak and learning to play both entail learning rules to the point where they can be forgotten or internalized. The *forgetfulness of being,* according to Hans-Georg Gadamer ([1962] 1976), is the phenomenon of being supported and guided by the totality of life experiences that are learned, reinforced, and stored away for use when called upon. We cannot, of course, consciously hold onto the vast supply of information that we learn on a day-by-day, moment-by-moment basis. As a result, our being is defined largely by what we have learned and temporarily forgotten, rather than by those thoughts, feelings, and experiences that we are aware of in any given moment. Fortunately, human well-being does not require that we consciously remember every step of the prior learning processes required for successfully meeting current challenges. We have the luxury of being guided in part by that which we have forgotten.

How does one reach the point of functional forgetfulness? Through rules, according to Gadamer—the *rules of the game* that initially guide us in the development of complex activities, including the activities of language and play. According to Gadamer, the *language game* develops similarly to other forms of structured play. The infant, equipped with the capacity to eventually learn speech, initially stumbles into life experiences capable only of feeling, grabbing, and uttering. Through the ongoing coaching of parents or other caregivers, she begins to connect particular utterances with specific experiences or objects. As the proper utterances are linked with their appropriate experiences and objects, they are reinforced by the caregivers. Gradually the developing child comes to understand that certain utterances or words stand for certain experiences and objects. As that understanding evolves further, and progressively more words are connected with a progressively larger array of experiences, the child begins to follow a set of rules: by consciously uttering certain words, she is likely to bring about certain responses. Eventually, the words, experiences, objects, and responses become linked in the child's mind. The words and their associated experiences become one: a word no longer stands for something, it becomes that thing.

Whereas early on the child struggles to recall the proper utterance, she eventually employs speech with little conscious reflection; the use of words becomes virtually automatic. She no longer struggles to remember the rules; they are now internalized, guiding her toward easier access to those experiences she desires. The forgetfulness of being frees her conscious energy from the need to search for such basic words as "mother" or "father," allowing her to use that energy to learn new words, or more complex rules for playing an increasingly complex game. This process of learning the rules of the language game, according to Gadamer, is repeated throughout our lives across domains of experience, as we confront new activities with their own set of governing rules.

Through his development of the game metaphor, Gadamer argues that our early struggles to master the basics of language result not only in the eventual acquisition of a vast and immensely complicated set of linguistic rules, but also in the inevitability of being ruled by language. The language game we learn to play ultimately comes to play us. We are restricted in our knowing of the world by the very language we create to describe it. Just as the young child accesses opportunities for satisfaction through language, older children and adults also access opportunities in the world through their recognition of those opportunities via language. It can be argued, then, that our ability to know the world and to take advantage of its opportunities is directly related to our ability to understand it, and our understanding of it is both opened up and limited by language.

As discussed in Chapters One and Two of this volume, Gadamer ([1962] 1976), describes the always-developing composite of learned and internalized experiences as the *forestructure of understanding*. This forestructure stores the rules of language that guide our understanding of any new experience. As described by the hermeneutic circle, we are thrown into new experiences from our current forestructure of understanding, which is then revised based on what we learn from the new experience. In this sense, the language-based rules of the game are always evolving.

We can see, then, how language shares the structure of play. Leary's theatrical dialogue shows how actors initially struggle to learn their lines. At first the lines allow the actors to fit uneasily into the flow of the play. With coaching from the director, however, the actor learns rules or exercises for connecting the lines to particular emotional or existential experiences. As the actor begins to access these experiences through the passionate delivery of her lines, the experiences become part of the play, part of her lines, part of her. The more authentically, or unselfconsciously, the actor can access experience, the less she needs to rely on the conscious use of her lines or particular techniques. The genuine actor, from this perspective, is one who loses herself in the play—one who, as Gadamer states, becomes lost in play. This is similar to the fluent speaker who becomes lost in speech, who is guided by speech more than speech is guided by her.

The play of Leary's theatrical dialogue is similar in structure to more natural forms of child and adult play. We learn rules for playing with blocks, playing house, playing with dolls and trucks, playing basketball, and playing the stock market. In each case, we initially struggle to master the rules of those games, which eventually come to play us. The child playing with blocks can get lost in her play, as can the investor playing the stock market. With every experience of being lost in play, a sense of freedom or buoyancy is gained. We can let our guard down as the rules become automated. In doing so, we are freer to *be*, freer to be played by the pleasures and opportunities of life. But at what risk? Is there a danger to the forgetfulness of being? Are we played against our will, or behind our backs, by the socializing influence of language? As the chapters in this cluster indicate, the rules of the game, because they are ruled by language, have dramatic implications for the development and education of youth.

LANGUAGE, PLAY, AND POWER

If, as Gadamer suggests, we are socialized into the rules of language, which then socialize us into the rules of additional games, such as the games of relationships, education, employment, and life opportunities in general, what are the implications of language development in schools? As discussed earlier in the introduction of Ramírez and Bravo's contribution to this cluster, these authors discovered profound limitations faced by the Latino immigrant students in their study, resulting from problems with writing and speaking English, that were due in part to a school system that was not responding to their unique needs, strengths, or interests. Because Ramirez and Bravo's students did not possess the language skills required to successfully compete in their English-speaking school, they were not only undereducated, they were also systematically disempowered in a variety of ways. According to the authors, their students experienced school as an alienating context, remote from their everyday lives. As a result, development for these students occurred primarily outside of school, and apart from any context of formal education.

It can certainly be argued that formal schooling is not a prerequisite for healthy development, given the current status of many of our public school systems. It can also be argued, however, that development devoid of adequate educational opportunities restricts a young person's capacity to define more broadly the alternatives for healthy living. Ramírez and Bravo cite the revolutionary educator Paulo Freire (1970), who argues in his groundbreaking work *Pedagogy of the Oppressed* that economically poor people require the "tools" of language above and beyond all else if they are to have an opportunity to compete in contemporary society. Freire's stance is similar in some respects to that of Jurgen Habermas (1971, [1983] 1990; see Chapter Two), who points to the distortions of language that keep people separated and, in the case of the economically poor, oppressed. Only through the development of communicative competence, Habermas argues, can people come together across differences to resolve their problems and create mutual opportunities for advancement. Development of such competence, however, requires contexts that promote it. Unfortunately, as

Ramírez and Bravo point out, our schools all too frequently are not those contexts.

Critical educator Lisa Delpit (1988) has long argued that the relationship between language and power is essential to public school education. Black children and other children of color, according to Delpit, must learn the rules of the game that dictate success within the white power structure in this country. Delpit makes the argument that white educators typically take the rules for granted, because those with power are the least aware of it. By taking the rules of operation for granted, by not making them explicit even to ourselves, we cannot, from this perspective, teach them to those who need them most—the racially and economically disenfranchised students in our schools.

Delpit's stance is consistent with Gadamer's notion of the forgetfulness of being. Just as we learn, forget, and are directed by the rules of language, we also learn, take for granted, and are guided by the power structures into which we are educated and otherwise socialized. Once we achieve power, we assume it and become less cognizant of its influence. If we as applied developmentalists are to remain ethical in our work with children, however, we cannot afford to remain blind to our authority or to the lack of power experienced by the youth with whom we work. In a certain sense, whether we are teachers, counselors, or youth workers in some other capacity, we must attempt to reverse the natural process of the forgetfulness of being, and remain aware of the rules into which we have been socialized and that have brought us privilege. The students we counsel and educate deserve the opportunity to learn those rules as well.

Hayward's study provides a detailed look at the intersecting roles of power and language in counseling and teaching. Discussing his experience as a black man attending Harvard University, Hayward states that he initially viewed himself as a "savior" for many of the African American children he counseled in his elementary school training experience. His race, dialect, hairstyle, and connections to the university all, he believed, would serve to help black children bridge the gap from where they were to where they might one day be. What he learned, however, was that his power to connect children with health and opportunity was located less in his race, his appearance, and his affiliations than in the content of his interactions. Hayward witnessed what he deemed to be demeaning and humiliating treatment of many children in the public school where he trained. Observing language being used as a powerful tool of destruction within certain segments of the school, he sought to reverse that process through his work.

Interestingly, Hayward began to see the extent of his own power through his ability to connect with a white student. Having originally desired to work strictly with African American children, he felt somewhat disappointed by his assignment to work with this student. Upon further reflection, however, he recognized that his resistance stemmed from his assumption that he had little to offer students who were from different racial backgrounds. Initially, when the student responded positively to him, Hayward attributed the student's affect to a desire to get out of class: after all, in counseling one did not have to do school work! However, as their relationship developed further, Hayward began to see that the student's responses to him were genuine, and based more on their interactions than on his external qualities. As he became aware of his power, he began to develop and use it more explicitly, not only with his white student but with his black students as well.

Hayward identified the locus of his power in *love*, which he framed as the antithesis of the disrespect he witnessed in some of the students' interactions with teachers. Love, in Hayward's language, consists of genuine respect and care for the children, communicated through firm expectations ("tough love"), consistently positive treatment, and clear statements of support and affection. One can take from his study the lesson that positions of authority come with the power to love respectfully. In the world of public education, a language of love can be complicated, and therefore needs to be thought through carefully. From Hayward's perspective, that thinking must occur, because to withhold love, respect, and affection is to disempower students, to indicate to them that they are not worthy of such responses. Just as those of us in positions of authority can forget the rules that got us here, we can also forget the power we have to genuinely uplift children through the quality of our interactions. Those in power, as Delpit argues, are the least aware of it. Hayward makes us wonder how many of us are truly aware of our power to love and to help children feel loved.

As the power of love is central to Hayward's investigation, the power of grief expressed through play is at the core of Edelschick's study. Although we are socialized into languages that help us to learn math, to make friends, and eventually, if we are lucky, to fall in love and hold a job, few of us receive adequate training in the expression of profound grief. Through her group work with middle school youth who had lost parents, siblings, and other family members, Edelschick discovered play as an entrée to communicating and grappling with those issues that are most difficult to talk about. By lightening her grief work through playful storytelling, drawing, and game playing, she enabled her students to release some of the tension that comes from holding pain inside. Through the release of finding and enjoying an outlet for that grief, the group members began to talk—of loss, happy memories, funny times together, anger, and the willingness to continue living in the absence of a loved one.

Edelschick's findings are as uplifting as they are saddening. Through her students' discussions of deciding whether to touch or kiss the bodies of their deceased family members as they lay in their funeral caskets, and through debates over the process of dead bodies decaying to skeletal form, the reader is pulled into the uncanny side of loss. By expressing this side of their experiences, Edelschick's students create a larger context for discussing the other sides, the sides that are not so uncanny but rather are brutally painful in the most realistic of terms.

An example of such realistic brutality is the story of Edelschick's student Elaine, who discusses the pain of living with the vivid image of her drug-addicted mother dying alone in a motel room. By sharing her pain with the group, Elaine was able to reconnect with her mother in important ways: she was able to connect with her through grief, and we might speculate, through breaking down the walls of secrecy and the shame that accompanies that secrecy. The grief group afforded Elaine a safe space in which to be public with her emotions about her deceased mother, and to do so in a manner that made room for a whole range of expression. Just as important for Elaine, the presentation of her mother's life and death made possible the sharing of related stories by the other group members. Elaine was not only supported in her grief, she was also able to open up possibilities for supporting others. This latter step, we would argue, helped her to feel that she was enhancing life, a profound experience for a young person confronted with the challenging task of grieving a complicated death. Edelschick poignantly captures the uniqueness of this opportunity through the stories of her students.

How does Edelschick's investigation shed light on the relationships among language, play, and power? Her work reveals the limitations inherent in the ordinary uses of language. The rules of language—both those remembered and those forgotten—can be of little help during times of unusual challenge and crisis. This can be especially true when we attempt to coerce language to work in a manner that contradicts our emotional state or existential disposition, or when there do not seem to be words available to capture what we are experiencing. On such occasions, play may be able to move beyond the confines of traditional language. Even though structured by language, the sometimes seemingly unstructured nature of free play can allow us to break the rules of ordinary expression, to move beyond the confines of the seriously spoken word. Edelschick's work exemplifies this phenomenon. By letting go of the control of language, play was given room to create openings—to create, as Edelschick says, a safe space to be. The safety of that space eventually made room for the more serious contents of speech.

We see here the reciprocity of language and play. Just as language guides play and allows us to understand its meaning, play can expand the limits of language; it can take us to new arenas of expression that allow for the expansion of understanding and future expression. Edelschick's students developed an expanded vocabulary for describing and understanding the experiences of life through their play in the group. Together they developed a broadened vocabulary for understanding loss. To do so, however, they first had to lose themselves, in the uncontrolled buoyancy of play.

Edelschick's work also illustrates the role of power in both language and play. She shows how language has the power to constrain expression, just as it has the power to make it possible. Play, too, has the power to constrain and make possible. It can constrain more serious expression, which leads many teachers and counselors to curtail it in the classroom and in counseling sessions. Genuine play requires empowered players—players who are free to participate fully, to help set the tempo, to get lost in the rhythms of spontaneity. But from where does such empowerment come? Quite frequently it comes from adults in positions of authority, such as parents, teachers, and other applied developmentalists. How do we who hold such positions exercise our authority to promote play, to help develop genuine players? We must start, it seems, with an understanding of the role of play in youth (and adult) development, and that start must be followed by our own willingness to relinquish some of our hard-earned authority. To let children play is to let go of control. To let go of control in a responsible fashion is to express faith in the development of self-control. Through the loss of self in play, the emergence of a more developed self is made possible.

FROM THE POWER OF PLAY TO THE POLITICS OF POWER

Ramírez and Bravo's work with Latino high school students provides further examples of the power of play for opening doors to the development of deeper human connections. Many of their male students were initially hesitant to communicate authentically through the language of the mainstream educational institution, a language that had too frequently left them feeling alienated and marginalized. Through the formation of a basketball team, Ramírez and Bravo began to reach a number of students who otherwise would likely have remained distanced. But the play of basketball, like that of all team sports, can evolve into a power hierarchy that can be both empowering and disempowering, depending of course on one's place in the pecking order. As a microcosm of the larger society, basketball requires an ongoing negotiation of the rules and roles of the game. Who is allowed to do what and when? Under what conditions does one pass or shoot? How important is winning versus "just playing"? Answers to all of these questions are dependent on the community of players.

As play becomes more organized, it often becomes more politicized. Organized play typically requires leaders. Leaders require followers or a constituency. In a certain sense, as play becomes more advanced, it begins to require work. And in an odd way, as we grow more sophisticated, it takes concentrated work to keep play within the realm of fun. As we learn to play the game of work, it can come to control and even deprive us of the sense of play. Ramírez and Bravo came to experience the hard work of playing basketball with a diverse group of high school students. The students had different ideas about how to play and what constituted good play. In addition, the team was composed of members from different Latino ethnic groups, which resulted in the development of an ethnically based political struggle within the basketball game.

Recognizing the basketball game for the political power it wielded, Ramírez and Bravo expanded their efforts from the school gym to the home playground of two of their discontented players. By doing so, they relinquished control of the game and communicated a willingness to play on the home turf of their students. This move proved to be a turning point in their work. The students were empowered to host their counselors in their own community. By extending their willingness to go to the students rather than insisting that the students come to them, Ramírez and Bravo implicitly acknowledged the value their students held for them. This was an educational experience far removed from those that the students had known previously. It suggested to them that they were meaningful to adults connected with the school, and as such it allowed them to return to school with an enhanced sense of self-worth.

We view the community-based work of Ramírez and Bravo as a political act, one stemming from the power dynamics that evolved during the course of playing basketball. The authors used the game of basketball to generate a sense of connection with their students. As that connectedness became politicized through the development of specific basketball roles, the authors validated the students' political stances by going to them to further negotiate a continuing relationship. Ramírez and Bravo could easily have used their power as school professionals to negotiate a different deal with the students: they could have bargained to keep the play situated on their own turf, the public school grounds. By taking the play to their students, they reversed the typical roles. They said, in a sense: "We are your constituency; we are here to serve your needs; you are the ones with the power." This is a difficult shift for most adults working with youth. It exemplifies the play of politics in youth development work, as well as the politics of play.

Hayward's case study presents an additional view of the politics of power in applied development work. As discussed earlier, he was struck by the capacity of teachers to use their power in a manner that he deemed counterproductive to the well-being of particular students. Why, we might ask, would a teacher use the disciplinary strategy described by Hayward of requiring a student to stand facing the wall with his back to the rest of the class? Was the strategy selected because the teacher felt it was likely to help the student to perform better in school by serving as a deterrent against misbehavior, late assignments, and the failure to complete homework? Or was it simply a form of punishment inflicted by a noncaring, frustrated teacher, one who should not be teaching "other people's children" (Delpit, 1988)?

Whatever the intentions of this teacher, he was likely socialized into his use of power the way children are socialized into language and play. He presumably worked hard to learn the organizing rules of teaching, including the management of student behavior. He perhaps was and is guided by a distinct philosophy of teaching and discipline. One wonders about the extent to which such a philosophy could be articulated. How has it evolved over his years of teaching? What has been internalized and forgotten? What is the structure of his "forgetfulness of being"—his "forgetfulness of being a teacher"? Are teachers and counselors capable of being lost in the power of teaching and counseling similarly to children's being lost in play? If so, what do the children lose in the process?

The questions posed here are not designed to elicit immediate answers. They are questions that have emerged from four very productive and provocative investigations. The best results of a well-done study, according to Gadamer, are more interesting questions. Each study in this cluster leaves us with important questions. We hope they do the same for you, the readers.

POLITICS AND ETHICS: IMPLICATIONS FROM CRITICAL HERMENEUTICS

If we are socialized into play, power, and politics by language, and if our playful, powerful, and political actions therefore reflect the rules of the games we have learned and long ago forgotten, what responsibility do we as educators and applied developmentalists have for critically examining our current positions? From the perspective of critical hermeneutics, particularly the work of Habermas (1971), it can be argued that we have an ethical responsibility to reflect systematically on those biases that have become deeply ingrained and therefore influence our communication outside of our awareness. Shaun Gallagher (1992) has expanded on the work of Habermas and others in his application of a range of hermeneutic approaches to education. In his overview of critical hermeneutics, Gallagher points to critical self-reflection as the espoused antidote to Gadamer's "forgetfulness of being." We have a deep responsibility, from this perspective, to counter the hidden forces that would allow us to hinder, unreflectively, the well-being of others.

Because of the inordinate power adults have over children and youth in education and applied development work, it seems only natural that those of us in these positions should critically examine on an ongoing basis the biases we bring to this work. A bias of critical hermeneutics, and one that guides much of our work, is that the education and development of children and youth, particularly those from low-income backgrounds, should be marked by overt strategies that help them recognize and overcome barriers to their well-being. Quite frequently, these barriers exist within applied developmentalists. Each of the four studies presented in this cluster uncovered barriers to growth that existed within the authors themselves. For Bravo and Ramírez, it was the lack of recognition of the cultural differences that existed within the larger Latino community. Edelschick was initially blocked by her bias that the grief group would benefit most from a carefully structured curriculum. Hayward saw his racial background as an impediment to working with white students, and overestimated it as the primary strength he possessed for working with black youth. Progress in Leary's work was temporarily slowed by his failed attempt to provide support to a Latina colleague who perceived his efforts as patronizing.

In each of these examples, the authors were able to uncover barriers to their progress through critical reflection. But critical reflection was part of their training. What happens to us long after our training has ended and there are no longer papers to write? Will we continue to reflect on our practice in a manner that helps to uncover prejudices that would otherwise remain hidden and restrictive to our work? These are more than questions for thought; they are questions of ethics.

As authority figures in the lives of children, applied developmentalists have an ethical responsibility not to harm children, not to hinder them, and not to make them pay for our ignorance. Within this line of ethical reasoning, we would argue that practice unreflected upon is unethical practice. Given our understanding of the development of language articulated at the outset of this chapter, we believe that all applied developmentalists are at tremendous risk of being played by the games we so painstakingly come to learn. We are at risk of becoming comfortable in our positions, or if not comfortable, overly accommodating to them. That is, we are at risk of moving through work the same way every day, of coming to see youth less as people to be genuinely cared for and more as "clients," "appointments," or "responsibilities" that take up our time. We are at risk for this even if we entered our fields with the best intentions. We are at risk for this because we are human. And because we are human, we are obligated to take ethical action to protect ourselves from placing others at risk. That action is the critical reflection that occurs through the multiple modes of dialogue articulated in Chapter Two.

Finally, from our perspective, applied development work of all sorts is both political and ethical by definition. By taking a position designed to foster the healthy development of youth, we have taken an implicit oath to improve the educational and life conditions that support us. Holding the position of teacher, for example, is a responsibility that comes with extraordinary political and ethical implications. Teachers are placed in the role of preparing "other people's children" (Delpit, 1988) for the world that awaits them. The ethical responsibilities that accompany this role speak for themselves. Politically, teachers have the responsibility of honestly responding to the best interests of their constituencies: the children themselves and their families. Similar arguments can be made for counselors, social workers, and other applied developmentalists.

Through the four investigations that follow, the rules of the game are applied to play, power, and politics from various angles. Our hope is that you, the readers, will take from these applications something of value for your own work: perhaps an idea, perhaps a helpful interpretation, but certainly, to borrow from Leary's theatrical dialogue, a question—a question that leaves you uneasy enough to push the dialogue a little further.

15

LANGUAGE AND POLITICS

Translating the Rules of the Game—
Ayer, AHORA y Mañana

John Ramírez Jr. and Marco Antonio Bravo

WE DECIDED TO COLLABORATE in the formation and writing of our phenomenological investigation for several reasons. First, having both grown up in Salinas, California, our worldviews stem from our agricultural experiences. Additionally, both of our educations from kindergarten through grade twelve were racially segregated, with the majority of students being Chicanos. Both of these factors have shaped our perspectives and our approaches to education and counseling. In addition to our similar backgrounds, our different disciplines have allowed for a collaborative analysis of the work that we conducted at our site: AHORA. Marco A. Bravo's academic background is rooted in language and literacy, while John Ramírez Jr.'s comes from a counseling perspective. These lenses, because they are both complementary and challenging to each other, allow us to view AHORA in a more holistic manner.

INTRODUCTION

AHORA! Bridge to the Future was established because the needs of the Latino students at Caplan High School were not being met. These students had, and continue to have, the highest percentage of school dropouts, the lowest SAT scores, and the lowest number of college applicants among the Caplan student body. Concilio Hispano, a non-profit, multiservice agency committed to providing programs to support the self-sufficiency and advancement of the Latino community, established the AHORA program to improve the plight of Latino students and to serve as an advocate for these students within the school system. The goal of AHORA is to help Latino students reach their potential by offering them tutoring, mentoring, counseling, alternative educational programs, and drug use education. AHORA is also committed to making the Caplan School accountable for its failure with respect to Latino students. The goal is to bend the system to fit students instead of bending the students to fit the system.

Though we have had to navigate through the sometimes rough waters of the program and the school politics, the learning experience we have received through interpreting AHORA's situation has served us well in uncovering new truths and understandings. Woolfolk, Sass, and Messer (1988) address the process we faced throughout the year: "One should use the standard hermeneutic methods of interpretation to generate hypotheses, but then one must subject these to relentlessly skeptical criticism" (p. 10). Throughout the year we have subjected our hypotheses about the program and the students to critical scrutiny.

GUIDING PHILOSOPHY OF AHORA

AHORA's director, Nelson Salazar, is responsible for the quality of the service provision and for ongoing evaluation of the program. It is imperative to discuss his philosophy within this study because it shapes the AHORA program. We interpret the director and the program through the lens of ontological hermeneutics (interpretation of being). The language Nelson uses to construct and oversee the program helps to define him, which in turn influences the manner in which the program is shaped. This is consistent with the hermeneutic framework discussed by Woolfolk, Sass, and Messer (1988), in which the authors state that "The 'everyday' activities that are always interpreted and reinterpreted come to represent who we are, how we understand" (p. 10).

We make sense of ourselves through our histories, so that is how we begin our attempt to reach an understanding of both the director and the AHORA program. Salazar arrived in the United States at the age of twenty-three, leaving El Salvador at the break of the Salvadoran revolution in 1980. The revolution was sparked by continually fraudulent elections, which reached a climax after the 1977 polls revealed that continued trickery had taken place. At this point the leftists lost all hope of reform through the democratic process and sought justice through violent means. This left Nelson's father without much choice other than to help his son escape from the country, because young males were being kidnapped off the streets and forced to join the repressive military. Those who refused to join were beaten, jailed, and often killed. Consequently, Nelson's father decided that he would "rather have his son far away and alive than with him in El Salvador, perhaps suffering or even dead" (Process Notes, Oct. 21, 1994). Nelson's background and experiences serve as the foundation of his philosophy. For example, having been an undocumented immigrant in this country, he is acutely aware of the realities and limitations that exist for the newcomers who make up a significant portion of the students who come to AHORA.

An example of Nelson's inside understanding of this population is his argument that we should not assume or imply that all of the AHORA students, or all of the Latino community for that matter, can necessarily go to college (Process Notes, Oct. 21, 1994). This is a crucial consideration when working with an immigrant population, because it is important not to make promises when for some, the barriers are rooted not only in language or grade point average but also in prejudice and public policy. The constant influx of Latino immigrants, who are leaving their native countries for reasons ranging from economic instability to political or military repression, is never ending because they are drawn to the myth of the American dream. Counselors, teachers, and administrators must realize that for many immigrants who enter this country illegally the American dream is a fallacy. By understanding this, we can more effectively counsel students. The difficult balance must be struck between realizing and communicating these limitations while encouraging undocumented students to do well in school, and assisting them with the process of acquiring amnesty so they can continue their educations once they become legal residents.

The director is also convinced that AHORA students must learn to take responsibility for themselves and their futures, and that this starts with taking responsibility at AHORA (Process Notes, Jan. 24, 1995). He argues that students must take on the responsibility of fundraising to finance potential events in which they may want to participate. He contends that we at AHORA should not act like "baby-sitters"; rather, we must teach our students to become self-sufficient so they can reach their full potentials within a system that continually fails them. To accomplish this, we have reinforced the communal backgrounds and nature of these students, while simultaneously preparing them to interact within what Lisa Delpit (1988) terms the "culture of power." As Delpit suggests, it is imperative that we teach these youths the rules necessary to function among society's gatekeepers (p. 282). Preparing students to negotiate the culture of power is possible by teaching them about the middle-class white values that are the foundation of this nation. We see it as our responsibility to provide the support and environment conducive to their learning, development, and empowerment. Without providing this necessary support, we are only mirroring the prejudices of the school system and society at large. By making the "rules of the game" explicit, we help to establish an environment that encourages critical dialogue and offers the possibility of emancipation.

RAISING SILENT VOICES: WRITING CLASS

Staggering dropout statistics bombard the Latino community in the United States. Headlines report that educators are worried about a 50 percent Hispanic dropout rate, yet no remedies are either suggested or supplied to alleviate the situation. We feel that the academic reasons behind this alarming rate are grounded in the lack of teaching the basic learning tools: critical reading and writing.

The lack of skills in our students, coupled with our feeling that there was a pressing need to create a voice for them, sparked the beginning of our writing course. The course began with a discussion of several assumptions about writing. Student feedback about their writing made it clear to us that there was a discontinuity between the style of their discourse and the writing they were being asked to produce at school. That is, the emphasis at the Caplan School fell on expository writing, contrary to what a large portion of the Latino population had seen in their home countries (Process Notes, May 3, 1995). Hence, we began by discussing explicitly the structure of writing required in the United States, as well as what would be asked of their writing skills at the Caplan school. We did not want to compromise the narrative style of writing the students were accustomed to producing, because as Gadamer (1976) states, "understanding, and especially understanding through language, is a primary form of being in the world" (p. 3). We believe that in order for our students to communicate their thoughts, it was necessary for them to understand that writing is a unique form of language that needs to be structured by various components.

Nonetheless, we think that counselors, like teachers, are responsible for becoming sensitive to students' diverse writing styles. It is our belief that only when teachers and counselors learn the language of the students will we become aware of our own prejudices about those students (Gadamer, 1976, p. 6). As a result of our mixed feelings, we related the message to students that their styles of writing were not wrong, yet what was going to be asked of them in college and future English courses would be a different structure of writing. Furthermore, we believe that the subject matter that students write about needs to be pertinent to their lives. Therefore, our group decided that our first assignment would be to write an essay on the recent passage in California of Proposition 187. The students, being recent immigrants (some illegal), decided that this was an interesting topic.

After examining the students' essays, we were able to diagnose some of the major problems in the writing of these second-language learners. Language certainly played a primary role in the slow acquisition of English writing skills. Due to lack of time, we decided to teach writing and reading strategies rather than going through the whole writing process, which we saved for our continuing individual sessions. We began with connectives and moved onto sentence structure and paragraph formation. That is, we emphasized the overall structure of an essay and helped the students to consider the different components that together constitute an essay.

Yet sometime after our assessments we realized that we needed to reinterpret what we were doing, because it seemed that the students may have been thinking that we were doing exactly what we were preaching against. That is, after looking at the magnitude of corrections we suggested in sentence structure, content, and paragraph formation, we revisited what we had originally discussed about the uniqueness of their writing. Upon reflection, we feel that the content of their writing is an area we should have left untouched. Packer and Addison (1989) discuss the notion that the concept behind the term *error* points to an ideal of "correctness" (p. 33). This is a sand trap to which we fell prey. Reframed optimistically, we can interpret this action of reflection and reinterpretation as our recognition of multiple truths at multiple points in time (Packer and Addison, 1989, p. 35). We believe this is an important way to learn about ourselves and our roles with students.

The students were initially frustrated with the writing and editing process, but with proper scaffolding they were able and willing to do drafts and group revisions. It was at this point in their growth that a strong voice was created among the students. When they began to lose their fears about writing, it became an ally in speaking their minds. More specifically, the writing course allowed the students to enter the hermeneutic circle of the school via the use of a common language, which they initially did not speak. Now, because they had gained a better grasp of this language, they could use it as Gadamer ([1962] 1976) describes language, as a "fundamental mode of operation in their being-in-the-world and the all-embracing form of the constitution of the world" (p. 3). For example, an undocumented immigrant found the space to voice his perceptions of the laws preventing him from receiving financial aid to attend the Massachusetts Institute of Technology, the university of his choice. He wrote: "Being an immigrant myself, I know how hard it is to survive in this new environment. I know the effort you have to make. The things you have to leave behind and forget because they are no longer a part of your everyday life. What is hard for me is having the grades and not being able to go to school like everyone else."

Our initial objective for the writing course was accomplished, yet much more was achieved and understood. At first we wished to correct the students' writing, not to listen to what they were trying to say. We focused on the technicalities of grammar, syntax, and structure, not at all reinforcing the writing style they were accustomed to producing. Consequently, we believe, we, like many of their other instructors, allowed our prejudices to further alienate the students by reinforcing feelings of inadequacy. Were it not for the interpretive process of hermeneutics, which forces us to take responsibility for our roles, we would not have taken the time to realize that we were perpetuating a cycle of judgment that often marks these students' educational experiences, and in so doing, building new barriers for them.

BASKETBALL AS A MEDIUM FOR COUNSELING

A major force for AHORA, as discussed previously, is director Salazar's philosophy and commitment to the students. Salazar believes that the formation of relationships between staff and students is necessary to create an environment of open dialogue and growth. The primacy that Salazar places on communication between the staff and students led him to suggest that we use half of our time at AHORA to create a basketball team. We believed as well that this would be a great experience. Nakkula and Selman (1991) support this approach, positing that when individuals interact through play, they form relationships that allow them to uncover aspects of themselves that are important for their development (p. 210). We took the opportunity to utilize the basketball team as a medium through which we could meet students and implement different counseling components: to discuss issues pertaining to the Latino community and the importance of college and education, to serve as male role models, and to talk over general life issues while engaged in an activity that builds collaboration and relationship skills. These are components we felt were missing in their educational experiences, and our team gave us a natural way to integrate these into daily relationships.

Through dialogue and misunderstanding, we have been able to determine where the students are coming from, while simultaneously offering them insight into our perspectives. Our development with this group grew from our experiences together, both on and off the basketball court. These experiences can be viewed through the application of Speight, Myers, Cox, and Highlen's (1991) "Influences on Worldview" philosophy (p. 32). We first approached the students from a universal human point of view. Due to a conflict, we began to look at the cultural specifics that existed among this diverse group of students.

In the early stages of the team, we lacked knowledge of the ethnicities of the players. Thus we were guilty of generalizing the players as simply that: players. We only realized the cultural distinctions between players when a fight broke out between two ethnically different players (Process Notes, Nov. 6, 1994). The fight ensued after a Puerto Rican student fouled one of the Dominican players, and as tempers flared, so did left and right hooks. At the conclusion of the fight, profanities regarding ethnicity were yelled. This caused us to ask AHORA staff and students if there were any racial problems among the Latinos at the Caplan School. We found out that, indeed, differences existed among documented and undocumented Latinos. For example, we learned that Puerto Ricans were considered by other Latinos to be assimilated because of their legal status, while Dominicans and Salvadorans were considered "mojados."[1] This experience of not understanding the underlying conflicts in the game allowed us to realize and then examine the biases we had when we began the basketball team. We learned the racist implications involved in our assumptions that the Latino community is monolithic, and this led us to reexamine our thinking and to focus on the uniqueness and differences that occur within and across ethnic groups.

Learning about the rich ethnicity represented on our team facilitated the growth of the relationships we sought. That is, through our contact with the players and their realization and acknowledgment that our desire was to better understand and help them, we established trust and rapport that then allowed them to view us as resources they could tap. The basketball team has been a major factor in our connecting with students as a group as well as on an individual level. It is important to note that this increased connection and understanding came only after we confronted misunderstanding and entered into a process of reinterpretation through the return arc of hermeneutics.

William is an excellent example of how the basketball team provided a space for real communication. William felt that on our team he could be himself and not be reprimanded for it. However, because William had persistent problems with authority in school, we asked: Could we be more effective in reaching him by using basketball as an engaged activity (Gadamer, [1966] 1976, p. 15)? What if we played basketball where he and his friends played? This approach, to go to where the students played ball, proved effective with a former Raza Unida player, Raul, who had quit the team along with his brother Mario because, in his words, the other players were "Huns"[2] (Process Notes, Apr. 25, 1995). We had continually attempted to bring Raul back to the team, because he was failing his classes, but he would not return.

It was not until then that we realized that the key to reaching these two individuals was to engage in a basketball game at Gore Park, which they often referred to as "our park." Pederson (1991) argues that it is important to take a broad multicultural perspective to help avoid stereotyping. We agree with Pederson's contention that we as counselors are required to establish and maintain "an accurate and profound understanding of the world around each client" (p. 10). We therefore decided that we not only had to listen to the input of our counselees, but we also had to step into and interact with the students in their worlds.

Through interacting in their worlds, we began to experience first-hand the stressors that students experience. This allowed us to better engage in the interpretation process: first from their world (forward arc), then from our reinterpretations (return arc), and then from the repetition of the process through our continual engagement in "their ball park." Because we are able to continually interpret and reinterpret within the hermeneutic circle, we can provide students with more individual support in confronting the walls within the school system and those that exist in the "real world" (Wehmiller, 1992). This interaction also provides support for us as counselors, because it allows us to interact outside of our worlds and thus provides a reinterpretation of our worldviews, which engenders critical analysis and allows for growth to transpire.

After we played basketball with Raul and Mario in an area in which they felt safe and comfortable, and in which they could interact in their usual manner, they began to see us differently. We have continued to play basketball at Gore Park, even as we take study breaks from writing this chapter. We have noticed the respect and the "chumship" (Sullivan, 1953) that we have developed with the Reyes brothers. Mario, the older brother, seems to protect us when we are at the park, making sure that the others realize that we are with him and that we are "cool."

Moreover, both brothers have now become regulars at AHORA. Their ability to connect with us outside of AHORA and to understand who we are and where we are coming from has allowed them to trust us and thus to participate in, and make use of, the resources at AHORA. As a result, we have been asked to assist Mario with his application to Northeastern University. It is important that he feels he wants our help, because he is graduating and may not have anyone he can trust to assist him with the application process next year. Raul has also committed himself to bettering his academic situation. In fact, he approached us to help him get his "act together" (Process Notes, Apr. 24. 1995). He stated that he was doing poorly in school and needed help. So we helped him by providing tutoring and counseling. Fortunately, Raul's choice to reinterpret his academic situation after we entered his world helped him to realize his own power (Pederson, 1991, p. 11), and has helped him to take school seriously again.

OPPORTUNITIES BLOCKED AND OPENED

The basketball team was a medium for building rapport with the AHORA students in order to facilitate the building of our relationships. Building compatibility with the basketball team enabled us to move from being just two more counselors at AHORA to being primary resources for a group of students who continue to be neglected and ignored by the Caplan School. By gaining the players' acceptance, we also gained the respect of other AHORA students and became resources for many of them. Because of our time constraints, we focused mostly on assisting seniors with their college essays. As we mentioned earlier, these students encountered numerous barriers with their writing because of language. The barriers did not end with language, however. Several students faced constraints to furthering their educations because of legal status, which introduced them to the white supremacist structure that exists within the school and also within this society.

This sentiment was echoed by the recent passage of Proposition 187 in California and President Clinton's State of the Union Address, in which he echoed the rhetoric of Proposition 187's commitment to cutting public aid and social services to undocumented immigrants. The justification for this racist legislation was that immigrants, Latinos in particular, have been continually entering this country and becoming dependent on the state. This stereotype has plagued the media and the minds of many Americans for many years, and particularly since the passage of Proposition 187 in November 1994.

Vicente's presence in the United States runs counter to the stereotype and rhetoric that fueled the passage of Proposition 187. We began working with Vicente early last semester and were made aware of his legal status. At that point we began to investigate the possibility of him attending college. Vicente was accepted to several top universities, but he was not able to attend any of them because of his legal status, which created another wall for Vicente to contend with. Fortunately we learned that state schools do not ask for legal status upon acceptance. Therefore, Salem State College became an option for Vicente. The Language Intensive Program at Salem State would provide Vicente with an opportunity to develop his verbal and written skills in English. When Vicente went for a tour of Salem State, Eileen de los Reyes, director of the Language Intensive Program, realized Vicente's potential and scheduled an appointment for him with the director of the honors program (Process Notes, May 5, 1995). After conversing with the director of the honors program, Vicente was guaranteed admission to the program following the completion of his freshman year.

It is ironic that students with similarly high-level abilities are kept out of the higher-education system because of the backlash spreading across this nation. It appears that Latinos are being scapegoated once again because of the country's economic recession. We therefore believe that it is important to teach Latino students white middle-class values so they can function within the system, but we must also discuss institutional racism with them so they will be prepared when they encounter racist situations in college and in the workforce (Delpit, 1988; Mehan, Hubbard, and Villanueva, 1994). Awareness of the white supremacist structure will allow these students to engage in rather than withdraw from dialogue that either states or implies racism. Further, we can teach them to step out of discussions to critically assess racist situations as well as their own biases, and how both of these influence communication.

Viewing the white supremacist structure from a critical hermeneutic perspective defines our goals as beyond just understanding (Woolfolk, Sass, and Messer, 1988). In our opinion, individual growth is important, but the overall human experience must also be changed. For this to become a reality, we must begin the cultural revolution that Paulo Freire defines in *Pedagogy of the Oppressed* (1973). This process begins with providing the oppressed with a critical analysis of their realities (via language acquisition) so that they may begin to develop critical thinking and communication skills in order to empower themselves to overcome their oppression. Accordingly, we need to aid students in critically analyzing their situations and raising their informed voices.

The most important factors we face in making a college education a reality for our students are obstacles such as financial aid, affirmative action, and bilingual education. Because of the recent federal cuts in student aid, several of the AHORA students are facing the possibility of having to attend a junior college because the universities that accepted them are not providing sufficient funding. Another national agenda being discussed is the abolishment of affirmative action. How can people of color compete with mainstream students when they are faced with a myriad of unique risk factors? Furthermore, the governor of the state of Massachusetts is trying to abolish bilingual education. Without bilingual education, how can monolingual Spanish-speaking Latinos enter the school system? This conservative backlash is obviously meant to attack people of color. Because this trend is so pervasive and limiting, it is crucial to address these political issues when attempting to provide counseling and direction to students of color.

NOCHE LATINA

A night of dance, song, and poetry was what the event entailed, or at least that is what was mentioned on the three hundred letters sent out to the Cambridge Latino community. We believe that Noche Latina was the climactic point of our experience with AHORA, because we had reached our goal of creating a sense of unity and familiarity between students and staff. This celebration of student talent brought together the various individual relationships we had formed throughout the year.

For us, Noche Latina was a way to open communication between AHORA and parents. Often, because of the language barrier, Spanish-speaking parents are alienated from schools. This night was created to bridge home and school, or at least to create an atmosphere in which parents could get to know the campus. As a result of this commitment to parents, many of them responded to the letters sent home, showing more than just interest in coming to the event. That is, several parents wanted to present their talents alongside the students (Process Notes, Feb. 22, 1995). For one night, the walls that stood not only between the school and parents but also between the parents and AHORA were brought down, permitting unobstructed communication to take place. Parents showed gratitude for the opportunity to finally meet the staff who interacted on a daily basis with their children.

Noche Latina created a space for expression. There were multiple issues on the minds of many students that our initial biases blinded us from seeing. For example, we were skeptical about the dedication the students would show toward the event (Process Notes, Feb. 17, 1995). Our doubts were put to rest when we saw Ricardo and his dance group practicing daily. At first, his dedication surprised us, and then we had to question: How many other times had we underestimated students' abilities? Upon reinterpreting our notes from last semester, we found various other incidents in which this sort of doubt was evident. It is disturbing to realize that we could get caught up in the barriers the school creates—such as assuming that teachers' and administrators' negative assessments of these students were correct—when our goal is to emancipate students from systems that discredit them.

One individual's performance at Noche Latina stood out in particular because it spoke explicitly to the conditions in which we as Latinos find ourselves living (Process Notes, Mar. 3, 1995). Alain had once made reference to his frustration about the enormous Latino dropout rates and the lack of representation of Latinos in colleges (Process Notes, Oct. 16, 1994). On this particular night, he was given a forum to speak his mind to a larger audience. Many people who sat in the audience related to Alain's rap, "Latino Originale." This was evident from the ecstatic ovation he received upon the completion of his performance. To provide a sense of how truly powerful Alain's rap was, we present a piece of his lyrics (Alain Montes, 1995):

La gente de este país no quieren aceptar
que somos poderosos y queremos progresar

somos una raza de tres en uno
y a la gente le da emvidia y fugurio
al saber que somos indios, hispanos, y Africanos
y ellos no son nada comparados.

Anger fills these words, which emphasize the negative views attached to Latinos by "mainstream America." It further explains the reality of the Latino heritage by illuminating the three races that make up Latinos, known as the "meztisaje" (mixed blood).

The termination of Noche Latina was very difficult for both the students and the staff. After the performances were over, all those involved (directly and indirectly), including parents, relocated to the AHORA office. Salsa, chips, and passionate conversations led the event well into the night. This event reinforced an AHORA identity among the students, staff, and larger community, and stands as a symbol of a year of growth and development.

CONCLUSION

Many changes have taken place this year—changes in the students, in us, and in our relationships. We began our practicum experience at AHORA with a narrow view of the Latino population. Our limited experience with Latinos, other than Chicanos, caused us to enter our site with a Chicanocentric view of Latinos. However, through our willingness to engage with our interpretations and reinterpretations of our worldviews and prejudices, we were able to engage in the hermeneutic circle and reevaluate our limited perspectives.

This understanding of the need for reinterpretation was further supported by the note-taking process. The possibility of documenting and reevaluating the everydayness of ourselves and of our relationships with students enriched our (re)interpretations. This ability to step in and out of the hermeneutic circle allowed for a deeper, more profound understanding of the human experiences we encountered. This increased understanding was documented over time and can be detected in our ability to build trust among AHORA students. This in turn removed the walls that existed between the Latino students and the AHORA staff. The change was precipitated and reinforced through our experiences in our writing class, on our basketball team, and with Noche Latina.

These different forms of learning—through writing, creativity, community-building, and play—have allowed us to become immersed in a mutual growth process for both the students and ourselves. As a result, twenty-five of our students have continued their education past Caplan High (last year there was only one student from AHORA who attended college), equipped with the analytical tools and knowledge to interact critically within the "culture of power," yet still maintaining their individual identities. The camaraderie and commitment formed between us continues to flourish, and many of these students will return to AHORA as mentors and tutors. We will continue to (re)interpret our biases and use the experience and insight we have gained through working and playing with AHORA students in our future discourse and counseling.

NOTES

1. A derogatory term meaning "wetback," used to describe undocumented immigrants from Mexico and Central America. The term makes reference to the fact that these people needed to cross a body of water to reach the United States.
2. The students use this term, which means "ball hog," to describe someone who does not pass the ball.

16

ENTERING PLAY

Lessons of Grief, Joy, and Growth

Tara Edelschick

I HAVE SPENT THIS YEAR AT HARVARD, I now realize, learning how to play: learning how to play with the students and how to be playful with my own thoughts and growth, learning to be with my students, not out in front of them, pulling and cajoling them to join me. It has been a frightening, exhilarating, humbling, and joyful process. I hope that by remaining with this chapter, not out in front of it, cajoling it to make nice, neat little conclusions, I can capture some of the essence of my growth this year.

This investigation is a story. I feel it is important to acknowledge that I am not telling the students' stories. They are theirs to tell. This is the story of my interpretation of our experiences together.

In my last study, I wrote:

> My recognition of the hermeneutical constraints and my desire for the possibilities leads me to the research question I bring to my work, the question that is the focus of my story: *How does facilitating, rather than controlling, group interactions and experiences allow for more growth and a sense of personal agency for both my students and me?*
>
> Actually, I did not begin the year with this question in mind. But writing the first paper for this class, as well as work I have done in other classes, has changed me. I started working with the group

late; and by the time I started working with them, something felt different. It is not that I had transcended my beliefs and needs; it is just that I was more aware of them. The question examines my growth as well as that of the students. I feel it is necessary to examine my own growth if I am going to attempt to gauge theirs [Phenomenological Investigation I, p. 5].

When I wrote that investigation, I was still struggling to understand the ideas and terminology of hermeneutics. I used hermeneutics as a strict prescription for interpretation: describe your biases, or forestructure; ask your question; and describe your backwards arc, or conclusions. While this exercise was invaluable at the time, I now feel comfortable with the language of hermeneutics and am immersed in the process. This semester I am not observing the hermeneutic circle (Addison, 1989) from afar; I am in the circle.

I understood this shift for the first time when I began to think of a research question for this investigation. I realized that my questions no longer concerned the role of facilitation versus control, the topic of my study last semester. My forward projection this semester has more to do with developing new questions than with coming to a new understanding. My questions are now about play: how to play, and how play enhances understanding and meaning. My forestructure of understanding has changed, and I am interpreting events from a different vantage point. For the first time I truly understand the explanation of the circularity of interpretive inquiry provided by Packer and Addison in *Entering the Circle* (1989): "interpretive inquiry does not try to ensure that knowledge is built upon a 'foundation,' but instead places emphasis on recognizing and appropriating a 'starting place' for hermeneutic inquiry in practical understanding" (p. 99). Entering into this circle has changed me. I hope this paper echoes that change as I explore my newly found questions and concerns.

METHODOLOGY

Discussing the validity of interpretation, Packer and Addison write, "Interpretation always begins from concerned engagement. . . . What is uncovered in the course of a true interpretation is a solution to the problem, the confusion, the question, the concern, and the breakdown in understanding that motivates our inquiry in the first place" (1989, p. 279). I was first drawn to this quote because it seemed to explain so much about what students in the two groups I was facilitating did and did not find meaningful. When the work and play of our groups centered on the issues and concerns that students were struggling with most, the room was charged with an almost electric quality of exploration and emerging understandings. When it did not, I felt as though I was pulling a three-hundred-pound twelve-year-old through a week-long calculus convention. What they might learn would inevitably be meaningless because the interpretation did not begin from concerned engagement.

I soon realized that this quotation was an equally valuable guide for my own interpretations. What about my work was truly engaging? What were my deepest concerns? Where did my understanding of myself and the groups break down? These may seem like obvious questions, even easy to answer. For me, however, it took virtually the entire semester to answer them. They were slow in developing, and it is with questions that my journey this semester ends, not where it began.

Naturally this process dictates the methodology of this investigation. My chapter traces my work this semester and its influence on an *emerging question*. I could, I suppose, take the question as it is now unfolding and go back to reinterpret the sessions with the groups. But that would seem quite artificial. I am excited by this odd turn of events. My interpretation of what was happening in the groups led to my questions, not the other way around. My methodology will respect that.

With this understanding, I will outline the basic elements of my methodology:

1. The interpretation will be guided by play, not by a specific interpretive question, as my last investigation was. By play, I mean an unguided, unpredictable, and complex exploration of the systems and chaos I encountered in my work (VanderVen, 1996). I have found that play guides my students as they make meaning of their lives, and that play can serve the same function for me. This investigation is in some ways a playful exploration of play. I do not yet know where it will lead. This is an important aspect of my methodology.

2. As in my first paper, I will acknowledge and describe my forestructure with the insight I have into its meaning and effects. I will explore the traditions in my personal and professional life that influence how I interact with students.

3. My data are process notes that I took within two days of each group meeting. On one occasion, I recreate a session from memory, noting the possible distortions that may have occurred over time.

THE STORY: ACT I

In February, I began a six-week grieving group for six seventh graders who had lost a significant loved one to death. I cofacilitated the group with two hospice volunteers, Nancy and Robin. In many ways, this group changed my life and how I will work with children. This story is about a piece of that change.

During the first week of the group, three things grabbed my attention, two while I was in the group and one only after discussing the session with someone else: (1) these children said things more eloquently and easily through drawings than they did while speaking; (2) if I was not respectful of where a student was and what she was ready for, I could push my agenda on her, superseding her own; and (3) there is precious little space in children's lives to explore and play with issues of death.

On the first day of our group we drew two pictures: one of their families just before the death and one just after. It was only *after* everyone started drawing that Eileen began to tell the story of her mother's death. Her mother was a drug addict who died alone in a motel. The story was difficult for her to tell. Once Eileen spoke, others joined in the conversation, more relaxed than they had been while taking turns telling their stories. They were passing crayons, asking questions, and responding to one another.

The pictures themselves told wonderful stories. Kim's "before" picture was a tightly clustered family with no space separating them. Her "after" picture was a line of unsmiling people, each separated by about an inch. Eileen's "before" picture included her mother, her father, and herself. Her "after" picture was a big picture of her face, entitled "Self-Portrait." In their drawings the students were expressing aspects of their lives and how they understood them.

Earlier, when each child was taking a turn describing the person who died and how they died, Eileen had passed, fighting hard to keep back her tears. When I put my hand on her knee, she started to cry. I kept it there and she wept quietly. With my hand still on her knee, Eileen started drawing and telling her story. Later, I met with Gail, a social worker who does grief work, to review the session. In my notes from that meeting I wrote:

> I related to her the story of touching Eileen's knee. Well, she changed my mind about how I interpreted the encounter. I assumed that touching Eileen sent her the message, "It's OK to cry. I'll

support you." Gail made the point that touching anyone who is on the verge of tears will send them over the edge and they *will* cry. Now, maybe Eileen wanted to cry and maybe she didn't. She may have been fighting really hard to keep her defenses up, and for good reason. Essentially, I took that choice away from her. Gail suggested, instead, creating a space and explicitly telling the students that if they want help—someone to hold their hand, put their arm around them, or hold them while they cry—all they have to do is ask. Now this seems almost obvious, even trivial. But I find it sort of revolutionary: space to make choices that are right for you, and support for those choices [Process Notes, Feb. 1, 1996].

It *was* revolutionary, and it inspired my thinking about how I can really be with the children where they are, not out in front of them, pulling them along to where I think they should be.

I also learned in this first session how little space there is for children to talk about death. Students shared things on our first day that they said they had not told anyone before. Paula, who is almost fourteen and lost her father three years ago, cried for the first time since her twelfth birthday, when she vowed she was too old to cry about it any longer. Kim shared that she believed it was her fault that her father died, and others followed with similar statements. I wondered: Why would they open up like this on the first day to a group they hardly knew? I learned in later sessions, from this group and a subsequent grieving group, that it seems that no one wants to listen to these children's stories. The adults in their lives seem to react either by crying or by telling them that they should be over it already. For example, Brent's family forbids him to discuss his mother. Dean, who thinks that his uncle committed suicide, cannot get anyone in his family to answer his questions. Eileen's teachers get upset and tell me to stop when I try to explain what she is going through. The students, who embrace every game and activity with enthusiasm, laughter, and tears, are looking for places to explore the meaning of death. Unfortunately, they find too few safe spaces.

During the second session, we discussed stages of the grieving process and students drew pictures of where they were in their process. Eileen drew a broken heart, with a bunch of "Shhhs" all around it and said that the broken heart represented her caterpillar phase and the "Shhh"s were her cocoon stage of wanting to be left alone. Kim's picture was very disturbing. It showed a screaming mother and a knife, "'cause sometimes I want to die and be with him [her father]." In these pictures, it is clear that they are struggling with so much. About Dean's picture, I wrote:

Dean's picture had this on it: [? Questionless].

T: What does this mean?

D: Questionless. It means I don't have any questions.

T: You don't have any questions at all? None?

D: None.

T: I thought you said that they're not sure how he died. He just died in bed.

D: Well, they think it might have been his medicine. He fell in a fire and he was taking medicine.

T: Pain medicine?

D: Mmmhmm.

T: And he took too many?

D: [Nods.]

T: So you do know how he died.

D: [Nods.]

He took the picture back and scribbled something on it. When he shared it with the group, it looked like this: [? Questions].

T: You do have questions?

D: Yeah.

T: What are they?

D: Why? and Who's next?

T: Those are important questions [Process Notes, Feb. 8, 1996].

Two things in this encounter struck me. First, Dean was clearly using the drawing as a form of play, exploring, and wishing, almost a make-believe. What would it mean to have no questions? How could he convince himself that there were no questions, and how could he live with questions that no one will answer? How could he tell us that he had questions and how would we react? Second, my willingness to engage in Dean's play and to take his drawing seriously created a space for Dean and me to explore some things together, to come to a new understanding and new set of questions. Only much later did we discuss suicide and Dean's dilemma over how to move on without having all of the answers. For this day, it was enough to admit there were some questions. Dean taught me this—it is enough to admit there are some questions.

Near the end of that second session, I had another experience that taught me the value of engaging in children's stories and the spontaneity of their revelations:

JOHN: I had a dream last week that my family was home watching TV and my grandma knocked on the door. I yelled at my mom not to let her in. My mom said, "But it's your grandma." I told her I didn't care. "Tell her to go away."

T: When your grandma was staying with you when she was dying, did you sometimes wish she would go away?

J: [Nods yes.]

T: How did you feel about wishing that?

J: Bad, like I shouldn't feel that.

T: You know, it's very normal to wish that. It's hard to watch someone die. And besides, with your grandma there, there probably wasn't much time for family stuff like watching TV.

J: [Nods.]

T: Wishing she would leave didn't make her die any faster.

J: I know [Process Notes, Feb. 8, 1996].

We then went on to explore the guilt that many of the students discussed in a previous session. John brought his dream to the group, hoping to make sense of it. In a space that respects the seemingly nonsensical, like dreams and pictures, it is safe to explore and question. I believe that John was showing us that he believed the group was a safe place in which to explore, and by doing so he made it safer for others to do so as well.

I will now look at an incident in which, after deciding to have a pizza party for our last session, the students decided not to participate in the scheduled activity but instead had a lively discussion of decaying bodies. After our fourth session, I wrote:

> The group got into an animated discussion about wakes, which led to an equally animated discussion about how bodies decay. Surprisingly, I only flinched mildly at the idea of not doing our activity.... Two weeks ago, when we asked about the wake, we didn't get a reaction. I guess they feel more comfortable with each other and with the topic of death.
>
> They talked about kissing or not kissing the dead bodies, how "it felt kind of gross," how funny the bodies looked in makeup and wigs. "You mean it's someone's job to put makeup on dead people?!" Then they were talking about how a body becomes a skeleton: "Don't you know? Bodies are biodegradable." John says, "Do you think maybe we can not talk about this during our party?" Laughter. Eileen says, "Hey, you know, I heard when a body

decays, it looks just like pizza." Peals of laughter [Process Notes, Feb. 29, 1996].

The ability to tell jokes and share the truth of their experiences, to question the mysteries of life as well as the facts, is a wonderful aspect of children's play that I had forgotten. I wanted to discuss their beliefs in the afterlife, and they really wanted to know if your hair falls out when you die and what happens to your eyeballs. Their jokes and their laughter were so perfect and will stay with me for many years. I wrote at the end of my notes that day, "Guilt over playing tag at the wake and humor side by side. It felt good" [Process Notes, Feb. 29, 1996].

For me, the last day of the grieving group was magical. Two reasons for this stand out as I write this chapter. The first is how differently each student articulated what the group meant to her or him. Kim brought in a cake that said "Be Happy!" and told us that she had a little more hope now. Dean wrote Paula a note that said, "Paula, I want to thank you because when you cried on the first day and no one laughed at you, I knew it was OK to show my feelings." Each student wrote that it meant a lot to him or her to know other kids who are going through what they are. In the second group, Erica said that she now knew she did not have to be "over it" in two weeks. Chandra said that it was all right that she wasn't a perfect kid while her mother was sick. Each child said something different, and I understood what it meant to be with children, where they are, struggling with what matters to them. No predetermined objectives could have predicted what meaning each of the students would make of the group. It was their space: a space in which to explore, question, and play. In my notes on the second grieving group I wrote:

> Now, for the big finale. Everyone wrote to the person who died on a little card and tied it to the end of a helium balloon. At the end of the session, we went outside with the balloons. I had them all close their eyes, think of the person, and make a wish for their own future. Then, on the count of three, they released the balloons into the air. All heads up. All voices quiet. All eyes teary, especially mine. Kim: "I always thought that my dad was that way," pointing away from where the balloons were headed. "Hmmm," she said. I couldn't get them to go back into school. Just sat there watching the balloons. After school, I saw Eileen standing outside with her friends, every once in a while peeking up to see if she could find it.
> ME: Can you still see it?
> EILEEN: Nope [shaking head].

ME: Maybe she got it.

Eileen beamed and nodded her head. Maybe she got it [Process Notes, Mar. 14, 1996].

So, what do I make of all of this? How do I understand what happened in this group and inside me? In my last investigation I wrote about how my experiences growing up led me to want to control things, to "fix everything . . . to be everything, do everything and meet everyone's needs. . . . I am adeptly sensitive to the feelings of others, especially feelings of pain and suffering; and I am most comfortable when responding to that pain. As a teacher, it meant that I would try to solve my students' problems *for them,* not letting them learn how to struggle with and resolve them on their own" (Phenomenological Investigation I, 1996, p. 4). What I did not realize was how this need to control things left little room for play. With my students, I am again learning how to play, learning how important play is in their lives and in mine. I have learned that there is a logic to their play. It is not childish, but wonderfully childlike.

Shaun Gallagher (1992) describes Hans-Georg Gadamer's notion of play, stating that play is a necessary component of growth and meaning making. Gadamer believes that for an experience to be most meaningful, we must lose ourselves in the play of the experience. VanderVen (1996) states that play is necessary for children to see themselves as continual learners and understand the characteristics of chaos. When John brings in a dream or Dean revises his picture to convey a new understanding, they are changing their stories, their play, and making new sense of their world. By respecting that play, I hope to help them value the changing nature of it, the changing nature of their stories and their understanding. They can create new endings to their stories; they can revise their pictures and reinterpret their dreams.

Describing its functions, VanderVen (1996) says that play is symbolic, that it allows the participant, or player, to let one thing stand for another. Again and again, I saw the students symbolically drawing and representing their experiences. When they were joking about decaying bodies, they were saying that it's now OK to smile. At first I was concerned that the students would think sending balloons up into the sky was corny. Instead, as Gadamer describes in his model of play and growth, they lost themselves in the play of it. VanderVen says that children connect various experiences into meaningful patterns and integrate puzzling experiences through play. Students in the grieving group were making these types of connections, understanding how their questions and patterns of grief were similar to, and different from, others in the group. They were asking new questions and putting others to rest. They were reexamining some beliefs while fiercely defending others.

I also learned that if I want to connect with children, I must play *with* them. I cannot organize their play for them, although I can, following their cues, help guide the play. I must be willing and able to play with them, to be in relationship with them, so I can help them make sense of the play and work with them in creating new alternatives in their stories.

Gallagher (1992) discusses what makes an experience hermeneutically relevant, and I think it is appropriate to bring that discussion in here. He says, "In the case of play there is no distinction to be made between means and ends as if interpretation were to be made practical in a particular application. . . . The notion of self-transcendence in play indicates that the player is not in control of the play and therefore cannot set the game up as a means to an end" (pp. 160–161). I have often misunderstood this aspect of play, thinking that I could devise neat little games and activities that would lead students to a predetermined end. I realized throughout this year that this is not possible. When play is relevant, we cannot dictate its outcome. No one can control play; if we could, it would not be play. I saw this starkly when I realized that each student had made a different meaning of the group. I also saw how useless it was to force play the day the students ignored the planned activity and devised their own play because it was more relevant to their concerns.

THE STORY: ACT II

I am particularly grateful for the effect the grieving group has had on my work with the Peer Outreach Group (POG). I wrote about this group last semester:

> This paper is the story of my work with a group of seventh graders at the Hancock Middle School. The group consists of twelve students, both racially and behaviorally diverse, selected to participate in a Peer Outreach Group that meets weekly throughout the year. My goal for the group is to help the students gain the skills, self-esteem, and courage to make better decisions for themselves in all areas of their lives and to eventually use their skills to help others. During the year, we focus on building self-esteem, cultural pride, and respect for others, developing skills such as effective communication, risk taking, trust, and courage [Phenomenological Investigation I, 1996, p. 1].

After finishing work on an art exhibit about themselves, we began conflict resolution training. Each week, more and more students talked about leaving the group, and they were all singing a chorus of "We're bored. We want to play games." What I was slowly learning about play in the grieving group came to influence my work in the POG. I will present two sessions that I believe demonstrate some of that change.

At the beginning of March, Rob Aylward, who is evaluating the project's effectiveness, and I decided that it would be nice for him to see one of the POGs in action. All of the students except Jonathan wanted Rob to join us, so they convinced Jonathan to agree to a vote. "Jonathan eventually agreed to let Rob in if he participated. But he did it somewhat begrudgingly and nervously. I felt helpless to help the group see that voting is not an ideal way to resolve conflict. This is the second time they have resorted to voting and people felt left out and unheard" (Process Notes, Mar. 1, 1996).

The session was not a complete disaster. During the following session, we spent a lot of time talking about how Jonathan felt. I include this episode to show the lack of connection between the conflict resolution lessons and resolving actual conflict in our group. I could not understand why this disparity existed. Was it simply a matter of time? Perhaps they needed time to integrate the lessons into their own lives. Or was it something more? I had a sense that it was due to the fact that the lessons were not meaningful to them. They just were not getting it. They would often tell me, "Tara, this just isn't real. We couldn't really do this stuff." How could I help the students make the connections? I needed more clues to help me understand what was really happening with them.

Luckily, the students presented me with many clues over the next weeks, often complaining that they were bored, that they did not see how this conflict resolution stuff could really work, and that they wanted to play. On the fifth of April, we had a session where it all became clear to me. I will recreate it as fully as possible from my memory.

As usual, I came in with a plan, an agenda. But before I could begin, Allison jumped in.

ALLISON: I'm not gonna mention any names, but last week a group of kids started making fun of me. Someone in this group was with them and I don't think that's very nice.

CHRIS: I know you're talking about me!

TARA: What happened?

CHRIS: I was with them, cuz they're my friends. But I didn't say anything. Nothing at all.

This led us into a discussion about what others might have done in the situation. To my surprise, they all said they would have done what Chris did—not join in, but not ask them to stop either. When we were talking about why they would not stop it, Stacey said, "Well, we're not even friends." My heart almost skipped a beat. Sad little faces around the room were nodding their heads or saying, "Yeah, we're not friends."

This led to a discussion about how much the group "sucks." "We never do anything." "Why do we have to teach these stupid lessons anyway?" On and on. Not my best moment with kids, but I kept trying to listen and avoided trying to convince them that it wasn't so bad.

This was a painful session for me and I suspect it was painful for many of the students as well. We had spent five months together and they could not call themselves friends. I felt like a failure, and spent a few days sulking and berating myself. Eventually I decided to see the session as a turning point. The students were telling me quite clearly what they wanted, and if I listened to them I could help them achieve it.

I spent the following week thinking about what they were saying. They wanted to be friends, and clearly that had to come before teaching them and their classmates how to resolve conflict. They were also telling me how they wanted to go about making friends. They wanted to play. It seems so obvious to me now. But it took a long time for it to sink in. After considering how to handle it, I decided to share with them how I had been feeling and what I was thinking. I am including extensive notes from that day because it was such an important day, for the group and for me.

> TARA: I want to start by sharing with you what I've been thinking about this week. I'm a teacher, and as a teacher, I have a need to feel like you feel better about yourselves at the end our time together. I thought that if you went into classrooms to teach about conflict resolution, you would be proud and know that you had something to offer other kids. But I wasn't listening to you and what would make you feel better. We live in a society where people don't listen to women, don't listen to

minorities or immigrants, and don't listen to children. I work
hard to fight this and yet I didn't listen to you. I am sorry.

A lot of stunned faces, open mouths and wide eyes.

After a few minutes, I said I realized after the last session that
many of them still didn't feel like friends, and that that's what they
were saying they wanted to do. "So we can spend the next three
sessions becoming friends." Lots of nods. "Yeah!"

[Later,] I gave each of them a cup with activity cards in it, activities they had suggested and ones I thought they might like. At this
point, I jokingly asked, "Did anyone pick 'Tour the library'?"
David had.

ALLISON: What are we gonna do? We just can't vote.

BRENDA: If we vote, David's gonna lose and feel bad.

TARA: That *is* tough.

Then they got into pairs and came up with a plan to accommodate everyone. What struck me was how kind they were with each
other. They decided that I would take David to the library on my
own. And when we finally got down to deciding between two activities that significant numbers of students each wanted, they agreed
to combine them on the same day. At first I was going to push them
to choose [between the two], but then I realized that they had
devised a creative, loving solution and I should let it be.

Finally, we spent the last half hour playing "freeze tag." Two
people enter the circle and act out an escalating conflict . . . until
someone can think of a collaborative solution. They yell "Freeze!"
and switch places with someone and resolve the conflict. It was a
perfect combination of their wish to play (they've been asking to
act out commercials) and my wish to help them think in new ways
about friendship and conflict. I was psyched. Everyone left looking
so happy. It felt good. I hope they felt as good about it as I did
[Process Notes, Apr. 12, 1996].

So much happened in this session that it is difficult to capture it all. I
will highlight what was most significant to me. First, I was moved by
the students' shock and then their pleasure when I apologized to them.
They attend a school and live in a culture that has so little respect for
children and what children care about that I think it took a minute for
this to sink in. Second, I was moved by how naturally and respectfully
they decided how to spend their next three meetings. Once we articulated what the group was going to be about—making friends—they
quickly went to it.

Finally, I want to say something about the nature of the play here. I still brought in an activity and it was still about resolving conflict. What was different was that the play was relevant, to use Gallagher's term. There was no prescribed ending. This was not an activity to prepare them to teach, but a game that allowed them to explore different roles and ways of being in relationship. It was a game that dealt with the issues they were grappling with: how to become friends and resolve their own conflicts. This play, like that in the grieving group, was an end unto itself. It allowed the students to make connections between their experiences and what they had "learned" about conflict resolution. They were trying on new roles and beginning to understand how it might feel to react in new ways.

So I have realized that I cannot control their play experience. Margaret Wheatly (in VanderVen, 1996) writes, "It seems that the very experiences these children seek out are the ones we avoid: disequilibrium, novelty, loss of control, surprise. These make for a good playground" (p. 75). If the students were going to use their play as a way to create understanding and new possibilities, then I could dictate neither the play nor the outcomes. This realization came easier in the grieving group, but was just as significant when it finally came in my POG work.

Gallagher (1992, p. 161) says, "To the extent that play is more like a mystery than a technical problem, that is, to the extent that the player is directly, immediately affected in play and cannot attain objective detachment so as to stand apart and unaffected, or to the extent that the player is genuinely at play, there is no question at all of attempting to make the game interesting." Too much of my work with the POGs had been a technical endeavor: "Here's how we make an 'I Statement'." No wonder the students were always bored! In fact, I was bored. I was not allowing myself to engage in their struggles, to be where they were and not where I wanted them to be. Thankfully, the students ached for something more interesting and meaningful. They insisted that we play and that I learn how to play with them.

THE QUESTION

So here I am—at the end and the beginning of my exploration, having come to a question and ready to take that question forward, allowing it to influence me and change with new experiences. At the beginning of the investigation I asked why I would want to abandon my outline, allowing the play between me and this text to lead me in an unforeseen direction. Now I know. I have arrived at my question—a question whose form and content were only a glimmer to me at the beginning of this study but are now a meaningful expression of both my growth thus far and my hope for continued growth in the future. There does not seem to be a tidy or clever way to finish a chapter that ends with a question. Instead, I will do just that—end with my question: *How can I develop my ability to play, to be lost in the moment and embracing the ambiguities of life, so that I might better engage with students in their play as they too struggle to make meaning out of the ambiguities and problems in their own lives?*

17

WHAT'S LOVE GOT TO DO WITH IT?

Combining the Influences of Race and
Love to Create an Effective Black Counselor

Randy B. Hayward

IN MY FIRST PHENOMENOLOGICAL INVESTIGATION, I documented my process of coming to realize that I view the world through a specific lens that has been created by my experiences. Through the study of hermeneutics I came to understand that my interactions shape how I see the world. The prejudices I possess, which stem from these experiences, inform my subsequent interpretations of myself, people, and events. As Meichenbaum (1988) writes, "Events are not merely 'out there' to be revealed, but rather our (pre)conceptions influence the very nature of what is revealed" (p. 86). Understanding my current interpretations depends on how well I understand my history and what that history means to me. I have not always entered situations with the realization that my history and beliefs play an integral part in shaping my choices and actions. It is when I began to reflect consciously on my life that I realized how my history affects my ways of thinking, and that this causes me to enter into every situation with prejudgments and biases that may benefit or hinder the people with whom I interact.

Packer and Addison (1989) suggest that "we are thrown into future ways of acting that are made possible by our cultural and personal history. . . . We live toward a future whose possibilities are both created and limited by the present and the past" (p. 33). To understand my beliefs and assumptions as they relate to the major question I pose in this second investigation, the reader should know some things about my history:

> I grew up in Detroit, Michigan, in a family of ten: my parents, five boys, and three girls. My history, by today's standards, is "dysfunctional." My parents moved from rural Georgia to Detroit in the late forties with the hope that they would not have to deal with what seemed like an insurmountable barrier for blacks in the South: racism. Racism was shaping my parents' existence before my siblings and I were born. My parents grew up in the thirties and forties with concrete barriers to housing, jobs, and education. Without many options, they settled into one of many black ghettos in Detroit.
>
> Living in an area with many risk factors such as narcotics, crime, and homicide, my parents felt they had to be vigilant, with the hope that their children would not succumb to these risks. My oldest brother did succumb to drugs. My parents, recognizing that they had already lost one child to the problems that plague our community, were not willing to lose another. So, along with their increased protectiveness came a bombardment of warnings: "Don't drink," "Don't do drugs," as well as, "Know who you are associating with." Then came the philosophy by which many blacks have to live: "You have to work twice as hard as white folk to make it in this world." From that point on, most of my experiences have been shaped by the color of my skin.
>
> As a thirteen-year-old paperboy, I did not have just one route; I had three. This required me to work twice as hard as was expected of a boy my age. Later, after I had grown up, I served eight years in the Air Force, even though I only wanted to serve four years. In the Air Force, retirement was the goal to strive for. I did not want to quit, even though I felt unwanted and on the periphery because I was black. "Work hard and prove yourself," the voice of my parents rang loud, preventing me from leaving the Air Force. Later, when I was completing my undergraduate studies, raising two kids alone, working two jobs, and taking part-time classes at another university, I heard their familiar voices telling me to persevere even though I felt overwhelmed with responsibility. I had become the man I never thought I could be, nor wanted to be: my father. My father was a hard worker who always said that a black man must prove himself by showing that he can do the work as well as, if not better than, the white man. My father proved this through his actions, not just his words. He worked harder because he was black. Like him, I enter every situation with this prejudgment. As

Gadamer ([1962] 1966) states, "prejudices . . . constitute the initial directness of our whole ability to experience" (p. 9). As a black man I view my life through a lens developed from the similar experiences of other black men, including my father. Part of that lens dictates that I work twice as hard.

I left the Air Force after eight years in order to work with youth who had been marginalized due to circumstances beyond their control. When I reflect on this decision, I believe it had a lot to do with watching my oldest brother abuse drugs and alcohol, as well as seeing how his actions affected our whole family. I eventually went to work as an outreach worker at an organization that helped place young adults in their own apartments in the community rather than in group homes ["Where I Come from, What I Bring," 1995].

I believe that in order to understand my personal growth this year, I must evaluate it from two points in time. The first point is the starting position, that is, the beginning of the year and my first phenomenological investigation, and the second is my present position, from which this current evaluation is taking place. In this investigation I will present my growth and change, while simultaneously interpreting that growth and change over time. The major components of this interpretation will be: the students I counsel, the system in which I do my work, and me. I define the system as the physical building, the rules put in place by the school system, the ideology of the teachers, and the students who are governed and affected by the school system. My interpretation of growth and change will be analyzed by answering the following question: Other than my race and ethnicity, what do I provide for the students that makes me an effective counselor and mentor?

METHODOLOGY

The data I am using for this research are my year-long counseling notes, related course readings and notes, and written observations and experiences derived from working at the Nichols Elementary School and at the Jordan School, located in a private children's development center. I will use these data to inform my interpretations and to retell the history of the pair therapy and group counseling sessions I conducted at my sites. These data, as they relate to pair therapy and group counseling, will help me to reconstruct the history formed in the triad of pair therapy and in group counseling. It will therefore help me to reveal patterns that played an integral part in my personal growth and change over the year.

The analysis of my growth and change has at its core the under-standing I have gained through our year-long practicum course and by conducting my previous phenomenological investigation. In my previ-ous investigation I wrote, "I do not always enter situations thinking that my history and beliefs are playing an integral part in helping to shape my choices" (Phenomenological Investigation I, 1995). This statement explains how I operated in the world at the time of writing it: I did not connect my actions with my past.

After engaging in critical reflection, I have been able to operate with a heightened level of consciousness. The difference between the last study I wrote and this one, though they were both written through crit-ical reflection, is that the counseling work I have done recently is done with the understanding that my history informs my practice. As a result of writing my first paper, I returned to my sites in January 1996 attempting to do my work with the awareness of the prejudices informing it. At that time, I was beginning to understand how my biases benefited or hindered the people with whom I interacted.

Packer and Addison (1989) state that "we live toward a future whose possibilities are both created and limited by the present and the past" (p. 34). To me this statement means that I must always attempt to understand my past because it is always shaping and dictating my present and future. Although I strive to surpass my limitations, I now know there are boundaries stemming from my experiences. For exam-ple, experiencing white racism limits the trust I have in white folk. This limited trust may cause me to miss out on friendships or other oppor-tunities that may involve white folk. I cannot undo the past, which is marked by oppression, but I should try not to be limited by it. However, just as the past can limit, it can also create possibilities. For example, even within the bounds of white racism, possibilities have been created in my life because of my hardworking parents, caring sib-lings, and positive role models, who all give me the momentum I need to push myself towards a brighter future.

Just as there is much to be learned by looking at the limitations and possibilities created by my personal and cultural histories, there is also something to be learned by looking critically at the history of my expe-riences at my site placements. In reviewing these experiences, I will not be reconstructing this history in order to reveal it to the reader, but instead I will analyze the history in order to make meaning of it, for the purpose of directing me toward more informed ways of working with young people. My reconstruction uses the theory of critical hermeneu-tics, which "is about taking apart oppressive structures in order to rebuild them in healthier ways" (Michael Nakkula, Lecture Notes, Oct. 3, 1995). In terms of the work at my sites, this means looking at the ways in which the sites act as a hindrance or barrier to the children's development, and then using this knowledge to make my work in those environments more beneficial for the children. To look forward and create positive change for the children, I must first look back.

HISTORIES

Revisiting My Personal History

My experience of going back to graduate school and doing an internship was in part shaped by my past. In my first investigation I analyzed my history to explore how my prejudices informed my decision to do the work of pair therapist and group counselor. As noted in my first investigation, Gadamer ([1962] 1966) states, "prejudices . . . constitute the initial directedness of our whole ability to experience" (p. 9). I came to understand that at the forefront of my historical lens was the belief that black men need support systems in place to survive in a society that seems determined to destroy us. I recognized that I had survived to manhood because of a loving environment that fostered an ethic of hard work, and that I therefore saw a need to work with black boys in order to teach them how to navigate through our racist society. This decision was constituted by my prejudice that black boys need the help of someone black who understands them.

History of My Experiences at My Site Placements

I entered pair therapy and group work thinking that I could "save" the black boys with whom I would work. I felt they needed someone to rescue them from the many negative influences they faced, and often I felt like their savior. One tool I was given to save the children was pair therapy. Pair therapy is supposed to enhance the social and interpersonal skills of two paired students during a forty-five-minute therapy session once a week. When I was first given this tool, I thought it was a naive practice based on false hopes for fast cures. Given that I was not a counselor, and did not believe in the "learn as you do" model, I did not see how I would be effective in this setting. I wondered how this counseling modality could help address more pressing issues such as poor academic performance, volatile homes, uninvolved parents, and uncaring teachers.

Initially, I attempted to shut pair therapy out of my work, and in supervision I was forced to look at my motives for wanting to do so. Over time, I learned to capitalize on the ever-present teachable moment. A teachable moment can be any instance that lends itself to exploring, challenging, and educating children. In seeking out these teachable moments I learned to listen, not only to the students' spoken words but also to what they were not saying. Had I not questioned my initial decision not to utilize pair therapy, I would have missed this opportunity for personal and professional growth. The critical questioning of my thoughts and actions, both individually and in supervision, helped me in my professional development and therefore in my service to children.

At the Nichols Elementary School, pair therapy is set apart from the overall systemic functioning of the school. It happens within the school but is not governed by the school's ideology. Therefore, I believe, the students do not see pair therapy as part of the "system." The system, as I understand it, and as I believe the kids also see it, is very controlling. In contrast, pair therapy does not look to control; it looks to enhance skills that are vital in everyday social interactions. These skills include the ability to respect, to compromise, to be tolerant, and to show leadership. One could argue that public education affords similar opportunities, but I disagree. The school requires kids to behave in certain ways (that is, "no talking in line," "walk in a single file," and "don't talk out of turn"). Many of these controlling rules discourage the formation of self-identity and restrict critical thought. Although I work in this environment, pair therapy allows me an opportunity to help the students combat some of these control mechanisms. The students I work with know that for at least forty-five minutes once a week, they will not be forced to walk in straight lines. They also know that they will be asked to speak up and to think critically about their interactions in the world. Furthermore, I believe the students feel I am someone who cares for them. In my first investigation, I reflected on creating this type of environment through pair therapy:

> What I have come to realize is that there are few places in the public school system where students are allowed to express themselves. Sometimes the behavior exhibited at school is the manifestation of bad experiences in their home environments or in their communities. Pair therapy provides the "therapeutic space" in which students can express themselves. "Therapeutic space" is not meant simply to describe the physical place where therapy is conducted or the therapy itself, rather it is "the physical, temporal and interper-

sonal space in which the child and the therapist interact" (Donovan and McIntyre, 1990, p. 111). This "space" is made up of rules, trust, safety, and consistency and has a lot to do with the expectations and the forms of self-expression exhibited by the boys during pair therapy. The boys and I are responsible for orchestrating this "space," which will allow or hinder exploration and creativity [Phenomenological Investigation I, 1995].

Five months ago I would never have thought that I would be applauding pair therapy. But as I saw a controlling environment smothering students, I knew that pair therapy could be a vital tool to engage them in their own learning. Still, I did not lose sight of an even bigger problem: the marginalization of the young black boys with whom I worked. It was these young boys who had been targeted as most needing the services of pair therapy, partly because their teachers felt that pair therapy would serve as some sort of behavior modifier. This could not have been further from the truth. An example of how pair therapy was viewed by some teachers comes from an encounter I had with a fifth grade teacher. She was explaining that the student I counseled was missing class time because of pair therapy. She added that this allowed her not to have to bother with his behavior. She felt that his behavior in class was "disruptive" to her teaching, and that maybe I could do better with him (control him is what I understood her to mean). However, instead of using pair therapy to control him, I used it to enlighten the student about his ability to learn. Instead of focusing on what he was doing to others, I asked him to think about how he was affecting his own progress, and in turn how his progress, or lack of it, affected others.

I came to realize this year that before I could get such a student to a point of reflection, I had to learn more about his context, both in and away from school. Yet many teachers do not take the time to learn about the kids they teach. They only feel that they must teach, and if that teaching is hindered, they should try to control or remove the student. In learning this perspective, I began to understand what role I could play in this system: the role of insider. Such a role could greatly benefit the students. Still, at first I did not want to play this role. I wanted no part of the dogmatic system I observed at the Nichols Elementary School. I even went as far as to say that I would not work in any public school. I have since changed my position.

My change of heart should not be taken lightly. Sometimes it is a struggle to go to the Nichols School, and other times I cannot wait to spend time with the young boys I counsel. My change in position—from not wanting to work in a public school system to feeling that it is my duty—is complex. The most basic thought that allowed for this change is the fact that the kids need someone in their lives to care for them. I realized this year that I may not be the sole someone, the savior, but I do see the need for the services I offer in a public school setting, because so many children, and especially young black boys, are stifled. I also recognize that students need positive role models with whom they can identify. Over the year I have begun to think about issues of racial identity in counseling and to question what I have to offer beyond my racial identity.

Seven months ago I thought my braids, my black vernacular, and the color of my skin were enough for these kids to identify with me. I wanted them to have someone working with them who looks like them. In my first investigation, I explored the relevance of race and ethnicity for therapy:

> For me, my race and ethnicity are the two factors that most critically shape the therapeutic space. These two factors alone fueled my decision to work only with black boys. Having heard all my life that black men had to work twice as hard as white folk, I knew black boys were at a disadvantage. I felt they needed help from someone who understood them. I had come to the site with so many assumptions about "these kids"! I had a father who lived in my home; they did not. Therefore, I concluded, they needed someone to teach them the things that my father taught me. They lived in poverty, and therefore I assumed their homes were unstable. All of these assumptions were based on the fact that I had not experienced many of these conditions myself. Someone was there to help me out of my impoverished surroundings, and I assumed that these children were assigned to counseling because they needed to be provided with protective factors not present in their homes. I did not know what these protective factors were, but I thought that as a counselor I could do better than the homes these children were coming from. Looking back I see that I never asked myself if these kids had other role models. Given the neighborhoods and environments I believed they were coming from, I just assumed they did not have any positive supports. I was the counselor who did not ask questions because I thought I already had the answers. I had not thought to ask about the boys' histories [Phenomenological Investigation I, 1995].

What I did not realize was that I too would have to learn about these children and offer them something more than just my blackness. It is possible that had I not worked with David, the only white student whom I counseled, it may have taken me longer to realize that I was offering students more than just ethnic and cultural identity. Reflecting on my work with David offered me a better understanding of this important fact.

DAVID: HELPING ME SEE BEYOND MY SKIN. David was a fifth grade white male who was assigned to pairs because of behavioral problems that interfered with his academics. When I was told I would have David in one of my pairs, I was not pleased. In all honesty, I felt I was not there for the white students, but given that he was paired with a black student I agreed to work with him. I was not trying to be cruel; I was naive and I believed that I did not have anything to offer David because he was white. I wondered: Given that I was not white, how could he identify with me? I now realize that I left out a major component: my services. For the first three or four months, I did not question why David appeared glad to see me, or why he demanded my presence each week. I took it as a sign that he was just glad to be out of his teacher's class. David's teacher constantly used his harshest punishment against David, making him face the wall. In this teacher's class, students who do not follow his rules are made to stand facing the lockers for an entire day. His rules include: Do not talk out loud! Do not laugh in class! or the dreaded, You will do twice as much tonight! I think this form of punishment is not only mean and controlling but also barbaric. David was often forced to face the lockers, so I thought it was no wonder that during the first three months I knew him he appeared to gravitate from class towards me; I assumed it was because it appeared that I was not part of the school system. What I did not take into account was that I offered David something he was not getting in school: care and the room to express himself.

David showed genuine interest when I spoke to him or placed my hand on his shoulder. When I had to reprimand him, he showed remorse. One day I saw David at the lockers and, as I normally do, asked him why he was there. He said because his teacher did not appreciate being told by him that he "did not want to hear it." I was shocked. David went on to explain that he politely listened to the teacher yell at him, and when the teacher was finished he tried to explain himself. The teacher would not listen, so when he began to speak again, David said he "did not want to hear it." Other students who told me about the incident said David was a "bad student" or "crazy" for talking to the teacher in the manner he did. However, I silently applauded David because he stood up for what he felt was unjust. I was sure he knew the consequences would be to face the lockers, given that he had been sent there for lesser offenses. Nonetheless, David stood his ground. Why had he not acted this way with me? This question made me analyze my interactions with David within the triad of pair therapy as well as in our one-to-one contact.

In my analyses of my interactions with David, I discovered that it is more than racial identification that plays a part in developing therapeutic relationships. David knew to expect me every Tuesday at 1:00 P.M., and my arrival offered him consistency. With consistency came trust. David knew that for at least forty-five minutes a week he could say whatever he felt without fear of repercussions.

I also showed David I cared for him. Although I was often stern with him when I discussed his failing grades or missed homework assignments, I was sure to place my hand on his shoulder as a gesture of affection. I knew that a simple gesture of a hand on his shoulder, a handshake, or a pleasant smile showed him that I cared. Often practitioners forget that we must love the children we serve. And sometimes practitioners do not know the difference between control and tough love. Tough love is the offering of words or actions out of love that the recipient may not like or easily accept because they are challenging. Control is used to stifle, whereas tough love provides direction. This direction is intended to be beneficial to the recipient and is offered through love and care. David knows that he has a place in which he will be cared for and given expectations that will challenge him.

Over the course of this year I have come to recognize the necessity of providing a caring, safe, and trusting environment for all of the students I counseled. But it was with David that I first noticed the importance of these counseling attributes. The other thirteen students, twelve black and one Latino who identifies as black, were benefiting from my services, but I assumed it had more to do with my race and ethnicity than anything else. This assumption was established during my first pair session with Shaka and Jamal, two students at the Jordan School.

SHAKA: RACE AND LOVE. Within the first few minutes of pair therapy with Shaka and Jamal, Shaka said that he felt I would understand them better. I understood Shaka to mean that because of my race we could identify with each other. This assumption came from the knowledge that Shaka did not know anything about me personally or professionally other than the fact that I was black. Shaka had sitting before him someone he saw as a therapist but who looked like any of a number of black males from his community. The difference was that as his therapist I was in a different role than he may have been accustomed to, so I was in a position of possibly being seen as a positive role model.

Having me, a black man, as his therapist may have allowed Shaka to feel less vulnerable. His contact throughout the school day, other than forty-five minutes per week, is with an all-white staff. So it is possible that Shaka felt I would understand him better given that I am also black. For example, I noticed that Shaka spoke to me differently than he did to the white staff members. I believe that Shaka used his black vernacular with me because he knew I would understand him. Shaka often said that he felt the teachers did not know him or where he was coming from.

My race may have allowed Shaka to identify with me initially, but race alone was not going to allow me to build a meaningful relationship with him. Still, because of our race, I believe Shaka may have been more eager to submit to the process of building a relationship than if I had been white. I have come to the realization that in order to engage, one must be willing to submit. By submission, I mean one must be willing to open one's self up to a process of growth. We are continually asking students to do this; however, submitting and allowing one's self to grow must be a two-way process. Both parties, the teacher and the learner, must accept growth and open up to the process of change and development. Failure to have both parties submit usually leads to resistance on someone's part. The sad fact is that those in authority—teachers, therapists, or counselors—tend not to see their own resistance. I feel, therefore, that they see submission as a responsibility of only the student or client and not their own.

I further realized that therapeutic love is a crucial developmental experience when I saw Shaka show the same care to his white therapist (Dennis) whom he has seen over the last three years. Dennis and I felt it was important for Shaka to have the opportunity to see that we worked together in an alliance of care for him. So, together we took Shaka to McDonald's for breakfast. We had some concerns that our joint presence might overwhelm Shaka or make him feel anxious. I was pleasantly surprised to witness Shaka move through his two worlds, that of his white therapist and his black therapist, so easily and comfortably. I was even more shocked to see that Shaka showed a tremendous amount of genuine care for his white therapist. Shaka talked to his therapist in a pleasant voice, and at times held his hand. As a result of this experience, I was forced to ask myself the question: What caused Shaka to have this trust and care in his white therapist?

Had I continued to believe that race was the sole factor in allowing me to connect to these black children, I would not have been able to find an answer to the question I just posed. Dennis has recognized that he can offer advice, care, understanding, and patience only if he engages with Shaka. This engagement will add to Shaka's continued growth as well as to Dennis's. My own growth came in part through my realization that a black-white client-therapist bond could be as beneficial for both individuals as the bond between a black therapist and black client as long as care and nurturance were the foundation of their bond.

CONCLUSION

My growth and change has been uncovered as I have charted the change and growth in my relationships with the students with whom I have worked. I entered a system and have questioned my place from day one. I have also learned to reflect critically on and question myself. This dual process of questioning the system and myself has forced me to become more critical of my own beliefs as well as the beliefs of the people and systems around me. Through my systematic questioning I have realized that I initially operated from a lack of awareness about the reasons I practiced in particular ways. As my lack of consciousness was brought to a more conscious level, my practice became better informed. This has not only benefited me, but it has also benefited the students and systems within which I have worked.

There was something within my history that caused me to see race as the most vital factor in working with black youth. I recognized that I was limiting the contributions I was making to the children by seeing only race as a factor. In addition to race, we must offer care and nurturance to children if we hope to connect with them. But before we can find that connection, we must be willing to review and interpret our own histories as well as the histories of the children. This critical process of reflection should be done continually in order to push the margins of our own understanding of self. The tearing down and reconstruction of self and others, although not easy, is necessary if we want to better serve children.

18

THEATRICAL DIALOGUE

A Hermeneutic Analysis of Change in One Act

Robert W. Leary

THE FOLLOWING SCRIPT IS INTENDED for live performance. It represents a year's worth of hermeneutic inquiry, and attempts to answer, through a methodology that integrates theory, research, and practice, both my initial and my emerging questions.

I (the investigator, represented by the main character in the play, Rob) worked as an intern at the Massachusetts Prevention Center and recorded my experiences there. Most of these notes were reflective, recounting my experiences at points during the year, and were recorded immediately after the experiences occurred. I analyzed these notes and recorded the questions that, upon further reflection, arose for me in the analysis. These questions, along with my personal reflections on my work at the Prevention Center, can be found in the three papers I have written since I began the practicum course. These data and investigations are integrated into the dialogue of this play. In short, Rob asks questions, a vignette is presented and processed, and new questions are asked. The change over time becomes apparent in the new questions asked, that is, through the return arc of the hermeneutic circle.

THE CAST

ROB: Hermeneutic Investigator

MEMBERS OF THE HERMENEUTIC CIRCLE: Hans-Georg Gadamer, Shaun Gallagher, Martin Heidegger, Paul Ricoeur, Robert Steele, Jurgen Habermas, Richard Addison, Donald Spence, Dorothy Smith

MIKE NAKKULA: Practicum Professor

FRAN: Intern Coordinator at the Prevention Center

ANNA: Intern Supervisor and Youth Development Specialist

SHUNA: Co-director of Teenage Girls InFormed (TGIF)

MEMBERS OF TGIF: Dionne, Tia, Shironda, Tracy

HEYWORTH PEER EDUCATORS: Nancy, Kathy, Thom, John, Leslie

CHUCK: Alcohol and Other Drug (AOD) Educator at Heyworth

MICHAEL: Dean of Student Activities at Heyworth

STAGE NOTES

The stage is bare, except for a giant circle hanging upstage in front of the scrim. The circle is lit from above. Enter the members of the Hermeneutic Circle, a sort of Greek chorus. They stand in a circle and speak in unison unless otherwise noted.

CIRCLE: Truth is a question. Questions lead to answers, which in turn lead to questions. The process of understanding is a process of asking ever more intricate—

[*Rob enters, unseen by the Circle. He stands to their right, listening and observing.*]

GALLAGHER: —questions.

CIRCLE: The process is a circle. A hermeneutic circle.

HEIDEGGER: Uncovering—

STEELE: —questioning—

PACKER AND ADDISON: —and evaluating—

RICOEUR: —action—

GADAMER: —and understanding.

ROB: So, what do you want to know? I started this year so full of hope, so full of confidence. I really thought I knew what was going to happen. I was quoting Augusto Boal left and right, talking about oppression, hoping against all hopes that I would actually help students.

[*Enter Mike Nakkula.*]

MIKE: You did know what you were doing. You said that you'd taught drama, and as I noted in your practicum placement interview, you have quite a clinical background.

[*Mike exits, stage right.*]

ROB: Yeah, but I had so many questions.

CIRCLE: We must look for a starting place, one that will vary from inquiry to inquiry, not an absolute foundation.

ROB: Yeah, yeah, yeah. So what was my starting place? I entered the circle with my own beliefs, and my own questions. I didn't know if the work I wanted to do with young people would be effective. But I had to answer the questions put forth to me by the mighty Doctor Mike Nakkula and his teaching fellows, Dorothy Smith and Sharon Ravitch. I had to clarify where I was starting from, like you said.

CIRCLE: *Not* an absolute foundation.

ROB: OK, so you've said that. Twice now. I think I understand.

GADAMER: Ask yourself this: What do you bring? The answer is important, but more important are the questions that arise from your answer.

ROB: I really don't think that's enough, though. I had to identify the lens through which I would be viewing my work, so the answer to that *is* important.

GADAMER: Yes, yes, the lens is very important. But to identify the lens, you must ask yourself what it is you bring to this work. And much value can be found in the answers you provide to the question. But of even more value is what you find in the questions that arise from your answers.

ROB: I see. I brought hope. I brought years of living as an alcoholic, an addict, nearly forgetting what it was like to really feel human. I brought the experience of struggling to get back into everyday life, to be happy just to be alive. I brought three years as a recovering addict, drug- and alcohol-free. I brought a lot of information about alcohol and drugs, and why people use them. I brought my experiences in the theater: my passion for it, and all the headaches that eventually drove me away from it. I brought my memory of losing myself in performance, in characters, my fear of losing my tenuous hold on recovery to the lure of the stage, and the flight from reality it had consistently brought me. I brought an awareness of the healing and education that the theater can bring. And I brought a need to try to prevent others from becoming addicts, especially young people, through that healing.

GALLAGHER: What questions do you hear yourself asking?

STEELE: Look at it from "odd angles." Ask these questions: What are you telling us, and why? Why is it important that you are an addict?

ROB: [*Frustrated*] It's important because it's who I am! It is the reason why I want to do what I want to do. The theater is a love I've worked hard to accept in myself. It's wrapped up in my addiction!

HABERMAS: You're getting defensive. That sort of communication won't help matters.

ROB: Will it make any difference in my work that I am an addict, that I have a personal sneak peek into what the Prevention Center wants me to prevent? Will it affect the peer leaders with whom I work? Will I be able to foster an understanding of what it's like to be an addict? To prevent kids from becoming addicts? To develop a compassion in the kids I work with for people who are addicted, so that they don't see them as criminals or bad people but as people who are sick and in need of treatment? And still help the kids learn to make healthy decisions? Or even to just help them understand what addiction is and where it comes from? Will I learn to leave my own history of addiction at the door? Or will I find that I am self-centeredly pulling that information out when I should keep it to myself? Will this knowledge help the girls in Teenage Girls InFormed, TGIF, the theater company I co-direct, to portray their characters better? Will they even want to ask me what it's like to be an addict, or how I became one? And if they do ask, will it help them to know? What does it mean, anyway?

CIRCLE: Right!

ROB: So what if I want to answer these questions? I mean, no offense to the Circle, but I really want to know whether or not my experiences are valuable to the kids with whom I work. These questions aren't just there to lead me to more "intricate questions." They're also part of my career, what I want to do, and whether or not my history matters for that. I think the answers to these questions are crucial to my ability to work effectively with students, and with my colleagues.

[The members of the Circle move to the back wall, facing upstage.]

ROB: Back in November, Shuna and I held a retreat for the members of TGIF. We did a drawing activity, called LifeMaps, in which the participants use pictures and symbols to represent their own histories, achievements, goals, and experiences. The questions we asked them to answer were: Where do you come from? What is something you're proud of? What is one of your goals? and What was your first experience with alcohol? We all drew our life maps, and in order to answer my questions about addiction, I included my experience of being in recovery in the "something I'm proud of" section.

[Rob joins TGIF members at the table.]

DIONNE: And so that's Boston, and that's where I come from and this is my first experience with alcohol, you see the 7-Up and the Seagram's Seven, and my goal is to go to college. You're next.

ROB: OK, so the truck and the bricks represent the Army, because I grew up in a military family and I'm not really from anywhere; and my first experience with alcohol was my father's Rob Roys. See the cherry, he used to let me eat them. And this represents my graduation from college last year, something that I never really thought would happen, because of my being an addict. And this represents my being in recovery from alcoholism and addiction for three years now; and my goal is to do more work in the theater, to combine it with my work in prevention, because I really like doing theater and think it's a fun and powerful way to get messages across to people. Art moves people, and I want to use it to move people into healthy decisions, healthy lifestyles, into living without abusing drugs and alcohol. So who's next?

SHIRONDA: I'll go—

[*Rob walks down stage center to talk to the audience. The TGIF members leave and the Hermeneutic Circle moves back into a circle.*]

ROB: Yeah, so that's it. We didn't talk about my history in rehearsals again. And I was fine with that: I didn't want to make it an issue, and I'm glad I got to put it on the table. I think I have my answer, though. Nobody was really interested in my experiences with addiction, at least not in TGIF. Why, I think they pretty much forgot about it.

CIRCLE: Do you presume that simply because the girls do not seem to care about it that it does not matter? Have you not yet realized that who you are and what you bring affects the way you perceive your work as well as your interactions? And that every interaction, upon reflection, affects your interpretations of every interaction that follows? And that these interpretations can lead you to make decisions that can affect other people's lives?

ROB: Y'all sure do ask a lot of questions.

DOROTHY: That's what we're here for.

ROB: Not to say y'all aren't right, either. Every interpretation of an interaction, upon reflection, *does* affect the way I look at the world, at my work. What's significant, to *me* anyway, was that I have a personal source of inspiration, motivation, *whatever;* it's why I need to do this work. And that when I talk to Tracy, the recovering alcoholic, about her character, I have a clear picture of what she, the character, is feeling, and when Tracy asks me what she could be doing better, I have something meaningful to tell her. I understand the meaning of addiction, the effects, the implications.

DOROTHY: Has she ever asked you to tell her?

ROB: No.

DOROTHY: So why'dya bring it up?

ROB: Look who's jumping the gun now! The reason I brought it up is because I have that belief, that understanding, and it's a resource. Even though I know that nobody has to use it, they can if they want to. That's how that experience changes the way I look at all of this, how my *hermeneutic* perspective has changed. I identified my lens, asked a question, conducted a kind of test, evaluated what happened, and now I see how my perspective has changed. I see that I don't even have to mention that I'm an addict, an alcoholic, for it to affect my interactions with young people.

CIRCLE: But that is not the end of the changes, and that is only one question.

ROB: Yeah, yeah, I know, I know. There are all sorts of changes, all sorts of questions, and every question leads to ever more intricate questions.

DOROTHY: I'm glad to see you're catching on.

ROB: I came to a realization over the winter. A realization that led me to a whole new question, a question about hermeneutics. This question changed the way I conceptualize the creativity of acting and the rehearsal process.

CIRCLE: Questions, questions, questions—

[*Rob steps forward to deliver the following monologue to the audience, gesturing to the Circle when appropriate.*]

ROB: I told you before about my love of the theater. It's not just the performance that fascinates me but the process of preparing for that performance. I love that process: digging inside myself, pulling out the tough stuff and the fun stuff, getting to know it, love it, embrace it. I love knowing my own emotions so well that I can call on them when I need to, freeing myself of my inhibitions so I can be spontaneous in every sense of the word. This was what the theater was for me, and I want to share it and use it for a better purpose than just bringing in a dollar or providing entertainment. That's why I was so glad to find out about TGIF and to be asked to be a part of it. I saw the company itself as a workshop for the actors to explore their own selves—their feelings, opinions, biases, and stresses. And a chance for

them to experience addiction, almost firsthand, through their characters, and to impart the lessons of that experience to the audiences
they touched. As we progressed through the year, though, and I read
more about hermeneutics, I began to realize that there were more
similarities between acting and the circle.

RICOEUR: Interpretation is always a form of reading; all interpretation
is analogous to textual interpretation.

ROB: Right! And so, what is the foundation of acting if not the first
cold read-through of a play? The emotive reading of a text before an
audience? The performance is literally the interpretation of a text. The
script is the text, the way the actor reads it, the interpretation. It is a
hermeneutic activity. The actor moves forward in his interpretation of
the text by performing, then steps back to assimilate the feedback he's
given by the director or by the other actors. The feedback is integrated—

GALLAGHER: [*Interrupting*] Accommodated!

ROB: *Accommodated.* And the new interpretation is presented in order
to undergo the process again—

CIRCLE: A *circle*!!!

ROB: Yes, a circle. But still, that's not all. I asked myself, What is the
mark of a good actor? For me, it is her ability to realistically portray
her character, to read the lines and interpret the text as if they were *not*
scripted, as if she did not know what she would be saying next, and to
"fill in" the emotional content of those lines. In building her character,
the actor uses her own emotional experience as the meat of her character's feelings. She must work from her past experiences and feelings to
move into the lines and become the character.

CIRCLE: The movement between what is known and what is portrayed
is circular in fashion.

ROB: Yes! The actor knows, understands, herself. She draws her experience into the present, into the lines she says, and gives them new meaning. The new and the old meaning blend, and her interpretation of the
lines is changed. Whereas once there were only lines and distant emo-

tional experiences, there are now lines infused with emotions. These are presented and then revised through the feedback the actor receives from the director.

CIRCLE: A circle.

ROB: A circle. For example, watch what happened at this rehearsal for TGIF back in November. [*Shironda, Dionne, Tia, Tracy, and Shuna enter, and the Circle spreads out against the scrim.*] Shironda is supposed to open her monologue in intense anger. Yet her lines sounded more like apathy than anger.

SHIRONDA: Stop. No more facts. No more figures. No more.

ROB: Shironda. Try again, only this time, more. More anger. We need more emotion from you.

SHIRONDA: I just can't. I can't be angry, I don't feel angry.

SHUNA: Maybe if you tried to remember a time when you were angry, you could use that feeling to get the effect we need.

SHIRONDA: OK. [*Still pretty flat*] Stop. No more facts. No more figures. No more. No more.

ROB: OK. Let's try something different. Shironda, what in your life made you really angry?

SHIRONDA: I was accused of stealing when I didn't.

ROB: I need a volunteer. How about Tia? Accuse Shironda of stealing your notebook. Accuse her until she gets angry.

SHIRONDA: OK, but I don't see how this is gonna work.

TIA: [*Getting up*] Hey! You stole my notebook!

SHIRONDA: No, I didn't. You lost it.

TIA: No, you stole it. You're always stealing things.

SHIRONDA: I didn't take it— This isn't working.

SHUNA: OK, Tia, really accuse her of stealing it. Just keep at her until she really gets angry.

[*Tia keeps accusing her, pointing her fingers at her, yelling, growing in volume and intensity until Shironda's pleas of innocence can no longer be heard.*]

SHIRONDA: STOP!!!!!

[*Rob steps out of the scene to talk to the audience. Shuna and the TGIF group leave and the Circle re-forms.*]

ROB: Shironda wasn't able to portray the anger her character needed because she wasn't reaching into her experience and finding the anger she was capable of feeling. The exercise gave her that experience, and she was able to use that feeling to begin her monologue. She found her starting point, reinterpreted her lines, moved forward into them with a new understanding of where she was going. When she completed her monologue, she moved back to reexamine it, and interpreted it again, understanding it in a new way, understanding the impact of starting with anger.

GADAMER: I think the exercise gave her more than that. That it was more than just an experience. I think that she experienced the profound sensation of play, that for a moment she wasn't playing her part like some game, that rather she became a part of the play, a part of the game!

ROB: As an actor, it is important that she "become" her character. In becoming a character, she isn't just saying lines, "she," as it were, is gone. There is only the character, and she is the character, and she is saying and feeling the lines, saying them naturally and without the need to think them through. She is lost in the character, she has surrendered her *self* to the play!

GADAMER: Play fulfills its purpose only if the player loses himself in the play. The actual subject of play is obviously not the subjectivity of an individual who, among other activities, also plays, but it is instead the player being played himself.

ROB: I think so. I have the hardest time understanding you when you talk like that.

GADAMER: Sorry. My language, the language of hermeneutics, has become internalized.

ROB: Okay. But it's not as if she has disappeared and the character has taken over. She is the character, but when she emerges she is the same person she was when she became the character.

GADAMER: But in becoming the character, she has had an experience. An experience of being another, living in the world of another.

ROB: A world that she created, and yet that is not exactly hers! And because the characters these girls are playing have all been profoundly touched by alcohol, I would say that they, the girls, stand a chance of being touched as well.

GADAMER: The world of the game will change you, but you must accommodate to the experience of being played!

ROB: Of course. So anyway, that's not it. I mean, I have other questions, questions I never realized I would be asking. The first question came from an experience I had with a group of college peer leaders at Heyworth College. Originally I went there with Anna and Fran for an introductory meeting with the alcohol-and-other-drugs educator, the dean of student activities, and the peer counselors there. Some strange and unexpected things happened, which led to new questions and discoveries that are important to my work in prevention and education because they could change how I work.

[*The Hermeneutic Circle unfolds against the scrim, and eight of the peer leaders from Heyworth, along with Chuck (the AOD educator), Michael (the dean), Fran, and Anna enter with chairs.*]

ROB: I really thought everything was going fine. I got the feeling that Chuck and Jack really believed that I knew how to teach them about alcohol and other drugs.

PACKER: That's what you were there for.

ROB: Right. And it was my first time, too. But nothing prepared me for what happened, for how it changed my perspective, or for the new questions I was forced to contemplate.

[*Rob sits and becomes part of the scene with Anna, Fran, and the Heyworth people. Fran is standing, miming that she is writing on a chalkboard, while the others sit.*]

FRAN: So that's it. We've set the schedule, and this looks like it's going to be great!

CHUCK: [*Standing*] Thank you so much for coming. [*Shakes Rob's hand, and Fran's too, but not Anna's.*]

[*Rob and Anna head down stage to talk. As they do, the Heyworth people and Fran clear the stage and exit.*]

ROB: I think this is gonna be great. I'm really excited to be working with college kids, you know? That's the age group I've wanted to be working with all along. So what do you think?

ANNA: I don't know—

ROB: What?

ANNA: Did you see that?

ROB: See what?

ANNA: That Chuck guy.

ROB: Yeah, what about him?

ANNA: Did you see how he treated me? Like I wasn't even there.

ROB: What did he do? I was so nervous about being here, starting with the new group, I didn't notice.

ANNA: He shook your hand, and he shook Fran's hand, but not mine. When we started, he didn't even introduce himself to me. I just sat there, and he ignored me. The fat guy, too. Fran had to introduce me to him, draw his attention to me. He didn't need to have his attention drawn to you, did he?

ROB: No. That's really strange, since you're my supervisor.

ANNA: You are gonna learn a lot during this training, Rob. [*Pause*] I'm glad you're doin' this with me. I've never worked with an all-white group before, and I think you're gonna learn a lot.

[*Anna exists. The Hermeneutic Circle re-forms center stage.*]

CIRCLE: What are you wondering?

ROB: [*Pause*] I'm wondering why Chuck didn't shake Anna's hand. I mean, I don't want to think it, but I would guess from what she says it's 'cause she's Latina, and for some reason that's not enough for him to respect her.

CIRCLE: What do you think of that?

ROB: I mean, I'm sure he didn't mean to do that, but, but from what I've learned this year it seems that—

CIRCLE: Seems that what?

ROB: It just bugs me. I mean, Anna's my boss! I just don't usually think about shit like that. Like he should treat everyone the same. And I didn't even notice! It, it, it—

DOROTHY: Nothing like a scratch on the lens to help you see it more clearly.

ROB: You're right. Now I'm beginning to wonder whether all the Heyworth people are gonna be like that.

CIRCLE: Is there a question?

ROB: Yeah. How am I gonna learn from this? And I've never done this before, so how can I be of any help to Anna? I don't have any self-confidence. And I was just so amazed that that Chuck guy would want to talk to me that I didn't notice what Anna was experiencing. I think she's right, I am gonna learn a lot, but how on earth am I gonna learn it if I can't even see it? I want to know what I can do, as a white guy, to get these kids to think before they act, to open their minds, to value diversity.

CIRCLE: Do you?

ROB: Do I what?

SPENCE: Value that diversity? Do you realize when you're being offensive? Do you think that just because you are not thinking hateful thoughts that you are immune from racism?

ROB: Now hold on, that's a huge issue.

SPENCE: You're right. It is a huge issue. But it's on the table; it's on your mind, and it's certainly on Anna's mind.

ROB: She told me once that she thinks about that all the time when she's dealin' with white people. That she always feels like she has to prove herself. This sure as hell didn't go into my first paper. It was too unexpected. [*Pause*] Hey! There's a change right there! I didn't even think about that. I mean, I went to Mike's class, so I couldn't help but think about race. Everything seemed to be goin' all right so I never thought about it. With Anna bringing it up, putting it in my face, everything about what I do at work changes, especially at Heyworth. I've become open to seeing more, hearing more, thinking about more, and dealing with it.

CIRCLE: What is your lens?

ROB: Race. And whether or not these white kids at Heyworth take Anna seriously. I mean, it would hurt us both to have to tell them who's the boss and who's the intern, to set up some kind of power structure for them to buy into in order to get her the respect she simply deserves—

CIRCLE: The system.

ROB: What?

CIRCLE: The system. You are talking about the system.

ROB: The system? You mean how we do things, the structure we set up? How we present ourselves?

GADAMER: In a manner of speaking, yes. How does the system interact with you, how do you interact with the students, and how do the students interact with the system? How are they affected? How are you affected? And, how can you affect the system?

ROB: Those are tough questions. You're so postmodern.

GADAMER: I am just a simple man, no real—

ROB: [*Interrupting him*] Quiet, I'm thinking. I want to set up a system to promote equality so we can all feel free to be who we really are. Peer leadership trainings aren't as much about giving the peers information as getting them to look inside themselves, to think about the issues we bring up with regard to alcohol and other drugs, and other issues as well. So my question is, How can Anna and I use the system to teach the Heyworth people about alcohol, drugs, and peer leadership, but also get them to learn more about diversity and to value Anna for who she is in the process? Will anything we do to that effect work?

CIRCLE: So what happened?

ROB: OK, as I thought it would be, it's hard to say. The first night, Anna and I presented on our own and everything went pretty well.

[*The Heyworth students and Anna enter.*]

ROB: The curriculum went according to our plan: we split up the activities; I led some, she led some, both of us led the rest together. [*Rob does not enter the scene yet, and the Hermeneutic Circle is still together.*]

ANNA: [*To the Heyworth students*] OK, so this is the first time I've worked this curriculum, and the first time I've worked with a group like you guys, and I just wanted to get that up front before we got started—

[*The Circle spreads out against the back wall again.*]

ANNA: So that's that. Now Rob, you have the next activity, right?

ROB: Right! Thanks, Anna, and good job! So next, we're gonna do a little activity called "LifeMaps"—

[*They all freeze. Rob steps out of the scene and speaks directly to the circle.*]

ROB: That was my big mistake. After that session was over, Anna yelled at me for saying "good job" to her after a couple of the exercises. She was really angry with me because she thought my commending her showed that I assumed she didn't know what she was doing. And she was furious because of the way she felt the kids perceived it. Like I felt I was in charge of her, and therefore needed to encourage her at every step. She felt undermined by me.

RICOEUR: That sounds like quite a hermeneutic conundrum. Where did the misinterpretation begin?

ROB: Well, let me start with the lens I walked in with. I said before that I wanted the kids to respect Anna for who she was, not treat her the way Chuck did. And so I wanted there to be a sense of equality between the two of us, one that, if the kids didn't automatically assume it would be there, we could project into the room. And I acted with that in mind, and probably took every action with that rationalization behind it.

HEIDEGGER: And so that was your misunderstanding?

ROB: No, that's not it. I say "good job" to people because I think everybody needs encouragement. What I came to understand later is that Anna's experience of being told "good job" is that it is patronizing and even racist.

STEELE: I see. So when someone says "good job" to Anna, particularly a white person, it comes off to her as a power play.

ROB: That's *my* understanding, from our conversations anyway. My intention was good, but I didn't know enough about Anna to act the way I did. If I had been better able to take perspective, I wouldn't have said that! [*Pause*] It's amazing, you know, this pulling-apart of understanding, misunderstanding—looking at it and trying to understand how it works, how these things change, the lines of experience that lead one person to one interpretation and others to completely different ones.

HABERMAS: But the communication didn't end there, did it?

ROB: No, of course not. I said "good job" to Anna one time after that, but it was at the end of the training, and she started it—she said "good job" to me. I said the same back to her, and it was all right. We'd been working together long enough that I better understood her and therefore knew when and when not to say things, when it was appropriate and when not. And that, too, is a change.

[*Gallagher steps out of the circle, jumping up and down.*]

GALLAGHER: Tell us! Tell us! We love changes!

ROB: Me, too. The change was in how we worked together, how we grew in relationship to one another. But I'll get back to that in a minute. We never finished talking about race.

CIRCLE: Right!

ROB: So, we kept looking for "teachable moments," and one finally fell into our laps.

[*The circle opens up again, and the Heyworth students begin playing a game.*]

ROB: We were about halfway through the training, working on a set of activities about media images and messages and how they relate to alcohol. The activity we were doing was a form of "Win, Lose, or Draw, in which there were two teams, and the "artist" for each team had to get an anti-drunk-driving slogan across to his or her teammates by drawing pictures. Anna and I didn't realize that one of the slogans from the curriculum, "*Passe la llave,*" was in Spanish. Both Anna and I speak Spanish, so we didn't think much of it. But then the teams protested—

NANCY: This is in Spanish! How am I supposed to get them to say this?

ANNA: How do you think?

ROB: [*Part of the scene now*] Anna, what do you think we should do?

KATHY: We can't do this. It's in Spanish. We don't speak Spanish.

THOM: We could do it—

JOHN: We could try—

ROB: [*To the Circle*] So they did it in Spanish. Some of the peers knew how to speak Spanish, so we had them do the drawings for English and then translate. It took them a little while, but they did it. The learning opportunity came afterwards, when we processed the exercise. [*Heyworth students move to sit down at the table.*] We went through why each slogan was important, and then it occurred to me to ask what it was like not to be able to understand the message.

LESLIE: It was hard. Like, I wanted to be useful, to know what they were trying to say, but I can't speak the language.

JOHN: It was probably no harder for us, probably less frustrating, than it is for all the people in this country who don't speak English.

ANNA: Yeah, right. So why is it important to have these messages out there, in other languages?

JOHN: Because it's not just English speakers who need to know about drinking and driving. Everybody needs to think about it.

ROB: Because they need to be able to make healthy decisions, right?

THOM: Right.

[*Rob gets up from the table and walks back to center. The Hermeneutic Circle forms back into a circle again, and the Heyworth students exit.*]

ROB: I'm glad I got the chance to do this activity with them in that way.

ANNA: Yeah. I've done that activity with kids before, but there were always Latinos there. I think some of them really got thinking on that one, about feeling excluded. Do you think anything changed?

ROB: Well, some of them, some of them are still pretty closed-minded. That one woman—

ANNA: I don't think anything gets through to her. But John, and Thom, and Leslie, they seemed to get the message.

ROB: I do think so.

ANNA: I told you you were gonna learn something. [*She exits.*]

ROB: Yeah—

CIRCLE: Well?

ROB: Well, that's it. The training went on for a few more sessions, and then we were done.

CIRCLE: Did anything change? Did your activities do anything?

ROB: I'm not sure. It's really hard to tell.

GALLAGHER: No glaring changes, huh?

ROB: Nope.

GADAMER: Did they at least come to a hermeneutic understanding of Anna's dilemma, or did you have an epiphany, or did—

ROB: Nope. But I now think more about race, and about different points of view, and I try to analyze my assumptions, and be open to others' experiences, but mostly it's just working with people, one-on-one and in groups, and knowing that relationships take time to build, and that misunderstanding is inevitable, but not absolute. But being there, and being there for the people with whom I work. Watching. Being ready for the tiny changes, and appreciative of them when they happen. The growth I went through this year was a small, daily process. The changes, in and of themselves, were minute. But I look at things a little differently now—not so excited, but still enthusiastic. Not so self-centered, but more open. Not without confidence, but with a greater understanding of the expanse of that which I do not know.

STEELE: That sounds so boring. Think about what you're not saying. There's a wealth of information there to be explored. Perhaps if you—

ROB: You know, sometimes I think you ask too many questions. I remember once, Mike Nakkula said in class—

MIKE: [*Entering as Rob speaks*] The important thing is the experience of being there. Showing up, being present. The drama can be misleading. [*He exits.*]

CIRCLE: Ooooooh.

ROB: So that's it. [*To the circle*] What were the changes? [*To the audience*] There were plenty more. Trust me. Suffice it to say, I know less than I did at the beginning. But I am open to more now. I've seen a little of the way people work in groups, and how they think and act without taking others' perspectives. I now ask: How do I act without seeing, and how do my actions, invisible to me, affect those around me? I'm open to understanding that the best of intentions can wreak the worst of havoc. I've been shown up, and I've grown up in the process. I've learned to come from a place of knowing that I do not understand, and to act accordingly, and to look at my actions and the feedback they generate and try to learn more, not so that I can act "right," but so I can learn more about the questions I need to be asking. I have learned to see that I am part of a system, and that that system is part of a greater system, with one thing acting on another, and creating changes in systems removed from the ones I inhabit. Was it worth it? Sure. Do I need them? [*Motions to the Circle*] Sure. But now, I have learned to ask my own questions. [*Turns to leave, then looks back at the audience*] So what did *you* learn?

[*He turns, and walks off. All lights out, except those directly above the Hermeneutic Circle. They exit in a line, looking forward first, then backward, and the last lights go down as they leave the stage.*]

19

COMING FULL CIRCLE

The Return Arc of Reflection

"SO, WHAT DID *YOU* LEARN?"

Leary's concluding question in the preceding chapter is a useful place for us to begin this return arc of reflection. We expect that each reader will reflect back on the book and make meaning of it in different ways, depending on the places from which you were projected into it—the prior exposure you had to hermeneutics and various forms of applied development work with youth, your needs and interests, and the practical and political demands you are confronted with in your life and work.

We were projected into the writing of this book from the impassioned perspectives of teaching and learning over the past five years about a hermeneutics for applied developmental theory, research, and practice. What we learned and taught through discussion and reading has been transformed through our writing. We complete this book having written a different message than that which we set out to communicate. The message is different because it was constructed, deconstructed, and continuously revised from a starting point that was radically transformed through the clarifying process of writing. Consistent with Ricoeur's (1981) contention, however, that writing "fixes" one's thoughts on the page, thereby releasing them for an infinite array of public interpretations over which the author has little to no control, we recognize that what we view as a clear message will, from our perspective, be misunderstood, misapplied, and misappropriated in any number of ways. We have learned to appreciate this inevitability, even as we remain a bit apprehensive. We are appreciative knowing that every interpretation holds the power to push understanding the next step forward.

As we reflect on what in our message has been transformed through writing, we leave the reader with a brief summation of what we have learned more clearly. Perhaps our most poignant clarification has been in the ethical domain of our work: a hermeneutic approach to theory, research, and practice in the applied developmental arena is a thoroughly ethical endeavor. In practice, applied developmentalists' interpretations influence the lives of those in our care; in research, our interpretations depict the thoughts, feelings, behaviors, and even character of real people, who run the risk of having their lives influenced by our research "findings"; in theory building, our interpretations may be used to view people and to construct approaches to working with them in potentially constructive and destructive ways. When as interpreter we sit in a position of power, it is particularly critical to recognize the ethical implications of what we consider to be true. It is equally important to recognize that what we view as true is shaped by our cultural values, principles, and ways of being, and therefore that our truths are necessarily biased. Using our authority to act on these truths unreflectively is not only irresponsible, it is also unethical.

RESEARCH AND PRACTICE TOWARD EMANCIPATION

Heightened awareness of the ethical responsibility associated with interpretive authority need not be immobilizing. It can, in fact, prompt us to act more fervently on our beliefs, particularly when those beliefs are co-constructed through genuine appreciation of the viewpoints of others, including perspectives that seem to contradict our own. Ethically informed action must embrace as broad a range of opinion as possible. To discard contradictory ideas unreflectively is to weaken the platform from which we practice, whether that practice is applied developmental work, such as counseling or teaching, or research. We use the word *platform* to acknowledge the political basis from which so much of interpretation and communicative action proceeds. Herein lies an additional lesson we have learned more clearly through writing this book: not only is interpretation saturated in ethics, it is also thoroughly political.

Most of us conduct our work from a specific political platform. Quite often, however, that platform is not consciously distinguishable to us. *The forgetfulness of being,* Gadamer's ([1962] 1976) term for those lessons that have been so thoroughly internalized that they are not readily available for conscious recognition, captures the often concealed influence of politics on our interpretive actions. What exactly do we mean here by politics? We mean a broad range of things, including the politics of discourse in education, in the workplace, and in the larger society. Through our students' use in their chapters (the phenomenological case studies) of the educator Lisa Delpit's work, we learned more clearly about the role that language plays in the school lives of many low-income children, particularly children of color. When children are socialized into a different dialect than the one their teachers speak, and are misunderstood as a consequence, they are placed at an educational disadvantage. Like Delpit, we view this as a critical example of the politics of interpretation.

As Delpit points out, teachers do not consciously place select groups of students at a disadvantage because of linguistic differences; they place them at a disadvantage unintentionally. Nonetheless, this unintentional act can have crippling ramifications. When teachers and students misinterpret each other's actions based on a misunderstanding of words, students pay the price. That price can include a spiraling cycle of alienation from school and an interpretation of self as unintelligent or incapable of learning. Allowing such interpretations to proliferate is politically harmful, whether they stem from conscious design or unconscious ignorance.

Although Delpit's work focuses on teachers, her exemplary model of misunderstanding is equally applicable to counseling and clinical practice. As McDonough's phenomenological investigation (Chapter Twelve) into the role of language in client-centered counseling so vividly portrays, even the best-intended efforts to communicate nondirectively with clients are directed by unconscious political leanings. McDonough's deconstruction of his language use with a high school student uncovers numerous white middle-class biases that he was unconsciously communicating and that his working-class client was assimilating into his own responses during the counseling sessions. Although these biases are not inherently harmful, they are, as McDonough points out, implicitly disrespectful of his client's linguistic background. An implication of McDonough's study is that those with more power tend to impose their communication styles on those with less power. The burden of being understood, at least approximately, then falls on those with less power, who are expected to accommodate to the speaking style of those with more power. Although McDonough's study is derived from a therapeutic context, the lessons, we argue, are applicable to any number of settings and relationships.

The authors of the phenomenological investigations presented in this book conducted their research and practice primarily in school-based settings, but they carried out their work through a variety of approaches. Through each of these approaches, from in-school suspension counseling to theatrical expression, political dimensions of interpretation were uncovered. Cheng (Chapter Eleven) examined the politics of speaking and listening that influenced the learning possibilities for herself and her Asian students; Seaton (Chapter Six) connected his experiences growing up black in urban Philadelphia with the sometimes political obstacles faced by black middle school students in Boston. Cheng's and Seaton's studies are framed as confrontations of oppression, both political and psychological. A similar framing can be placed on each of the investigations in this book. This common framing did not occur by coincidence. Hermeneutic research and practice lead to the uncovering of barriers. Those barriers tend to cut across various domains: political, personal, and professional. As the phenomenological investigations portray, hermeneutic research within our framework attempts to uncover these barriers, not only to enhance understanding but also to clarify the focus of both politically and personally informed applied developmental practice.

A HERMENEUTIC INTERPRETATION OF EMPATHY

The linking of the personal and political, or psychology and politics, is at the core of what separates our hermeneutic framework for applied developmental practice from more traditional approaches, such as client-centered, psychodynamic, and cognitive-behavioral counseling. Each of these latter approaches addresses the role of oppression in human functioning, but generally at the intrapsychic or interpersonal levels. Even larger systems approaches tend to emphasize family and organizational dynamics from strictly psychological or behavioral perspectives. Our framework begins with an exploration of such perspectives, but consistent with critical theorists such as Habermas, it places them within larger historical and sociopolitical contexts. Students struggling with academic and behavioral problems in school, for example, not only are treated for these individual difficulties, but also are helped to uncover and identify barriers to their school performance that exist within the structure of their school. These barriers can include teacher preferences for particular learning and communication styles, or disciplinary practices that the students deem to be unjust (see Hayward's analysis, Chapter Seventeen). Once the barriers are uncovered, an applied developmentalist working from our hermeneutic orientation assists her clients in constructing strategies for confronting and transcending these barriers.

What is unique about the manner in which applied developmentalists working within our framework connect with their clients? The answer might be clarified through a hermeneutic interpretation of empathy. Because the students or clients with whom we work in low-income, urban school settings commonly confront barriers in their day-to-day functioning that many applied developmentalists have never experienced and will never experience, we should not pretend to understand the magnitude or existential quality of our students' challenges. This does not mean that we cannot connect with such students. By exploring aspects of the students' histories with them, and the various barriers in the students' current functioning, we are able to join the student-clients as strategists for their futures.

A hermeneutically informed strategizing of this sort is part client-centered empathy, part behavior modification, and part political planning and analysis. Hermeneutic applied developmentalists move quite rapidly beyond a purely empathic form of listening that focuses primarily on emotional content to connect strategies for modifying behavior to larger systemic or political issues. We operate from an assumption that helping people to place their own situations within larger cultural, historical, and political contexts serves to facilitate the client's liberation from excessive self-blame. For children and youth, such contextualizing is largely oriented toward the future. Hermeneutically oriented applied developmentalists work to help youth recognize a future context of possibility, one worth connecting to through a productive actualization of their interests, hopes, and dreams. When plans for a productive future become real for young people, they grow less enslaved by their historical circumstances, including such immediate histories as school failure and interpersonal turmoil. Without a future to grow toward realistically, they tend to live too exclusively in the past, a past mistakenly interpreted as the totality of their experience due to repetitious reinforcement.

Empathy in the hermeneutic sense, then, is not strictly connecting in the moment. It is also connecting with the student or client at the level of what she wants and needs for the future. Hermeneutic empathy is a genuine joining with another through the co-construction of interpretations. This joining does not require a full understanding of the other; it requires a desire and ability to connect with another in the exploration of possibilities. Realistically connecting with disenfranchised students in the manner described in this book requires a mutual exploration of the barriers that exist beyond the individual, and strategies for transcending those barriers. Without this external systemic or political layer of analysis, the joint exploration can be counterproductive and sabotaging of future progress. For students to grow in a healthy manner, they need a realistic assessment of what confronts them. Genuinely joining in this assessment is essential to empathy within our hermeneutic framework.

THE DIALECTICS OF INTERPRETATION AND CHANGE

Throughout this book we have emphasized the utility of hermeneutics for clarifying interpretation and for promoting change. We have attempted to articulate the dialectical relationship between interpretation and change, particularly when interpretation is focused on human being. In literary criticism, critics debate the extent to which truth is located either in the text to be interpreted or in the interpretive process itself. Readers enjoy the challenge of trying to decipher an author's intent, just as they enjoy making their own idiosyncratic meaning through the reading process. As applied developmentalists we must take our interpretive responsibilities quite differently. We work hard to make sense of precisely what students and clients mean by their communication: here we have an extra responsibility in deciphering the author's intent. But even in this context, we always make meaning of our clients' life texts in our own idiosyncratic ways that often have little to do with the messages the clients intend to communicate. It is the commitment to clarifying the misunderstanding the practitioner knows is inevitable that forms the core of the hermeneutic method in applied development work. Whether a teacher is working with a student, a counselor with a client, or even a coach with a player, clarification of misunderstanding is the key to growth and change.

Because the range of adults working with youth to promote their development is so vast, the hermeneutic framework is not limited to use by psychologists, social workers, counselors, and other health care providers. Teachers can promote the sort of change encouraged throughout this book through multiple modes of communication, including classroom dialogue, interpretive writing assignments, and community development exercises. Coaches can promote personal and interpersonal growth by interacting with their athletes in a manner that encourages the athletes not only to appreciate and develop their own talents but also to appreciate those of their teammates. Because the benefits of the hermeneutic framework can be developed within so many contexts, we adopted the term *applied developmentalist* for this book. By utilizing it throughout, we intended to communicate that our model should not be restricted to the mental health professions.

In addition to the flexible term *applied developmentalist* capturing a broad range of practice-oriented youth work, it also allows us to identify with researchers. Our hermeneutic framework is as focused on research as it is on practice. In fact, the roots of our particular hermeneutic approach extend deeply into Gadamer's work, specifically into his writings on the organizing and integrating function of hermeneutics as a worldview that prepares us to think, conduct research, and carry out practice from a self-consciously prepared point of view. Central to that point of view are rigorous attempts to contextualize the meaning of findings—from research, practice, and everyday life—within the personal and historical traditions in which those findings were uncovered. The truth or validity of findings, from this perspective, is always a matter of interpretation—interpretation grounded in personal and historical traditions.

The hermeneutic methodology for theory, research, and practice, laid out in fairly thorough detail in Chapter Two, is an attempt to articulate specific methods for advancing the contextualizing process. Human service providers and social scientists are required to contextualize their findings, but rarely are they provided with detailed guidance for carrying out that task. Our methodological articulation is an initial step toward rectifying that problem. In a nutshell, our methodology is a multidialogical approach: it presents a framework for connecting critical dialogue across interactive contexts.

Toward what end is the hermeneutic methodology carried out? Toward the end of ongoing application. For applied developmentalists, both research and practice activities are conducted for the purpose of enhancing life-conditions for youth. Those conditions can be internal or external. As hermeneutically oriented applied developmentalists we are not ideologically wedded to changing systems rather than individuals, or vice versa. We work with individuals who need individual support, and within systems that require systemic reform. We are, however, ideologically devoted to confronting the barriers that keep youth and all people oppressed. And there are times, we believe, when those barriers are as much internal as they are external. Our ideological leanings are very much rooted in critical hermeneutics, particularly in the work of Jurgen Habermas and his emphasis on communicative barriers and the development of communicative competence.

In looking back at the various obstacles and interventions described in the phenomenological investigations, we see compounded communication problems. Virtually every investigation described barriers to communication in both the intern's work with youth and the youths' struggles with family, peers, and school. Depending on the angle and on the cultural and intellectual tradition from which one looks, the communication problems can be interpreted quite differently. Consequently, the primary work stemming from our hermeneutic approach to understanding and intervening in problems is the work of clarifying communication, beginning with the clarification of our own communication. And once again, the heart of the clarification process is dialogue.

So, as we complete this clarification of what we have tried to communicate through this book, we would like to direct you to dialogue. Read yourself into the situations presented in the phenomenological investigations. Read your ideas and approaches into the methodology presentation. Discuss your reactions to this book with a colleague, friend, or partner. What questions come up for you? Is your understanding pushed beyond the point from where you started?

As you discuss your reactions with others, let us leave you with our bias. Dialogical methodology is not just a technique, it is an ethic. However informed the individual, she is informed by her own biases and prejudices. We are all, quite simply, limited by what we know, intuit, and feel. But we need not act repeatedly from the same limitations. Our limits can change through dialogue; they can be expanded, shifted, altered. To remain stagnant in the same biases is to select an overly limited worldview. Those of us who work with youth, who work in some way with the lives and futures of flesh-and-blood human beings, have an ethical responsibility to move beyond ourselves. We all have our own truths, but the expanded truth that comes from dialogue might be the one that is needed by the next child we meet. It would be unfortunate to miss the opportunity to find out. It would be unethical not to try.

BIBLIOGRAPHY

Addison, R. "Grounded Interpretive Research: An Investigation of Physician Socialization." In M. Packer and R. Addison (eds.), *Entering the Circle: Hermeneutic Investigation in Psychology.* Albany, N.Y.: State University of New York Press, 1989.

Anderson, E. *Streetwise: Race, Class, and Change in an Urban Community.* Chicago: University of Chicago Press, 1990.

Asante, M. K. "The Afro-Centric Idea in Education." *Journal of Negro Education,* 1991, 62, 170–180.

Brown, L. M., and Gilligan, C. *Meeting at the Crossroads: Women's Psychology and Girls' Development.* Cambridge, Mass.: Harvard University Press, 1992.

Delpit, L. "The Silenced Dialogue: Power and Pedagogy in Educating Other People's Children." *Harvard Educational Review,* 1988, 59, 280–298.

Delpit, L. *Other People's Children: Cultural Conflict in the Classroom.* New York: Free Press, 1995.

Dilthey, W. The Development of Hermeneutics. In H. Rickman (ed. and trans.), *Wilhelm Dilthey: Selected Writings.* Cambridge: Cambridge University Press, 1976. (Originally published 1900.)

Donovan, D., and McIntyre, D. "Child Psychotherapy." In J. Simeon and H. Ferguson, eds., *Treatment Strategies in Child and Adolescent Psychiatry.* New York: Plenum Press, 1990, pp. 177–197.

Fine, M. "Why Urban Adolescents Drop Into and Out of High School." *Teachers' College Record,* 1986, 87, 393–409.

Fine, M. *Framing Dropouts: Notes on the Politics of an Urban Public High School.* Albany: State University of New York Press, 1991.

Fine, M. *Disruptive Voices: The Possibilities of Feminist Research.* Ann Arbor: University of Michigan Press, 1992.

Fowers, B. J., and Richardson, F. C. "Why Is Multiculturalism Good?" *American Psychologist,* 1996, 51(6), 609–621.

Frank, J. D., and Frank, J. B. *Persuasion and Healing.* Baltimore: Johns Hopkins University Press, 1991.

Freire, P. *Pedagogy of the Oppressed.* New York: Seabury, 1970.

Freire, P. *Education for Critical Consciousness.* New York: Seabury, 1973.

Gadamer, H.-G. "On the Problem of Self-Understanding." In *Philosophical Hermeneutics* (D. E. Linge, trans.). Berkeley: University of California Press, 1976. (Originally published 1962.)

Gadamer, H.-G. "The Universality of the Hermeneutical Problem." In *Philosophical Hermeneutics* (D. E. Linge, trans.). Berkeley: University of California Press, 1976. (Originally published 1966.)

Gadamer, H.-G. *Philosophical Hermeneutics* (D. E. Linge, trans.). Berkeley,: University of California Press, 1976.

Gadamer, H.-G. *Reason in the Age of Science* (F. H. Lawrence, trans.). Cambridge, Mass.: MIT Press, 1981. (Originally published 1976.)

Gadamer, H.-G. *Truth and Method* (2nd ed.) (J. Weinsheimer and D. G. Marshall, trans.). New York: Continuum, 1993. (Originally published 1960.)

Gallagher, S. *Hermeneutics and Education.* New York: State University of New York Press, 1992.

Geertz, C. *Interpretation of Cultures.* New York: Basic Books, 1973.

Gergen, K. J. "If Persons Are Texts." In S. B. Messer, L. A. Sass, and R. L. Woolfolk (eds.), *Hermeneutics and Psychological Theory: Interpretive Perspectives on Personality, Psychotherapy, and Psychopathology.* New Brunswick, N.J.: Rutgers University Press, 1988.

Gilligan, C. *In a Different Voice: Psychological Theory and Women's Development.* Cambridge, Mass.: Harvard University Press, 1982.

Goldner, V. "Making Room for Both/And." *Networker,* Mar./Apr. 1992, pp. 55–61.

Goleman, D. "Violence Against Women in Films." *Response to the Victimization of Women and Children,* 1985, 8(1), 21–22.

Habermas, J. *Knowledge and Human Interests* (J. Shapiro, trans.). Boston: Beacon Press, 1971.

Habermas, J. "A Review of Gadamer's *Truth and Method.*" In F. R. Dalmayr and T. A. McCarthy (eds.), *Understanding and Social Inquiry.* Notre Dame, Ind.: University of Notre Dame Press, 1977.

Habermas, J. *Moral Consciousness and Communicative Action* (C. Lenhardt and S. W. Nicholson, trans.). Cambridge, Mass.: MIT Press, 1990. (Originally published 1983.)

Hegel, G. *Phenomenology of Mind* (J. B. Baillie, trans.). Atlantic Highlands, N.J.: Humanities Press, 1977.

Heidegger, M. *Being and Time* (J. Macguarrie and E. Robinson, trans.). New York: HarperCollins, 1962. (Originally published 1927.)

hooks, b. *Teaching to Transgress: Education as the Practice of Freedom.* New York: Routledge, 1994.

Husserl, E. *The Crisis of European Sciences and Transcendental Phenomenology: An Introduction to Phenomenological Philosophy* (D. Carr, trans.). Evanston, Ill.: Northwestern University Press, 1970.

Husserl, E. *Logical Investigations.* 2 vols. (J. Findlay, trans). Atlantic Highlands, N.J.: Humanities Press, 1976. (Originally published 1900, 1901.)

Ibrahim, F. A. "Effective Cross-Cultural Counseling and Psychotherapy: A Framework." *The Counseling Psychologist,* 1985, *13,* 625–683.

Ibrahim, F. A. "Contributions of Cultural Worldview to Generic Counseling and Development." *Journal of Counseling and Development,* 1991, *70,* 13–19.

Kant, I. *Critique of Pure Reason* (M. Muller, trans.). New York: Doubleday, 1966.

Karcher, M. J. "From Perspective-Taking to Emotion-Making in a Middle School Pair." In R. L. Selman, C. L. Watts, and L. H. Schultz, (eds.), *Fostering Friendship: Pair Therapy for Treatment and Prevention.* Hawthorne, N.Y.: Aldine de Gruyter, 1997.

Kegan, R. *The Evolving Self.* Cambridge, Mass.: Harvard University Press, 1982.

Kim, H.-G. "Do You Have Eyelashes?" In C. Gilligan, A. Rogers, and D. Tolman (eds.), *Women, Girls, and Psychotherapy: Reframing Resistance.* New York: Hawthorne, 1991.

Kingston, M. H. *The Woman Warrior: Memoirs of a Girlhood Among Ghosts.* New York: Random House, 1976.

LaFarge, V. "Termination in Groups." In J. Gillette and M. McCollom (eds.), *Groups in Context.* Reading, Mass.: Addison-Wesley, 1990.

Lorde, A. *Sister Outsider: Essays and Speeches.* Trumansburg, N.Y.: Crossing Press, 1984.

Maddi, S. R. "On the Problem of Accepting Facticity and Pursuing Possibility." In R. L. Woolfolk, L. A. Sass, and S. B. Messer (eds.), *Hermeneutics and Psychological Theory: Interpretive Perspectives on Personality, Psychotherapy, and Psychopathology.* New Brunswick, N.J.: Rutgers University Press, 1988.

Margonis, F. "The Co-Optation of 'At-Risk': Paradoxes of Policy Criticism." *Teachers College Record,* 1992, *94*(2), 343–360.

Mehan, H., Hubbard, L., and Villanueva, I. "Forming Academic Identities: Accomodation Without Assimilation Among Involuntary Minorities." *Anthropology and Education Quarterly,* 1994, *25*(2), 91–117.

Meichenbaum, D. "The Ubiquity of Interpretation: Commentary on Donald P. Spence." In S. B. Messer, L. A. Sass, and R. L. Woolfolk (eds.), *Hermeneutics and Psychological Theory: Interpretive Perspectives on Personality, Psychotherapy, and Psychopathology.* New Brunswick, N.J.: Rutgers University Press, 1988.

Messer, S. B., Sass, L. A., and Woolfolk, R. L. (eds.). *Hermeneutics and Psychological Theory: Interpretive Perspectives on Personality, Psychotherapy, and Psychopathology.* New Brunswick, N.J.: Rutgers University Press, 1988.

Mio, J. S., and Iwamasa, G. "To Do or Not to Do: That Is the Question for White Cross-Cultural Researchers." *Counseling Psychologist,* 1993, *21*(2), 197–212.

Mueller-Vollmer, K. (ed.). *The Hermeneutics Reader.* New York: Continuum, 1988.

Nakkula, M., and Selman, R. "How People 'Treat' Each Other: Pair Therapy as a Context for the Development of Interpersonal Ethics." In W. M. Kurtines and J. Gewirtz (eds.), *Handbook of Moral Behavior and Development*. Hillsdale, N.J.: Erlbaum, 1991.

Packer, M. J., and Addison, R. B. (eds.). *Entering the Circle: Hermeneutic Investigation in Psychology*. New York: State University of New York Press, 1989.

Parry, A. "A Universe of Stories." *Family Process*, March 1991, *30*, 37–54.

Pederson, P. B. "Multiculturalism as a Generic Approach to Counseling." *Journal of Counseling and Development*, 1991, *70*(1), 6–12.

Ponterotto, J. G. "The Nature of Prejudice Revisited: Implications for Counseling Intervention." *Journal of Counseling and Development*, 1991, *70*(1), 216–224.

Ponterotto, J. G. "White Racial Identity and the Counseling Professional." *Counseling Psychologist*, 1993, *21*(2), 213–217.

Ponterotto, J. G. *Handbook of Multicultural Counseling*. Thousand Oaks, Calif.: Sage, 1995.

Random House College Dictionary. New York: Random House, 1975.

Ricoeur, P. *Interpretation Theory: Discourse and the Surplus of Meaning*. Fort Worth: Texas Christian University Press, 1976.

Ricoeur, P. "The Model of the Text: Meaningful Action Considered as a Text." In J.B. Thompson (ed. and trans.), *Hermeneutics and the Human Sciences*. Cambridge: Cambridge University Press, 1981.

Rogers, C. R. *Client-Centered Therapy*. Boston: Houghton Mifflin, 1965.

Sampson, E. E. "Identity Politics: Challenges to Psychology's Understanding." *American Psychologist*, 1993, *48*, 1219–1230.

Sartre, J.-P. *Being and Nothingness: An Essay on Phenomenological Ontology* (H. E. Barnes, trans.). New York: Philosophical Library, 1956.

Schleiermacher, F. *Hermeneutics: The Handwritten Manuscripts* (H. Kimmerle, ed.; J. Duke and E. Forstman, trans.). Missoula, Mont.: Scholars Press, 1977. (Originally published 1819.)

Selman, R. L. *The Growth of Interpersonal Understanding: Developmental and Clinical Analyses*. New York: Academic Press, 1980.

Selman, R. L. "Fostering Intimacy and Autonomy." In W. Damon (ed.), *New Directions for Child Development: Today and Tomorrow*. San Francisco: Jossey-Bass, 1989.

Selman, R. L. "Assessment of Personality Development: Which Analysis When?" *Psychological Inquiry*, 1993, *4*(1), 49–53.

Selman, R. L., and Schultz, L. H. *Making a Friend in Youth: Developmental Theory and Pair Therapy*. Chicago: University of Chicago Press, 1990.

Selman, R. L., and others. "Friendship and Fighting: A Developmental Approach to the Study of Risk and Prevention of Violence." *Development and Psychopathology*, 1992, *4*, 529–558.

Speight, S. L., Myers, L. J., Cox, C. I., and Highlen, P. S. "A Redefinition of Multicultural Counseling." *Journal of Counseling and Development,* 1991, *70,* 29–36.

Spence, D. P. *Narrative Truth and Historical Truth: Meaning and Interpretation in Psychoanalysis.* New York: Norton, 1982.

Spence, D. P. "Rhetoric Versus Evidence as a Source of Persuasion: A Critique of the Case Study Genre." In M. Packer and R. Addison (eds.), *Entering the Circle: Hermeneutic Investigation in Psychology.* New York: State University of New York Press, 1989.

Sue, D. W. "Confronting Ourselves: The White and Racial/Ethnic–Minority Researcher." *Counseling Psychologist,* 1993, *21*(2).

Sue, D. W., and Sue, D. *Counseling the Culturally Different: Theory and Practice.* New York: Wiley, 1990.

Sullivan, H. S. *The Interpersonal Theory of Psychiatry.* New York: Norton, 1953.

Taylor, C. "The Politics of Recognition." In A. Gutmann (ed.), *Multiculturalism and "The Politics of Recognition."* Princeton, N.J.: Princeton University Press, 1992.

VanderVen, K. "Play, Proteus and Paradox: Education for a Chaotic—and Supersymmetric—World." In D. Fromberg and D. Bergen (eds.), *Play from Birth to Twelve: Contexts, Perspectives and Meanings.* New York: Garland, 1996.

Webster's Dictionary. New York: PMC, 1992.

Wehmiller, P. L. "When the Walls Come Tumbling Down." *Harvard Educational Review,* 1992, *62*(3), 373–383.

Woolfolk, R. L., Sass, L. A., and Messer, S. B. "Introduction to Hermeneutics." In S. B. Messer, L. A. Sass, and R. L. Woolfolk (eds.), *Hermeneutics and Psychological Theory: Interpretive Perspectives on Personality, Psychotherapy, and Psychopathology.* New Brunswick, N.J.: Rutgers University Press, 1988.

INDEX

A

Aaron, 164

Absences, silent, 185–186

Addison, R., 20, 49–50, 51, 52, 109–110, 116, 119, 124, 133, 148, 155, 157, 160, 162, 163, 165, 203, 205, 230, 243, 266, 277, 291–292, 294, 304

African American counselors, 122–136, 291–302

AHORA, 262–275

Aleida, 161–162

Alienation: loss and self-understanding related to, 182–185; from self, 77–78; in therapeutic relationship, 95–98

Allison, 287, 288

Anderson, E., 60, 134

Anger: and loss, 235, 237–240; and voicelessness, 211–213

Anna, 304, 313–321

Applied development work: and access to truth, 170; and arc of reflection, 323–330; background on, 323–324; communication and power in, 31–32; concept of, xviii; and dialectics of change and interpretation, 328–330; and emancipation, 324–326; and empathy, 326–328; ethics as foundation for, xvi–xviii; goal of, 57; hermeneutic framework for, 11–12, 34–36; interpretation in, xx–xxv; method and being in,

28–34; mission of, 12, 34; origins of, xxv–xxvii; phenomenological case studies in, xxi–xxiii, xxvii–xxviii; political issues for, 260; and practice, 53–62; prejudice and misunderstanding in, 30–31; and research, 41–53; and socializing influence of language, 245–330; text making in, 29, 32–34, 44–46; and theory, 36–41; uncovering in, 167–243

Arc of projection, in hermeneutic circle, 3–21, 25

Arc of reflection: in hermeneutic circle, 25, 46, 323–330; and hindsight, 93

Asante, M. K., 20, 130

Asian Americans, and voicelessness, 204–205, 208–213

Authority: ambiguity toward, 138, 143; in therapeutic relationship, 101–103

Aylward, R., 286

B

Barr, 151

Basketball, counseling with, 267–270

Bayla, 149–150

Behavioral psychology, 177–178

Being: forgetfulness of, 9, 33, 249, 253, 324; in language, 25–26; and method, 22–34

CPSIA information can be obtained at www.ICGtesting.com
Printed in the USA
BVOW01*2049120614

356003BV00005BA/18/P

9 780787 909574